Market Integration Through Data Protection

Law, Governance and Technology Series

VOLUME 9

For further volumes:
http://www.springer.com/series/8808

Mario Viola de Azevedo Cunha

Market Integration Through Data Protection

An Analysis of the Insurance and Financial Industries in the EU

Springer

Mario Viola de Azevedo Cunha
Centro de Estudos e Pesquisas no Ensino
do Direito – Rio de Janeiro State University
Centro, Rio de Janeiro
Rio de Janeiro
Brazil

ISBN 978-94-007-6084-4 ISBN 978-94-007-6085-1 (eBook)
DOI 10.1007/978-94-007-6085-1
Springer Dordrecht Heidelberg New York London

Library of Congress Control Number: 2013933339

Printed on acid-free paper

Springer is part of Springer Science+Business Media (www.springer.com)

To my wife Danielle and to my son Lorenzo, for making me feel special every single day of my life.

Book Abstract

In the context of the continuous advance of information technologies and biomedicine, and of the creation of economic blocs, this book is devoted to the analysis of the role data protection plays in the integration of markets, with a special emphasis on financial and insurance services. Moreover, it is also concerned with the identification of differences in the data protection systems of EU member states and with the development of common standards and principles of data protection, keeping in mind the need to establish a high level of data protection without unnecessarily constraining the flow of information.

The book is divided into four parts. The first one deals with the evolution of the right to privacy, focusing on the last few decades, taking into account the development of new technologies. In this part, an analysis of the European framework of data protection and of its developed standards is carried out. Then, in the second part, the interaction between data protection and the industries selected as case studies, namely insurance, banking and credit reporting, is discussed. This discussion concentrates on specific issues, such as generalisation and discrimination, adverse selection and the processing of sensitive and genetic data, which are the main issues that affect the processing of personal data in these industries.

The focus of the third part is the analysis of the legislation of three EU member states (France, Italy and UK). In order to perform this comparative exercise, some important issues are taken into account: the concepts of personal, data protection principles, the role of the data protection authorities, the role of the data protection officer, data subjects' rights, the processing of sensitive data, and the experience of the case studies in processing data. Moreover, issues related to the specific member states are also considered.

Finally and subsequently to the comparative analysis, some recommendations are proposed for updating EU legislation on data protection, so as to reduce the barriers to the establishment of an internal market, mainly for financial and insurance services.

Acknowledgements

To write this book I received the help of many people and I owe a significant intellectual debt to all of them. I am particularly indebted to my supervisor at the European University Institute, Prof. Giovanni Sartor, who gave me support and guidance. I am also indebted to Prof. Andrew Murray—my external co-supervisor, who helped me greatly when I was a visiting researcher at the London School of Economics and Political Science and later helped me to understand the 'Common Law System' and the issues regarding consent. Another important person in my research is Prof. Jacques Ziller, who 'convinced' me to embrace the topic I discuss in this book.

Others from academia and elsewhere have helped me in my research. They are: Justice Luiz Fux from the Brazilian Supreme Court, Prof. Gustavo Tepedino, Prof. Nilo Batista and Prof. Carlos Edison do Rêgo Monteiro Filho from Rio de Janeiro State University, Prof. Luiz Edson Fachin from Paraná Federal University, Prof. Christopher Millard from Queen Mary–University of London, Prof. Yves Poullet from University of Namur, Prof. Hans Micklitz from the European University Institute, Alfonso Scirocco from the European Economic and Social Committee; Ricardo Sanchini from the *Garante per la protezione dei dati personali* (Italy); David Reynolds and Richard Ansell from the UK Information Commissioner; Anne-Christine Lacoste, Bénédicte Havelange, Delphine Harou, Eva Dimovné Keresztes, Giovanni Buttarelli, Isabelle Chatelier, Herke Kranenborg, Hielke Hijmans, Katarzyna Cuadrat Grzybowska, Laurent Beslay, Maria Verónica Pérez Asinari, Martine Blondou, Michaël Vanfleteren, Nathalie Vandelle, Peter Hustinx, Rosa Barceló, Sylvie Picard, Xanthi Kapsosideri and Zsuzsanna Belenyessy from the European Data Protection Supervisor, Aurélie Banck, Céline Bonneau, Florence Raynal and Marie Leroux from the *Commission Nationale de l'Informatique et des Libertés* (France); Athena Bourka from the Hellenic Data Protection Authority; Manuel Garcia Sanchez from the *Agencia Española de Protección de Datos*; César Alonso Iriarte and José Manuel de Frutos Gomes from the European Commission; Juan Antonio Travieso from the *Dirección Nacional de Protección de Datos Personales* (Argentina); and Stefano Barbaroto and Chiara Stolfi from *Associazione Nazionale fra le Imprese Assicuratrici* (Italy).

I would like to say a special thanks to *Fundação Escola Nacional de Seguros* (Brazilian National School of Insurance) and to Capes Foundation (Brazilian Ministry of Education) for having provided the necessary financial support for the completion of this research.

I would also like to acknowledge and thank Benjamin Farrand and Mike Wiesmeier for their valuable proofreading assistance which helped to make the text much more readable. However, any mistake and lack of clarity remains entirely my fault.

The Ph.D.—the period during which I have written a great part of this book—however, is not just a matter of work, and one of the most valuable experiences I have had during my stay in Florence are the friendships I have developed. These friends are: from the EUI (sorry if I forgot someone), Norberto Andrade, Ida Federica Pugliese, Adriana Bessa, Alessandro Chechi, Samantha Ribeiro, Timo Hiller, Lucas Lixinski, Lúcio Feteira, Marco Botta, Rozeta Karova, Vassilis Tzevelekos, Edurne Iraizoz, Claire Staath, Jonathan Murray Bright, Evaldo Xavier Gomes, Marcílio Toscano Franca Filho, Alessandra Franca, Alessandra Becucci, William Baugniet, Devina Saha, Ana Espírito Santo, Hélder Ferreira do Vale, Rashad Ibadov, Igor Medina de Souza, Fabiano Corrêa, Bruno Boto, Pedro Lomba, Domingos Paiva de Almeida and Alessandra Vannini; from Florence (outside of the EUI community), Gabriele Mazzota, Isabella Mariani, Mike Wiesmeier, Donatella Costantini (*in memorium*) and all the guys from Palestra Fiodan. I am also thankful to older friends from Brazil, who have always supported this life project. They include Sergio Duque Estrada, Elisabeth de Santiago, Therezinha Vollú, Antônio Francisco Alves Neto, Fernando Freeland Neves, Fábio Falles, Paulo de Almeida Santos, Leonardo d'Almeida Girão, Rafael Viola and Danilo Doneda (actually, Danilo and I became friends—and partners in many projects—while I was in Florence). All of them, my old and not-so-old friends, have contributed in different ways to my PhD and to this book.

I would also like to say a special thanks to all teachers of the Language Centre of the European University Institute, who are always available, both to review papers and clarify any doubts we may have regarding a specific language. The ones that I had the pleasure to have as teachers are: Edurne Iraizoz, Camilla Salvi, Nicky Owtran, Nicki Hargreaves, Sylvain Capelli, Cecilia Picchi, Annarita Zacchi, Phil Jakes and Eleonore Eckmann.

A special thanks goes also to the administrative staff of the EUI, especially to Alessandro Coccioli, Natasha Tsigler, Saverio Bertaccini, Antonio Corretto, Siobhán Gallagher and Françoise Thauvin, who have always tried to make things easier for me. The same gratitude goes to the team of the *mensa* (both in Badia and Schifanoia): Antonella, Fiamma, Loredana, Cinzia, Paola, Guia, Lorena, who have made my life in the EUI more 'tasteful' and pleasant.

Now, more than ever, I recognise the importance of family in my life, and in the period that I was in Florence (where I wrote this book), apart from my wife, I am very thankful to my cousins Márcia and João and to their daughters Gabriella and Giovanna, for providing me with family support. I am also enormously indebted to my uncles and aunts, Sergio, Sônia, Silvio, Paulo, Dora, Elaine, for giving to me—and to my whole family—the necessary support in the most difficult moments of our lives. I am sure that I will never be able to pay back what you have done for us. I would also like to say a special thanks to my grandmother Conchetta, who has always predicted good things for me.

Finally, my deepest gratitude goes to my mother, Suely, and to my brother and sister, Breno and Kamille, who are the most beautiful example of a family one could have. I love you so much!!!

Contents

Introduction

> *We should not judge a man's merit by his great qualities, but by the use he makes of them.*
> François VI, Duc de La Rochefoucauld Prince de Marcillac (1613–1680)[1]

The study of privacy opens to the researcher the possibility to deal with a number of interesting and complex issues. Questions regarding unlawful and abusive interferences in private and family life, and violation of honour and reputation are just a few examples of how privacy raises the debate. Amongst all the issues involving the right to privacy, the one that, in my opinion, currently creates more challenges for the law is the protection of personal data. The continuous advance of information technologies and biomedicine has not only made the collection of personal data more rapid, but has also opened the possibility for the collection of new kinds of personal data, such as biometric and genetic data.

Furthermore, the creation of economic blocs, which increases trade between member states, intensifies the flow of personal data, making it necessary to establish a uniform trade environment in order to guarantee the protection of personal data within the bloc, avoiding different levels of protection between member states. Such different levels of protection could create barriers to the free movement of goods and services that use personal information as an important raw material for their activities.[2]

[1]La Rochefoucauld, François. La Rochefould Collected Maxims and other reflections—New translations with parallel French text. Translated by E.H. Blackmore; A.M. Blackmore and Francine Giguère. Oxford World's Classics. Oxford University Press, 2007. P. 119.

[2]Doneda, Danilo; Viola de Azevedo Cunha, Mario. Data Protection as a Trade Resource in Mercosur: A Data Protection Framework as an Integrative Tool. In Franca Filho, Marcilio Toscano; Lixinski, Lucas and Olmos Giupponi, Maria Belen (editors), The Law of Mercosur. Oxford: Hart Publishing, 2010. P. 366.

Therefore, a data protection framework would be of interest not only to those countries that feel the need to protect their citizens from the effects of abusive use of their personal information, but also to regional blocs of countries that, in addition to protecting their citizens' interests, would be keen to make their laws regarding data protection compatible and even interchangeable, in order to render transactions involving the transfer of personal data as 'noise-free' as possible.[3]

The European Union (hereinafter EU) adopted a model of data protection that pursues this balance, stimulating the free movement of services and goods, without restricting individuals' fundamental rights, mainly the right to privacy and data protection.[4] The approach used in the EU model is the one of harmonisation of member states' laws in this specific area. However, as will be shown in this book, there are still significant differences in the way member states have implemented the Directives in this field, leaving open room for more harmonisation at the EU level.

In fact, privacy and data protection are no longer to be seen "as a barrier to international communications and trade, but as a necessary condition without which individuals will not use the public networks for commercial transactions."[5]

In this context, this book is devoted to the analysis of the role data protection plays in the integration of markets, with a special emphasis on financial and insurance services. Moreover, it is also concerned with the identification of differences in the data protection systems of EU member states and with the development of common standards and principles of data protection, keeping in mind the need to establish a high level of data protection without creating unnecessary constraints for the flow of information.

The book is divided into four parts. The first one deals with the evolution of the right to privacy, focusing on the last few decades, taking into account the development of new technologies. In this part an analysis of the European framework of data protection and of its developed standards is carried out. Then, in the second part, the interaction between data protection and the industries selected as case studies, namely insurance, banking and credit reporting, is discussed. This discussion concentrates on specific issues, such as generalisation and discrimination, adverse selection and the processing of sensitive and genetic data, which are the main issues that affect the processing of personal data in these industries.

The focus of the third part is the analysis of three EU member states' legislation (France, Italy and UK). In order to perform this comparative exercise, some important issues are taken into account: the concepts of personal and anonymous data, data protection principles, the role of the data protection authorities, the role

---

[3]Ibid. P. 367.

[4]Jentzsch, Nicola. Financial Privacy: An International Comparison of Credit Reporting Systems. 2nd ed. Berlin: Springer, 2007. P. 119. "Data protection is one of the few fields, where the EU proved to be more successful in exporting its standards than the U.S. One of the reasons is the demanding "extraterritorial principle" in the EU Directive. According to this principle, personal data on Europeans should be only exported to countries that provide adequate data protection."

[5]Bennett, Colin; Raddb, Charles D. The governance of privacy—Policy Instruments in Global Perspective. Cambridge: MIT Press, 2006. P. 92.

of the data protection officer, data subjects' rights, the processing of sensitive data, the processing of genetic data and the experience of the case studies in processing data. Moreover, issues related to the specific member states are also considered. The issues analysed in this part are the ones dealt with by the respective Member States differently from what is provided for by Directive 95/46/EC.

Finally and subsequently to the comparative analysis, some recommendations are proposed for updating EU legislation on data protection, so as to reduce the barriers to the establishment of an internal market, mainly for financial and insurance services. The book concludes by emphasising the important role that data protection can play in the process of market integration.

Despite the fact that research in the field of data protection and market integration has seen important development in recent years,[6] the impact the former has on the latter is still a rather unexplored area of research and analysis, continually evolving and demanding new legal answers and frameworks. Following this rather poor state of the art, the impact of data protection on the integration of markets remains a subject of significant ambiguity and controversy. Moreover, there has not been sufficiently deep discussion about the constraints that different implementations of communitarian[7] legislation by member states of a regional bloc can create for the integration of specific markets, namely the financial and insurance ones. Therefore, we need to consider how data protection rules should be applied, how they should evolve in a progressively globalised world, and what new solutions may reduce barriers to market integration.

---

[6] See, for instance, the 'Law and Financial Markets Project', of the London School of Economics and Political Science (LSE), led by Prof. Roger McCormick, focusing on the interaction between law and financial markets, and the 'Comparative Research Project on Self-Regulation', of the European University Institute (EUI), coordinated by Prof. Fabrizio Cafaggi, aiming at identifying the legal framework applicable to self-regulation in different systems, in the areas of media, internet, advertising and financial markets. None of these projects, however, take the approach proposed here, either from the viewpoint of a comparative analysis between two integration processes or from the one related to the role data protection can play for the integration of markets, especially of financial and insurance services. For more information about these two projects see http://www.lse.ac.uk/collections/law/projects/lfm.htm and http://www.eui.eu/Documents/DepartmentsCentres/Law/Professors/Cafaggi/self-reg2.pdf. Accessed 7 January 2011. Other interesting research projects are the one carried out by the Project Group 'Restatement of European Insurance Contract Law', coordinated by Prof. Helmut Heiss of the University of Zurich and the one developed by the Scuola Superiore Sant'anna (Pisa, Italy), entitled Insurance law between market development and individual protection' and coordinated by Prof. Gagliardi. Again, the former only analyses issues exclusively related to insurance law and not other fields of law that could have an impact over the integration of the insurance market and the latter analyses the interaction between insurance law and tort law in a European perspective, without analysing the consequences in a cross-border environment—and focusing only on tort law. For more details about these projects see http://aida-portugal.org/pdf/bc18d3af669a52ac20f164d7c9681d5d.pdf and http://www.lider-lab.sssup.it/lider/research/research-lines.html#. Accessed 11 January 2011.

[7] The term 'communitarian' is used here to refer to legislation produced at the regional level.

Chapter 1
The Protection of Personal Data: Evolution and Standards in Europe

This chapter deals with the evolution of the right to privacy, focusing on the last few decades, taking into account the development of new technologies and the threats security issues pose to privacy. It starts by giving an overview of the discussions on the right to privacy and to data protection, presenting a brief distinction between the European and the North American approach to that subject. Then, it concentrates on the European Framework of Data Protection, both at the Council of Europe and at the European Union levels, analysing its main legal instruments, with particular emphasis on Directive 95/46/EC because it is the one which applies to the processings of personal data carried out by the case studies of this book. Regarding this latter Directive, the book focuses on the legal grounds for data processing, on storage and data transfer issues—including the adequacy procedure—and on institutional and regulatory bodies.

1.1 The Right to Privacy: From the "Right to Be Let Alone" to Data Protection[1]

The need to protect privacy started to be discussed only at the end of the nineteenth century, an important example being the famous article "The right to privacy", written by Louis Brandeis and Samuel Warren.[2] In this article the authors dealt with many aspects of the right to privacy, including what is now called 'informational

[1] Some portions of this section were included in an article written by the author and Danilo Doneda. Doneda, Danilo; Viola de Azevedo Cunha, Mario. Data protection as a trade resource in Mercosur: a data protection framework as an integrative tool. Op. cit.

[2] Brandeis, Louis; Warren, Samuel. The Right to Privacy. Harvard Law Review. Vol. IV, December 15, 1890, No. 5. Available at http://groups.csail.mit.edu/mac/classes/6.805/articles/privacy/Privacy_brand_warr2.html. Accessed 5 January 2010.

M. Viola de Azevedo Cunha, *Market Integration Through Data Protection*,
Law, Governance and Technology Series 9, DOI 10.1007/978-94-007-6085-1_1,

privacy', from which data protection derived, focusing on "the invasion of privacy brought by public dissemination of details relating to a person's private life."[3]

After the end of the Second World War, as a response to the atrocities committed,[4] many rights were elevated to the status of human rights, including the right to privacy,[5] which was included in many international documents, examples being the Universal Declaration of Human Rights (hereinafter UNDHR) and the European Convention on Human Rights (hereinafter ECHR). In these documents, it was ensured that "No one shall be subjected to arbitrary interference with his privacy, family, home or correspondence, nor to attacks upon his honour and reputation. Everyone has the right to the protection of the law against such interference or attacks."[6]

However, the discussions over the protection of personal data only came into the picture in the 1960s,[7] although personal data has been collected for credit purposes since the nineteenth century.[8] A famous example of the first debates about informational privacy is the 'National data center' case, in the United States, where some governmental agencies intended to unify their databases, but such initiative was blocked by the US Congress on the grounds of privacy protection, because it posed serious risks to individual privacy.[9]

---

[3]DeCew, Judith. Privacy. Stanford Encyclopedia of Philosophy. 2006. Available at http://plato.stanford.edu/entries/privacy/. Accessed 13 March 2010.

[4]See, for instance, Lazer, David; Mayer-Schönberger, Viktor. Statutory Frameworks for Regulation Information Flows: Drawing Lessons for the DNA Data Banks from other Government Data Systems. 34 J. L. Med. & Ethics (2006): 368. "Take as an extreme example the effort in the 1930s by the Netherlands to redesign their population information systems. The clear purpose of this endeavor was to improve administrative efficiency. However, part of the data that they collected, for innocent reasons, was each citizen's religious affiliation. Catastrophically, these data systems fell into the hands of the Nazis, and, arguably, as a result, Dutch Jews were killed at a much higher rate than any other Jews in Western Europe during the Holocaust."

[5]Winn, Jane K. Can a duty of information security become special protection for sensitive data under US Law? In Pérez, Maria Verónica; Palazzi, Pablo (editors). Défis du Droit de la Protection de la vie privée—Perspectives du droit européen et nord-américain. Cahiers du Centre du Recherche Informatique et Droit. 31. Bruylant: Bruxelles, 2008. P. 245. "The scope of the special protections accorded to sensitive data under EU Law is in some respects a reflection of modern European history. Countries such as Germany enacted strong data protection laws following World War II as a reaction to the horrors of the Nazi regime."

[6]Article 12 of the Universal Declaration of Human Rights. In the same sense, is Article 8 of the European Convention of Human Rights.

[7]See, for instance, Sartor, Giovanni. Prefazione. In Monducci, Juri; Sartor, Giovanni (editors). Il codice in materia di protezione dei dati personali. Cedam: Padova, 2004. P. XI; and Bennett, Colin; Raddb, Charles D. Op. cit. P. 84. "The institutions of the Council of Europe first became interested in privacy and data protection in the late 1960s, when a Committee of Experts was established to advise on how best to protect privacy in the face of modern computing advances".

[8]About the origin of credit records see, Jentzsch, Nicola. Op. cit. P. 63; and, Gelpi, Rosa-Maria; Julien-Labruyère, François. Histoire du crédit à La consommation—doctrines et pratiques. Paris: Éditions la découverte, 1994. P. 213.

[9]Solove, Daniel. Understanding Privacy. Cambridge: Harvard University Press, 2008. P. 118.

With the increase in trade in the twentieth century, many credit information agencies were created, culminating in the development of huge consumer information databases[10] aiming at facilitating credit.[11] Such increases in trade and in the automated processing of personal data made personal information an essential element for many business activities.[12]

On the one hand, personal data has become an important commodity in our society. Its processing is involved in many aspects of the daily lives of individuals, governments and companies, ranging from the conclusion of commercial transactions to the fight against terrorism and organised crime.[13] On the other hand, the

---

[10]Cate, Fred H. et al. Financial Privacy, Consumer Prosperity and the Public Good. Washington: Brookings Joint Center for Regulatory Studies, 2003. P. 3. "By 1969, there were 2,200 credit bureaus, collecting data from 400,000 creditors and public records, to maintain credit files on more than 110 million consumers." Currently, these credit bureaus have grown and they have revenues that amount one billion dollars per year. See Jentzsch, Nicola. Op. cit. P. 37. "As of 2006, two of them—Equifax and Experian—were publicly traded companies. In 2001, Experian had revenues of US$ 1.2 billion, Equifax US$ 1.1 billion and TransUnion US$ one billion. (. . .) The coverage rates of the economically active population range from 30% for smaller agencies to 90% for the large ones."

[11]DeCew, Judith Wagner. In Pursuit of Privacy—Law, Ethics, and the Rise of Technology. Ithaca and London: Cornell University Press, 1997. P 146–147. "Virtually every transaction today is recorded in a computer, and a recent consequence is the routine collection and transfer of personal information in digitalized form. The sale of such data for profit in the American private sector is now a multimillion-dollar business dominated by three leading credit bureaus: TRW California, Equifax in Atlanta, and Trans Union Credit Information in Chicago. The sheer volume of information stored and repeatedly resold is stunning: these information sponges keep more than 400 million records on 160 million individuals. In 1988 TRW revenues were $335 million, with 155 million individual files; Trans Union revenues were $300 million with 155 million files; Equifax revenues were $269 million, with 100 million files—and they are not the only ones in the business."

[12]Robinson, Neil; Graux, Hans; Botterman, Maarten; Valeri, Lorenzo. Review of the European Data Protection Directive. Available at http://www.ico.gov.uk/upload/documents/library/data_protection/detailed_specialist_guides/review_of_eu_dp_directive.pdf. Accessed 23 February 2010. P. 12/13. "2.1.1 Economic drivers affecting privacy

Personal data can be described as the lifeblood or basic currency of the information economy, being arguably a key asset, a central organising principle and a critical enabler for business competitiveness in today's world. A number of studies describe the link between micro-economics, the use of personal data and the increase in contribution to Gross Domestic Product (GDP), national competitiveness and economic growth. Using personal data can lead to efficiency gains in existing marketplaces because organisations understand their customers' preferences better, and may create markets for wholly new services and companies. Small, micro and medium sized-businesses can take advantage of personal data to reach a small or highly defined customer base."

[13]In the United States, for example, the insurance industry has a joint database called MID (Medical Information Bureau) that collects information about the health status of the insurance applicants. See Allen, B.; Mosely, R. 'Privacy and Health Insurance: Can Oil and Water Mix?' In Almeder, R.F.; Humber, J.M. (editors). Privacy and Health Care—Biomedical Ethics Reviews. Totowa: Humana Press, 2001. P. 135. "The MID is an insurance-industry clearinghouse that collects information on insurance applicants submitted by member insurance companies and releases that data to other insurance companies who may be considering the applicant's request for new or increased coverage. The MIB contends that its files do not contain raw medical data, but merely

processing of personal data increases the risk of privacy violation and of abusive control over individuals, justifying the implementation of legal instruments with the aim of balancing the interests of the actors involved.

Data protection instruments were mainly developed in the last decades.[14] Such regulations have their basis in the data protection principles that started to be drafted at the beginning of the 1970s, the so called Fair Information Principles,[15] which influenced almost all data protection legislation[16] and were the main inspiration for the first international documents to deal with this subject, Convention 108 of the Council of Europe[17] and the Organisation for Economic Co-operation and Development (OECD) Guidelines[18]:

> The basic framework for the European Union Data Protection Directive emerges from an American privacy report written for the Department of Health, Education, and Welfare (HEW) in 1973 as part of the effort that led to the passage of the Federal Privacy Act of 1974. The HEW report recommended a code of Fair Information Practices, which have influenced many laws in the United States. The HEW report also helped to shape the OECD Privacy Guidelines of 1980, which form the basis of privacy laws in countries around the world.[19]

These principles or recommendations are that: (a) There must be no personal-data record-keeping systems whose very existence is secret; (b) There must be a way for an individual to find out what information about him is in a record and how it is used; (c) There must be a way for an individual to prevent information

---

codes noting that some member insurers have declined or restricted coverage based on categories of medical data it ascertained. MID policy states that other member insurers are not allowed to make underwriting decisions based on the information from the MID. Rather, the information merely serves as a red flag alerting the insurer considering the application that the applicant has sought coverage before and the category of the data, which may lead the insurer considering coverage to conduct their own investigation or request for information from the applicant's medical record. It is impossible to verify whether this is how the information is actually used." About the MID database see also Kass, Nancy E. The implications of Genetic Testing for Health and Life Insurance. In Rothstein, Mark A. (editor). Genetic Secrets: Protecting Privacy and Confidentiality in the Genetic Era. New Haven and London: Yale University Press, 1997. P. 301/302.

[14]The first data protection legislation was adopted in 1970 by the German Land of Hesse, however, laws that dealt deeply with data protection were only adopted in the second half of the 1970s, being good examples the French and the German law. See, for instance, Sartor, Giovanni. Prefazione. In Monducci, Juri; Sartor, Giovanni (editors). Op. cit. P. XIII; and Solove, Daniel J. The digital person: technology and privacy in the information age. New York University Press, 2004. P. 105.

[15]U.S.A., Records, computers and the rights of citizens. Report of the Secretary's Advisory Committee on Automated Personal Data Systems, 1973, Available at: www.aspe.hhs.gov/datacncl/1973privacy/c3.htm. Accessed 7 March 2011.

[16]The first country to adopt a National Data Protection Law was Sweden, in 1973. See DeCew, Judith Wagner. Pursuit of Privacy—Law, Ethics and the Rise of Technology. Op. cit. P. 152.

[17]Council of Europe Convention n. 108/1081 for the protection of individuals with regard to automatic processing of personal data.

[18]Organization for Economic Co-operation and Development. Guidelines on the Protection of Privacy and Transborder Flows of Personal Data. Available at www.oecd.org/document/18/0,2340,en_2649_34255_1815186_1_1_1_1,00.html. Accessed 20 December 2008.

[19]Solove, Daniel. Understanding Privacy. Op. cit. P. 186–187.

about himself obtained for one purpose from being used or made available for other purposes without his consent; (d) There must be a way for an individual to correct or amend a record of identifiable information about himself; and (e) Any organization creating, maintaining, using, or disseminating records of identifiable personal data must assure the reliability of the data for their intended use and must take reasonable precautions to prevent misuse of the data.

The recent legislative developments in the area were driven by the need to balance all the interests involved: on the one hand, the privacy interests of individuals and, on the other, the need to enable the lawful processing of personal data by the entities that need personal data to operate more effectively.[20]

It can be seen, therefore, that since "the right to be let alone" developed by Brandeis and Warren, the right to privacy has been gaining a much broader scope, with a more protective level than the one initially thought by these authors.[21] As Solove argues:

> (...) some of the privacy problems we face today are different in nature, and do not track traditional conceptions of privacy. They involve efforts to gain knowledge about an individual without physically intruding or even gathering data directly from them (aggregation), or problems that emerge from the way that the data is handled and maintained (insecurity), the way it is used (secondary use), and the inability of people to participate in its processing (exclusion). Modern privacy problems emerge not just from disclosing deep secrets, but from making obscure information more accessible (increased accessibility) or from consistent observation or eavesdropping (surveillance).[22]

This new aspect of privacy, also called informational privacy, is the focus of this work. It is important, however, to distinguish between the two major approaches to privacy, the European and the North American, because depending on the approach adopted the protection given to privacy will be slightly different.

In the United States (hereinafter US) the protection of privacy "is more oriented toward values of liberty, especially liberty against the state",[23] its approach being

---

[20]International Finance Corporation (IFC)—World Bank Group. Credit Bureau Knowledge Guide. Available at http://www.ifc.org/ifcext/gfm.nsf/AttachmentsByTitle/FI-CB-KnowledgeGuide-E/$FILE/FI-CB-KnowledgeGuide-E.pdf. Accessed 14 April 2009. P. 3. "Credit reporting legislation should carefully balance the ability of the creditors to share information with the individual's right to privacy."

[21]This enlargement of the scope of privacy was object of discussion in the EU Member states, being a good example the words of the former president of the Italian Data Protection Authority, Professor Stefano Rodotà: "Emerges a deep link between freedom, equality, democracy, dignity and privacy, that oblige us to observe this last one for over its historical definition as 'the right to be let alone'." See Rodotà, Stefano. Relazione de 2004 dal attività svolta dal Garante per la protezione dei dati personali—Discorso del Presidente da Garante. Available at http //www.garanteprivacy.it/garante/navig/jsp/index.jsp?folderpath=Attivit%E0+dell%27Autorit%E0%2FRelazioni+annuali+al+Parlamento%2F2004%2FVersione+PDF. Accessed 23 December 2010. Unofficial translation by the author.

[22]Solove, Daniel J. A Taxonomy of Privacy. In University of Pennsylvania Law Review, Vol. 154, nº 3. January 2006. P. 560.

[23]Whitman, James Q. The Two Western Cultures of Privacy: Dignity Versus Liberty. In The Yale Law Journal. Vol. 113:11512003–2004. P. 1161. About the US approach to privacy, see also

much more in "the form that it took in the eighteenth century: It is the right to freedom from intrusions by the state, especially in one's own home."[24] According to Grodzinsky and Tavani:

> The notion of privacy in the US has evolved during the past two centuries from one that initially was concerned with governmental intrusion (as expressed in the Fourth Amendment to the US Constitution), to worries about governmental interference involving one's personal decisions (expressed in important court decisions in the 1960s), to current concerns about access to and control of personal information.[25]

Moreover, the US Supreme Court has been applying the idea of a "reasonable expectation of privacy", i.e., the expectation that American society has over its own privacy. For example, in *California v. Ciraolo*, the US Supreme Court decided that there was no privacy violation in "a police aerial observation made from an altitude of 1,000 ft of a home where marijuana was suspected".[26] In another case, *Miller v. Brooks*, the same Court found a violation of privacy in the use of cameras in places where there was "a reasonable expectation of privacy, such as a restroom or bedroom".[27] In what concerns the case studies of this book, "in *United States v. Muller*, the Court concluded that a person does not have a reasonable expectation of privacy in her financial records kept by her bank."[28] As highlighted by Solove:

> The Supreme Court has concluded that the Fourth Amendment protects against government searches whenever a person has a "reasonable expectation of privacy". Additionally, the Supreme Court has held that the Constitution preserves a "zone of privacy" encompassing decisions people make about their sexual conduct, birth control, and health, as well as protects their personal information against unwarranted disclosures by the government.[29]

The US, "Unlike the European Union, which adopted a general directive providing for large-scale privacy protection, (...) has not enacted measures of similar scope. Instead, Congress has passed a series of statutes narrowly tailored

---

Ferretti, Federico. The Law and Consumer Credit Information in the European Community—The Regulation of Credit Information Systems. London: Routledge-Cavendish, 2008. P. 140; and Westin, Alan. Privacy and Freedom. New York: Atheneum, 1968. P. 27.

[24]Whitman, James Q. Op. cit. P. 1161. Some authors in the US defend a property dimension to privacy and data protection, leaving to the individual the possibility to decide whether personal information can be used or not. In this sense see, for instance, Lawrence Lessig advocates a property right for privacy instead of the protection of dignity. Lessig, Lawrence. Code and other laws of cyberspace. New York: Basic Books, 1999; Westin, A. F. Privacy and Freedom. New York: Atheneum, 1968; and, Agre, Philip E.; Rotenberg, Marc (editors). Technology and Privacy: The New Landscape. Cambridge: MIT Press, 1998.

[25]Grodzinsky, Frances S.; Tavani, Herman T. P2P networks and the Verizon v. RIAA case: Implications for personal privacy and intellectual property. Ethics and Information Technology (2005) 7. Springer. P. 245.

[26]Staples, Willian G. (editor). Encyclopedia of Privacy. V. 2. Westport: Greenwood Press, 2007. P. 545–546.

[27]Ibid. P. 546.

[28]Solove, Daniel. Conceptualizing Privacy. In California Law Review, Vol. 90. 2002. P. 1151.

[29]Solove, Daniel. Understanding Privacy. Op. cit. P. 3.

to specific privacy problems."[30] By contrast, the EU adopts a completely different approach towards data protection in all of its aspects, considering it as a "form of protection of a right to respect and personal dignity."[31] "The core continental privacy rights are rights to one's image, name, and reputation, and what the Germans call the right to informational self-determination."[32] In fact, the Charter of Fundamental Rights of the EU, adopted on 7 December 2000, recognised in Article 7 the right to respect for private and family life and in Article 8 the right to the protection of personal data, giving to this latter the status of an autonomous fundamental right,[33] confirming the importance of such a right for European society. In effect, with the entry into force of the Lisbon Treaty, the Charter formally became part of the EU legal framework. According to Article 6(1) of the Treaty on European Union, the Charter has now "the same legal value as the Treaties".[34]

At the same time, the EU Directives dealing with data protection try to ensure a balance between the individual rights and the lawful use of personal data also by private parties. Indeed, Directive 95/46/EC is entitled the directive "on the protection of individuals with regard to the processing of personal data and on the free movement of such data", since the free flow of information is one of the

[30] Solove, Daniel. Privacy and Power: Computer Databases and Metaphors for Information Privacy. Stanford Law Review, Vol. 53. 2000–2001. P. 1440.

[31] Wong, Rebbecca. Privacy: Charting its Developments and Prospects. In Klang, Mathias; Murray, Andrew. Human Rights in the Digital Age. London: Glasshouse Press 2005. P. 158. "It was eloquently stated by Reidenberg that 'Europe treats privacy as a political imperative anchoring in fundamental human rights. European democracies approach information privacy from the perspective of social protection.'" The US and the EU diverge in the way they regulate privacy. The former one has adopted a more sectoral approach and the later one a general approach, with the adoption of a General Directive on Data Protection. See, for instance, Solove, Daniel. Understanding Privacy. P. 185.

[32] Whitman, James Q. Op. cit. P. 1161. This author also highlights the fact that "On the one hand, European interest in personal dignity, threatened primarily by the mass media; on the other hand, American interest in liberty, threatened primarily by the government." Ibid. P. 1219.

[33] "Il secondo, analiticamente disciplinato nell'articolo 8 della Carta, assume il carattere di autonomo diritto fondamentale, ormai distinto da quello alla tutela della vita privata." Rodotà, Stefano. In Panetta, Rocco. Libera circolazione e protezione dei dati personali. Tomo I. Milano: Giuffrè Editore, 2006. Preface—P. VIII.

[34] See Consolidated Version of the Treaty on European Union available at http://eur-lex.europa.eu/LexUriServ/LexUriServ.do?uri=OJ:C:2008:115:0013:0045:EN:PDF. Accessed 21 January 2010. Even when the Charter was not a binding document, the European Court of Justice had recognised the rights included in the Charter as an integral part of the general principles of Community law. See Laval Case (Case C-341/05). Grand Chamber of the European Court of Justice, Judgement of 18 December 2007. OJ C 51 of 23.02.2008, P. 9. "Although the right to take collective action must therefore be recognised as a fundamental right which forms an integral part of the general principles of Community law, the observance of which the Court ensures, the exercise of that right may none the less be subject to certain restrictions. As is reaffirmed by Article 28 of the Charter of Fundamental Rights of the European Union, it is to be protected in accordance with Community law and national law and practices."

instruments for the consolidation of the European internal market,[35] one of the main bases of the former EU first pillar.[36] This approach is identified, for example, in Recital nº 3 of the Directive, when it recognises that "the establishment of the internal market in which (…) the free movement of goods, persons, services and capital is ensured require not only that personal data should be able to flow freely from one Member state to another, but also that the fundamental rights of individuals should be safeguarded."[37]

Nevertheless, as a consequence of the terrorist attacks of 11 September 2001 in the US, the development of the protection of privacy had suffered an interruption. Such a change had consequences not only in the US but also in Europe.[38] Immediately after the terrorist attacks, the US Congress approved two laws that imposed restrictions to individual privacy and data protection. The first one was the US Patriot Act of October 2001 (Uniting and Strengthening America by Providing Appropriate Tools Required to Intercept and Obstruct Terrorism Act of 2001),[39] which authorised a series of agencies and governmental bodies to have unrestricted access to public and private databases, and to interconnect such databases.[40] The

[35]European Commission Press Release: IP/95/822. Council Definitively Adopts Directive on Protection of Personal Data. July 25, 1995. Available at http://www.ieee-security.org/Cipher/ConfReports/ECprivdirective.html. Accessed 5 March 2010. "I am pleased that this important measure, which will ensure a high level of protection for the privacy of individuals in all Member states, has been adopted with a very wide measure of agreement within the Council and European Parliament' commented Single Market Commissioner Mario Monti. 'The Directive will also help to ensure the free flow of Information Society services in the Single Market by fostering consumer confidence and minimising differences between Member states' rules.'"

[36]The three former pillars of the EU were: (1) Community; (2) Common Foreign and Security Policy; and Police and Judicial Co-operation in criminal matters. See http://europa.eu/scadplus/glossary/eu_pillars_en.htm. Accessed 23 February 2010. This pillar structure was dissolved by the Lisbon treaty, which made other important changes in the EU. See General Secretariat of the Council of the EU ~Information Note – Treaty of Lisbon (December 2009). Available at http://www.consilium.europa.eu/uedocs/cms_data/docs/pressdata/en/ec/111652.pdf. Accessed 21 October 2010. "On 1 December 2009 the European Community was replaced by the European Union which succeeds it and takes over all its rights and obligations. The Treaty on European Union keeps the same name and the Treaty establishing the European Community becomes the Treaty on the Functioning of the European Union".

[37]"(…) la tutela della privacy rivela una duplice funzione: di garanzia per i consumatori e di sviluppo per le imprese operanti nel mercato." Panetta, Rocco (editor). Libera circolazione e protezione dei dati personali. Giuffrè: Milano, 2006. P. 402. In the same sense, see also Doneda, Danilo; Viola de Azevedo Cunha, Mario;. Data protection as a trade resource in Mercosur: a data protection framework as an integrative tool. Op. cit.

[38]Rodotà, Stefano. La vita e le regole – Tra diritto e non diritto. Milano: Feltrinelli, 2006. P. 82. "La prospettiva di una più forte tutela attraverso strumenti giuridici, tuttavia, è contraddetta dalle tendenze legislative avviate dopo gli attentati dell'11 settembre 2001. Negli Stati Uniti, il Patriot Act consente a una serie di soggetti pubblici un accesso pieno a qualsiasi banca dati pubblica o privata, cancellando così la garanzia offerta dai divieti di interconnessione. Diventa problematica la possibilità di sottrarre il corpo elettronico allo sguardo totale di poteri non controllabili."

[39]Available at http://epic.org/privacy/terrorism/hr3162.html. Accessed 1 March 2010.

[40]Rodotà, Stefano. La vita e le regole—Tra diritto e non diritto. Op. cit. P. 82.

Act authorises, for example, the access to the history of calls emails, medical and financial files, amongst other provisions.

The second Act was the Aviation and Transportation Security Act,[41] which imposed on all air companies that fly from abroad to the US the duty to disclose passenger data (PNR Record) to the Customs and Border Protection Administration (CBP) before airplanes take off. This law had a real extraterritorial effect, since air companies must transfer the personal data of their clients collected in other countries, i.e., outside of US jurisdiction.

Such a rule generated a huge discussion in the EU due to its impact on individual data protection, forcing negotiations between the EU and the US with the aim of ensuring adequate levels of data protection from a European perspective. Air companies would be subject to sanctions imposed by national data protection authorities if they supplied US authorities with the information required, because such behaviour would violate most data protection laws of individual EU member states.[42]

In parallel to the adoption of these Acts, the idea of "nothing to hide"—if someone did not commit anything illegal he has no reason to be worried about his privacy, since he has nothing to hide—gained more support in the US Government. Following this idea, it may seem that there is never a threat to privacy: either the person has nothing to hide or she/he carries out illegal activities and, in this case, the person could not claim a violation of privacy.[43]

The idea that privacy should be restricted to fight terrorism gained some support also in the EU,[44] especially after the terrorist attacks in Madrid (March, 2004) and in London (July, 2005).[45] It is not by chance that "over the past two decades, in

---

[41] Available at http://frwebgate.access.gpo.gov/cgi-bin/getdoc.cgi?dbname=107_cong_public_laws&docid=f:publ071.107.pdf. Accessed 1 March 2010.

[42] See the US-EU PNR Agreement. Available at http://www.dhs.gov/xlibrary/assets/pnr-2007agreement-usversion.pdf. Accessed 1 March 2010. For a deeper analysis of the PNR Agreements between the EU and the US see Botta, Marco; Viola de Azevedo Cunha, Mario. La protezione dei dati personali nelle relazioni tra UE e USA: le negoziazioni sui trasferimento dei PNR (2010), Diritto dell'informazione e dell'informatica, Vol. 26, n°. 2, 315–341.

[43] Solove, Daniel. I've Got Nothing to Hide and Others Misunderstandings of Privacy. San Diego Law Review, Vol. 44, 2007. Available at https://ssrn.com/abstract=998565. Accessed 4 September 2008. "According to the nothing to hide argument, there is no threat to privacy unless the government uncovers unlawful activity, in which case a person has no legitimate justification to claim that it remains private."

[44] See, for instance, Human Genetics Commission. Nothing to hide, nothing to fear? Balancing individual rights and the public interest in the governance and use of the National DNA Database. November 2009. Available at http://www.hgc.gov.uk/UploadDocs/DocPub/Document/Nothing%20to%20hide,%20nothing%20to%20fear%20-%20online%20version.pdf. Accessed 10 January 2011. P. 48.

[45] See, for instance, Hijmans, Hielke; Scirocco, Alfonso. Shortcomings in EU Data Protection in the Third and the Second Pillars. Can the Lisbon Treaty be expected to help? In Common Market Law Review 46. Netherlands: Kluwer Law International, 2009. P. 1489/1490; and Puccinelli, Oscar Raúl. Apuntes sobre la evolución normativa y el desarrollo conceptual de los derechos <<de>>y<<a>> la protección de datos. In Pérez, Maria Verónica; Palazzi, Pablo (editors).

response to a series of national and international events, legislation has been passed and enacted in the UK that has shifted the balance of individual privacy rights away from the individual increasingly towards the right of the state to protect society from dangerous individuals and deliver economic efficiency."[46]

Now the sharing of personal information of citizens between police authorities in different EU member states becomes an essential element in the framework of the international cooperation against terrorism and organised crime.[47] In Europe, the systems for the exchange of information between national police forces within the Europol[48] and Schengen[49] are examples of this new approach to the transnational flow of personal data.

Indeed, the need to assure the security of citizens is a strong argument for restricting privacy. However, as highlighted by the Article 29 Working Party[50] in its opinion on the need for a balanced approach in the fight against terrorism, "Measures against terrorism should not and need not reduce the standards of protection of fundamental rights which characterise democratic societies".[51] Such measures also include the rights to privacy and data protection.

Défis du Droit de la Protection de la vie privée—Perspectives du droit européen et nord-américain. Cahiers du Centre du Recherche Informatique et Droit. 31. Bruylant: Bruxelles, 2008. P. 117.

[46]Bennett, Louise. Reflections on privacy, identity and cosent in on-line services. Information Security Technical Report 14 (2009): 120.

[47]Council Conclusions on an Information Management Strategy for EU internal security. 2979th JUSTICE and HOME AFFAIRS Council meeting Brussels, 30 November 2009 . Available at http://www.consilium.europa.eu/uedocs/NewsWord/en/jha/111549.doc. Accessed 5 March 2010. "Effective and secure cross border exchange of information is a precondition to achieve the goals of internal security in the European Union." In the same direction goes the Communication from the Commission to the European Parliament and the Council—An area of freedom, security and justice serving the citizen (COM(2009)0262 final). Available at http://eur-lex.europa.eu/LexUriServ/LexUriServ.do?uri=CELEX:52009DC0262:EN:HTML Accessed 5 March 2010. "The fight against these criminal phenomena will involve systematic exchange of information, widespread use of European investigative tools and, where necessary, the development of common investigative and prevention techniques."

[48]See http://www.europol.europa.eu/. Accessed 1 March 2010.

[49]See http://europa.eu/legislation_summaries/justice_freedom_security/free_movement_of_persons_asylum_immigration/l33020_en.htm. Accessed 1 March 2010.

[50]The functioning of the Article 29 Working Party will be explained in item 1.3.1.4 of this chapter.

[51]Article 29 Working Party on Data Protection. Opinion 10/2001 on the need for a balanced approach in the fight against terrorism. Adopted on 14 December 2001. Available at http://ec.europa.eu/justice_home/fsj/privacy/docs/wpdocs/2001/wp53en.pdf. Accessed 22 January 2010. In this Opinion, The Working Party also "underlines the obligation to respect the principle of proportionality in relation to any measure restricting the right to privacy as required by Art. 8 of the European Convention on Human Rights and the relevant case-law". Besides, such measures, according to the Working Party, should correspond to an "imperative social need".

Furthermore, the advances of information technologies and biomedicine,[52] especially in the field of genetics and biometrics, and the advent of the Internet provide challenges for data protection. There are many situations where there is a clash between privacy (and data protection) and the use of these new technologies for gathering personal information, such as caller ID, drug testing of employees, surveillance cameras, global position systems and biometric access control systems.[53] In the words of SOLOVE:

> In the past decade, we have undergone a dramatic transformation in the way we shop, bank and go about our daily business—changes that have resulted in an unprecedented proliferation of records and data. The small details that were once captured in dim memories or fading scraps of paper are now preserved forever in the digital minds of computers, vast databases with fertile fields of personal data. Our wallets are stuffed with ATM cards, calling cards, frequent shopper cards, and credit cards—all of which can be used to record where we are and what we do.[54]

The processing of new types of personal data, such as genetic data, generates a discussion about the scope society wants to give to the right to privacy. The use of such data, which presents a high discriminatory potential, requires an adequate level of protection that goes beyond the one given to other kinds of personal data, since through some genetic tests it is possible to identify, accurately, whether someone will develop or not a specific disease[55] and also if an individual is part of a specific ethnic group, giving margin for discrimination. In effect, the need to reassess the scope of privacy seems to become increasingly evident, in a society where "it is

---

[52]Slobogin, Christopher. Privacy at Risk—The new government surveillance and the fourth amendment. Chicago and London: University of Chicago Press, 2007. P. 10. "The easiest way to get useful data is to contact one of the many companies, usually called commercial data brokers, that use computers and the Internet to dig up <<durt>> from public and not-so-public records. One such a company is SeisInt, a concern owned by LexisNexis that operates a program known as Accurint (for accurate intelligence). According to its advertising, Accurint can, in mere seconds, <<search [ ] more than 20 billion records... dating back 30 years and more,>> armed with no more than a name, address, phone number, or social security number. Through this process, the company says, it can obtain information about a wide array of transactions, including bankruptcies and corporate filings; criminal conviction and criminal and civil court data (including marriage and divorce information); driver's license and motor vehicle records; firearms, hunting, fishing and professional licenses and permits; Internet domain names; property deeds and assessments; and voter registration."

[53]DeCew, Judith. Privacy. Stanford Encyclopedia of Philosophy. 2006.

[54]Solove, Daniel. Privacy and Power: Computer Databases and Metaphors for Information Privacy. Stanford Law Review, Vol. 53. 2000–2001. P. 1394.

[55]Moraes, Maria Celina Bodin de. O conceito de dignidade humana: substrato axiológico e conteúdo normativo in Constituição, Direitos Fundamentais e Direito Privado (org. Ingo Sarlet). Editora Livraria do Advogado, Porto Alegre: 2003. P. 128. The use of genetic information on insurance contracts is already a reality. In the UK life insurers are authorised to ask information about genetic tests results for some late onset single gene disorders. That is the only exception to the moratorium, which prohibits the use of genetic data on life insurance policies. In Webster, Mandy. Data Protection in the Financial Services Industry. Aldershot: Gower Publishing Limited, 2006. P. 150.

possible to insert a chip under the skin—with health information or which permits the localization of kidnapped people, dangerous criminals, convicts in free of parole, or just the identification of a person (....)".[56]

Even the EU, which has considered data protection as paramount, has established the duty of data retention[57] in the communications sector as a tool for the fight against crime,[58] even though it is a serious limitation of individual privacy.[59] This demonstrates the need for new solutions that reconcile security and individual freedoms.[60] In this regard, in November 2008 the EU adopted the Council Framework Decision 2008/977/JHA with the aim of providing a general rule regarding data protection in the field of police and judicial co-operation in criminal matters.

Given the differences between the US and EU models, and considering that the latter provides a better balance between the interests involved,[61] and that it

[56]Rodotà, Stefano. Transformações do corpo. Revista Trimestral de Direito Civil, Vol. 19, jul/set. Renovar: Rio de Janeiro, 2004. P. 94/95. Unofficial translation by the author.

[57]Some EU Member States Courts have rejected National Legislation implementing the Data Retention Directive. See, for instance, the German Federal Constitutional Court Decision. Available (in German) at http://www.bundesverfassungsgericht.de/pressemitteilungen/bvg10-011. Accessed 2 September 2012.

[58]See Article 1 (1) of Directive 2006/24/EC of the European Parliament and of the Council of 15 March 2006 on the retention of data generated or processed in connection with the provision of publicly available electronic communications services or of public communications networks and amending Directive 2002/58/EC. Available at http://eur-lex.europa.eu/LexUriServ/LexUriServ.do?uri=OJ:L:2006:105:0054:0063:EN:PDF. Accessed 8 April 2011.

[59]FINANCIAL TIMES. German court ruling on data law sends out shock waves. Available at http://www.ft.com/cms/s/0/c6191de8-2663-11df-aff3-00144feabdc0.html?nclick_check=1. Accessed 18 March 2010. "legislation in the European Union, requiring the storage of at least 6 months' worth of telephone and internet data, was contrary to the country's fundamental law. The constitutional court in Karlsruhe ordered the immediate destruction of all the data currently held on telephone calls, e-mails and text messages in Germany, and cancelled the legal basis for police and intelligence agencies to request such information." For a deeper analysis of the privacy impact of the Data Retention Directive, see European Data Protection Supervisor. Opinion on the Evaluation report from the Commission to the Council and the European Parliament on the Data Retention Directive (Directive 2006/24/EC). Available at http://www.edps.europa.eu/EDPSWEB/webdav/site/mySite/shared/Documents/Consultation/Opinions/2011/11-05-30_Evaluation_Report_DRD_EN.pdf. Accessed 16 June 2011.

[60]See European Data Protection Supervisor. Opinion on the proposal for a Directive of the European Parliament and of the Council on the retention of data processed in connection with the provision of public electronic communication services and amending Directive 2002/58/EC (COM92005) 439 final). "13. The impact of the proposal on the protection of personal data needs a thorough analysis. In this analysis, the EDPS will take the foregoing elements into account and he will conclude that more safeguards are needed. A simple reference to the existing legal framework on data protection (in particular, the directive 95/46/EC and 2002/58/EC) is not sufficient."

[61]As "Colin Bennet observes, '[t]he approach to making privacy policy in the United States is reactive rather than anticipatory, incremental rather than comprehensive, and fragmented rather than coherent. There may be a lot of laws, but there is not much protection.'" Apud Solove, Daniel. Privacy and Power: Computer Databases and Metaphors for Information Privacy. Stanford Law Review, Vol. 53. 2000–2001. P. 1444.

has already been exported to some foreign states,[62] the analysis in this book will concentrate on its data protection framework and not on the US one.[63] Moreover, the EU experience as a regional bloc is the best benchmark that can be found in terms of harmonisation of data protection legislation, with the aim of allowing the free flow of information within the bloc and fostering the market integration of services that use personal information as their raw material.

The European data protection framework consists of four levels, each of them applying to different actors. The first one, which applies not only to European Union member states but also to the other Council of Europe member states, is composed of Convention 108/81 of the Council of Europe (CoE) and its additional protocol of 2001. The second level, which applies to EU and EEA member states,[64] with a focus on the former EU first pillar, comprises Directives 95/46/EC (General Data Protection Directive), 2002/58/EC (Directive on privacy and electronic communications), and 2006/24/EC (Data Retention Directive).[65] The third level is covered by Regulation (EC) nº 45/2001, dealing with the processing of personal data by EU institutions and bodies. Finally, the fourth level applies to member states in relation to former EU third pillar activities and is regulated by Council Framework Decision 2008/977/JHA.[66] These four 'spheres' of data protection rules will be analysed in the following sections.

1.2 Council of Europe Convention 108/1981

The Convention nº 108/81 of the Council of Europe was the first international binding document to deal with data protection.[67] Its first article states that its objective and purposes are "to secure in the territory of each Party for every

[62]For example, Canada, Japan, Argentina and Uruguay have adopted Data Protection Legislation inspired by the EU model.

[63]Recently the US Government presented to the US Congress a Bill of Consumer Privacy Rights, aiming at creating "a framework for protecting privacy and promoting innovation in the global digital economy". White House. Consumer Data Privacy in a Networked World: A Framework for Protecting Privacy and Promoting Innovation in the Global Digital Economy. February 2012, Washington. Available at http://www.whitehouse.gov/sites/default/files/privacy-final.pdf. Accessed 07 April 2012.

[64]The EEA is the European Economic Area and is composed by EU and EFTA Member states. See http://ec.europa.eu/external_relations/eea/. Accessed 23 February 2010.

[65]Directives 2002/58/EC and 2006/24/EC were recently amended by Directive 2009/136/EC of 25 November 2009.

[66]There are other legal instruments dealing with data protection within the former third pillar, such as the Schengen Agreements, Europol and Eurojust, but they do not provide for general rules as the Council Framework Decision 2008/977/JHA does.

[67]This Convention was ratified by all EU Member states. See Hijmans, Hielke; Scirocco, Alfonso. Op. cit. P. 1489.

individual, whatever his nationality or residence, respect for his rights and fundamental freedoms, and in particular his right to privacy, with regard to automatic processing of personal data relating to him". This provision clearly recognises the need to protect personal data.

In turn, article 2 of the Convention presents a definition of personal data, stating that it comprises "any information relating to an identified or identifiable individual ("data subject")". The European Court of Human Rights, in a ruling of December 2008, decided that "fingerprints, DNA profiles and cellular samples, constitute personal data within the meaning of the Data Protection Convention as they relate to identified or identifiable individuals."[68] Although the cellular samples, fingerprints and DNA profiles themselves are not exactly data—it is true that data related to an individual can be extracted from them—the Court considered that they deserve the same protection as other personal data.

The second Chapter (articles 5 to 8) of the Convention establishes the basic principles of data protection, which are: (a) a fair and lawful collection and processing of data; (b) the storage has to be made for specific and legitimate purposes and the use has to be compatible with such purposes; (c) such collection and use has to be adequate, relevant and not excessive in relation to the purpose of the storage of the respective data; (d) data has to be maintained accurately and kept up to date; and (e) preserved in a form which permits the identification of the data subjects for no longer than is necessary for the purposes for which data are stored. The Convention also brings a definition of 'sensitive data'[69] and establishes some rights for individuals that have to be guaranteed by the member states, such as the right to access, to rectification and to erasure, with the necessary remedies to exercise such rights.[70]

Still regarding the use of sensitive data, in 13 February 1997 the Committee of Ministers adopted Recommendation n° R(97)5 on the protection of medical data, which in its article 1 defines medical data as "personal data concerning the health of an individual", including "data which have a clear and close link with health data as well as to genetic data". The recommendation also brings a specific definition for genetic data as "data, of whatever type, concerning the hereditary characteristics of an individual or concerning the pattern of inheritance of such characteristics within a related group of individuals", considering in such definition "any genetic

[68]European Court of Human Rights. Case of S. and Marper v. The United Kingdom (Applications nos. 30562/04 and 30566/04)—Judgment of 4 December 2008. Available at http://cmiskp.echr.coe.int/tkp197/view.asp?action=html&documentId=843941&portal=hbkm&source=externalbydocnumber&table=F69A27FD8FB86142BF01C1166DEA398649. Accessed 13 April 2009.

[69]Article 6—Special categories of Personal data revealing racial origin, political opinions or religious or other beliefs, as well as personal data concerning health or sexual life, may not be processed automatically unless domestic law provides appropriate safeguards. The same shall apply to personal data relating to criminal convictions.

[70]This basic principles and rights created by Convention n° 108/81 will be analysed deeply when we discuss the Directive 95/46/EC.

information (genes) in an individual or genetic line relating to any aspect of health or disease, whether present as identifiable characteristics or not."[71] Although it is not a binding document,[72] it suggests to the member states the adoption of safeguards for individuals concerning the use of their personal data in the health care sector.

Returning to Convention nº108/81, it created a Consultative Committee composed by one representative of each Member State of the Council of Europe,[73] the functions of which are: (a) to make proposals with a view to facilitating or improving the application of the convention; (b) to make proposals for amendment of this convention in accordance with article 21; (c) to formulate its opinion on any proposal for amendment of the convention; and (d) at the request of a Party, express an opinion on any question concerning the application of the convention.

Twenty years later, in 2001, influenced by Directive 95/46/EC, the additional protocol to the convention created the duty for CoE member states to "provide for one or more authorities to be responsible for ensuring compliance with the measures in its domestic law giving effect to the principles stated in Chaps. 2 and 3 of the Convention and in this Protocol." Such authorities have to be independent and to have "powers of investigation and intervention, as well as the power to engage in legal proceedings or bring to the attention of the competent judicial authorities violations of provisions of domestic law giving effect to the principles mentioned in paragraph 1 of Article 1 of this Protocol."[74]

---

[71] "Dalla semplice lettura del testo normativo si evince che, sebbene la Racomandazione del Consiglio d'Europa sia referita alla protezione dei dati sanitari, la definizione di dato genetico in essa contenuta va senz'altro letta in modo molto ampio, rientrando in essa anche informazione genetiche aventi caractteristiche, per così dire, <<trasversali>>, cioè non necessariamente di tipo medico." Bianca, Cesare Massimo; Busnelli, Francesco Donato. La Protezione dei Dati Personali. Tomo II. Milano: CEDAM, 2007. P. 1351.

[72] About the legal effects of Recommendations see Batellaan, Pieter; Coomans, Fons. "The International Basis for Intercultural Education including Anti-Racist and Human Rights Education: A selection of articles from relevant documents, adopted by the governments of member states of the United Nations, UNESCO, the Organisation on Security and Co-operation in Europe, and the Council of Europe. Second edition. International Association for Intercultural Education (IAIE) in co-operation with UNESCO: International Bureau of Education (IBE) and the Council of Europe 1999". Available at http://arno.unimaas.nl/show.cgi?fid=113. Accessed 13 April 2009. "3.2 Recommendations—It is common usage for international organizations, such as the United Nations, UNESCO or the Council of Europe, to draft and adopt recommendations. Recommendations can generally be defined as non-binding suggestions of international organs. Recommendations are usually addressed to the Member states of an international organization, but they do not legally bind them."

[73] Article 18—omissis.

2. (. . .) Any member state of the Council of Europe which is not a Party to the convention shall have the right to be represented on the committee by an observer.

[74] See Article 1 of the Additional Protocol to the Convention for the protection of individuals with regard to automatic processing of personal data, regarding supervisory authorities and transborder data flows.

The Convention played a very important role in the establishment of a European Data Protection Framework and worked as inspiration for the other spheres of the framework.[75]

Considering that this work will focus its analysis on the processing of personal data by insurance companies, banks and credit information suppliers, Regulation nº 45/2001 and Council Framework Decision 2008/977/JHA will be only briefly analysed, because they do not apply to these sectors, and instead efforts will be concentrated on Directive 95/46/EC.[76]

1.3 The European Union Data Protection Framework

1.3.1 Directive 95/46/EC

This Directive provides the legal basis for data protection. It works as well as an important tool for the integration process especially when it comes to the establishment of the European internal market. Its main purposes are: "(1) to allow for the free flow of data within Europe, in order to prevent the member states from blocking inter-EU data flows on data protection grounds; and, (2) to achieve a harmonized minimum level of data protection throughout Europe".[77]

In fact, recital 3 of Directive 95/46/EC recognises that the free flow of personal data and the protection of such data are essential for the establishment and functioning of the internal market.[78]

Therefore, the free flow of information between EEA member states has been playing an important role in the creation of the internal market.[79] As Kuner argues,

---

[75]The Council of Europe is currently discussing the review of Convention 108/81. See Kirk, Jeremy. Data Protection Convention Undergoes a Rewrite. Available at http://www.pcworld.com/businesscenter/article/245376/data_protection_convention_undergoes_a_rewrite.html. Accessed 07 April 2012.

[76]Directives 2002/58/EC and 2006/24/EC will not be analysed because they apply only to the electronic communications sector, and only supplement Directive 95/46/EC in that matter.

[77]Kuner, Christopher. European Data Protection Law and Online Business. New York: Oxford University Press, 2003. P. 17.

[78]Recital 3. Whereas the establishment and functioning of an internal market in which, in accordance with Article 7a of the Treaty, the free movement of goods, persons, services and capital is ensured require not only that personal data should be able to flow freely from one Member state to another, but also that the fundamental rights of individuals should be safeguarded;

[79]"The legal basis of the General Directive was Article 100[a] of the Treaty of Rome (currently Article 95 of the Amsterdam Treaty), which provides for the adoption of 'measures for the approximation of the provisions laid down by law, regulation or administrative action in Member states which have as their object the establishment and functioning of the internal market' and mandates 'a high level of protection' in matters concerning consumer protection (. . .)." In Kuner, Christopher. European Data Protection Law and Online Business. (Oxford University Press, New York, 2003) p. 29.

"Information has become the new raw material of the world economy. Just as, in past centuries, iron, wood, and coal were the foundation upon which the economy was based, so nowadays it is data and Information."[80]

According to Article 1(1)(2) of Directive 95/46/EC,[81] the object of the directive is to protect fundamental rights and freedoms of natural persons, in particular the right to privacy in relation to the processing of personal data without restricting or prohibiting the free flow of personal data within the bloc.[82]

Such a flow of information is of vital importance for the free movement of services, especially the financial and insurance ones, since their businesses depend on the gathering of personal data. However, even after 15 years of the adoption of the directive, there are still differences between member states' legislation. These differences bring into discussion the need to modify the directive[83] since it is creating barriers for the establishment of the European internal market,[84] at least of

---

[80]Ibid. Preface—P. ix. In the same sense, see Robinson, Neil; Graux, Hans; Botterman, Maarten; Valeri, Lorenzo. Op. cit. P. 12; Reden, Armgard von. Data Protection Activities in the Private Sector. Speech at the 21st International Conference on Privacy and Personal Data Protection. Available at http://www.pcpd.org.hk/english/infocentre/files/von-reden-paper.doc. Accessed 15 March 2009. P. 8; and Panetta, Rocco (editor). Libera circolazione e protezione dei dati personali. Milano: Giuffrè Editore, 2006. P. 864.

[81]Article 1—Object of the Directive

1. In accordance with this Directive, member states shall protect the fundamental rights and freedoms of natural persons, and in particular their right to privacy with respect to the processing of personal data.
2. Member states shall neither restrict nor prohibit the free flow of personal data between member states for reasons connected with the protection afforded under paragraph 1.

[82]"This means that Member states cannot impose legal restrictions on data transfers or data flows to another Member state based on the level of data protection in such other Member state." In Kuner, Christopher. European Data Protection Law and Online Business. Op. cit. P. 29. It is important to notice that all Member states of the European Union have to observe the provisions of Directive 95/45/EC what guarantees a standard level of personal data protection and allows free data transfers or data flows among Member states.

[83]"La directive du 24 Octobre 1995 qui constitue le socle commun à tous les pays de l'Union européenne en matière de protection des données personnelles devrait être modifiée dans les années à venir pour s'adapter aux technologies du 21ème siècle. D'ores et déjà, un certain nombre de travaux sont engagés dont la mise en cohérence et la coordination s'avèrent nécessaires.

Depuis plusieurs mois, la CNIL constate une augmentation du nombre de projets liés, directement ou indirectement, à la révision de la directive européenne relative à la protection des données personnelles. (...) Face à ce constat, la nécessité de la mise en cohérence et de la rationalisation de ces travaux s'impose. Le lancement de la consultation publique annoncée par M Jacques Barrot devrait y contribuer." In Commission Nationale de L'Informatique et des Libertes. L'impressionnante profusion des initiatives tendant à la révision de la directive de 1995 sur la protection des données. Published on 30 March 2009. Available at http://www.cnil.fr/index.php?id=2538&tx_ttnews%5btt_news%5d=432&tx_ttnews%5bbackPid%5d=1&cHash=c8572d9b47. Accessed 5 April 2009.

[84]Robinson, Neil; Graux, Hans; Botterman, Maarten; Valeri, Lorenzo. Op. cit. P. 26. "Problems with national implementations can be indicative of insufficient harmonisation with the provisions

financial services, as will be shown in the next chapter.[85] As highlighted by Andrew Charlesworth in an article of 2003:

> the harmonization process has struggled in the face of the Member States' "margin of appreciation" when implementing the Directive, and as a result across the EU, Member States' data protection laws are anything but uniform.[86]

Directive 95/46/EC is divided into three basic parts: (a) data protection itself, with the establishment of legal grounds for the processing of personal data; (b) the control over storage, transfer and flow of data; and (c) the creation of a regulatory and institutional structure to monitor the application of its provisions within the EEA area.[87] The next topics will be dedicated to them.

1.3.1.1 Legal Grounds for the Processing of Personal Data

In its first part, Directive 95/46/EC deals with the conditions for the legitimated processing of personal data. The first of all we need to consider is consent, the role of which was already recognised in the national data protection rules preceding the directive, such as the French ones. However, for the consent to be valid it is essential

---

of the Directive; for instance, if implementation functions well in some countries but not in others, this may indicate that the Directive leaves too much margin for interpretation."

[85]See Expert Group on Credit Histories. Report. May 2009. Available at http://ec.europa.eu/internal_market/consultations/docs/2009/credit_histories/egch_report_en.pdf. Accessed 21 January 2010. P. 27. "The various national approaches to data protection are also reflected in differences in the authorised purposes and the authorised actors for exchanging credit data, which can be an issue when sharing credit data cross-border. Therefore, it is strongly recommended that the Commission organise discussions with data protection authorities in order to elaborate a common set of practices and a common interpretation of the Data Protection Directive across the EU, with regards to the processing of credit data both nationally and cross-border."

[86]Charlesworth, Andrew. Information Privacy Law in the European Union: E Pluribus Unum or Ex Uno Plures? Hastings Law Journal, vol. 54, 2002–2003. P. 951.

[87]Paul M. Schwartz identifies four elements in what he called 'the European approach'. These elements are: "the creation of a statutory fabric that defines obligations with respect to the use of personal information; the maintenance of 'transparent' processing of personal information; the assignment of special protection for sensitive data; and the establishment of enforcement rights for the individual and effective oversight of the treatment of personal information." The author also refers to the creation of independent governmental agencies. Scwartz, Paul M. European Data Protection Law and Medical Privacy. In Rothstein, Mark A. (editor). Genetic Secrets: Protecting Privacy and Confidentiality in the Genetic Era. New Heaven and London: Yale University Press, 1997. P. 392–393 and 411.

that the data subject is able to give free[88] and informed[89] consent.[90] In this regard, Article 7 (a) of Directive 95/46/EC establishes that "member states shall provide that personal data may be processed only if: (a) the data subject has unambiguously given his consent."[91]

For the consent to be free and informed, the data subject has to have an exact understanding of why his personal data will be collected, the destination that will be given to it and, thus, be able to consciously express his consent.[92] Unfortunately, it is not always the case.[93] For example, on consumer credit contracts, if the data

---

[88]Article 29 Working Party on Data Protection. Working Document on the processing of personal data relating to health in electronic health records (HER). Adopted on 15 February 2007. Available at http://ec.europa.eu/justice_home/fsj/privacy/docs/wpdocs/2007/wp131_en.pdf. Accessed 10 March 2009. P. 8. "Consent must be given freely: 'Free' consent means a voluntary decision, by an individual in possession of all of his faculties, taken in the absence of coercion of any kind, be it social, financial, psychological or other. Any consent given under the threat of non-treatment or lower quality treatment in a medical situation cannot be considered as 'free'. Consent given by a data subject who has not had the opportunity to make a genuine choice or has been presented with a fait accompli cannot be considered to be valid."

[89]Ibid. P. 9. "Consent must be informed: 'Informed' consent means consent by the data subject based upon an appreciation and understanding of the facts and implications of an action. The individual concerned must be given, in a clear and understandable manner, accurate and full information of all relevant issues, in particular those specified in Articles 10 and 11 of the Directive, such as the nature of the data processed, purposes of the processing, the recipients of possible transfers, and the rights of the data subject. This includes also an awareness of the consequences of not consenting to the processing in question."

[90]Article 29 Working Party on Data Protection. Opinion 15/2011 on the definition of consent. Adopted on 13 July 2011. Available at http://ec.europa.eu/justice/policies/privacy/docs/wpdocs/2011/wp187_en.pdf. Accessed 6 August 2011. P. 6. "Consent is also a notion used in other fields of law, particularly contract law. In this context, to ensure a contract is valid, other criteria than those mentioned in the Directive will be taken into account, such as age, undue influence, etc. There is no contradiction, but an overlap, between the scope of civil law and the scope of the Directive: the Directive does not address the general conditions of the validity of consent in a civil law context, but it does not exclude them. This means, for instance, that to assess the validity of a contract in the context of Article 7(b) of the Directive, civil law requirements will have to be taken into account. In addition to the application of the general conditions for the validity of consent under civil law, the consent required in Article 7(a) must also be interpreted taking into account Article 2(h) of the Directive."

[91]The Article 29 Working Party created four criteria to verify if the consent is valid: '(...) consent must be a clear and unambiguous indication of wishes; consent must be freely given; consent must be specific; consent must be informed.' In Kuner, Christopher. European Data Protection Law—Corporate Compliance and Regulation. 2.ed. Oxford: Oxford University Press, 2007. P. 67.

[92]Article 2(h) of the Directive 95/46/EC establishes that data subject's consent shall mean any freely given specific and informed indication of his wishes by which the data subject signifies his agreement to personal data relating to him being processed. As highlighted by the Article 29 Working Party, "Consent is related to the concept of informational self-determination. The autonomy of the data subject is both a pre-condition and a consequence of consent: it gives the data subject influence over the processing of data." Article 29 Working Party on Data Protection. Opinion 15/2011 on the definition of consent. Op. cit. P. 8–9.

[93]Ibid. P. 10. "Consent is sometimes a weak basis for justifying the processing of personal data and it loses its value when it is stretched or curtailed to make it fit to situations that it was never intended

subject refuses to give the information asked for by the bank, he/she will not be able to conclude the contract nor to choose another lender because lenders use the same standard contractual terms.[94] Accordingly, the data subject would not have a real choice and his consent would not be freely given.[95]

Therefore, there are two basic requirements related to consent: the awareness of the implications of a specific data processing and the availability of acceptable alternatives regarding the manifestation of the consent.

Departing from these two basic requirements, the analysis in this section will concentrate on the data protection principles which empower or even substitute consent, because the other legal grounds which authorize the processing of personal data provided for by art. 7 of Directive 95/46/EC[96] do not rely on consent by default.

In relation to the awareness of the data processing implications, it is ensured by the application of the information principle. This principle creates an obligation for data controllers to inform data subjects about the purposes of the processing, the addresses of the data collected, if third parties will have access to their data and the conditions for the exercise of data subjects' rights.

In this regard, article 6(1)(a) and (b) of the directive imposes that the purposes of the data collection have to be specified at the moment of the collection, when

to be used in. The use of consent 'in the right context' is crucial. If it is used in circumstances where it is not appropriate, because the elements that constitute valid consent are unlikely to be present, this would lead to great vulnerability and, in practice, this would weaken the position of data subjects in practice."

[94]Ferretti, Federico. Op. cit. P. 191–192. "(...) when an individual deals with a business organisation, particularly a large one, there is pressure on the individual to behave in compliance with that organisation's standard terms of business. In such a situation, there is unequal bargaining Power between the two that clearly influences whether or not the consent of the individual is freely given. (...) In consumer credit, in fact, it is not just individuals who normally deal with large lenders, but also other lenders in the marketplace make use of the same type of standard terms, as they are part of a network system, a membership that owes its alleged business success to extensive coverage in terms of scale and scope, which has the propensity to universality. Thus, consumers sign up to the standard terms of a given lender or seek another lender, but then all other lenders would be part of the reporting network and impose the same terms."

[95]Robinson, Neil; Graux, Hans; Botterman, Maarten; Valeri, Lorenzo. Op. cit. P. ix. "Exercising choice—many services are only provided after sufficient personal data is released, but if important services are denied when we are unwilling to supply that data, do we still have a real choice?"

[96]Article 7—Member States shall provide that personal data may be processed only if: (a) the data subject has unambiguously given his consent; or (b) processing is necessary for the performance of a contract to which the data subject is party or in order to take steps at the request of the data subject prior to entering into a contract; or (c) processing is necessary for compliance with a legal obligation to which the controller is subject; or (d) processing is necessary in order to protect the vital interests of the data subject; or (e) processing is necessary for the performance of a task carried out in the public interest or in the exercise of official authority vested in the controller or in a third party to whom the data are disclosed; or (f) processing is necessary for the purposes of the legitimate interests pursued by the controller or by the third party or parties to whom the data are disclosed, except where such interests are overridden by the interests for fundamental rights and freedoms of the data subject which require protection under Article 1 (1).

all potential uses of the data have to be identified and the data subject adequately informed.[97]

The second requirement, of the existence of acceptable alternatives regarding the expression of consent, is not so easy to achieve. Let us take again the example of the consumer credit contract. As highlighted above, in this type of contract the data subject has no alternative and, therefore, the consent cannot be considered as a legal ground for the processing of personal data because the second requirement is not fulfilled. In fact, the directive does not require the consent of the data subject when the "processing is necessary for the performance of a contract to which the data subject is party".[98] Therefore, the mere fact of entering into a contract, according to the directive, supplies the 'need' of consent.

Moreover, there are many situations where there is no contract involved, in which the consent is a requirement for a consideration.[99] Even in those situations, the bargaining power of the data subject is significantly reduced, since he/she has only two options: either he/she gives his/her consent or he/she does not get the consideration offered.[100]

Therefore, when these two requirements are not properly fulfilled, consent cannot be considered as a relevant legal ground for the processing of personal data.[101] This shows, indeed, that consent itself cannot be the only legal ground to legitimise a specific processing activity in the situations not covered by article 7 (b) to (f)[102]; it

---

[97]Carey, Peter. Data Protection: A Practical Guide to UK and EU Law. 2.ed. New York: Oxford University Press, 2004. P. 54.

[98]Article 7(b).

[99]The Black's Law Dictionary defines 'consideration' as "Something (such as an act, a forbearance, or a return promise) bargained for and received by a promisor from a promisee; that which motivates a person to do something, esp. to engage in a legal act." It is in this sense that this word is used here. Garner, Brian A. (editor in chief). Black's Law Dictionary. 9th Edition. West, 2009. P. 347. Indeed, the European Court of Justice has employed the term 'consideration' with this same meaning. See, for instance, Geraets-Smits and Peerbooms. (Case C-157/99) Judgment of the Court of 12 July 2001. Paragraph 58.

[100]Article 29 Working Party; Working Party on Police and Justice. The Future of Privacy: Joint contribution to the Consultation of the European Commission on the legal framework for the fundamental right to protection of personal data. Adopted on 01 December 2009. Available at http://ec.europa.eu/justice/policies/privacy/docs/wpdocs/2009/wp168_en.pdf. Accessed 21 October 2010. P. 17. "There are many cases in which consent can not be given freely, especially when there is a clear unbalance between the data subject and the data controller (for example in the employment context or when personal data must be provided to public authorities)."

[101]We will see in Chap. 3 that some Member states have adopted a different interpretation of free consent.

[102]Bennett, Colin; Raddb, Charles D. Op. cit. P. 122. "The position that personal data must be collected and disclosed with the consent of data subjects is also an important empowering principle. This may be a precondition for processing, although it may not be necessary where laws stipulate other legitimate grounds: protecting vital interests of the data subject, adherence to other legal requirements, contractual reasons and so on."

is only one step that has to be followed by other steps in order to make the processing lawful and fair.[103]

Other and more important legal grounds that authorise the processing of personal data are the principles of finality (or purpose),[104] of proportionality,[105] of data quality[106] and of information.[107] The latter principle was already explained when the issue of awareness of the implications of the processing was discussed.

According to the finality principle personal data can only be processed for the purpose it was collected,[108] not being admitted for further use incompatible with this initial purpose.[109] Conforming to the proportionality principle, the data collected has to be relevant and compatible with the purposes of the collection,[110] and not

---

[103]The Directive 95/45/EC brings some exceptions concerning the obligation to obtain the consent of the data subject. One of them is the case where the data is necessary for the performance of a contract to which the data subject is party or in order to take steps at the request of the data subject prior to entering into a contract. See Carey, Peter. Data Protection: A Practical Guide to UK and EU Law. 2.ed. Op. cit. P. 7.

[104]Article 29 Working Party on Data Protection. Working Document on the processing of personal data relating to health in electronic health records (HER). Op. cit. P. 6. "Use limitation principle (purpose principle): This principle partially embodied in Article 6(1)(b) of the Directive, among others, prohibits further processing which is incompatible with the purpose(s) of the collection."

[105]Poullet, Yves. La loi des données à caractère presonel: um enjeu fondamental pour nos sociétés et nos démocraties? La In *LEGICOM n° 42–2009/1. La régulation des données personnelles*. Paris: Victoires Éditions. P. 66. "La proportionalité tout d'abord—elle s'entend tant de l'existence même du traitement que du contenu de celui-ci."

[106]See Article 6(d) of Directive 95/46/EC.

[107]There are other data protection principles in the Directive that are recognised by the doctrine, but some of them are included in the ones that we mentioned (legitimacy and transparency) and the others are not relevant for the limits on use and collection of personal data, which are the focus of this topic. See Kuner, Christopher. European Data Protection Law and Online Business. Op. cit. P. 17–18. "The content of the General Directive is often expressed in terms of six main principles which underlie it:

Legitimacy: personal data may only be processed for limited purposes;

Finality: personal data may only be collected for specified, explicit and legitimate purposes and may not be further processed in a way incompatible with those purposes;

Transparency: the data subject must be given information regarding data processing relating to him;

Proportionality: personal data must be adequate, relevant and not excessive in relation to the purposes for which they are collected and further processed;

Confidentiality and security: technical and organizational measures to ensure confidentiality and security must be taken with regard to the processing of personal data; and

Control: supervision of processing by DPAs must be ensured."

[108]The Directive provides for some exemptions and restrictions to this rule in its article 13.

[109]About the limits imposed by the finality principle see, for instance, Article 29 Working Party on Data Protection. Working Document on Genetic Data. Adopted on 17 March 2004. Available at http://ec.europa.eu/justice_home/fsj/privacy/docs/wpdocs/2004/wp91_en.pdf. Accessed 10 May 2008. P. 6; and Viola de Azevedo Cunha, Mario; Doneda, Danilo; Andrade, Norberto. La re-identificazione dei dati anonimi e il trattamento dei dati personali per ulteriori finalità: sfide alla privacy. In Ciberspazio e Diritto. Vol. 11, n° 4. Dicembre 2010. P. 6–7.

[110]Article 29 Working Party on Data Protection. Working document on biometrics. Adopted on 1 August 2003. Available at http://ec.europa.eu/justice_home/fsj/privacy/docs/wpdocs/2003/wp80_en.pdf. Accessed 10 March 2010. P. 6. "According to Article 6 of Directive 95/46/EC, personal

excessive.[111] In this sense, the proportionality principle forbids companies from asking for information not related to the contract they are seeking to conclude with the data subject. Some authors advocate, especially in the field of employer-employee relationships, the existence of a 'right to lie' in situations where the information required is incompatible with the proportionality principle.[112]

Accordingly, if a company obtains personal data for specific purposes, such as the conclusion of a contract, this company must not make this information available to other companies of the same economic group, unless such future use is compatible with the initial use and could have been foreseen by the data subject at the moment of the initial collection.[113] Furthermore, the kind of data that can be transmitted to third parties must be related to the object of the contract concluded between the data subject and the controller (or a third party, as in the case of credit bureaus in relation to banks), and has to be linked to the new destination of such data; for example, a new contract.[114]

Lastly, the data quality principle underlies articles 5 and 6(1)(a) of the Directive 95/46/EC[115] which establish that personal data have to be kept accurate and up to date.

---

data must be collected for specified, explicit and legitimate purposes and not further processed in a way incompatible with those purposes. In addition, personal data must be adequate, relevant and not excessive in relation to the purposes for which they are collected and further processed (purpose principle). (. . .) Furthermore, an evaluation of the respect for proportionality and the respect for legitimacy is necessary, taking into account the risks for the protection of fundamental rights and freedoms of individuals and notably whether or not the intended purpose could be achieved in a less intrusive way."

[111]Article 29 Working Party on Data Protection. Working Document on the processing of personal data relating to health in electronic health records (HER). Op. cit. P. 9. "The data quality principle: This principle in the Directive requires personal data to be relevant and not excessive for the purposes for which they are collected. Thus, any irrelevant data must not be collected and if it has been collected it must be discarded (Article 6(1)(c)). It also requires data to be accurate and kept up-to date."

[112]Simitis, Spiros. From the General Rules of Data Protection to a specific regulation of the use of Employee Data: Policies and Constraints of the European Union. Comparative Labor Law & Policy, Vol. 19. P. 358, 359. "The term may surprise, even bewilder, but the meaning is nonetheless clear: Employers are entitled to seek information, but they must limit themselves to the relevant data for the particular employment relationship; and when they transcend the proper limit of their power, the employee (or applicant) is not required to be truthful in response."

[113]The use of personal data for purposes different from the ones it was collected for will be further discussed in the following item (1.3.1.1.1).

[114]Carey, Peter. Op. cit. P. 54.

[115]See Articles 5 and 6(1). About the fairness of the processing of personal data see Webster, Mandy. Data Protection in the Financial Services Industry. Aldershot: Gower Publishing Limited, 2006. P 22–23. The author presents the criteria used by the UK Information Commissioner to evaluate if there is a fair and lawful processing of personal data. "Some of the questions the Information Commissioner will ask when assessing fairness are:

Was the person supplying the data under the impression that it would be kept confidential by the data controller and was that impression justified by the circumstances?

Was any unfair pressure used to obtain the information? Were any unjustified threats or inducements made or offered?

To sum up, the legal grounds for the processing of personal data provided for by Directive 95/46/EC (to be observed by EU [and EEA] member states), which complement or substitute consent in the situations not covered by article 7 (b) to (f), are the principles of information, finality, proportionally and data quality.[116] The principle of information provides the precondition for the realisation of the other principles: the data subject must be informed about the purposes of the collection, the destination of the data, whether that data will be transferred to third parties and any other relevant detail.

This is not to say that consent should not exist. Indeed, consent should remain for all situations not covered by the other legal bases contained in article 7 of Directive 95/46/EC as a necessary formal step to ensure that there is a relationship between the data subject and the data controller. However, it will only be a legal ground authorizing the processing of personal data when the two basic requirements related to consent are present. Just to illustrate, when the processing of data is the activity which satisfies the intents of the data subject, for example when he/she wants to upload a video or images in a website or social network showing his/her personal data, and consents to that, it will work (and should work) as a legal basis for such processing. The outcome will not be the same when the data subject is "required to consent to receiving behavioural advertising to register with a social network service, without further specification or alternative options."[117]

The Processing of Personal Data for Further Purposes

As discussed above, the finality principle is one of the legal grounds for the processing of personal data. According to this principle, personal data has to be processed for specific purposes and cannot be used for further purposes which are not compatible with the initial purpose (or purposes),[118] as required by Directive

Was the person improperly led to believe that they must supply the information, or that failure to provide it might be disadvantage them?

(...) Personal data must be processed in accordance with any relevant legal requirements, both civil and criminal."

[116]Article 29 Working Party on Data Protection. Opinion 15/2011 on the definition of consent. Op. cit. P. 7. "Moreover, obtaining consent does not negate the controller's obligations under Article 6 with regard to fairness, necessity and proportionality, as well as data quality. For instance, even if the processing of personal data is based on the consent of the user, this would not legitimise the collection of data which is excessive in relation to a particular purpose."

[117]Ibid. P. 18.

[118]Bensoussan, Alain. Informatique et libertes. Paris: Éditions Francis Lefebvre, 2008. P. 47. "Dans la mesure ou les données sont d'utilisation polymorphe, il est difficile de justifier de limitations trop restrictives. Pour cette raison, la loi a prévu que les données pouvaint être utilisées pour des nouveaux traitements, sous reserve que l'utilisation ne sois pas <<incompatible avec les finalités initiales>> (L. 1978, art. 6)."

95/46/EC.[119] Therefore, a relation of proportionality has to exist between the new purpose, the interests involved and the finality of the initial processing.

It is important to notice that both the European Data Protection Supervisor and the Data Protection Authorities of the EEA member states have admitted in some cases the use of personal data for a purpose different than the one for which the data were initially collected. The further use is possible only when it is proportional in relation to the initial collection and its aims. To analyse whether the principle of proportionality is observed in the new intended processing, some requirements have been developed by National Data Protection Authorities, the most relevant being the following: (1) the data subject should be able to anticipate that his data would be processed for this new purpose (even if the purpose was not literally mentioned in the moment of the collection)[120]; (2) the data to be processed should be indispensable for the intended activity; and, (3) the new purpose should present a relevant public interest.[121] Only if these requirements are satisfied is the processing for purposes different than the one(s) for which data were initially collected lawful.[122]

In the insurance, banking and credit reporting industries—which are the case studies of this book—, personal data collected for a specific purpose are usually processed later for different ones, such as for targeted marketing, fraud prevention and detection, and debt collection.[123]

Processing of personal data for marketing purposes, although quite common, has been the focus of much criticism.[124] On the one hand, this processing takes place without the consent of the data subject and, on the other, it may have the

---

[119]See Article 13.

[120]Sarmento e Castro, Catarina. Op. cit. P. 231.

[121]See Comissão Nacional de Proteção de Dados de Portugal. Parecer nº 22/2001. Available at www.cnpd.pt/bin/decisoes/2001/htm/par/par022-01.htm. Accessed 23 February 2010; and Information Commissioner's Office. Guidance on electronic mail marketing. Available at http://www.ico.gov.uk/for_organisations/topic_specific_guides/marketing.aspx. Accessed 25 January 2010

[122]The UK Information Commissioner in "The Guide to Data Protection" gives some guidance regarding the use of personal data for further purposes. Information Commissioner's Office. The Guide to Data Protection. Available at http://www.ico.gov.uk/upload/documents/library/data_protection/practical_application/the_guide_to_data_protection.pdf. Accessed 23 February 2010. P. 8. "As you develop the goods and services you offer, you should think about whether your customers are likely to reasonably expect you to use their personal data to offer them these products. If you are unsure about this, you should explain your intentions and, at the very least, give your existing customers an easy way to opt out. If you intend to make a significant change to what you do with personal data, you will usually need to get your customers' consent."

[123]See Viola de Azevedo Cunha, Mario; Doneda, Danilo; Andrade, Norberto. Op. cit. P. 8.

[124]In the UK data subjects have the right to prevent processing of personal data for direct marketing purposes and once the data controller receives a notice requiring to cease or not to begin processing of personal data it has to comply with it, since there are no exceptions to this right. See Information Commissioner's Office. Data Protection Act 1998: Legal Guidance. Available at http://www.ico.gov.uk/upload/documents/library/data_protection/detailed_specialist_guides/data_protection_act_legal_guidance.pdf. Accessed 29 March 2011. P. 55.

consequence that some consumers are deprived of access to specific products or advantages.

At the European Level, the European Commission approved—based on a proposal presented by the Federation of European Direct Marketing—the European Code of Practice for the use of Personal Data in Direct Marketing.[125] This code, in its item 2.4, gives guidance on how to verify the legitimacy of processing personal data for a purpose different from the one for which such data were collected. In particular, it requires that the new purpose is compatible with the notified one, by considering the following factors: "whether the new purpose(s) is substantially different from the purpose(s) for which data were collected, whether data subjects could reasonably have foreseen or whether it is probable that they would have objected to if they had known."[126]

The UK Information Commissioner reached similar conclusions when he decided that the processing of personal data could only be carried out for direct marketing purposes with the consent of the data subject, unless three other conditions are met: (1) data were obtained in the course of a sale or negotiations for a sale of a product or service; (2) the messages are only marketing similar products or services; and, (3) a simple opportunity to refuse to marketing is given to data subjects when their data are collected, and if they do not opt out at this point, they are given a simple way to do so in future messages.[127]

The other usual purpose for which personal data are further processed by banks, insurance companies and credit bureaus is fraud detection and prevention. In this case it seems that the exemption regarding the processing of personal data for the "prevention, investigation, detection and prosecution of criminal offences, or of breaches of ethics for regulated professions"[128] would apply and, for that reason, the further use would be legitimate. A good example of such use for fraud detection and prevention is the experience of the DVLA (Driver and Vehicle Licensing Agency), the British public body responsible for the licensing of drivers and vehicles, which discloses information related to vehicles, its owners and drivers to public authorities and other interested parties that prove a 'reasonable cause' for needing the information. As will be seen in the analysis of the UK Data Protection System (Chap. 4), the prevention and detection of fraud is considered by DVLA as a reasonable cause.[129]

---

[125]This Code was also approved by the Article 29 Working Party. See Opinion 4/2010 on the European code of conduct of FEDMA for the use of personal data in direct marketing. Adopted on 13 July 2010. Available at http://ec.europa.eu/justice/policies/privacy/docs/wpdocs/2010/wp174_en.pdf. Accessed 19 October 2010.

[126]Available at http://www.fedma.org/getfile.php/342991.1014.xacscqtseu/FEDMACodeEN.pdf. Accessed 21 January 2010.

[127]Available at http://www.ico.gov.uk/for_organisations/topic_specific_guides/marketing.aspx. Accessed 23 February 2010.

[128]Article 13(1)(d) of Directive 95/46/EC.

[129]DVLA. "Request of Information". Available at www.dft.gov.uk/dvla/foi/Disclosure/ReleaseofInfo.aspx. Accessed 23 February 2010.

It is worth noting, however, that the Article 29 Working Party argues that "if data are collected for the purpose of assessing solvency in credit applications, the same data cannot be used automatically for other purposes, even if they form part of the activities of financial institutions, such as anti-money-laundering procedures."[130] Besides, the Working Party recommends that data stored by credit registers should not be disclosed to entities out of the credit sector.[131]

As far as the collection of debts are concerned, the requirements of proportionality and legitimacy are observed, since the "processing is necessary for the purposes of the legitimate interests pursued by the controller or by the third party or parties to whom the data are disclosed, except where such interests are overridden by the interests for fundamental rights and freedoms of the data subject which require protection under Article 1 (1)."[132] In this same direction was the position adopted by the UK Information Commissioner in his Guide to Data Protection, where a transfer of personal data to a debt collection agency without the consent of the data subject is considered to be legitimate once the consumer had moved from his address without informing to his creditor his new address, and also by the fact that the creditor's right to collect the debt should prevail over the data subject's right of not having his data disclosed to a debt collection agency.[133]

Finally, another kind of processing of personal data for further purposes used by the analysed industries, is statistics. Recital 26 of Directive 95/46/EC states that "the further processing of personal data for historical, statistical or scientific purposes is not generally to be considered incompatible with the purposes for which the data have previously been collected provided that member states furnish suitable safeguards". The UK Data Protection Act 1998, contains a similar provision, where Section 33 recognises that the "further processing of personal data only for research

---

[130] Article 29 Working Party. Contribution to the public consultation of DG MARKT on the report of the Expert Group on Credit Histories. http://ec.europa.eu/justice/policies/privacy/docs/wpdocs/2009/wp164_en.pdf. Accessed 29 March 2011. P. 5.

[131] Ibid. P. 5. "The Article 29 Working Party recommends that access to credit registers should be limited to the credit sector and not extended to entities from other sectors, such as utilities providers (electronic communications). If this were not the case, credit referencing and blacklisting would ultimately overlap. It would also become extremely difficult to determine which data are relevant and not excessive for the purposes sought by this processing, contrary to Article 6(1)(a) and (b) of Directive 95/46/EC.

[132] Article 7(f) Directive 95/46/EC.

[133] Information Commissioner's Office. The Guide to Data Protection. Op. cit. P. 111–112. 'A finance company is unable to locate a customer who has stopped making payments under a hire purchase agreement. The customer has moved house without notifying the finance company of his new address. The finance company engages a debt collection agency to find the customer and seek repayment of the debt. It discloses the customer's personal data to the agency for this purpose. Although the customer has not consented to this disclosure, it is made for the purposes of the finance company's legitimate interests—i.e. to recover the debt. (. . .) In the example on the previous page, it is clear that the interests of the customer are likely to differ from those of the finance company (it may suit the customer quite well to evade paying his outstanding debt). However, passing his personal data to a debt collection agency in these circumstances could not be called 'unwarranted'".

purposes[134] in compliance with the relevant conditions[135] is not to be regarded as incompatible with the purposes for which they were obtained". Hence, the further processing of personal data put in place by the analysed industries is regarded as proportional and legitimate according to EU legislation.

The processing of data for statistical purposes attracts the discussion on the definition of anonymous data, which will be carried out in the next chapter (Sect. 2.1).

1.3.1.2 Data Subjects' Rights and Storage of Personal Data

The second part of the Directive 95/46/EC regulates the storage, transfer and flow of information. These aspects are of pivotal importance, especially in a period where "the world economy is transforming itself from an industrial-based economy to an information-based economy, in which the free exchange of information has become the life-blood of modern business life."[136]

To illustrate some aspects of data subjects' rights and storage of personal data, case-studies will be used, that involve databases which process both negative and positive information, to be understood as follows:

> **Negative Information**: Negative information consists of statements about defaults or arrears as well as charge-offs and bankruptcies. It may also include statements about lawsuits, liens and judgements that are obtained from courts. This kind of information may be collected about individuals or companies. It is also called black information. Negative information is information about contractual breaches.
>
> **Positive information**: Positive information consists of assets and liabilities as well as guarantees. It sometimes includes detailed statements about outstanding types of credit, amount of loans and repayment patterns as well as further information like employment and family history. The extent to which positive information is collected depends on the data protection regime prevailing. Such facts may be collected about individuals or companies. It is also called white information. Positive information are facts about contracts compliant behaviors.[137]

Banks and insurance companies, as a first step, consult databases to confirm the authenticity of the data concerning the potential client and to obtain other

---

[134]"'research purposes' includes statistical or historical purposes (. . .)". Section 33(1) of the UK Data Protection Act 1998.

[135]Relevant conditions means "the conditions—(a) that the data are not processed to support measures or decisions with respect to particular individuals, and (b) that the data are not processed in such a way that substantial damage or substantial distress is, or is likely to be, caused to any data subject." Section 33(1)(a) and (b) of the UK Data Protection Act 1998.

[136]Nugter, A.C.M. Transborder Flow of Personal Data within the EC: A comparative analysis of the privacy statutes of the Federal Republic of Germany, France, the United Kingdom and The Netherlands and their impact on the private sector. Deventer: Kluwer Law and Taxation Publishers, 1990. P. 1.

[137]Jentzsch, Nicola. Op. cit. P. 32.

information that might be important for accurate risk analysis. However, as the use and maintenance of such databases cannot be unrestricted, some measures have to be implemented at the national level, in order to guarantee to data subjects the rights provided for by article 12 of the Directive 95/46/EC.[138]

The first of these rights is the right to be communicated to by the controller "in an intelligible form of the data undergoing processing and of any available information to their source".[139] It is worth noting that, in spite of the fact that no provision in the Directive establishes the moment when the communication has to be made, there is a view that the data subject must be informed before information is included into the database, in order to avoid errors and problems with the information stored, as highlighted by the Article 29 Working Party, according to which "one way of avoiding errors and problems would be to lay down a reasonable period between notification of the data subject and the actual entering of the information on the joint file, and this procedure could also apply to files on breaches of monetary obligations."[140]

Another important right is the one that allows data subjects to gain access to their information and to check whether information related to them is being processed, the purposes of the processing, the categories of data concerned and the recipients or categories of recipients to whom the data are disclosed.[141] After gaining access to such information, the data subjects will have the possibility to rectify, erase or block the processing of data if there is any inaccuracy.[142]

---

[138]Article 12. Right of access

Member States shall guarantee every data subject the right to obtain from the controller:

(a) without constraint at reasonable intervals and without excessive delay or expense:

confirmation as to whether or not data relating to him are being processed and information at least as to the purposes of the processing, the categories of data concerned, and the recipients or categories of recipients to whom the data are disclosed;

communication to him in an intelligible form of the data undergoing processing and of any available information as to their source;

knowledge of the logic involved in any automatic processing of data concerning him at least in the case of the automated decisions referred to in Article 15(1);

(b) as appropriate the rectification, erasure or blocking of data the processing of which does not comply with the provisions of this Directive, in particular because of the incomplete or inaccurate nature of the data;

(c) notification to third parties to whom the data have been disclosed of any rectification, erasure or blocking carried out in compliance with (b), unless this proves impossible or involves a disproportionate effort.

[139]Article 12(a), second paragraph.

[140]Article 29 Working Party on Data Protection. Working Document on Blacklists. Adopted on 3 October 2002. Available at http://ec.europa.eu/justice_home/fsj/privacy/docs/wpdocs/2002/wp65_en.pdf. Accessed 9 May 2008. P. 8 - fn 8.

[141]Article 12(a) first paragraph.

[142]Article 12(b) and Article 6(1)(d).

Many studies conducted both in the US and in Europe identified a huge problem of inaccuracy in credit reporting databases. For example, a report by the Consumer Federation of America and the National Credit Reporting Association contained analyses of the information in the credit reports issued by the three large U.S. credit bureaus: TransUnion, Equifax, and Experian. The authors analyzed a random sample of credit reports and found that 82.4% of the files contained inconsistencies in the category of the balance on revolving accounts or collections and 96.1% of the files had inconsistencies in the category of account's credit limit. In 43.1% of the files, conflicting reports existed for the same accounts on how often the consumer's payment had been late by 30 days. The study estimates that, based on inaccuracies contained in credit reports, nearly 40 million people may be mistakenly classified as sub-prime borrowers in the mortgage market.[143] The same conclusion was reached by a report produced by Pam Dixon of the World Privacy Forum which focused on Choicepoint, a data aggregation company[144] based in the US who "sells information and data services to insurers, businesses, government agencies, and direct marketers."[145] According to "her sample, 90% of the reports obtained contained errors; frequently these errors were serious, such as individuals being identified by the wrong sex."[146]

These examples show the importance of enforcing data subjects' rights—especially in a cross-border scenario—, in order to ensure the quality of personal data stored in databases. In this sense, a data subject will have, at any moment, the right to request the controller of the database for access to his/her personal data stored, and, if he/she finds an error, he/she can request rectification, erasure or blocking[147] of the respective data. In case the data controller refuses to give access or to rectify, erase or block the data in question, the data subject will be able to use not

[143]International Finance Corporation (IFC)—World Bank Group. Op. cit. P. 42. This problem of inaccuracy in credit reporting databases is also recognised by Ferretti, Federico. Op. cit. P. 171. "In the absence of data from the EC, the US experience—where consumer credit reporting is most developed—shows that errors do occur on a large scale. According to the Federal Reserve Board, 70% of the 600 million credit files maintained by the three largest CRAs have missing or inconsistent credit information, and 78% are missing at least one account in good standing."

[144]"A data aggregator is an organization such as Acxiom and ChoicePoint involved in compiling information from detailed databases on individuals and selling that information to others." Definition from Wikipedia. Available at http://en.wikipedia.org/wiki/Data_aggregator. Accessed 16 September 2012.

[145]Solove, Daniel J.; Hoofnagle, Chris Jay. A model regime of privacy protection. University of Illinois Law Review, Vol. 2 (2006): 362.

[146]Ibid: 388.

[147]The data subject has the right to block the possibility of any processing operation concerning a specific information if data protection guarantees have not been observed. See Spoto, Giuseppe. I diritti dei consumatore. In Panetta, Rocco. Op. cit. P. 407. "Il 'blocco' proibisce al titolare o al responsabile qualsiasi altra operazione di trattamento diversa dalla mera detenzione."

only administrative measures through national supervisory authorities[148] but also judicial remedies regulated by national rules of the member states.[149]

It is true, however, as claimed by Viktor Mayer-Schönberger, that in practise individuals do not often exercise their data subject's rights:

> While creating a complex new rights regime, in reality these rights are rarely exercised. Few request access to their data, and even fewer enforce their rights through legal action. In fact, over a ten-year period in Germany, not a single case was brought by an individual claiming her privacy rights were infringed, even though Germany's data protection law shifts the burden of proof in asserting harm from asserting harm from potential plaintiffs to processors of personal data.[150]

Another important issue is related to the period during which personal data can be stored. Article 6(1)(e) of the Directive 95/46/EC establishes that "data should be kept for no longer than is necessary for the purposes for which the data were collected or for which they are further processed".

However, unlike in the US, where the Fair Credit Reporting Act "bars creditors from inquiring about, or denying credit on the basis of, bankruptcies of the prospective borrower that occurred more than 14 years earlier, or any other adverse information relating to events (including arrests and convictions) that occurred more than 7 years earlier",[151] in Directive 95/46/EC there is no such provision nor is there any unanimous view on how long this period should be.[152] For instance, Article 29 Working Party, in its Working Document on Blacklists, observes that in some member states information related to a default "may not be maintained once a debt has been paid off, even when overdue, while in others the information may stay on record for a maximum period which varies from one country to another." According to the Working Party, in any case, however, "the principle of updating information entails an obligation clearly to reflect the fact that the debt has been paid off even if the entry on non-payment is maintained beyond the date of full repayment."[153]

In this respect, there appears to be a clear need for further harmonisation in order to reduce the barriers for the creation of the EU internal market for financial and insurance services.[154] These differences will become more evident in the analysis of the selected member states (Chaps. 3, 4, 5).

---

[148] Article 28.

[149] Article 22.

[150] Mayer-Shönberger, Viktor. Useful Void: The Art of Forgetting in the Age of Ubiquitous Computing. Faculty Research Working Paper Series, John F. Kennedy School of Government—Harvard University. RWP07-022 (April 2007): 9.

[151] Posner, Richard A. The 1978 James McCormick Mitchell Lecture: Privacy, Secrecy, and Reputation. 28 Buffalo L. Rev. 1 (1979). P. 42.

[152] Article 6(1)(d).

[153] Article 29 Working Party on Data Protection. Working Document on Blacklists. Adopted on 3 October 2002. Available at http://ec.europa.eu/justice_home/fsj/privacy/docs/wpdocs/2002/wp65_en.pdf. Accessed 9 May 2008. P. 5.

[154] When I use the expression 'financial services' I refer not only to banks but also to insurance companies and credit bureaus.

1.3.1.3 Data Transfer to Third Countries (Adequacy)

Another relevant point that can have impact on the activities under analysis in this book concerns the transfer of personal data to third countries. Directive 95/46/EC establishes restrictive rules regarding the adequate level of data protection of the third country, "without prejudice to compliance with the national provisions adopted pursuant to the other provisions" of Directive 95/46/EC.[155]

Article 25(2) presents the criteria to be adopted to verify the level of adequacy of the third country, taking into account "the nature of the data, the purpose and duration of the proposed processing operation or operations, the country of origin and country of final destination, the rules of law, both general and sectoral, in force in the third country in question and the professional rules and security measures which are complied with in that country."

According to the procedure referred to in Article 31(2),[156] the European Commission can decide whether a third country ensures or not an adequate level of data protection and the member states have to adopt measures to comply with such a decision, unless some derogations provided for by Article 26 are applied, such as when "the transfer is necessary or legally required on important public interest grounds, or for the establishment, exercise or defence of legal claims".[157] This means that in some situations the transfer of personal data to third countries can be concluded without ensuring an adequate level of data protection and without the consent of the data subject.

Deborah Hurley and Viktor Mayer-Schönberger advocate that

> The EU Directive contains a significant extraterritorial provision that the flow of personal information from any EU member country may be halted, if the jurisdiction to which it is being transferred is deemed not to have an adequate level of protection for personal data. The United States is generally viewed as lacking an adequate level of protection for personal information, due to the absence in the United States of "omnibus" legislation. The issues of U.S. adequacy and the adequacy of data protection policies of U.S. companies, the intentions of the EU and its member countries to enforce the extraterritorial provision of the Directive, and possible recourse to various international bodies by the EU and the United States or other non-EU countries that might also be affected by the Directive have all been matters of debate and inter-governmental consultation. (. . .) More recently, protection of personal information has been included in the proposed work program of the World Trade Organization (WTO) on electronic commerce, which is to be taken up in the next round of trade negotiations.[158]

Actually, as a consequence of this 'adequacy requirement', many foreign states are seeking recognition from the EU Commission of the adequate level of protection of their national data protection frameworks, in order to facilitate the flow of

[155] See Article 25(1).

[156] See Article 31.

[157] See Article 26(d).

[158] Hurley, Deborah; Mayer-Schönberger, Viktor. Information Policy and Governance (January 2000): 13–14.

personal data coming from the EU Member States and reduce transaction costs in many areas.[159] Nevertheless, until now only Andorra, Faeroe Islands, Israel, Switzerland, Canada, Argentina, Guernsey, Jersey, Isle of Man[160] and more recently Uruguay[161] were recognized by the EU Commission as having adequate legal frameworks. However, "Current and emerging trade powers such as China, India, Brazil, Japan and Russia, are not included, and the US is only covered through the 'Safe Harbor' Privacy Principles (and to a lesser extent the transfer of PNR data to the Bureau of Customs and Border Protection)."[162]

1.3.1.4 Institutional and Regulatory Bodies

The last part of Directive 95/46/EC establishes a regulatory structure to be created by the member states with the aim of controlling the accomplishment of its provisions and also of national rules that incorporate such provisions. Article 28(1)(2) requires that each state creates supervisory authorities.[163]

These authorities must have investigative powers, effective powers of intervention and powers to engage in legal proceedings.[164] These powers are justified by the fact that such authorities are responsible for monitoring the application of the Directive's rules in the member states, playing an important role in the development of the internal market and a free area of data transfer and data flow.

---

[159] See Doneda, Danilo; Viola de Azevedo Cunha, Mario. Data protection as a trade resource in Mercosur: a data protection framework as an integrative tool. Op. cit.

[160] See http://ec.europa.eu/justice/data-protection/document/international-transfers/adequacy/index_en.htm#h2-2. Accessed 12 September 2012.

[161] See European Commission. 2012/484/EU: Commission Implementing Decision of 21 August 2012 pursuant to Directive 95/46/EC of the European Parliament and of the Council on the adequate protection of personal data by the Eastern Republic of Uruguay with regard to automated processing of personal data (notified under document C(2012) 5704). Available at http://eur-lex.europa.eu/LexUriServ/LexUriServ.do?uri=OJ:L:2012:227:0011:01:EN:HTML. Accessed 12 September 2012.

[162] Robinson, Neil; Graux, Hans; Botterman, Maarten; Valeri, Lorenzo. Op. cit. P. 33.

[163] Article 28

Supervisory authority

1. Each member state shall provide that one or more public authorities are responsible for monitoring the application within its territory of the provisions adopted by the member states pursuant to this Directive.

These authorities shall act with complete independence in exercising the functions entrusted to them.

2. Each Member state shall provide that the supervisory authorities are consulted when drawing up administrative measures or regulations relating to the protection of individuals' rights and freedoms with regard to the processing of personal data.

[164] See Article 28(3).

Besides this supervisory structure, Article 29 of the Directive creates a Working Party on the Protection of Individuals with regard to the Processing of Personal Data (known as the Article 29 Working Party), which is an independent advisory body, composed of the representatives of the Data Protection Authorities of all EEA member states and of a representative of the EU Commission, and having as its main tasks[165]: (a) to examine any question covering the application of the national measures adopted under this Directive in order to contribute to the uniform application of such measures; (b) to give the Commission an opinion on the level of protection in the Community and in third countries; (c) to advise the Commission on any proposed amendment of this Directive, on any additional or specific measures to safeguard the rights and freedoms of natural persons with regard to the processing of personal data and on any other proposed Community measures affecting such rights and freedoms; and, (d) to give an opinion on codes of conduct drawn up at the Community level.[166]

Considering the fact that the Working Party is composed of representatives of all member states who work in the field of data protection, it is possible to say that it has a privileged view of the situation of all member states concerning the issues that arise from the processing of personal data, and can identify whether there are differences between the laws or practices of Member states, and propose solutions.[167] However, the Article 29 Working Party "has been criticized as both lacking transparency in its deliberations, and flexibility in its opinions. In the opinion of a significant number of data controllers, this has resulted in varying degrees of over-regulation by the Member States."[168]

Concerning the activities which are the focus of this analysis, although there is no special provision in the Directive, it has full application and obliges the member states to adopt legislation that will affect and regulate the processing of personal data by such sectors. Despite the lack of transparency and flexibility alleged by some sectors, Article 29 Working Party has been drawing a lot of opinions that are not binding documents but give directions which should be followed by the member states, since they represent the views of the national data protection authorities. Some of these opinions deal with issues directly related to insurance companies, banks and credit information suppliers.[169] Finally, it is important to note that the

---

[165] See Article 30 (1).

[166] Robinson, Neil; Graux, Hans; Botterman, Maarten; Valeri, Lorenzo. Op. cit. P. 9. "At the European level, codes can be validated by the Article 29 Working Party. Only two organisations have achieved European level validation so far: the International Air Transportation Association (IATA) and the Federation of European Direct and Interactive Marketing (FEDMA)."

[167] See Article 30 (2)(3)(4).

[168] Charlesworth, Andrew. Op. cit. P. 933.

[169] See, for instance, Article 29 Working Party on Data Protection. Working Documents on Blacklists and on Genetic Data. Op. cit.

'soft law'[170] approach adopted by the Article 29 Working Party does not bind either the national data protection authorities or the data controllers.

1.3.2 Regulation 45/2001

According to Article 286 of the Treaty establishing the European Communities "From 1 January 1999, Community acts on the protection of individuals with regard to the processing of personal data and the free movement of such data shall apply to the institutions and bodies set up by, or on the basis of, this Treaty"[171] and "Before the date referred to in paragraph 1, the Council, acting in accordance with the procedure referred to in Article 251, shall establish an independent supervisory body responsible for monitoring the application of such Community acts to Community institutions and bodies and shall adopt any other relevant provisions as appropriate."

In this sense, the European Parliament and the European Council adopted Regulation (EC) n° 45/2001 on the protection of individuals with regard to the processing of personal data by the Community institutions and bodies and on the free movement of such data, with the aim "to insure both effective compliance with the rules governing data protection of individuals' fundamental rights and freedoms and the free flow of personal data between member states and the Community institutions and bodies or between the Community institutions and bodies for purposes connected with the exercise of their respective competences."[172] The Regulation has a structure very similar to the one of Directive 95/46/EC and for this reason the analysis here will focus on some specific points—which to a small

[170]Mörth, Erika. Introduction. In Mörth, Erika (editor). Soft Law in Governance and Regulation: An Interdisciplinary Analysis. Cheltenham: Edward Elgar Publishing, 2004. P. 6. "We, therefore, adhere to Snyder's (1993a) definition of soft law quoted above: 'rules of conduct which, in principle, have no legally binding force but which nevertheless may have practical effects' (p. 198)".

[171]Article 16 of the Treaty on the Functioning of the European Union, which replace Article 285 TEC, has the following reading:

Article 16 (ex Article 286 TEC)

1. Everyone has the right to the protection of personal data concerning them.
2. The European Parliament and the Council, acting in accordance with the ordinary legislative procedure, shall lay down the rules relating to the protection of individuals with regard to the processing of personal data by Union institutions, bodies, offices and agencies, and by the Member states when carrying out activities which fall within the scope of Union law, and the rules relating to the free movement of such data. Compliance with these rules shall be subject to the control of independent authorities.

The rules adopted on the basis of this Article shall be without prejudice to the specific rules laid down in Article 39 of the Treaty on European Union.

[172]Recital 13 of Regulation (EC) n° 45/2001.

or large extent differ from the General Data Protection Directive—, such as the processing of personal data for further purposes, the role of the European Data Protection Supervisor (hereinafter EDPS), the role of the Data Protection Officer (hereinafter DPO) and the obligation data controllers have to inform data subjects.

The first issue is the possibility of using personal data for a purpose different from the one the data was collected for. Article 6 of Regulation 45/2001 states that this is only possible "if the change of purpose is expressly permitted by the internal rules of the Community institution or body".[173]

The EDPS, which is the institution in charge of ensuring that EU institutions and bodies process personal data in accordance with this Regulation, recognised the possibility of using personal data for a different purpose than the one for which it was originally collected, provided it is compatible with the original purpose.[174]

Another important provision deals with the processing of special categories of data,[175] which can be processed only under specific exceptional circumstances. One important exception concerns data relating to offences, criminal convictions or security measures, the processing of which can be authorised by the EDPS even if it is not regulated by the Treaties or other instruments adopted. The EDPS has

---

[173] Article 6

1. Personal data shall only be processed for purposes other than those for which they have been collected if the change of purpose is expressly permitted by the internal rules of the Community institution or body.
2. Personal data collected exclusively for ensuring the security or the control of the processing systems or operations shall not be used for any other purpose, with the exception of the prevention, investigation, detection and prosecution of serious criminal offences.

[174] See European Data Protection Supervisor. Opinion on the Proposal for a Council Framework Decision on the protection of personal data processed in the framework of police and judicial co-operation in criminal matters (COM (2005) 475 final). Available at http://www.edps.europa.eu/EDPSWEB/webdav/site/mySite/shared/Documents/Consultation/Opinions/2005/05-12-19_data_protection_EN.pdf. Accessed 23 February 2010. "They can be used for that original purpose and might then be processed for another purpose provided it is compatible with the original one (data collected on an individual convicted of drug trafficking could be used in the framework of an investigation concerning a network of drug dealers, for instance). This approach reflects well the principle of purpose limitation, as it is also enshrined in Article 8 of the Charter of Human Rights for the European Union and is thus consistent with current data protection legislation." See also European Data Protection Supervisor. Opinion on the Communication from the Commission on an Action Plan for the Deployment of Intelligent Transport Systems in Europe and the accompanying Proposal for a Directive of the European Parliament and of the Council laying down the framework for the deployment of Intelligent Transport Systems in the field of road transport and for interfaces with other transport modes. Available at http://www.edps.europa.eu/EDPSWEB/webdav/shared/Documents/Consultation/Opinions/2009/09-07-22_Intelligent_Transport_Systems_EN.pdf. Accessed 23 February 2010.

[175] Article 10 (1) The processing of personal data revealing racial or ethnic origin, political opinions, religious or philosophical beliefs, trade-union membership, and of data concerning health or sex life, are prohibited.

also the power to "determine the conditions under which a personal number or other identifier of general application may be processed by a Community institution or body."[176]

Moving to data subjects' rights, the Regulation provides for some 'extra' provisions concerning information to be given by data controllers which includes: (a) the legal basis of the processing operation; (b) the time-limits for storing data; and (c) the right to have recourse at any time to the EDPS,[177] including data obtained from the individual or not.

The EDPS was, in fact, created to supervise the application of the Regulation.[178] It is an independent supervisory body "responsible for monitoring and ensuring the application of the provisions of this Regulation and any other Community act relating to the protection of the fundamental rights and freedoms of natural persons with regard to the processing of personal data by a Community institution or body, and for advising Community institutions and bodies and data subjects on all matters concerning the processing of personal data."[179] His powers include: (a) the prior checking of processing operations that are likely to present specific risks to the rights and freedoms of data subjects; (b) the consultation, which means that Community institutions and bodies when drawing up administrative measures or legislative proposals with regard to the processing of personal data have to consult the EDPS[180]; and (c) to hear and investigate complaints made by EU staff.[181]

The Regulation also creates the obligation for the different institutions and bodies of the European Union to appoint a Data Protection Officer (DPO) with the task of:

(a) Ensuring that controllers and data subjects are informed of their rights and obligations pursuant to this Regulation;
(b) Responding to requests from the European Data Protection Supervisor and, within the sphere of his or her competence, cooperating with the European Data Protection Supervisor at the latter's request or on his or her own initiative;
(c) Ensuring in an independent manner the internal application of the provisions of this Regulation;
(d) Keeping a register of the processing operations carried out by the controller, containing the items of information referred to in Article 25(2);

---

[176] Article 10(6).

[177] Articles 11(1) and 12(1).

[178] The EDPS was implemented by Decision nº 1247/2002/EC of the European Parliament, of the Council and of the Commission of 1 July 2002.

[179] See Article 41 of Regulation 45/2001.

[180] "The EDPS endeavours to become an authoritative advisor who contributes to the quality of the legislation of the European Union, in so far as matters concerning the processing of personal data are concerned." In European Data Protection Supervisor. "The EDPS as an advisor to the Community Institutions on proposals for legislation and related documents". Policy Paper. Available at www.edps.europa.eu. Accessed 10 March 2011. P. 1.

[181] See Article 46.

(e) Notifying the European Data Protection Supervisor of the processing operations likely to present specific risks within the meaning of Article 27.[182]

Both structures, the EDPS and the DPO, are the ones in charge of ensuring the compliance with data protection rules among the EU institutions and bodies.

1.3.3 Council Framework Decision 2008/977/JHA

Council Framework Decision 2008/977/JMA (hereinafter Decision), different from the previous instruments, regulates data protection in the former third pillar of the EU (Police and Judicial Co-operation in Criminal Matters). Its Recital n. 11 states that "It is necessary to specify the objectives of data protection within the framework of police and judicial activities and to lay down rules concerning the lawfulness of processing of personal data in order to ensure that any information that might be exchanged has been processed lawfully and in accordance with fundamental principles relating to data quality. At the same time the legitimate activities of the police, customs, judicial and other competent authorities should not be jeopardised in any way." In the same direction is its Article 1(1),[183] which defines as its main purpose the establishment of a balance between data protection and judicial and police activities.

Recital n. 12 highlights the need to ensure the accuracy of the data, taking into account the nature and the purpose of the processing. In the same line, Recital n. 15 states that the exercise of data subjects' rights of rectification, erasure or blocking of personal data when it is inaccurate, incomplete or no longer up-to-date, should be carried out in accordance with national law. In what concerns particularly the right to be informed, Recitals n. 26 and 27 provide for some 'guidance', leaving to the member states the regulation at the national level of "The modalities of the right of the data subject to be informed and the exceptions".

The Decision also points out the need to "ensure that the competent national supervisory authorities (which should exercise their functions with complete independence) are consulted prior to the establishment of filing systems" that represent specific risks for fundamental rights and freedoms, such as "processing by means of

---

[182] Article 24(1).

[183] Article 1 (Purpose and scope)

1. The purpose of this Framework Decision is to ensure a high level of protection of the fundamental rights and freedoms of natural persons, and in particular their right to privacy, with respect to the processing of personal data in the framework of police and judicial cooperation in criminal matters, provided for by Title VI of the Treaty on European Union, while guaranteeing a high level of public safety.

new technologies, mechanisms or procedures."[184] Article 23 describes the situations where this prior consultation is necessary.[185]

It is important to notice that this Framework Decision does not apply to the acts "governing the functioning of Europol, Eurojust, the Schengen Information System (SIS) and the Customs Information System (CIS), as well as those introducing direct access for the authorities of member states to certain data systems of other member states (...). The same applies in respect of the data protection provisions governing the automated transfer between member states of DNA profiles, dactyloscopic data and national vehicle registration data pursuant to the Council Decision 2008/615/JHA of 23 June 2008 on the stepping up of cross-border cooperation, particularly in combating terrorism and cross-border crime."

Article 1(2) of the Decision lists the situations where its provisions concerning data protection have to apply to processing operations of personal data for the purpose of prevention, investigation, detection or prosecution of criminal offences or execution of criminal penalties,[186] what does not include the processing of personal data in a specific member state when the data was collected in its territory. In other words, the Framework Decision only applies to the cross-border transfer of personal information.[187]

The operations covered by the Framework Decision have to observe some legal grounds, which are established by the application of the principles of lawfulness,

---

[184]See Recitals n. 32 and 34.

[185]Article 23 (Prior consultation)

Member states shall ensure that the competent national supervisory authorities are consulted prior to the processing of personal data which will form part of a new filing system to be created where:

(a) Special categories of data referred to in Article 6 are to be processed; or (b) the type of processing, in particular using new technologies, mechanism or procedures, holds otherwise specific risks for the fundamental rights and freedoms, and in particular the privacy, of the data subject.

[186]2. In accordance with this Framework Decision, member states shall protect the fundamental rights and freedoms of natural persons, and in particular their right to privacy when, for the purpose of the prevention, investigation, detection or prosecution of criminal offences or the execution of criminal penalties, personal data:

(a) are or have been transmitted or made available between member states;
(b) are or have been transmitted or made available by member states to authorities or to information systems established on the basis of Title VI of the Treaty on European Union; or
(c) are or have been transmitted or made available to the competent authorities of the member states by authorities or information systems established on the basis of the Treaty on European Union or the Treaty establishing the European Community.

[187]Hijmans, Hielke; Scirocco, Alfonso. Op. cit. P. 1499. "Transfers to third countries of data where only one member state is involved are not covered."

proportionality and purpose.[188] Therefore, personal data can only be processed by competent authorities for specific, explicit and legitimate purposes[189]—the prevention, investigation, detection or prosecution of criminal offences or execution of criminal penalties—, that have to be the same purposes for which data were collected.[190]

However, there are some exceptions that allow the processing of personal data for other purposes. These exceptions include the further processing that is compatible with the initial one, the processing authorised by competent authorities according to the applicable legal provision and the processing which is necessary for the intended purposes and respected the proportionality with the initial purpose. It is also possible to engage in further processing "for historical, statistical or scientific purposes, provided that member states provide appropriate safeguards, such as making the data anonymous."[191]

Following the 'instructions' of Recital n. 15, Article 4 regulates the rectification, erasure and blocking of personal data, stating that inaccurate data shall be rectified and, "where this is possible and necessary", completed or updated. However, it does not define what 'possible and necessary' is, leaving margin for different interpretation.[192]

Nevertheless, Articles 16, 17, 18 and 19 recognise some data subjects' rights, such as the right to be informed about the collection or processing of personal data by competent authorities in accordance with national law; the right of access—at least to receive a confirmation from the controller or national supervisory authority if their personal data were transmitted or made available, including information on the recipients or categories of recipients of such data, and communication of the data undergoing processing, or at least a confirmation from the national supervisory authority that all necessary verifications[193] and rights of rectification, erasure and blocking have taken place.[194]

---

[188]See Article 3(1).

[189]See Article 1(2).

[190]See Article 3(1).

[191]See Article 3(2).

[192]A literal interpretation of such provision will lead to the conclusion that personal data transferred to other member states, International bodies or even private parties concerning criminal offenses, for example, can be inaccurate and out dated if it is not possible or necessary to rectify them.

[193]The Decision opens space for some 'extra' limitations on these rights, if it "constitutes a necessary and proportional measure":

(a) to avoid obstructing official or legal inquiries, investigation and procedures;
(b) to avoid prejudicing the prevention, detection, investigation and prosecution of criminal offences or for the execution of criminal penalties;
(c) to protect public security;
(d) to protect national security;
(e) to protect the data subject or the rights and freedoms of others. (Article 17(2)).

[194]According to Article 8(1) "The competent authorities shall take all reasonable steps to provide that personal data which are inaccurate, incomplete or no longer up to date are not transmitted

The Decision also has a provision concerning the processing of 'sensitive data', highlighting that it is permitted "only when it is strictly necessary and when the national law provides adequate safeguards".[195] The same applies for 'automated individual decisions', which can be authorised only by a law guaranteeing data subjects' legitimate interests.[196]

Furthermore, the Framework Decision also states that damages caused by an unlawful processing operation or by any act incompatible with the national provisions adopted pursuant to the Framework Decision, should entitle the respective data subjects to receive compensation from the controller or other authority competent under national law.[197]

Another important issue regulated by the Framework Decision is the transfer of personal data "to competent authorities in third States or to international bodies."[198] The Decision establishes the purposes of the transmission and the respective conditions to allow the transfer, that are: (1) the characteristics (and competences) of the recipient authority concerning the prevention, investigation, detection or prosecution of criminal offences or the execution of criminal penalties; (2) the need to obtain the consent[199] of the "member state that primarily collects information"; and; (3) the third State or international body has to ensure an adequate level of protection for the intended data processing.[200]

Finally, and probably the most controversial provision of the Framework Decision, is the one concerning the transmission of personal data collected within the framework decision to private parties in the member states, because these entities are not covered by its provisions but can come to process data collected within its legal framework. The Decision imposes some conditions for such processing. The competent authority of the member state from which the data were obtained needs to give its consent; no legitimate interests of data subjects prevent the transmission; and

or made available. To that end, the competent authorities shall, as far as practicable, verify the quality of personal data before they are transmitted or made available. As far as possible, in all transmissions of data, available information shall be added which enables the receiving member state to assess the degree of accuracy, completeness, up-to-dateness and reliability. If personal data were transmitted without request the receiving authority shall verify without delay whether these data are necessary for the purpose for which they were transmitted.' And "If it emerges that incorrect data have been transmitted or data have been unlawfully transmitted, the recipient must be notified without delay". The data must be rectified, erased, or blocked without delay in accordance with Article 4.

[195]See Article 6.

[196]See Article 7.

[197]See Article 19 (1). A judicial remedy for any breach of the rights guaranteed to the data subjects has to be provided for by national law (Article 20).

[198]See Article 13.

[199]There is the possibility to transfer data without prior consent, if it "is essential for the prevention of an immediate and serious threat to public security of a Member state or a third State or to essential interests of a Member state and the prior consent cannot be obtained in good time." However, "The authority responsible for giving consent shall be informed without delay." (Article 13(4)).

[200]See Article 13(1)(a), (b), (c) and (d).

the "transfer is essential for the competent authority transmitting the data to a private party for: (i) the performance of a task lawfully assigned to it; (ii) the prevention, investigation, detection or prosecution of criminal offences or the execution of criminal penalties; (iii) the prevention of an immediate and serious threat to public security; or (iv) the prevention of serious harm to the rights of individuals." The competent authority also has to inform the private party "of the purposes for which the data may exclusively be used", that are the ones listed in Article 14 (2)(c).

Considering this scenario, it is possible to say that, overall, Council Framework Decision 2008/977/JHA complies with data protection principles and standards, notably in the area of Police and Judicial cooperation in criminal matters. Nevertheless, some aspects of the Decision deserve criticism and for this reason should be reviewed, mainly in the parts concerning data subjects' rights, its scope of application and the lack of a formal forum of discussion.[201] These problems seem not to be solved in the Proposal for a Directive[202] recently put forward by the EU Commission.[203]

Concerning the scope of application, the Council Framework Decision should apply not only to cross-border transfers of personal data, but to all processing operations carried out by police and judicial authorities in criminal matters, including DNA Samples and dactyloscopic data, which are very important for police and judicial activities. Besides, it should also cover Europol, Eurojust, the Schengen Information System (SIS) and the Customs Information System (CIS).

With regard to data subjects' rights, the direct access to files should be guaranteed, or at least a similar level of information to the one provided for by the Schengen

---

[201]The EU Commission recently put forward a proposal for a 'DIRECTIVE OF THE EUROPEAN PARLIAMENT AND OF THE COUNCIL on the protection of individuals with regard to the processing of personal data by competent authorities for the purposes of prevention, investigation, detection or prosecution of criminal offences or the execution of criminal penalties, and the free movement of such data', but since the analysis carried out in this book concentrates on the financial and insurance industries, the analysis of the changes proposed by the EU Commission in the framework of Police and Judicial Cooperation in Criminal Matters will be left to future investigation. The EU Commission proposal is available at http://eur-lex.europa.eu/LexUriServ/LexUriServ.do?uri=COM:2012:0010:FIN:EN:HTML. Accessed 12 September 2012.

[202]European Commission. Proposal for a Directive on the protection of individuals with regard to the processing of personal data by competent authorities for the purposes of prevention, investigation, detection or prosecution of criminal offences or the execution of criminal penalties, and the free movement of such data ('the proposed Directive').

[203]"(...) the EDPS is seriously disappointed with the proposed Directive for data protection in the law enforcement area. A positive element of the proposed Directive is the fact that, contrary to the Framework Decision 2008/977/JHA, domestic processing will also be covered by the EU instrument. However, this widening of the scope of application only has added value if the Directive substantially increases the level of data protection in this area, which is not the case." European Data Protection Supervisor. Opinion on the data protection reform package. Available at http://www.edps.europa.eu/EDPSWEB/webdav/site/mySite/shared/Documents/Consultation/Opinions/2012/12-03-07_EDPS_Reform_package_EN.pdf. Accessed 23 September 2012. P. 4.

regime[204] should be given to data subjects instead of only "a confirmation from the national supervisory authority that all necessary verifications have taken place", as recognised by the Framework Decision. Furthermore, data quality should be assured in any case, since inaccurate and outdated data can lead to wrong analyses and, consequently, to violations of individual rights and freedoms.

Finally, the creation (or recognition) of a formal forum of discussion, which could be the Working Party on Police and Justice, is a necessary step to ensure a certain level of harmonisation between member states in this area.

The entry into force of the Lisbon Treaty brought many changes to the EU legal framework and some of them have had a direct impact on the processing of personal data in former third pillar activities, such as the ones regulated by the Framework Decision. Firstly, from an institutional point of view, the abolition of the pillar structure will allow a greater involvement of the European Parliament in the area of the former third pillar. According to Article 87 (2) of the Treaty on the Functioning of the European Union, the Council and the Parliament may adopt, on the basis of the ordinary legislative procedure, measures relating to "the collection, storage, processing, analysis and exchange of relevant information" between the police authorities of member states. This new ordinary legislative procedure became the main instrument regarding the cooperation between judicial and police authorities.[205] As a consequence, when adopting a new US-EU PNR agreement, just to give one example, the European Commission will have to take into consideration the opinion of the Parliament, which seems not to be so in favour of the terms of the former agreement, as can be inferred from the rejection of the SWIFT agreement,[206] since it shows that the Parliament will not approve any new piece of legislation nor the ratification of any international agreement if such instruments reduce the safeguards already established by the current data protection framework, as was the case of the previous PNR agreements, which were largely

[204] Joint Supervisory Authority. The Schengen Information System: a guide for exercising the right of access. Available at http://www.dutchdpa.nl/downloads_int/Guide_for_exercising_the_right_of_access.pdf. Accessed August 7, 2011. P. 7. "Right of indirect access—In this case the person sends his request for access to the national data protection agency of the State to which the request is addressed. The data stored in the SIS is verified by the data protection agency in the same way as for police files relating to national security, defence or public security."

[205] Art. 294 TFEU.

[206] The SWIFT agreement is a EU-US agreement regarding the transfer of bank transfers information to US authorities with the aim of fighting terrorism. It was finally approved by the Parliament on 8 July 2010. About the rejection of this agreement by the EU Parliament and its latter approval see European Parliament. SWIFT: MEPs to Vote on Backing or Sacking EU/US Data Sharing Deal. Available at http://www.europarl.europa.eu/news/public/story_page/019-68537-039-02-07-902-20100205STO68536-2010-08-02-2010/default_en.htm. Accessed 19 February 2010; and Digital Civil Rights in Europe. SWIFT Agreement Adopted By The European Parliament. 14 July 2010. Available at http://www.edri.org/edrigram/number8.14/swift-20-adopted-european-parliament. Accessed 12 September 2012.

criticized by the fact that they have reduced data protection safeguards and standards for EU citizens.[207]

Furthermore, the changes imposed by the Lisbon Treaty together with Council Framework Decision 2008/977/JHA will have an impact not only in the international agreements to be concluded by the EU, but also in the way that law enforcement data will be processed within the European Union territory.[208] In fact, Declaration 21 on the protection of personal data in the fields of judicial and police cooperation in criminal matters, annexed to the final act of the intergovernmental conference which adopted the Treaty of Lisbon, recognises "that specific rules on the protection of personal data and the free movement of such data in the fields of judicial cooperation in criminal matters and police cooperation based on Article 16 of the Treaty on the Functioning of the European Union may prove necessary because of the specific nature of these fields."[209] Again, despite the criticism it deserves, the Council Framework Decision is an important attempt to regulate the processing of personal data in the area of judicial and police cooperation in criminal matters.

In this new scenario, without the pillar structure, the area of judicial and police cooperation in criminal matters will also need to be taken into account in a possible review of the General Data Protection Directive, and that is the approach adopted by the EU Commission in the reform of the data protection legislation it is proposing.

1.4 Chapter Conclusion

In this chapter it was possible to have a brief overview of the different layers of data protection in Europe (European Union and Council of Europe levels). Additionally, it was possible to conclude that the EU model of Data Protection is the one which prevails, even over the North American one, and that it has been exported throughout the globe. However, despite being the model to be followed, it was shown that it still needs some improvements when it comes to harmonisation of rules and the consequent reduction of barriers to the flow of information and the associated services which use personal data as an important raw material for their activities. These differences in the implementation of the European Data Protection Framework, mainly of Directive 95/46/EC which are the focus of this book, will become more evident in Chaps. 3, 4, and 5 when the experience of three EU Member States will be considered.

---

[207] See Botta, Marco; Viola de Azevedo Cunha, Mario. Op. cit.

[208] A good example is the discussion about the EU PNR System. See European Parliament. EU Passenger Name Record Talks on Hold in Council Until Lisbon Treaty Is Ratified. Available at http://www.europarl.europa.eu/news/expert/infopress_page/019-61958-279-10-41-902-20091006IPR61955-06-10-2009-2009-false/default_it.htm. Accessed 10 October 2010.

[209] Available at http://eur-lex.europa.eu/LexUriServ/LexUriServ.do?uri=OJ:C:2010:083:0335:0360:EN:PDF. Accessed 10 October 2010.

Chapter 2
Data Protection and the Insurance, Banking and Credit Reporting Industries

In Chap. 1 the data protection framework at the EU level was analysed in order "to prepare the field" for the analysis which will be carried out in this chapter.

Here the focus will be the processing of personal data that take place in the financial, insurance and credit reporting industries. The insurance industry and the banking sector use personal data to develop their activities with more efficiency, and the credit information suppliers are an important part of this mechanism, since they help banks and insurance companies in their search for personal data about their potential customers.[1] Banks and insurance companies[2] use personal information[3] for risk analysis,[4] such as the risk of making a loss for example, in the case of

[1]The expression 'credit information suppliers' is used because there are basically two kinds of institutions that provide credit information: credit bureaus and public credit registers. Jentzsch, Nicola. Financial Privacy: An International Comparison of Credit Reporting Systems. 2.ed. Berlin: Springer, 2007. P. 61. For a definition of credit bureaus and public credit registers see International Finance Corporation (IFC)—World Bank Group. Op. cit. P. 7. "A credit bureau is an institution that collects information from creditors and available public sources on a borrower's credit history. The bureau compiles information on individuals and/or small firms, such as information on credit repayment records, court judgments, and bankruptcies, and then creates a comprehensive credit report that is sold to creditors. (...) A public credit registry is defined as a database managed by the public sector, usually by the central bank or the bank supervisor, that collects information on the creditworthiness of borrowers (persons or businesses) from supervised financial institutions, makes such information available to financial institutions, and is used primarily for supervisory purposes."

[2]International Finance Corporation (IFC)—World Bank Group. Op. cit. P. 7. "Consumer credit bureaus collect information in a standardized format from several types of lenders, such as banks, credit card companies, retail lenders, other non-bank financial institutions, and utility companies."

[3]DeCew, Judith Wagner. Pursuit of Privacy—Law, Ethics, and the Rise of Technology. Op. Cit. P. 147. "At little or no cost, the bureaus make it easy for almost anyone to find out another individual's income, employment status, marital status, driving record, real state holdings, credit limit, and even civil and criminal court records."

[4]International Finance Corporation (IFC)—World Bank Group. Op. cit. P. 5. "Credit bureaus help address the fundamental problem in financial markets known as 'asymmetric information', which means that the borrower knows the odds of repaying his or her debts much better than the

M. Viola de Azevedo Cunha, *Market Integration Through Data Protection*, Law, Governance and Technology Series 9, DOI 10.1007/978-94-007-6085-1_2,

insurance,[5] or related to defaults,[6] in the case of banks.[7] From such analyses they classify their potential customers (and sometimes their current ones) in different categories of risk, establishing different premiums or interest rates according to the risk profile, or even refusing to conclude a contract with a specific person.[8]

To perform such analyses, insurance companies and financial institutions collect as much information as possible about their potential customers,[9] and in some cases sensitive data is also collected,[10] trying to reduce the possibility of concluding a contract with a high risk of loss[11] or default. As highlighted by Jentzsch "(...)

---

lender does. The inability of the lender to accurately assess the credit worthiness of the borrower contributes to higher default rates and affects the profitability of the financial institution."

[5]"A ciò va aggiunto che la disciplina sulla protezione dei dati personali impatta sull'industria assicurativa in modo forse più significativo che in altre imprese, se si considera la struttura típica del negozio assicurativo, che pone, come vederemo, lo scambio di informazione e dati sul rischio tra assicurato ed assicuratore a fondamento della stabilità dell'impresa e della correttezza dell'operazione assicurativa." CUFFARO, Vincenzo et al. Il codice del trattamento dei dati personali. Torino: G. Giappichelli Editore, 2007. P. 557.

[6]Jentzsch, Nicola. Op. cit. P. 274. "Default: This term denotes the situation, where the borrower fails to meet his or her financial obligations. Default is often used to refer to accounts that are more than 180 days delinquent. (...) Delinquency: Delinquency is the situation where the borrower fails to pay when due. Usually, there are late fees applied after the delinquency occurred. The credit business usually distinguishes 30-day, 60-day and 90-day delinquencies with the latter being the most serious. Delinquencies that are over 30 days are usually reported to credit bureaus."

[7]Another use of personal information by those industries is production of consumer personal consumer profiles in order to allow them to offer new and specific products adapted to the needs of their consumers. See SOFSKY, Wolfgang. Privacy—A Manifesto. (Translated by Steven Rendall). Princeton & Oxford: Princeton University Press, 2008. P. 107. "On the commodity market other interests are dominant. Traders, banks, insurance companies, and advertising agencies collect information about customers in order to produce personal consumer profiles and open up new market niches. Anyone who knows his customers' buying habits can surprise them with special offers and try to bind them to him."

[8]Information Commissioner's Office. Credit Explained. Available at http://www.ico.gov.uk/upload/documents/library/data_protection/practical_application/credit_explained_leaflet_2005.pdf. Accessed 23 February 2010. P. 1. "No one has a right to credit."

[9]Ferretti, Federico. Op. Cit. P. 15–16. "Each file usually contains the name of the borrower, his/her date of birth, current address, previous addresses if any, linked addresses, marital and employment status, number of accounts, amounts, types, stage (loan under approval, withdrawn, denied) and terms of accounts, amount of monthly instalments, amount of residual instalments, historical data, number of defaults, amount of arrears, name of granting institutions, payment history (both regulars and in default), dates. In addition, information relating to people that have a financial relationship with him/her is usually included."

[10]In the US, "The Medical Information Bureau (MIB), a nonprofit institution, maintains a database of medical information on 15 million individuals, which is available to over 700 insurance companies." SOLOVE, DANIEL J. Privacy and Powever: Computer Databases and Metaphors for Information Privacy. Stanford Law Review, Vol. 53 (2000–2001): 1409.

[11]Meyer, Roberta B. 2004. The insurer perspective. In *Genetics and life insurance—Medical underwriting and social policy*, ed. Mark A. Rothstein. Cambridge: The MIT Press. P. 29. "Risk classification assures that premiums are financially prudent or adequate to enable the insurer to meet its contractual obligations to its policy holders. It allows the insurer to determine premiums

Banks and insurance companies screen and monitor applicants and there is a possibility to signal certain characteristics."[12] The reason why these industries were selected as the case-studies of this book is the fact that they have personal information as an important raw material for the development of their activities.

This chapter will concentrate on the more sensitive issues that arise from the processing of personal data carried out by the selected industries, such as the processing of sensitive and genetic data—including the discussions about adverse selection, generalisation and discrimination.

2.1 The Processing of Personal Data by Insurance Companies, Banks and Credit Information Suppliers[13]

After having justified the choice of insurance companies, banks and credit information suppliers as the case-studies in this book, I will focus on the data processing activities carried out by these industries. To conduct this analysis I will look at the provisions of Directive 95/46/EC because they guide national legislation in the field of data protection. In the next chapters I will show the differences in the implementation of the Directive in the selected member states.

The first point to be discussed is the definition of personal data. Article 2(a) of Directive 95/46/EC[14] defines personal data as "any information relating to an identified or identifiable natural person ('data subject')" considering an identifiable person as "one who can be identified, directly or indirectly, in particular by reference to an identification number or to one or more factors specific to his physical, physiological, mental, economic, cultural or social identity."[15]

---

that are appropriate to levels of risk. The more underwriting information available to the insurer, the more precise it can be in determining appropriate premiums. This protects both insurer and policy holders from the insurer becoming insolvent due to inadequate premiums."

[12]Jentzsch, Nicola. Op. cit. P. 43. "(...) Banks and insurance companies screen and monitor applicants and there is a possibility to signal certain characteristics."

[13]Some portions of this section were previously published in Viola de Azevedo Cunha, Mario. Data Protection and Insurance: The Limits on the Collection and Use of Personal Data on Insurance Contracts in EU Law, Global Jurist: Vol. 10: Iss. 1 (Topics), Article 6, 2010.

[14]Available at http://eur-lex.europa.eu/LexUriServ/LexUriServ.do?uri=CELEX:31995L0046:EN:HTML. Accessed 7 May 2009.

[15]Kuner, Christopher. European Data Protection Law—Corporate Compliance and Regulation. 2.ed. Oxford: Oxford University Press, 2007. P. 92. "The requirement that the data relate to an 'identifiable' person in the General Directive similarly means that a set of data which, taken together, could be matched to a particular person, or at least make identification of that person considerably easier, is considered 'personal data'. Thus, for example, data concerning 'all males over 50 living in city X' would not be considered personal data, since it probably could not be tied to a specific person, even if great time and expense were used. However, data concerning 'all males over 50 living in city X who are physicians, have two daughters, listen to Verdi operas and have vacation houses in the south of France' would probably be considered personal data, since it

Nevertheless, even amongst EU member states there are differences regarding the concept of personal data. For instance, Portugal considers information concerning deceased people as personal data,[16] while the UK does not.[17] For the purposes of the analysis carried out in this chapter the definition of personal data adopted by the Article 29 Working Party on Data Protection shall be taken, which includes:

> (...) any sort of statements about a person. It covers "objective" information, such as the presence of a certain substance in one's blood. It also includes "subjective" information, opinions or assessments. These latter sort of statements make up a considerable share of personal data processing in sectors such as banking, for the assessment of the reliability of borrowers ("Titius is a reliable borrower"), in insurance ("Titius is not expected to die soon") or in employment ("Titius is a good worker and merits promotion").[18]

Nonetheless, it is not enough to define only the concept of personal data; it is also necessary to deal with a special kind of data, sensitive data, which plays an important role in the activities under analysis (especially in insurance). Sensitive data are those data related to the intimate sphere of the individual, such as data about his ethnic origin, political or religious beliefs, sexual choices and health status.[19]

Despite the fact that Directive 95/46/EC does not use the expression 'sensitive data', in its Article 8(1)[20] it includes a 'special category of data' which fits into the definition of sensitive data.[21] Such definition, however, varies from one Member State to the other, as identified by Andrew Charlesworth:

> Where definitions were provided in the DPD, they were often so wide-ranging as to be rendered meaningless when passed through the implementation process. For example, while the definition of "sensitive data" (personal data revealing racial or ethnic origin, political

---

would be possible to link this description with a specific person or persons, even though the data set itself does not contain any names."

[16]The same applies to Italy as will be seen in the next chapter (Sect. 5.2).

[17]Webster, Mandy. Op. cit. P. 109. The differences in the concept of personal data in EU Member states will become evident in the analysis I will carry out in the Chaps. 3, 4 and 5.

[18]Article 29 Working Party. Opinion 4/2007 on the concept of personal data, adopted on 20th June 2007. Available at http://ec.europa.eu/justice_home/fsj/privacy/docs/wpdocs/2007/wp136_en.pdf. Accessed 21 January 2010. P. 6.

[19]"Tale potere di controlo si fa ancora più stringente com riferimento a quello che viene considerato il nocciolo duro della privacy, rappresentato dalle informazioni relative alla salute, alle abitudine sessuale, alle opinione politiche, alle opinione religiose. (...) In relazione a tali informazioni è stata elaborata da c.d. categoria dei <<dati sensibile>>, che necessitano di uma protezione particolare contro i rischi della circolazione, proprio per la loro intrinseca attitude ad essere strumentalizzati per fini discriminatori." In Bianca, Cesare Massimo; Busnelli, Francesco Donato. La protezione dei dati personali. Cedam: Torino, 2007. P. LXXIX. See also Doneda, Danilo; Viola de Azevedo Cunha, Mario. Risk and Personal Information: The Finality Principle and Data Protection in the Brazilian Legal System. RBRSi, Rio de Janeiro, Brazil, v. 3, n. 3, p. 133–150, 2009. Available at http://www.rbrs-i.com/img/upload/RBRSi%203-3%20Danilo%20Doneda.pdf. Accessed 21 January 2010.

[20]See Article 8 Directive 95/46/EC.

[21]The CoE Convention 108/1981 adopted the same expression—special categories of data—for sensitive data.

> opinions, religious or philosophical beliefs, trade-union membership, and the processing of data concerning health or sex life) in the Directive is quite broad to begin with, some Member States appear to have defined "sensitive data" considerably more widely than others. For example, Portugal includes data about the "private life" of the individual within the definition, thereby requiring express consent for collection of data on consumer and household habits, whereas in the UK such data would almost certainly be treated as "non-sensitive" personal data and would require a correspondingly lower degree of protection."[22]

This is another issue to be addressed in the upcoming review of the EU Data Protection Framework, since "The concept of 'sensitive data' is misguided. Sensitivity depends on context. It is best addressed by appropriate interpretation of the data protection principles. The conditions for processing sensitive data do not achieve their aim."[23]

Nevertheless, not all kinds of data used by the industries analysed in this book are covered by the General Data Protection Directive. Anonymous and statistical data, which are largely used for building risk models, are not considered as personal data within the meaning of Directive 95/46/EC or of the definition of the Article 29 Working Party. It is, therefore, important to define the concept of anonymous data. The Directive, despite not defining anonymous data, adopted the position that "the principles of protection shall not apply to data rendered anonymous in such a way that the data subject is no longer identifiable".[24] The doctrine points toward a definition in the same direction, considering as anonymous data anything that could not be linked to an identified or identifiable individual[25] and some EU member states have adopted legislation which goes in the same direction.[26] The characterisation of anonymous data, however, is fundamental, in the sense that information which cannot be related to an identified or identifiable person lead to the non-application of data protection rules. Many member states have included in their national legislations a procedure called anonymisation of personal data, which is requirement for the 'free' processing of such data in specific circumstances.[27]

However, the distinction between personal data and anonymous data is not absolute and the validity of anonymous data as an exception to the application of

---

[22]Charlesworth, Andrew. Op. cit., 940.

[23]Apud Ibid, 941.

[24]Recital 26 of Directive 95/46/EC.

[25]Gediel, José Antônio Peres; CORRÊA, Adriana Espíndola. "Proteção jurídica de dados pessoais: A intimidade sitiada entre o Estado e o Mercado." Revista da Faculdade de Direito—UFPR, n.47. 2008. P. 144.

[26]Article 4(1) (n) of the Italian Personal Data Protection Code (Legislative Decree no. 196 dated 30 June 2003) considers anonymous data as "any data that either in origin or on account of its having been processed cannot be associated with any identified or identifiable data subject."

[27]See, for instance, the French Act n° 78-17 of 6 January 1978 on data processing, data files and individual liberties, http://www.cnil.fr/fileadmin/documents/en/Act78-17VA.pdf. Accessed 1 August 2011.

data protection rules has been put into question,[28] since through some modern techniques of data processing it is possible to recover the link between the anonymous data and the respective data subject.[29] Back in 2000, a research conducted by the computer scientist Latanya Sweeney proved that through the combination of three 'anonymous informations' (zip code, sex and birthday) it was possible to identify 87% of North American citizens.[30] Arvind Narayanan and Vitaly Shmatikov, in another research, "were able to identify a large proportion of anonymized Netflix subscribers by matching data in their movie ratings against an additional online database."[31] In a recent study, Paul Ohm argues that anonymisation techniques are misleading, because there is a wide range of possibilities of re-identification of personal data, i.e., through the use of statistical and mathematical techniques and the combination of different databases it is possible to link the anonymous information to a data subject.[32] According to Ohm, every information can become personal information if combined with other relevant information (although anonymous).

It is worth noting that many IT systems are built taking into account the fact that the processing of personal data after the use of anonymisation techniques would be free from the incidence of the data protection legislation. Such approach, on the one hand, could be considered as the application of Privacy by Design principles, but, on the other hand, it could lead to many risks, because data considered as anonymous would be processed until being linked to their data subjects.[33]

---

[28]Information Commissioner's Office, Data Protection Act 1998: Legal Guidance, http://www.ico.gov.uk/upload/documents/library/data_protection/detailed_specialist_guides/data_protection_act_legal_guidance.pdf. Accessed 3 March 2010: 13. "The Commissioner considers anonymisation of personal data difficult to achieve because the data controller may retain the original data set from which the personal identifiers have been stripped to create the 'anonymised' data."

[29]Regarding the anonymisation of genetic data the situation is even more complicated. See MURRAY, Thomas H., "Genetic Exceptionalism and 'Future Diaries': Is Genetic Information Different from Other Medical Information?," in Genetic Secrets: Protecting Privacy and Confidentiality in the Genetic Era, ROTHSTEIN, Mark A. (New Heaven and London: Yale University Press, 1997), 63. "If a database contained sufficient information about the sequence, even if the person's name were not attached to the file, it might be possible to identify the individual whose sequence it is, in a manner similar to the method of genetic fingerprinting. So, although the practise of removing identifying information is usually thought to confer anonymity by making records impossible to trace to an individual, that may not be the case with records containing significant chunks of DNA sequence data."

[30]Sweeney, Latanya. Foundations of Privacy Protection from a Computer Science Perspective, http://dataprivacylab.org/projects/disclosurecontrol/paper1.pdf. Accessed 22 February 2011.

[31]Tene, Omer. Privacy: The new generations. International Data Privacy Law Vol. 1, No. 1 (2011): 17.

[32]Ohm, Paul. Broken Promises of Privacy: Responding to the Surprising Failure of Anonymization (August 13, 2009). University of Colorado Law School Legal Studies Research Paper No. 09–12, http://ssrn.com/abstract=1450006. Accessed 7 November 2010.

[33]An example of the risks is the software produced by Phorm, called WebWise, which was hardly criticized by data protection advocates. See Clayton, Richard. The Phorm 'Webwise'system, http://www.cl.cam.ac.uk/rnc1/080518-phorm.pdf. Accessed 7 November 2010.

The importance of this subject led to a discussion about the distinction between anonymous data for statistical purposes and anonymous data for data protection purposes. The Article 29 Working Party in its Opinion 1/2008 on data protection issues related to search engines stated that for data to be considered as anonymous and, therefore, out of the scope of the General Data Protection Directive, the anonymisation has to be complete and irreversible, in a manner that renders the data subject unidentifiable.[34] Such complete anonymisation, however, even if possible, is a difficult task, both from a technical viewpoint and in terms of adequacy to data protection rules.[35]

The European Data Protection Supervisor in some of his opinions developed a clear distinction between "anonymous" or "anonymised" data for data protection purposes, and "statistical anonymous data". The former would be "any information relating to a natural person where the person cannot be identified, whether by the data controller or by any other person, taking account of all the means likely reasonably to be used either by the controller or by any other person to identify that individual. Anonymised data would be anonymous data which previously referred to an identifiable person, no longer identifiable." From a statistical point of view, anonymous data "are data for which no direct identification is possible. This definition implies that the possibility of indirect identification would still qualify the data concerned as anonymous from a statistical point of view, but not necessarily from a data protection point of view."[36]

[34]Article 29 Working Party on Data Protection, Opinion 1/2008 on data protection issues related to search engines, adopted on 4 April 2008. http://ec.europa.eu/justice/policies/privacy/docs/wpdocs/2008/wp148_en.pdf. Accessed 4 January 2011, 20. In its opinion 4/2007, the Article 29 Working Party presents a definition of anonymous data that take into account 'the means likely reasonably to be used' for the identification of the data subject. See Article 29 Working Party, Opinion 4/2007 on the concept of personal data, Op. cit.: 21.

[35]Walden, Ian, "Anonymising Personal Data," International Journal of Law and Information Technology 10 n° 2 (2002): 226. "Achieving effective anonymisation may be a challenging task, from both a technical and compliance perspective. Sophisticated data analysis and data mining techniques on supposedly anonymous data may eventually yield data that does 'directly or indirectly' relate to a specific individual (…)."

[36]European Data Protection Supervisor. Opinion on the proposal for a regulation of the European parliament and of the council on European statistics (COM(2007) 625 final). Adopted on 20 May 2008. Available at http://www.edps.europa.eu/EDPSWEB/webdav/site/mySite/shared/Documents/Consultation/Opinions/2008/08-05-20_Statistics_EN.pdf. 25 Jan 2010: 4. In the same sense, see European Data Protection Supervisor, Opinion of 5 September 2007 on the proposal for a Regulation of the European Parliament and of the Council on Community statistics on public health and health and safety at work (COM(2007) 46 final), http://www.edps.europa.eu/EDPSWEB/webdav/site/mySite/shared/Documents/Consultation/Opinions/2007/07-09-05_Statistics_health_data_EN.pdf. Accessed 4 January 2011: 4. "18. The same analysis occurs with the notion of anonymity. Although, from a data protection view, the notion of anonymity would cover data that are no longer identifiable (see recital 26 of the Directive), from a statistical point of view, anonymous data are data for which no direct identification is possible. This definition implies that indirect identification of data would still qualify these data as anonymous, from a statistical point of view."

Regarding the issue of a person being "identified or identifiable", the Article 29 Working Party, in its opinion on the concept of personal data, tried to establish a distinction between these two concepts. For the Working Party "a natural person can be considered as 'identified' when, within a group of persons, he or she is 'distinguished' from all other members of the group. Accordingly, the natural person is 'identifiable' when, although the person has not been identified yet, it is possible to do it (that is the meaning of the suffix '-able')."

Directive 95/46/EC itself, in its recital 26, presents an indication on how to determine whether an individual is identifiable or not:

> (. . .) to determine whether a person is identifiable, account should be taken of all the means likely reasonably to be used either by the controller or by any other person to identify the said person (. . .)

This reasonableness referred to by the Directive is the key element in establishing the threshold for considering data as related to an identified or identifiable person and, as a consequence, personal data.[37] As highlighted by the Article 29 Working Party, "This means that a mere hypothetical possibility to single out the individual is not enough to consider the person as 'identifiable'".[38]

Recommendation R (97) 5 of the Committee of Ministers of the Council of Europe, on the protection of medical data, in its Article 1(1) states that data cannot be considered identifiable "if identification requires an unreasonable amount of time and manpower".[39] These criteria of time and manpower were taken into account by the German Data Protection Law:

> (. . .)'depersonalized' if a person can only be identified with 'a disproportionate amount of time, expense and labour'(. . .).[40]

As Waden argues, "The issue of effective anonymisation is ultimately one of fact for the regulator or courts to decide in the particular circumstances, although a statutory definition for anonymous data would provide criteria against which such an assessment could be made."[41]

This is an aspect which is missing in the Directive and that should be included in the discussions regarding its review. A possible solution would be to follow the same criteria established by both the German Data Protection Law and Recommendation R (97) 5 of the Committee of Ministers of the Council of Europe, i.e., if the necessary measures to identify the link between a person and a certain datum

---

[37]According to the Article 29 Working Party, the reasonableness is "Another general limitation for the application of data protection under the Directive." in Article 29 Working Party. Opinion 4/2007 on the concept of personal data, Op. cit.: 5.

[38]Article 29 Working Party. Opinion 4/2007 on the concept of personal data, Op. cit.: 13.

[39]Council of Europe. Committee of ministers recommendation no. R (97) 5 on the protection of medical data. 13 Feb 1997. Available at www.coe.int. 17 Nov 2009.

[40]Apud Walden, Ian, Op. cit.: 226. The cost of the identification was recognised by the Article 29 Working Party as one of the factors to be taken into account when analysing whether an individual is identifiable or not. Article 29 Working Party, Opinion 4/2007 on the concept of personal data, Op. cit.: 15.

[41]Walden, Ian, Op. cit.: 227.

are disproportionate, this datum will not be considered as personal data but as an anonymous one for the purposes of the application of data protection rules.[42]

Having defined the concepts of personal data, sensitive data and of data that are not covered by the directive (anonymous data), I shall now address the 'justifications' used by the respective industries for the processing of personal data and the negative effects that such processing can have on individuals' privacy.

2.1.1 *Risk Analysis and Adverse Selection*

Insurance companies, banks and credit information suppliers base their activities on risk analysis.[43] According to this kind of analysis, the insurer, the bank or the credit information supplier checks the probability of a person developing a certain disease, having an accident or dying, or of not paying a debt.[44] After that, they classify that person according to the categories of risk previously elaborated, what supports the decision concerning the premium to be paid[45] or the interest rate,[46] or even of not concluding a contract.[47]

---

[42]Sarmento e Castro, Catarina, Direito da informática, privacidade e dados pessoais (Coimbra: Almedina, 2005), 72.

[43]Liedtke, Patrick M. What's Insurance to a Modern Economy. The Geneva Papers, 2007, 32. P. 214. "An insurer also works as a risk expert and risk manager because he has to understand and assess the risks he will accept or decline for the scheme. If somebody buys into that scheme, a new relationship is established and has to be judged on its merits, not least vis-à-vis the existing participants and their risks. Whenever an insurer accepts a new risk into the scheme, this affects everybody who is already in the scheme. It is not just a decision that the insurer takes and where he has a direct obligation concerning the risk per se, he also has an obligation to his other business relations."

[44]Jentzsch, Nicola. Op. cit. P. 274. "Credit risk: The (estimated) probability that the borrower will not repay the amount owed on time. Although there are different definitions, credit risk in general usually is defined as delinquency or as default; this is being either 30, 60, 90 or 180 days late. The term is also used for a consumer's creditworthiness (credit rating). In information economics, this term is used as a short form for 'credit risk of the consumer,' where there is a separation in good credit risks and bad ones."

[45]Baker, Tom. Containing the Promise of Insurance: Adverse Selection and Risk Classification. University of Connecticut School of Law Articles Working Paper Series. 2001. Available at: http://lsr.nellco.org/cgi/viewcontent.cgi?article=1002&context=uconn/ucwps. Accessed 1 February 2008. P. 3. "Insurance risk classification is the process of sorting insurance applicants into categories believed to correspond to differences in expected risk. Common examples include sorting life insurance applicants by age, health insurance applicants by health status, workers compensation insurance applicants by type of industry, and property insurance applicants by the nature of the construction of the property to be insured (e.g., wood versus brick)."

[46]International Finance Corporation (IFC)—World Bank Group. Op. cit. P. 5. "Credit bureaus are essential to the success of credit markets. They serve as indispensable tools used by financial institutions to support their retail lending business."

[47]Viola de Azevedo Cunha, Mario. Privacidade e Seguro: a coleta e utilização de dados pessoais nos ramos de pessoas e de saúde. Cadernos de Seguro—Teses n. 33. Funenseg: Rio de Janeiro, 2009. P. 22.

To perform this analysis, they use as much information as possible about the potential customers,[48] concerning their habits, economic condition,[49] health status, including genetic data, and many others.[50] Moreover, not only information relating to the potential customers is used, but also to third parties, such as data related to family history of diseases or to grantors.[51] Both providers and their clients raise claims based on information asymmetry.

On the one hand, insurance providers and banks argue that individuals have better knowledge about their health status or financial situation than insurance companies or banks. When a potential customer does not give any particular piece of information or when a specific piece of data cannot be used for risk analysis, because of a legal provision, e.g., there is information asymmetry between the data subject and the provider of services—financial institution or insurance company—, leading to adverse selection.[52] Indeed, elderly people, with a higher risk of becoming

[48]Meyer, Roberta B. Op. cit. P. 29. "Risk classification assures that premiums are financially prudent or adequate to enable the insurer to meet its contractual obligations to its policy holders. It allows the insurer to determine premiums that are appropriate to levels of risk. The more underwriting information available to the insurer, the more precise it can be in determining appropriate premiums. This protects both insurer and policy holders from the insurer becoming insolvent due to inadequate premiums." In the same sense, see Expert Group on Credit Histories. Op. cit. P. 40. "Some EGCH experts agree that when assessing creditworthiness and indebtedness, the use of as much relevant data as possible is an advantage (provided it is correct)."

[49]Credit Bureaus and Public Registers usually collect and stored only credit information, that can be positive or negative, or even both, what varies from country to country. See International Finance Corporation (IFC)—World Bank Group. Op. cit. P. 12."Credit history information can be broadly divided into two categories: Negative information: credit history only contains information on defaults. The information may include amounts outstanding at default and the date of last payment. When the debt is repaid, information on delinquencies is deleted from the database . These types of databases are also often referred to as black lists. Among all consumer credit bureaus, 32% provide negative only information. Positive (and negative) or full-file information: credit history contains information on all open and closed credit accounts, including the amount approved, as well as the information on repayment. If a borrower has defaulted on payments, but eventually paid it off, the default information remains on file and is not deleted for a defined period of time. Among all consumer credit bureaus, 68% provide both negative and positive information." See also the Expert Group on Credit Histories. Op. cit. P. 38.

[50]International Finance Corporation (IFC)—World Bank Group. Op. cit. P. 7. "These individual credit reports generally contain personal borrower information and information on borrower credit accounts. The personal section usually captures the borrower's name; identification number, such as social security (if any); date of birth; former names; current and previous addresses; other forms of identification; employment history; alerts, such as ID theft or security freezes; and date of information update. The credit summary section contains information on all credit accounts (both open and closed) that the borrower may have had, all accounts in good standing, past due accounts, negative account history, and all inquiries made about the borrower for at least the past 12 months."

[51]Family history data will be discussed in Sect. 2.2 of this chapter.

[52]Adverse selection happens when one party has information before the transaction that would change the terms of the transaction if known to the other party—e.g. Someone knows that he/she has cancer but does not give this information to the insurance company and contract a life insurance. BAKER, Tom. Op. cit. P. 2. "Adverse selection" (sometimes called "anti-selection" in the insurance trade literature) refers to the theoretical tendency for low risk individuals to avoid

sick, and people with health problems, tend to seek insurance coverage more than young and healthy people. Insurance companies argue that the lack of information makes them increase the premiums, motivating adverse selection, because only high-risk people will agree to pay a higher premium.[53] Therefore, in the view of the insurance advocates "Adverse selection harms both insurers and their other clients, who collectively cover at unfairly advantageous rates."[54] In the case of credit, "Adverse selection arises when the creditor is not aware of some performance characteristics of the borrower" and the credit information suppliers are considered as an important tool because they complete "the information provided directly by a credit applicant—which may or may not be a true reflection of his/her credit risk or ability to repay the loan."[55]

On the other hand, consumers' advocates argue that individuals lack proper knowledge about how their information will be used, which creates, in a different sense, information asymmetry in favour of the strongest side of the contractual relationship.[56] The discussion about adverse selection is not simple, as it involves not only economic aspects but also some other relevant issues, such as the risk of discrimination it creates. A good example of this risk of discrimination can be found in the case of battered women in the US, during the late 1980s when:

> (...) some large U.S. insurers were refusing to sell life, health and disability insurance to battered women on the grounds that they posed an unacceptably high risk. In response to

---

or drop out of voluntary insurance pools, with the result that, absent countervailing efforts by administrators, insurance pools can be expected to contain disproportionate percentage of high-risk individuals (...). For example, adverse selection is said to explain the disparity in prices between group and individual health insurance in the United States. With group health insurance, an employer signs up employees as a group, so the insurer gets both the low and the high risks. With individual health insurance, people decide on their own whether to purchase insurance, and those who need it the most are the most likely to purchase it (assuming that they have financial means), with the result that insurers end up with more of the high risks in the pool and less of the low risks.

[53] Scolik, Hélio. O Prêmio Nobel de Economia de 2001 e a Informação Assimétrica. Available at http://www.vemconcursos.com/opiniao/index.phtml?page_ordem=assunto&page_id=274&page_print=1. Accessed 11 March 2007.

[54] O'NEILL, Onora. Insurance and Genetics: The Current State of Play. In Brownsword, Roger et al. (editors). Law and Human Genetics—Regulating a Revolution. Oxford: Hart Publishing, 1998. P. 129.

[55] Expert Group on Credit Histories. Report of the Expert Group on Credit Histories. May 2009. P. 13.

[56] Solove, Daniel. Understanding Privacy. Op. cit. P. 73. "Acquisti and Grossklags point to the problem of information asymmetries, when people lack adequate knowledge of how their personal information will be used, and bounded rationality, when people have difficulty applying what they know to complex situations. Some privacy problems shape behavior. People often surrender personal data to companies because they perceive that they do not have much choice. They might also do so because they lack knowledge about the potential future uses of the information. Part of the privacy problem in these cases involves people's limited bargaining power respecting privacy and inability to assess the privacy risks. Thus looking at people's behavior might present a skewed picture of societal expectations of privacy."

> this news, states began enacting legislation prohibiting insurers from discriminating against victims of domestic violence, and bills to do the same on a national level were introduced into the U.S. Congress. In the effort to defeat this legislation, the insurers' defense was that excluding battered women from the insurance pool was "actuarially fair." According to the insurers, the history of abuse meant that these women were much more likely to make life, health or disability insurance claims in the future than others, otherwise similarly situated women who were not domestic abuse victims. This higher risk meant that it was "actuarially fair" to exclude them from the insurance pool, just as insurers excluded other unacceptably high risks.[57]

Another example, given by Amitai Etzioni, demonstrates the risks behind allowing the use of some kinds of sensitive information in commercial transactions:

> (. . .) in the realm of medical privacy, if a person has a stroke, some banks that find out will call in the loans. There is little or no contribution to the common good in such interventions, but the intrusion is very high, indeed one of the highest intrusions one can imagine.[58]

Making selections on the basis of highly sensitive information—such as that mentioned in the examples—would disproportionately sacrifice the interests of certain people, on the basis of the fact that they belong to a certain disadvantaged class, ethnicity or simply genetic group. Therefore, the argument of information asymmetry and of adverse selection is not strong enough to legitimise the processing of all kinds of personal data for risk analysis, both in the field of insurance or credit. It is important to establish limits for that processing, which go beyond the legal grounds for the processing of personal data discussed above (Sect. 1.3.1.1), and those limits should include the non-discrimination principle.

2.1.2 Generalisation and Discrimination

In this part I will analyse the risks of discrimination posed by profiling techniques used by the selected industries, which work on the basis of generalisations. Generalisation takes place when an entire group is treated in a certain way because of the behaviour of a minority of that group.[59] Insurance companies, banks and credit information suppliers base most of their decisions on generalisations. When they design a risk profile or even when they analyse the risk a specific individual poses, they do that based on previous behaviours of certain people that are part of the same age, sexual, or ethnic group.[60]

---

[57]Baker, Tom. Op. cit. P. 12.

[58]Etzioni, Amitai. A Communitarian Approach: A Viewpoint on the Study of the Legal and Ethical Policy Considerations Raised by DNA Tests and Databases. Journal of Law, Medicine & Ethics, V. 34 (2006): 217.

[59]Schauer, Frederick. Profiles, Probabilities and Stereotypes. Cambridge: Belknap Press of Harvard University Press, 2003. P. 3.

[60]Ibid. P. 4. "(. . .) generalisation is the stock in trade of the insurance industry. Indeed, the insurance industry has its own name for this kind of decisionmaking. To be an actuary is to be

Such generalisations impose a heavy burden in the whole category of individuals who belong to this same group, even if they behave in a different way. For example, "When a teenage male acquires a driver's license, his family's insurance premium will rise dramatically, even if their son is a paragon of caution less likely to be involved in an accident than even most adults."[61] The main problem of those generalisations is the discrimination that they can create, since individuals who are part of targeted groups do not have the opportunity to demonstrate that the generalisations about their specific 'group' do not apply to them and they suffer very severe consequences for that.[62]

Although "All human beings—teenage males who drive cars, ex-convicts, used-car salesmen, Scots, accountants, and everyone else—deserve to be treated as individuals and not simply as members of a group",[63] generalisations are not necessarily always morally wrong, but some limits should be imposed on them. However, there are generalisations which are controversial, as the case of asking gay men to pay more for health insurance because they belong to a group who "have a statistical likelihood of contracting the HIV virus" or even the case of "people whose genetic makeup makes them more likely to suffer from cancer or heart disease".[64] Let us take the example of women of eastern European Jewish (Ashkenazi) origin. Medically speaking, such a 'group' of women has a higher risk of developing breast or ovarian cancer than average women, due to the fact that a mutation in the gene BRCA, which increases the risk of breast cancer, is more common in this group than in others.[65] If insurance companies used this generalisation for risk analysis purposes, they would probably deny coverage of breast or ovarian cancer in private health or life insurance policies to all women with an eastern European Jewish

a specialist in generalization, and actuaries engage in a form of decisionmaking that is sometimes called actuarial."

[61]Ibid. P. 4.

[62]Daniel Solove brings an interesting example of generalisation which discriminate an entire group of people. Solove, Daniel J. The digital person. Op. cit. P. 50. "(. . .) one bank routinely denied credit card applications from college students majoring in literature, history, and art, based on the assumption that they would not be able to repay their debts."

[63]Schauer, Frederick. Op. cit. P. 19.

[64]Ibid. P. 5. There are other examples of generalisations made by insurance companies that are considered to be controversial, such as being resident of a specific city or driving high-performance sport cars. See Schauer, Frederick. Op. cit. P. 5.

[65]UK National Cancer Institute. BRCA1 and BRCA2: Cancer Risk and Genetic Testing. Available at http://www.cancer.gov/cancertopics/factsheet/Risk/BRCA. Accessed 8 March 2010. See also The Oncologist. More Ashkenazi Jews Have Gene Defect that Raises Inherited Breast Cancer Risk Vol. 1, No. 5, 335–335, October 1996. AlphaMed Press. "The study shows the BRCA2 mutation is just as common among Ashkenazis as a similar mutation in the BRCA1 gene that also increases the risk of breast cancer in this ethnic group. Despite the similar frequency of the two mutations, the risk of breast cancer is more than three times higher in Ashkenazi women who inherit the BRCA1 mutation compared to those who inherit the BRCA2 mutation, the research indicates."

origin,[66] and, hence, would discriminate against the whole group. Frederick Schauer presents four reasons to consider this generalisation unjust:

> The first is that health insurance is crucially important, and in the modern world a person without health insurance is at considerable risk of suffering a medical and financial catastrophe. The second reason is that those who suffer from the generalization are women, and the fact that women are subject to financial discrimination in the workplace and elsewhere both compounds the magnitude of the financial risk and potentially exacerbates existing forms of gender discrimination. Third, the statistically relevant factor, eastern European Jewishness, is one that may foster or entrench existing prejudices about the otherness of Jews, about Jews as a distinct racial class, and about Jews as being in some way different from the bulk of the population. Fourth, and finally, using the generalization might be unjust simply because most eastern European Jewish women will not become afflicted with breast or ovarian cancer, and many will even have identifiable health factors or personal habits that lower the risk of such cancers substantially more than having an eastern European Jewish genetic background raises it.[67]

This author suggests that one possible solution would be to prohibit the use of ethnicity or race as patterns for generalisation to avoid their overuse,[68] although in the opinion of this author "'Discrimination', after all, is not necessarily pejorative, and to have discriminating taste is a virtue and not a vice. (. . .) the ability to discriminate even in individual cases is a function of the careful use of all the available evidence, and the available evidence itself takes the form of a series of generalisations."[69]

It is also my opinion that although not all kinds of generalisation should be avoided, some limits should be imposed to them, which affects the way both the insurance industry and the banking sector (including credit information suppliers) design their risk models and analyse the risk individuals represent. A limit to be

---

[66] Lenox, Bryce A. Genetic Discrimination in Insurance and Employment: Spoiled Fruits of the Human Genome Project. University of Dayton Law Review. Vol. 23. 1997–1998. P. 194; 196–197. "Genetic discrimination by employers and insurers presents a myriad of issues for individuals subject to genetic screening. Currently, there are several target groups for genetic discrimination: (1) people who are carriers for a recessive genetic disease (they carry the gene but will never become symptomatic); (2) people who carry a gene linked to a genetic disease, but are asymptomatic (they have the gene, but show no signs currently and may never become symptomatic); (3) family members with relatives that carry a known or presumed genetic defect; and (4) those with a genetic aberration not known to manifest any medical condition. Apparently, such genetic discrimination may occur in insurance and in the workplace in almost all targeted groups. (. . .) Further, 'the fact that genetic diseases are sometimes closely associated with discrete ethnic or racial groups such as African Americans, Ashkenazi Jews, or Armenians compounds the potential for invidious discrimination.' Finally, genetic discrimination impacts the creativity and productivity of people, possibly more than the actual disease itself. 'By excluding qualified individuals from education, employment, government service, or insurance, the marketplace is robbed of skills, energy, and imagination. Such exclusion promotes physical and economic dependency, draining rather than enriching social institutions.'"

[67] Schauer, Frederick. Op. cit. P. 36–37.

[68] Ibid. P. 187.

[69] Ibid. P. 214.

imposed upon the use of generalisations is the potential of discrimination they represent to specific groups of individuals,[70] such as based on race, ethnicity, religion, etc., which are considered by society as morally wrong.[71] Such limitations should apply to nonspurious generalisations, because spurious generalisations should not be used at all for risk analysis.[72]

Indeed, the proposed 'Principles of European Insurance Contract Law (PEICL)' developed by the Project Group 'Restatement of European Insurance Contract Law' in the framework of the European Network of Excellence on European Contract Law (CoPECL), set up by the European Commission,[73] forbid the use of nationality, racial or ethnic origin "as factors resulting in differences in individuals' premiums and benefits".[74] This approach is in line with one of the basic orientations of the European Union, included in article 19 of the Treaty on the Functioning of the European Union,[75] which establishes that "the Council, acting unanimously in accordance with a special legislative procedure and after obtaining the consent of the European Parliament, may take appropriate action to combat discrimination based on sex, racial or ethnic origin, religion or belief, disability, age or sexual orientation."

---

[70]Bagenstos, Samuel R. "Rational Discrimination", Accommodation, and the Politics of (Disability) Civil Rights. Virginia Law Review. Vol. 89, Number 5, September 2003. P. 856. "Thus a more plausible theory for what makes stereotyping based on the forbidden classifications of race, gender, and disability worse than other types of stereotyping is that stereotyping based on those classifications causes greater harm to the groups that are persistently on the 'wrong' side of society's stereotypical judgements." In the same sense, see Stein, Michael Ashley. Review Generalizing Disability. Michigan Law Review. Vol. 102, Nº 6, 2004. Survey of Books Relating to the Law (May, 2004). P. 1389. "Nonetheless, a prominent exception to the morality of decisionmaking based on broad classifications are instances where the sustainable empirical facts are themselves by-products of past discrimination against those groups."

[71]Schauer, Frederick. Op. Cit. P. 128. "(...) certain forms of generalization, even if nonspurious vis-à-vis legitimate goals, are nevertheless morally repugnant because of the way in which they may stigmatize or isolate members of certain traditionally oppressed or marginalized groups."

[72]Stein, Michael Ashley. Op. cit. P. 1374. "(...) spurious categories lacking statistical support and nonspurious categories that are empirically sustainable. The nonspurious category contains two further varieties: universal generalizations that are always true because of either definitional ('all bachelors are unmarried') or empirical ('all humans are less than nine feet tall') reasons, and those generalizations that are relatively truer for members of a particular group than they are in general ('bulldogs tend to have poorer hips than most other dogs,' or 'teenagers are relatively bad drivers in comparison to the overall driving population')".

[73]See http://www.copecl.org/. Accessed 13 March 2010.

[74]Basedow, Jürgen et al. (editors). Principles of European Insurance Contract Law (PEICL). Munich: Sellier European Law Publishers, 2009. P. 69.

[75]Available at http://eur-lex.europa.eu/LexUriServ/LexUriServ.do?uri=OJ:C:2008:115:0047:0199:EN:PDF. Accessed 13 March 2010.

2.1.3 The Processing of Sensitive Data

The problem of discrimination is more evident when the assessment of risk involves the processing of sensitive data, which is quite common in insurance contracts—but sometimes also in the banking sector.[76] There are many examples of situations in which the use of sensitive data is fundamental for the relationship between the individual and the data controller, such as the case of religious institutions, trade unions and political parties concerning their associates or affiliates. On the one hand, forbidding these institutions to collect and use sensitive data related to religious or political beliefs and to affiliation to a trade union would not bring any benefit to the individuals and, on the other hand, would make the relationship between the individuals and those institutions difficult. The use of sensitive data for these purposes was recognised by Directive 95/46/EC in its article 8(2)(d).

With regards to credit reporting and lending activities, since their main purpose is to evaluate the creditworthiness of potential (or current) customers,[77] it does not

---

[76]Data related to fraud is an example of the use of sensitive data in credit reporting activities. See Expert Group on Credit Histories. Op. cit. P. 40. "Data about fraud is often stored in central databases so that a creditor may check to see if a credit application may be related to a past fraud. Creditors store information about instances of fraud within their own business and employ experts and tools to detect and prevent fraudulent new credits and fraud activity in existing accounts."

[77]Directive 2008/48EC imposes to financial institutions the duty to assess the creditworthiness of the consumers, by consulting the relevant databases. It also creates to member states the obligation to ensure to creditors from other member states, in the case of cross-border credit, access to databases used in that member state for assessing the creditworthiness of consumers in a 'non-discriminatory' way. See Articles 8 and 9:

Article 8. Obligation to assess the creditworthiness of the consumer

1. Member states shall ensure that, before the conclusion of the credit agreement, the creditor assesses the consumer's creditworthiness on the basis of sufficient information, where appropriate obtained from the consumer and, where necessary, on the basis of a consultation of the relevant database. Member states whose legislation requires creditors to assess the creditworthiness of consumers on the basis of a consultation of the relevant database may retain this requirement.
2. Member states shall ensure that, if the parties agree to change the total amount of credit after the conclusion of the credit agreement, the creditor updates the financial information at his disposal concerning the consumer and assesses the consumer's creditworthiness before any significant increase in the total amount of credit.

Article 9. Database access

1. Each Member state shall in the case of cross-border credit ensure access for creditors from other member states to databases used in that member state for assessing the creditworthiness of consumers. The conditions for access shall be non-discriminatory.
2. If the credit application is rejected on the basis of consultation of a database, the creditor shall inform the consumer immediately and without charge of the result of such consultation and of the particulars of the database consulted.
3. The information shall be provided unless the provision of such information is prohibited by other Community legislation or is contrary to objectives of public policy or public security.

seem proportional to collect information other than credit related information, and this is the position adopted in most EU member states.[78] Only when banks and credit information suppliers process information to prevent criminal activities, such as fraud and money laundering, the processing of sensitive data would be acceptable.[79] In France, for example, the processing of information related to the nationality of the applicant for credit is considered to be proportional.[80] Nevertheless, this approach seems to contradict article 19 of the Treaty on the Functioning of the European Union, since it leaves space for a possible discrimination based on ethnic origin, once banks in France could deny credit to nationals of some states which have a specific ethnic origin.

The case of insurance is quite different from banking, and the need to process sensitive data in some situations seems to be clearly necessary, but it is obvious that not all sensitive data can be collected and used for insurance purposes. Data related to sex life, to religious or political beliefs and to ethnic origin, for example, even if they could have an influence on the evaluation of the risk, should not be used—at least as a rule—because it would impose on data subjects an excessive burden to prove that they do not have an increased risk, excessively exposing their private lives. Moreover, the evaluation of the impact of such data on risk analysis would be extremely subjective.

In the Test-Achats case, the European Court of Justice considered as invalid article 5(2) of Directive 2004/113/EC, precluding insurance companies to use gender

---

4. This Article shall be without prejudice to the application of Directive 95/46/EC of the European Parliament and of the Council of 24 October 1995 on the protection of individuals with regard to the processing of personal data and on the free movement of such data.

[78]Expert Group on Credit Histories. Op. cit. P. 40. "In most European markets today, however, some types of non-credit information cannot be processed. As far as this data would constitute infringements to the legislation, they might be considered as judicial data in the sense of some national laws implementing the Data Protection Directive. Judicial data is strictly protected and cannot, according to such laws, be processed except e.g. by the data controller use in the course of his/her own litigation. Centralisation of such data or its processing by a third party (creditor) would therefore not be admissible. In addition, data collected for a specific purpose (e.g. telecommunication services) must be, according to the Data Protection Directive, processed for that specific purpose and cannot automatically be transferred to another data controller with an incompatible purpose."

[79]Both insurance companies, banks and credit information suppliers process personal data for preventing criminal activities. There are some legal duties imposed to these activities regarding, for example, money laundering and paedophilia.

[80]See Chap. 3.

as a factor for risk analysis.[81] However, the interpretation the EU Commission adopted in its Guidelines on the application of Council Directive 2004/113/EC to insurance, in the light of the judgment of the Court of Justice of the European Union in Case C-236/09, was that the Court Decision

> (...) does not prohibit the use of gender as a risk-rating factor in general. Such use is allowed in the calculation of premiums and benefits at the aggregate level, as long as it does not lead to differentiation at the individual level. After the Test-Achats ruling, it therefore remains possible to collect, store and use gender status or gender-related information within those limits (...)[82]

Directive 95/46/EC presents in article 8(1) a list of data which fits the definition of sensitive data, establishing as a rule the prohibition of the processing of such data. Nevertheless, other paragraphs of article 8 provide for some exceptions to this rule. Paragraph 4 of Article 8 admits, when "substantial public interest" is involved, that other exemptions can be added to the ones of paragraph 1 by national law or by a decision of the supervisory authority. The processing of data relating to offences, criminal convictions or security measures should be carried out, as a rule, "only under control of official authority or if suitable specific safeguards are provided under national law." Nonetheless, such a rule is "subject to derogations which may be granted by the member states under national provisions providing for suitable specific safeguards" (Article 8(5)).

Accordingly, the processing of sensitive data requires a case-by-case analysis of the situations where their processing is intended. It is important to notice that the starting point for that analysis should be the adequacy of the processing operation to the finality, proportionality, data quality and information principles. It is my opinion that the idea of non-discrimination should be added to the processing of sensitive data, already discussed in Sect. 2.1.1, and which will be further developed in the next section (Sect. 2.2). Moreover, this analysis should also observe the provisions

[81]EUROPEAN COURT OF JUSTICE. Case C-236/09, Association belge des Consommateurs Test-Achats ASBL and others v. Conseil des ministres. Grand Chamber, 9 March 2010. Available at http://curia.europa.eu/jurisp/cgi-bin/form.pl?lang=en&alljur=alljur&jurcdj=jurcdj&jurtpi=jurtpi&jurtfp=jurtfp&numaff=C-236/09&nomusuel=&docnodecision=docnodecision&allcommjo=allcommjo&affint=affint&affclose=affclose&alldocrec=alldocrec&docdecision=&docor=docor&docav=docav&docsom=docsom&docinf=docinf&alldocnorec=alldocnorec&docnoor=docnoor&docppoag=docppoag&radtypeord=on&newform=newform&docj=docj&docop=docop&docnoj=docnoj&typeord=ALL&domaine=&mots=&resmax=100&Submit=Rechercher. Accessed 7 August 2011.

[82]European Commission. Communication from the Commission—Guidelines on the application of Council Directive 2004/113/EC to insurance, in the light of the judgment of the Court of Justice of the European Union in Case C-236/09 (TestAchats). C(2011) 9497 final. Brussels, 22.12.2011. Available at http://ec.europa.eu/justice/gender-equality/files/com_2011_9497_en.pdf. Accessed 17 September 2012. P. 5.

of national law implementing Article 8(2)(a),[83] what will be the focus of the next chapters (Chaps. 3, 4, 5).

I will use the example of life insurance, where, in general, insurers collect data related not only to the health status of the individual, but also about his habits (e.g. if someone smokes or practises sports). This latter kind of data will be the first one to be analysed in this context. The first parameter is the respect of the finality, proportionality, data quality and information principles. In fact, it seems to be reasonable for an insurance company to ask, for example, whether the potential insured party smokes, since smoking increases the probability of developing many diseases or of death.[84] In the same sense, it seems reasonable for the insurer to ask the insured party if he practises extreme sports, because this kind of sport has the same effect of increasing the probability of death or of injuries.

Also information about the ownership of sports cars may be relevant to risk assessment, although owning a fast car does not necessarily mean that the individual drives fast or dangerously, exposing him to a higher risk. It is difficult, therefore, to establish the limits for the processing of such data by insurers, or its legitimacy, and therefore, whether this kind of data is just part of the lifestyle of the individuals and should be protected as part of their privacy or not.[85] In my opinion, the adequacy of the processing of sensitive data will need to be assessed on a case-by-case basis and the starting point will be the incidence of the finality, proportionality, data quality, information and non-discrimination principles.

Insurers can also ask for information about the health status of the potentially-insured party, including previous treatments, surgeries and medicines that he has been using, with the purpose of accurately defining the risk and limits of

---

[83]Article 29 Working Party on Data Protection. Working Document on the processing of personal data relating to health in electronic health records (HER). Op. cit. P. 9. "In contrast to the provisions of Article 7 of the Directive, consent in the case of sensitive personal data and therefore in an HER must be explicit. Opt-out solutions will not meet the requirement of being 'explicit'. In accordance with the general definition that consent presupposes a declaration of intent explicitness must relate, in particular, to the sensitivity of the data. The data subject must be aware that he is renouncing special protection. Written consent is, however, not required."

[84]"Although tobacco deaths rarely make headlines, tobacco kills one person every 6 s. Tobacco kills a third to half of all people who use it, on average 15 years prematurely. Today, tobacco use causes one in ten deaths among adults worldwide—more than five million people a year. By 2030, unless urgent action is taken, tobacco's annual death toll will rise to more than eight million." In World Health Organization. Report on the global TOBACCO epidemic, 2008. Available at http:// www.who.int/tobacco/mpower/mpower_report_full_2008.pdf. Accessed 15 May 2008.

[85]In this sense, see International Labour Office—Report of the Director-General. Equality at work: Taking the challenges (Global Report under the follow-up to the ILO Declaration on Fundamental Principles and Rights at work). International Labour Conference, 96th Session, 2007. P. 49. "Discrimination base on lifestyle—182. Lifestyle and, more specifically, whether an individual leads a 'healthy' life, is becoming a factor in obtaining or keeping a job. Being overweight or a smoker or suffering from hypertension can be an occupational disadvantage in several industrialized countries. Virtually every lifestyle choice, including driving fast cars, has some health-related consequence; the question therefore is where to draw the line between what an employer can regulate and the freedom of employees to lead the life of their choices."

the coverage.[86] Nevertheless, member states can establish specific limits for this collection and use.[87]

Mainly in the case of insurance, the Committee of Ministers of the Council of Europe adopted in 2002 the Recommendation nº Rec (2002) 9 on the protection of personal data collected and processed for insurance purposes,[88] which considers as insurance purposes "any operation involving the collection and processing of personal data relating to cover for a risk, in particular under a policy or an insurance contract".[89] This Recommendation suggests that personal data for insurance purposes should be collected, in principle, from the data subject or his legal representative[90] and establishes the purposes for which personal data can be collected.[91] It also admits the use of criminal data, including information related

[86]Article 29 Working Party on Data Protection. Working Document on Blacklists. Op. cit P. 9–10. "As for blacklists including any other kind of especially protected data, such as health information, it should be pointed out that files of this kind on such questions are essentially compiled in connection with life insurance offered by companies in that sector. In such cases, in the absence of legal regulations incorporating the appropriate safeguards, these files may only be compiled with the data subject's free, specific, explicit and informed consent, which he is entitled to revoke. Even then, however, Article 6 of the Directive must be taken into account, as must, in particular, the proportionality of creating these files in relation to the end in sight. It is also necessary to establish that no specific rules in the Member state concerned prohibit this kind of practice even when the data subject has given his consent. (...) As specific examples of action in relation to this kind of blacklist, some national supervisory authorities have reprehended joint files centralised by a federation of insurance companies which included data on persons who had been refused life insurance on the grounds of their health problems. The supervisory authority ruled that these had to be deleted or legitimised in accordance with the Directive, as it took the view that it was not sufficient that this information should be available to the respective companies with life insurance contracts with those data subjects with which the nature of the contractual relations could provide grounds for holding this information."

[87]Article 29 Working Party on Data Protection. Working Document on the processing of personal data relating to health in electronic health records (HER). Op. cit. P. 18. "When structuring HER records, recurrent information demands should also be taken into consideration. One example: Under national law, private insurance companies might be entitled to receive some (limited) information concerning health records, when necessary in the context of fulfilling their contractual obligations towards insured patients. Granting access to private insurance companies to the HER of a patient seems unacceptable. For that reason a solution could be to establish a standardized special 'documentation package' which, when necessary, meets the legitimate information interests of the insurer and, if authorized by the patient, could be (electronically) transmitted to the private insurance company."

[88]This recommendation, however, is not a binding document. See Batellaan, Pieter; Coomans, Fons. Op. cit.

[89]Article 1(c) of the Appendix to the Recommendation.

[90]Article 4.2 of the Appendix to the Recommendation.

[91]4.4. Subject to the provisions of Principles 4.6–4.8, 8.1 and 13.1, personal data may only be collected and processed for the purposes of: a. preparing and issue of insurance; b. collecting premiums and submitting other bills; c. settling claims or paying other benefits; d. reinsurance; e. co-insurance; f. preventing, detecting and/or prosecuting insurance fraud; g. establishing, exercising or defending legal claim; h. meeting another specific legal or contractual obligation; i. prospecting new insurance markets; j. internal management; k. actuarial activities.

to criminal proceedings and convictions, under specific safeguards provided for by domestic laws of the member states, if it is "necessary to combat insurance fraud, for the granting of insurance or the payment of claims or any other insurance benefit".[92]

2.2 Genetic Predictive Tests and the Insurance Industry

The processing of genetic data determines particularly serious risks, as described by Stefano Rodotà:

> The violation of the private sphere, serious in itself, becomes even more worrying if taking into account the fact that, thanks to data obtained from any genetic material (saliva, hair, skin, blood), it is possible to obtain information not only about the identity of a person but also to make a forecast about that person. Since the genome can reconstruct the link between generations, data concerning a specific person can supply information about people from the same biological group. Past, present and future, therefore, can be examined through genetic data.[93]

In this section, only the processing of genetic data by insurance companies will be analysed, since credit information suppliers and banks currently do not use genetic information for risk analysis.[94] Firstly, a discussion about the definition of genetic data and its distinction from other kinds of health data will be carried out, then the claims used to justify its use will be analysed and, finally, some considerations about the future of genetic data processing by the insurance sector in the EU will be presented.

2.2.1 The Concept of Genetic Data and its Distinction from Other Health Data

The European Society Human Genetics 2000 considers genetic information as "[I]nformation that derives directly from the variation between people that exists in their chromosomes or DNA, or information that is being used to infer that a specific genetic variation or genetic influences might be present. The former includes cytogenetic and DNA test results and very specific biochemical changes.

---

[92]Article 4.7 of the Appendix to the Recommendation.

[93]Rodotà, Stefano. A vida na sociedade da vigilância: privacidade hoje. Rio de Janeiro: Renovar, 2008. P. 249. Unofficial translation by the author.

[94]Maybe in the future they will intend to use genetic information for risk analysis in long-term contracts, such as mortgages, but it is not a current scenario.

whilst the latter category of genetic information includes family history, clinical diagnosis, imaging, clinical chemistry, test results, etc."[95]

Similarly, the Unesco International Declaration on Human Genetic Data describes human genetic data as "Information about heritable characteristics of individuals obtained by analysis of nucleic acids or by other scientific analysis"[96] and genetic testing as "A procedure to detect the presence or absence of, or change in, a particular gene or chromosome, including an indirect test for a gene product or other specific metabolite that is primarily indicative of a specific genetic change."[97] The Proposal for a Regulation on Data Protection presented by the EU Commission on 25 January 2012 defines genetic data as "all data, of whatever type, concerning the characteristics of an individual which are inherited or acquired during early prenatal development."[98]

Nonetheless, not all kinds of genetic information are relevant for insurance risk analysis. Only genetic data obtained through predictive tests that detect the possibility of an individual developing a specific disease in the future[99] are relevant for such analysis and will be considered as such in this book.[100]

---

[95] Godard, Béatrice; Joly, Yann; Knoppers, Bartha Maria. A Comparative International Overview. In Rothstein, Mark A. Genetics and Life Insurance—Medical Underwriting and Social Policy. Cambridge: The MIT Press, 2004. P. 175.

[96] Article 2(i) of the Unesco International Declaration on Human Genetic Data. Available at http://portal.unesco.org/en/ev.php-URL_ID=17720&URL_DO=DO_TOPIC&URL_SECTION=201.html. Accessed 17 May 2008. See also Recommendation nº R(97)5 of the Council of Minister of CoE on the protection of medical data, which Article 1 defines genetic data as "data, of whatever type, concerning the hereditary characteristics of an individual or concerning the pattern of inheritance of such characteristics within a related group of individuals", considering in such definition "any genetic information (genes) in an individual or genetic line relating to any aspect of health or disease, whether present as identifiable characteristics or not."

[97] See Article 2(xii) of the Unesco International Declaration on Human Genetic Data. Available at http://portal.unesco.org/en/ev.php-URL_ID=17720&URL_DO=DO_TOPIC&URL_SECTION=201.html. Accessed 17 May 2008.

[98] Article 4(10) of the EU Commission's Proposal for a Regulation of the European Parliament and of the Council on the protection of individuals with regard to the processing of personal data and on the free movement of such data (General Data Protection Regulation).

[99] Juth, Niklas; Radetzki, Marian; Radetzki, Marcus. Genes and Insurance—Ethical, Legal and Economic issues. Cambridge: Cambridge University Press, 2003. P. 11. "Is the latter purpose of genetic testing that is of primary interest to insurance companies, that is the testing for diseases that have not yet revealed any symptoms."

[100] See Association of British Insurers. Code of Practice for Genetic Tests. June 2008. Available at http://www.abi.org.uk/Information/Codes_and_Guidance_Notes/41697.pdf. Accessed 23 February 2010. P. 2. "The Code is applicable to insurance where an applicant may disclose a predictive genetic test result."

Having defined the scope of genetic data, it is important to underline the distinction between genetic data and health data.[101] Genetic data has raised specific issues since it provides information about a possible future scenario, showing whether someone may develop a certain disease or not, whilst normal health data refers to the person's health situation in the present.[102]

Some authors claim that genetic tests do not give a predictable diagnosis about future diseases but about a current situation. However, the examples of genetic tests they give (such as tests to anticipate the formation a tumour),[103] as well as the definitions of genetic data they consider, differ from those used for the purposes of this work. As Onora O'Neill says, "To find genetic test results with predictive value for insurers one has to look to those that are relevant to late onset disorders with high predictive value, and in particular tests for single gene late onset disorders."[104]

In the following topics I will analyse the processing of genetic data for insurance risk analysis, which brings into discussion not only economic aspects but also many moral and ethical ones.[105] In this respect, the main objective of this section is to establish the limits—or legal grounds—for the processing of genetic data for insurance purposes in EU Law, taking into account the human dignity principle,[106]

[101]In this sense is the conclusion of the Article 29 Working Party on Data Protection concerning the extension of the protection given to sensitive data under the Directive 95/46/EC to genetic data. In Article 29 Working Party. Working Document on Genetic Data. Op. cit. P. 5.

[102]Lewicki, Bruno. A Privacidade da Pessoa Humana no Ambiente de Trabalho. Rio de Janeiro: Renovar, 2003. P. 201.

[103]Meyer, Roberta B. Op. cit. P. 39/40. "The second myth deals with the widely held misperception that genetic tests are always concerned with future rather than present disease. DNA-based genetic tests designed to diagnose cancers and other diseases by definition deal with conditions that are already present. They aid in early diagnosis of that disease that already exists. Genetic tests are being developed to define the genetic makeup of a tumor or disease-causing organism and to design therapies tailored to those genetic characteristics. For example, genetic tests are performed on the microorganism that causes tuberculosis to determine if a given Mycobacterium is resistant to conventional drug therapy. Another prognostic genetic test involves polymerase chain reaction of blood to detect malignant cells that are in the process of metastasizing from a primary site to distant body locations. The results may signal an unexpected need for aggressive chemotherapy. Because results of both diagnostic and prognostic genetic tests provide information relevant to the likelihood of premature death, they are likely to be critical to medical underwriting."

[104]O'neill, Onora. Insurance and Genetics: The Current State of Play. In Brownsword, Roger et al. (editors). Law and Human Genetics—Regulating a Revolution. Oxford: Hart Publishing, 1998. P. 126.

[105]Burley, Justine. An abstract approach to the regulation of human genetics: law, morality and social policy. In Somsen, H. The regulatory challenge of biotechnology. Cheltenham: Edward Elgar Publishing, 2007. P. 63.

[106]The Charter of Fundamental Rights of the European Union recognises human dignity as a inviolable right (Article 1).

which is one important principle of EU Law,[107] particularly when privacy and data protection issues are brought into question.[108]

2.2.2 *Claims for the Use of Genetic Data: Are They Enough to Legitimise It?*

The first requirement for the processing of genetic data is the consent of the data subject, as discussed in Chap. 1 (Sect. 1.3.1.1). Nonetheless, there are some specific considerations that must be made. Most of EU member states' legislation on data protection require the written consent of the data subject as one of the criteria to authorise the processing of sensitive data and, of course, of genetic data.[109]

However, to freely express their consent, data subjects must be informed about the criteria of underwriting to which such data are linked and about the implications in the price of the premium before giving their consent, as a way to comply with the finality, proportionality and information principles. Moreover, data subjects must be informed about the storage of their data, not only to protect their privacy but also that of their relatives, since through genetic tests it is possible to identify the probability of developing certain diseases related to specific genes that can affect the whole family of the data subject. The issue of the validity of consent is, therefore, a very important one when it comes to genetic testing.[110]

---

[107]See Omega Case (Case C-36/02) decided by the European Court of Justice. "34. As the Advocate General argues in paragraphs 82–91 of her Opinion, the Community legal order undeniably strives to ensure respect for human dignity as a general principle of law. There can therefore be no doubt that the objective of protecting human dignity is compatible with Community law, it being immaterial in that respect that, in Germany, the principle of respect for human dignity has a particular status as an independent fundamental right." In the same sense, see Rodotà, Stefano. La vita e le regole—Tra diritto e non diritto. Op. cit. P. 29. "L'inviolabilità della dignità umana, proclamata in apertura della Costituzione tedesca e della Carta dei diritti fondamentali dell'Unione europea, è garanzia che preclude a chiunque, fosse pure lo stesso interessato, di ridurne il significato e la portata. Libertà e dignità appartengono alla sfera di quel che non è negoziabile, è posto fuori del mercato."

[108]Niger, Sergio. Il diritto alla protezione dei dati personali. In Monducci, Juri; Sartor, Giovanni (editors). Il codice in materia di protezione dei dati personali. Cedam: Padova, 2004. P. 8. "La dignità umana costituisce uno dei valore fondativi della privacy, destinato ad assumere un rilievo sempre più grande per diffondersi e il rafforzarsi di tendenze che espongono, usando lespressione di E.J. Blounstein, la vita privata ad un public scrutiny."

[109]Viola de Azevedo Cunha, Mario; Marin, Luisa; Sartor, Giovanni. Peer-to-peer privacy violations and ISP liability: data protection in the user-generated web. International Data Privacy Law, 2012, Vol. 2, No. 2. P. 53.

[110]The relevance (or not) of consent as a valid legal basis for the processing of (all kinds) of data will be further analysed in Chap. 6.

Other issues must also be taken into account. The more important one, in my opinion, is related to the possibility of discrimination.[111] Many are the examples where there is a risk of discrimination related to the disclosure of personal genetic data by insurance companies. Janet L. Dolgin presents some examples of genetic discrimination, including (but not only) in insurance:

> Employers have refused to hire, and insurers to cover, individuals who test positive for harmful genetic alterations as well as individuals identified, through familial or ethnic associations, with groups linked with particular gene alterations. One study, carried out almost a decade ago, reported numerous instances of discrimination, especially in insurance and employment contexts, against individuals who tested positive for genetic alterations associated with illness. Some of those who suffered discrimination were carriers, at no risk of becoming ill with the condition in question. A more recent survey of people at risk of developing a genetic illness identified 200 cases of genetic discrimination among 917 respondents. A 1998 U.S. government resport concluded that '[g]enetic predisposition or conditions can lead to workplace discrimination, even in cases where workers are healthy and unlikely to develop disease or where the genetic condition has no effect on the ability to perform work'. Other reports indicate genetic discrimination in an even wider variety of contexts. Genetic information can influence institutional and legal decisions about parental rights, criminal sentencing and parole status.[112]

Nonetheless, the insurance market tries to justify the use of genetic data and to reject the accuse of discrimination by arguing that if the use of this kind of data is not allowed, adverse selection will be promoted, since individuals who know that they will be sick or will die prematurely would contract for more insurance than others who do not have this kind of information.[113] Or moving in the opposite direction, if they learn that they do not have an increased risk, it would affect their decision to purchase life or health insurance, or the amount of coverage.[114] In this context, it is possible to raise the question 'Is there a threshold where adverse selection would be at work and would justify the use of genetic information?' This book will address this question later, but it is possible to say that the sole argument of adverse selection is not strong enough to justify the use of genetic information without any safeguards for an individual's privacy.

The discussions about this issue that have been developed in the United States, where health care services are mainly covered by private insurance schemes, show the importance of the topic:

> Certain kinds of genetic information are deemed by some insurers to be relevant to evaluation of the magnitude of the risk being transferred, for example, a test result indicating the individual carries the gene for Huntington's disease. In theory, this additional source of information permits insurers to classify individuals more accurately into various categories

[111] Rodotá, Stefano. A vida na sociedade da vigilância: privacidade hoje. Op. cit. P.250.

[112] Dolgin, Janet L. Ideologies of Discrimination: Personhood and the 'Genetic Group'. Studies in History and Philosophy of Biological and Biomedical Sciences. Vol. 32, No. 4. Great Britain: Elsevier, 2001. P. 707.

[113] Meyer, Roberta B. Op. cit. P. 29–30.

[114] Rothstein, Mark A.; Horung, Carlton A. Public Attitudes. In Rothstein, Mark A. Genetics and Life Insurance. London: MIT Press, 2004. P. 1.

> of risk or to assess risk premiums more accurately. Thus, relevant genetic tests results, if disclosed, could enhance equity in insurance—the idea that people who have similar health or roughly the same life expectancy should pay equal premiums, and people who have worse health or a lower life expectancy should pay more.
>
> The general ethical problem that genetic information poses for insurance is twofold: discrimination by insurers against individuals who possess what are known (statistically) to be offending genes, and adverse selection—this is not in fact much different from the twofold problem that other kinds of health information, actual or predictable pose.[115]

Concerns about the risk of discrimination that emanate from the use of such data are reflected both in international and national instruments. Article 21 of the Charter of Fundamental Rights of the European Union prohibits any kind of discrimination based on genetic characteristics.[116]

In the same vein are the provisions of Article 11 of the Convention on Human Rights and Biomedicine of the Council of Europe,[117] Article 6 of the Unesco Universal Declaration on the Human Genome and Human Rights[118] and Article 7(a) of the Unesco International Declaration of Human Genetic Data.[119]

It is important to notice that Article 12 of the Convention on Human Rights and Biomedicine of the Council of Europe establishes that genetic predictive tests may be performed only for health purposes or for scientific research linked to health purposes, and are subject to appropriate genetic counselling.[120]

Moreover, many EU member states have edited rules concerning the processing of genetic data,[121] although Directive 95/46/EC does not have any provision

---

[115]Burley, Justine. Op. cit. P. 69.

[116]Article 21 Non-discrimination

1. Any discrimination based on any ground such as sex, race, colour, ethnic or social origin, genetic features, language, religion or belief, political or any other opinion, membership of a national minority, property, birth, disability, age or sexual orientation shall be prohibited.

[117]Article 11—Non-discrimination—Any form of discrimination against a person on grounds of his or her genetic heritage is prohibited.

[118]Article 6—No one shall be subjected to discrimination based on genetic characteristics that is intended to infringe or has the effect of infringing human rights, fundamental freedoms and human dignity.

[119]Article 7—Non-discrimination and non-stigmatization

(a) Every effort should be made to ensure that human genetic data and human proteomic data are not used for purposes that discriminate in a way that is intended to infringe, or has the effect of infringing human rights, fundamental freedoms or human dignity of an individual or for purposes that lead to the stigmatization of an individual, a family, a group or communities.

[120]Article 12—Predictive genetic tests—Tests which are predictive of genetic diseases or which serve either to identify the subject as a carrier of a gene responsible for a disease or to detect a genetic predisposition or susceptibility to a disease may be performed only for health purposes or for scientific research linked to health purposes, and subject to appropriate genetic counselling.

[121]"In Five European countries—Austria, Belgium, Denmark, France and Norway—any use of genetic information for business purposes is prohibited. In Four countries—France, Germany, Sweden, and the United Kingdom—a moratorium or partial moratorium on the use of genetic information by insurers has been established. In the Netherlands, the Medical Examination Act

regarding the processing of such data. One example is Law 12/2005 from Portugal, concerning personal genetic information and health information, which in article 11 establishes that "Nobody can be damaged, in anyway, as a consequence of possessing a genetic disease or of his own genetic heritage".[122]

In the United Kingdom, the use of genetic data for insurance purposes has been a subject of great concern. A parliamentary discussion in 1995 on this topic[123] led to the adoption of a Code of Conduct by the insurance sector containing limitations on the use of genetic testing for insurance[124] and, then, to the establishment of a moratorium of 5 years, agreed to by British life insurers and the National Government, meaning that during this period they cannot use genetic data for risk analysis. The only exception is for testing to detect the gene related to Huntington's disease,[125] which can be required by life insurance companies where the coverage intended by the potential insured party is superior to 500,000 pounds.[126]

(1998) prevents the acquisition of genetic information by insurers and employers below a certain amount of coverage." In EuroGAPPP. Genetics and public and professional policy in Europe. Available at http://ec.europa.eu/research/biosociety/pdf/bmh4_ct98_0550_partb.pdf. Accessed 5 March 2008. Although France appears twice in the citation, both as a country where the use of genetic information for business purposes is prohibited and as a country that established a moratorium, the correct one is the reference to a legal prohibition, according to article L.1141-1 of the Code of Public Health. Available at http://www.legifrance.gouv.fr/affichCode.do?cidTexte=LEGITEXT000006072665. Accessed 10 November 2010.

[122]Art. 11—Non discrimination principle

1. Nobody can be damaged, in anyway, as a consequence of possessing a genetic disease or of his own genetic heritage.
2. Nobody can be discriminated, in any way, as a consequence of the results of a genetic test, including for employment purposes, health or life insurance purposes, access to education and adoption, both for the adopted and for the adopter.
3. Nobody can be discriminated, in any way, in his right to a have a medical and psycho-social treatment and genetic counselling as a consequence of the refusal to do a genetic test. (Unofficial translation by the author).

[123]See UK House of Commons. Select Committee on Science and Technology Fifth Report. Available at http://www.parliament.the-stationery-office.co.uk/pa/cm200001/cmselect/cmsctech/174/17404.htm#a1. Accessed 13 January 2011.

[124]Leemens, Trudo. Genetics and Insurance Discrimination: Comparative Legislative, Regulatory and Policy Developments and Canadian Options. Health Law Journal Special Edition, 2003. Available at http://www.law.ualberta.ca/centres/hli/userfiles/Lemmens.pdf. Accessed 13 January 2011. P. 60.

[125]Rothstein, Mark A. Genetic Secrets: A Policy Framework. In Rothstein, Mark A. (editor) Genetic Secrets: Protecting Privacy and Confidentiality in the Genetic Era. New Heaven and London: Yale University Press, 1997. P. 474. "In the Netherlands, a 5-year moratorium trial period, in which no genetic information may be used in underwriting policies below 200,000 guilders (about $ 100,000), has been extended indefinitely while proposed legislation is debated in the Parliament."

[126]Genetic Privacy. Available at http://epic.org/privacy/genetic/. Accessed 16 February 2008. "Discrimination in life insurance: Life insurance applications generally require individuals to disclose information about themselves, their health and their lifestyles as a condition of obtaining

Even in the US, "the Health Insurance Portability and Accountability Act of 1996 prohibits insurance companies from relying on genetic information to establish eligibility for health insurance coverage. However, the statute does not define 'genetic information', and thus leaves open the possibility that insurers can refuse coverage on the basis of information obtained through medical histories."[127]

The insurance industry, in its turn, presents some arguments to justify the processing of genetic information and to legitimise the requirement of genetic tests, the relevant argument being one concerning family history data.[128] Private health and life insurers have been collecting information on current and past health or ill conditions of their potential customers, with the purpose of establishing the adequate premiums for specific risks. They argue that "when they infer a risk of illness from family history information, they are using genetic information, although of an imprecise sort."[129]

Some scholars claim that family history information is, in fact, more effective than genetic tests in identifying the predisposition of someone to the development of diseases in the future:

> Family history remains one of the most informative "genetic tests." No cost is involved and no blood sample is required. "Questions about parents' or siblings' disease, time from diagnosis and death will provide the insurer with the information that can predict the individual's risk of dying at a young age or become ill more effectively than results from genetic predisposition tests".[130]

On the other hand, unlike genetic data, a family history does not have the power to create in people the idea that they will definitively develop a certain disease in the future nor to exclude such a person immediately from insurance protection, since insurers usually analyse other sources of information to see whether the family history of diseases affects the risk status of the applicant. The family history data argument can, thus, be used the other way around, to prevent insurers from using

---

coverage. Some life insurers have asked individuals to take genetic tests in order to determine whether they are predisposed to diseases that could make them greater risks. Genetic testing for life insurance was a subject of a Parliamentary hearing in the UK. Because of the uncertain connection between genetic predisposition and the eventual development of disease in any specific individual, life insurers agreed to a voluntary 5-year moratorium on genetic testing with the exception of the test for Huntington's Disease on policies that would pay out more than 500,000 pounds." The processing of genetic data by the insurance industry in the UK will be better analysed in the appropriate topic (4.5.3).

[127]Dolgin, Janet L. Op. cit. P. 708.

[128]Meyer, Roberta. B. Op. cit. P. 35. "Insurers have used broadly defined genetic information in underwriting for a long time. Applications for policies commonly seek information on family history, cholesterol level, hypertension, coronary heart disease, cancer, diabetes, and many other impairments that may have a genetic basis, which is inherited, acquired, or both."

[129]O'Neill, Onora. Op. cit. P. 126.

[130]Uhlmann, Wendy R., and Sharon F. Terry. 1997. Perspectives of consumers and genetics professionals. In *Genetic secrets: Protecting privacy and confidentiality in the genetic era*, ed. Mark A. Rothstein. New Heaven: Yale University Press. P. 168.

genetic tests since they have other potentially less damaging ways of obtaining similar information, that is more in line with the idea of the proportionality principle.

Another important issue concerning genetic tests is the data subject's right not to know.[131] Genetic tests, as said before, simply detect a predisposition to the development of a certain disease, but not the certainty that this predisposition will be confirmed in the future.[132] In spite of its lack of certainty, a positive result in a genetic test can affect the life of the data subject, since he/she is made aware that he/she has a specific gene and that he/she might develop a serious disease in the future. It can also affect the family of the data subject since they have a common genetic heritage. In the words of Stefano Rodotà, the right to privacy is "the right to maintain control over our own information and to determine the way to construct our private sphere."[133] In the same direction is the opinion expressed by Nancy E. Kass, who considers the right to know as an exercise of the autonomy.[134]

Moreover, the disclosure to insurance companies of the results of genetic tests taken for medical or reproductive reasons could make people avoid doing such tests, which could lead to a "delay in medical treatment that might ameliorate a disorder, or even prevent its development."[135] Indeed, many countries have adopted

---

[131] Article 29 Working Party. Working Document on Genetic Data. Op. cit. P. 9. "Right not to know: It is the case where the person concerned chooses not to be informed of the results of the genetic test nor receive any further information (i.e. as to whether it is carrying a defective gene or is going to suffer a disease) particularly if the disease is highly serious and at the time there are no scientific means to prevent or treat it. The same applies to the family members who may wish to assert a right not to know about the results of a test taken by a family member to determine the presence or absence of a serious genetic disorder, preferring to live their lives without the shadow of such information. This is particularly true when there is no prevention or treatment available."

[132] Ibid. P. 7. "Predictive genetic tests are designed to identify genetic changes which are highly likely to lead to an illness at a later point in the life of the person tested. A particular problem associated with predictive diagnostics is that, even if genetic changes can be identified which are demonstrably linked to certain illnesses, it often cannot be predicted with certainty if and when a particular illness will occur in the later life of the person concerned."

[133] Apud Moraes, Maria Celina Bocin de. O conceito de dignidade humana substrato axiológico e conteúdo normativo. In Constituiçao, direitos fundamentais e direito privado, ed. Ingo Sarlet. Porto Alegre: Editora Livraria do Advogado. P. 128. Unofficial translation by the author.

[134] Kass, Nancy E. P. 306. "The threat to autonomy. Genetic tests are available for medical conditions for which there are no or limited treatments. This means that the decision whether to learn whether one is destined to have—or is at increased risk for—a certain condition is a matter of personal choice. Counselling programs have been established to help individuals who may be at risk for certain conditions for which no intervention is available decide if they want to learn whether they carry a gene mutation associated with a particular health condition later in life. Inherent to such counselling programs is the assumption that valid reasons exist both for wanting the information and for not wanting the information perhaps years in advance of becoming symptomatic.

Mandatory genetic screening—or 'conditionally mandatory' screening, that is, screening required as a condition of obtaining health insurance—would deprive individuals of this right to personal autonomy. No longer would the consequential psychological decision about whether to take a genetic test be left to the individual."

[135] O'neill, Onora. Op. cit. P. 129. In the same sense, see Kass, Nancy E. Op. cit. P. 306. "If insurance companies increasingly seek to use genetic information in their risk-screening process,

the position of not allowing the disclosure of genetic tests to insurance companies, even when the individual has taken the test previously.[136]

In this perspective, genetic testing or the disclosure of the results of such tests for insurance risk analysis presents complex issues that overlap those related to sensitive data in general. Consequently, the importance of the topic and the need to regulate it at the European level is evident,[137] since EU member states have adopted completely different approaches.[138] The Proposal for a General Data Protection Regulation recently put forward by the European Commission does not solve this problem, since it recognises consent as a valid legal basis for the processing of genetic data, leaving to Member States the decision on not admitting consent for legitimising the processing of genetic data.[139]

---

either by asking the applicants whether they have been tested on their own or by requesting copies of applicants' medical records, individuals will have an incentive to avoid testing until it is medically necessary. Obviously, once a patient presents with the symptoms and a diagnostic test is warranted, the test may have little additional impact in whether a person is considered insurable. (...) If one's access to health or life insurance were limited severely as a result of acquiring such information early of from sharing such information with one's physician, such public health benefits could not be realized."

[136]In the UK, if the individual discloses such information to an insurance company, this latter cannot take into account this information for risk analysis. See Association of British Insurers; Government of the United Kingdom. Mar 2005. Concordat and Moratorium on genetics and insurance. Available at http://www.dh.gov.uk/prod_consum_dh/groups/dh_digitalassets/@dh/@en/documents/digitalasset/dh_4106050.pdf. 23 Feb 2010.

[137]The European Parliament recognised the need to regulate the processing of personal data for insurance purposes at the European level, what, in the opinion of the Parliament should lead to a prohibition of such processing activity. See European Parliament. Resolution on the ethical and legal problems of genetic engineering. (Official Journal C 96, 17/04/1989, p. 165–171). Available at https://www.codex.vr.se/texts/EP-genetic.html. Accessed 16 February 2009. "As regards genome analysis for insurance purposes:

19. Considers that insurance companies have no right to demand that genetic testing be carried out before or after the conclusion of an insurance contract nor to demand to be informed of the results of any such tests which have already been carried out and that genetic analysis should not be made a requirement for the conclusion of an insurance contract;
20. Asserts that the insurer has no right to be notified by the policy holder of all the genetic data known to the latter." In the same direction was the position adopted by the World Medical Association in its Declaration on the Human Genome Project. World Medical Association. 2010. Declaration on the human genome project. Available at http://www.wma.net/en/30publications/10policies/20archives/g6/index.html. 26 Jan 2010. "Genetic discrimination in private insurance and employment—here is a conflict between the increasing potential of new technologies to reveal genetic heterogeneity and the criterion for private insurance and employment. It may be desirable, regarding genetic factors, to adopt the same tacit consensus which prohibits the use of race discrimination in employment or insurance. Genetic mapping may become a source of stigmatization and social discrimination, and the 'risky population' may turn into a 'defective population'."

[138]See footnote 280 (supra).

[139]See Article 9(2)(a) of the Proposal for a General Data Protection Regulation. European Commission. 2012. Op. cit. "Article 9—Processing of special categories of personal data—(1.) The processing of personal data, revealing race or ethnic origin, political opinions, religion or

2.2.3 *The Future of Genetic Data Processing Within the Insurance Industry*

Apart from the international documents about this subject, "the present and potential multiplication of dilemmas in the area of biomedicine creates the need to establish some external limits, which are of ethical and legal nature."[140] These limits are a way of preserving human dignity.[141] Allowing the unrestricted use of genetic information for risk analysis would impose a heavy burden on minority groups who present some genetic predispositions to develop specific diseases,[142] leading to a kind of genetic discrimination against these groups.[143] The question therefore is not so simple, involving other rights beyond the right to privacy, such as the right to non-discrimination and the right not to know. Thus, it imposes on the legislator the obligation to produce laws that not only regulate health and life insurance in the case

---

beliefs, trade-union membership, and the processing of genetic data or data concerning health or sex life or criminal convictions or related security measures shall be prohibited. (2.) Paragraph 1 shall not apply where: (a) the data subject has given consent to the processing of those personal data, subject to the conditions laid down in Articles 7 and 8, except where Union law or Member State law provide that the prohibition referred to in paragraph 1 may not be lifted by the data subject; or".

[140]Moraes, Maria Celina Bodin de. O conceito de dignidade humana: substrato axiológico e conteúdo normativo. Op. cit. P. 128. Unofficial translation by the author.

[141]Schwartz; Paul. M. Op. cit. P. 408. "Günter Wiese argues that private insurers might be tempted to practice adverse selection techniques to increase their profits and lower the premiums of their remaining clients: 'An exclusion of genetically encumbered persons from private insurance would be unsatisfactory for the society as a whole; the state and the general public of tax payers would be responsible for these individuals, after all, and the system of private insurance would end by being discredited. This exclusion would be especially problematic if, due to demographic trends, public social insurance benefits could only be set at a low level.' Profit maximizing by private companies that use personal genetic data does not increase the social wealth. Rather, it inefficiently shifts costs to taxpayers and, to a lesser extent, back onto health care providers who may be forced to provide uncompensated or undercompensated care."

[142]Francioni, Francesco. The International Legal Framework. In Francioni, Francesco (editor). Biotechnologies and International Human Rights. Oxford and Portland: Hart Publishing, 2007. P. 22. "Myriad Genetic claimed a patent relating to a gene probe 'for diagnosing a predisposition to breast cancer in Ashkenazi Jewish women'. The relevant gene mutation related to ovarian and breast cancer and was found to be prevalent in Ashkenazi Jewish population in the order of 1% as compared to 0.1% of the general population."

[143]Ibid. P. 21. "At the same time, genetic science and technology, especially in the field of medicine, are raising new possibilities of discrimination. From a general point of view, the most threatening type of discrimination can come from conceptualization of 'normality' based, rather than on the natural definition as a state of physical and mental wellbeing, on a genetic connotation, which includes the hidden predisposition to some health impairment or, conversely, the search for a certain quality of life."

of diagnosis of genetic diseases,[144] but which also prevent discrimination based on genetic tests in the admission procedure for a job post, just to give an example.

However, to produce such laws the legislator will have to deal with the problem of how to balance the interests involved—those of the data subjects, their families, the insurers and even members of the same ethnic group.[145] Should the relatives of the data subject have access to his/her genetic information, allowing them, for example, to adopt preventive therapies for the related disease? Should insurance companies be given access to genetic information, allowing them, on the one hand, to avoid increasing the premiums for everybody and, on the other, to specialise in the coverage of certain degenerative diseases?

The answer to these questions has to take into account the ambiguity of genetic tests in an actuarial perspective,[146] which has a direct impact upon the risk analysis:

> (...) a positive result on a gene test is actuarially ambiguous because being predisposed to developing a disease like breast cancer does not necessarily mean that death or disability will occur prematurely. A person found to have a BRCA mutation is likely to take steps that should result in earlier detection of tumors (and hence improved survival), and may even adopt a greater health consciousness and better preventive measures that could reduce her risk for a wide range of diseases and disorders. Furthermore, the very scientific advances that underlie the identification of a gene mutation also represent "an early step in the elucidation of the pathophysiology and the development of treatments and/or cures." What this means is that an actuary's prediction of the likelihood and timing of breast cancer in the person with the BRCA mutation will likely be invalidated by the radically improved ability of medicine to respond therapeutically in the future.[147]

---

[144] DeCew, Judith Wagner. P. 148. "Consider, for example, the dangers that can accompany advances in genetic tests. Tests for breast cancer genes, to cite one case, could potentially be extremely useful for patients who might benefit from extra vigilance to check for the disease. If confidentiality of the results cannot be assured, however, allowing information to be part of a doctor's or genetic counsellor's file could mean that patients are later identified as having <<preexisting conditions>>, jeopardizing medical insurance coverage for themselves and even their children."

[145] Rothstein, Mark A. Genetic Secrets: A Policy Framework. In Rothstein, Mark A. (editor). Genetic Secrets: Protecting Privacy and Confidentiality in the Genetic Era. New Heaven and London: Yale University Press, 1997. P. 471. "There is a legitimate concern that similar, surrogate measures for genetic traits could be adopted by one or more insurers if genetic testing were prohibited. For example, nonspecific diagnostic criteria could be used to predict the onset of a genetic disorder. Less likely, but more troubling, an insurer might refuse to insure members of a certain ethnic group because the group has a higher prevalence of a particular gene disorder, regardless of legal prohibition on such conduct."

[146] Rothstein, Mark A. Ibid. P. 468. "There is little evidence that the state of the art in genetics is sufficiently developed or that medical directors of insurance companies have the expertise in genetics to base medical underwriting on predictive genetic information. For example, among the results of a 1992 questionnaire survey of the medical directors of life insurance companies, 'more than one in four indicated that they believe that genes are composed of chromosomes rather than the other way around, and ... [o]nly half knew that DNA is composed of four nucleotides.'"

[147] Capron. A. M. Genetics and Insurance: Accessing and Using Private Information. In Paul, Ellen Frankel (editor). Social Philosophy & Policy: The Right to Privacy. Volume 17. Number 2. Bowling Green: Bowling Green State University, 2000. P. 255.

In the same vein, Onora O'Neill argues that, even in the case of genetic tests based on late onset single gene disorders, the outcomes may vary:

> Two widely discussed instances of late onset single gene disorders are Huntington's chorea and the hereditary forms of breast cancer that can be predicted on the basis of the BRCA1 and BRCA2 tests. (...) In these cases a good deal of actuarial information is already available, which makes it possible to use a genetic test result for predicting later onset of serious, even fatal, disease. However, even in these cases the outcome can vary: the ages for onset of disease and of death of those with genes for Huntington's or with the BRCA1 and BRCA2 genes vary greatly; a few of the former and the sizeable fraction of the latter live to old age and die of other causes.
>
> In other cases, the results of genetic tests are not linked to single gene disorders at all. This may be because the gene and its variants code for characteristics which are not disorders. Or it may be because a given gene, or some of its variants, have only a weak statistical link to some multifactorial disorder. Where genetic test results are weakly linked to disorders, other genetic, environmental or life-style factor will also be at work. In these cases a given test result may not provide a sound basis for actuarially significant predictions. Some of those with a given gene that is statistically associated with a disorder may be protected against the disorder by other genes, or by medication, or by lifestyle. For example, clotting factor can protect against haemophilia; a special diet against the retardation associated with PKU.[148]

The best option seems to be the one that forbids the use of genetic data for insurance purposes, at least until there is a real understanding of the relationship between a positive result in a predictive genetic test and the effective development of the respective disease in the future.[149] Thus for most genetically related illnesses a moratorium would be justified. Also the Article 29 Working Party recommends this approach:

> The Working Party believes at this stage that the processing of genetic data in the field of insurance should be prohibited in principle and only authorised under really exceptional circumstances, clearly provided for by law. (...) In some cases insurance applicants might, as a result of an unfavourable finding in a genetic test, be required to pay exorbitant premiums for insurance cover or even be regarded as uninsurable on the basis of a potential illness which may even never arise. This position is in line with the positions adopted in most Member states, where the processing of genetic data in the field of insurance does not constitute a legitimate purpose.[150]

And the Recommendation nº R(92)3 of the CoE Committee of Ministers on genetic testing and screening for health care purposes:

---

148 O'neill, Onora. Ob. cit. P. 126–127.

149 Rodotà, Stefano. La vita e le regole—Tra diritto e no diritto. Milano: Feltrinelli, 2006. P. 72. "Solo assicurando che i risultati dei test genetici non potranno essere conosciuti e utilizzati da assicuratori e datori di lavoro, che potrebbero utilizarli per discriminare, le persone possono liberamente ricorrere a quei test e così tutelare efficacemente il loro diritto alla salute."

150 Article 29 Working Party Working. Document on Genetic Data. Op. cit. P. 10. This position is very close to the precautionary principle used against the production and commercialization of genetic modified organisms. About this subject see Martini, Luca. Il Diritto Internazionale e Comunitário della Bioetica. Torino: G. Giappichelli Editore, 2006. P. 73–144.

> Insurers should not have the right to require genetic testing or to enquire about results of previously performed tests, as a pre-condition for the conclusion or modification of an insurance contract.[151]

As highlighted above (Sect. 2.2.2), even in the US, since 1996, a Federal Legislation "forbids insurance companies from using genetic information (both test results and family history) to exclude from group health insurance".[152] Moreover, the US President signed in 21 May 2008 the Genetic Information Non Discrimination Act, which forbids the use of genetic information for health insurance underwriting.[153]

Nonetheless, considering the differences between EU member states, the topic needs to be broadly debated.[154] Society should decide whether genetic information can be used for other purposes that are not health related and the way in which this kind of information should be treated.[155] I am of the opinion that the use of genetic tests should only be admissible for late onset single gene disorders and over a certain amount of coverage, like in the UK moratorium.

Another option would be to obligate insurance companies to consider also other sources of information—and to allow the concerned data subjects to produce information that would minimise the effects of a predictive genetic test result. A system such as the one created by the Aeras Convention,[156] in France, which establishes a mechanism regarding persons with a high health risk in terms of access to credit and insurance, could be a good source of inspiration.[157]

---

[151] Principle 7.

[152] O'Neill, Onora. P. 127.

[153] Available at http://www.whitehouse.gov/news/releases/2008/05/print/20080521-7.html. Accessed 4 September 2008.

[154] Burley, Justine. Op. cit. P. 78.

[155] Rothstein, Mark A. Genetics and Life Insurance. London: MIT Press, 2004. P. xii. "(...) We have to decide the degree to which genetic information of relevance in medical settings should be available for use in other settings. We have also yet to decide whether this information should be treated the same way as other health information or whether it is somehow unique. Finally, we have yet to determine the extent to which access to results of genetic tests by third parties will dissuade people from undergoing testing."

[156] Available at http://www.aeras-infos.fr/sections/les_documents_offici/la_convention/texte_de_la_conventi/downloadFile/file/convention_aeras.pdf?nocache=1167154356.09. Accessed 18 October 2010.

[157] The French Code of Public Health imposed the adoption of a national convention regarding the access to credit for persons who, deal to their age, health status or disability, present a higher risk (risque aggravé), to be concluded between the "National Government, Trade Associations of the Credit Institutions, Insurance Companies, mutual insurance companies and institutions of precaution (prévoyance) as well as national organisations representing patients and the users of the health system approved under the terms of article L. 1114-1 or representatives of persons with disabilities" (Article L. 1141-2 of the Code of Public Health), aiming at facilitating the access to credit by those persons. Unofficial translation by the author.

The Convention Aeras was signed on 6 July 2006 and entered into force on 6 January 2007. According to the convention, the lending institutions, besides analysing the financial status of the applicant for credit, can request that such person subscribes an insurance policy to

2.3 Chapter Conclusion

In this chapter I observed that different kinds of data, such as the genetic ones, are now largely used by companies in order to better know their clients. However, this type of information has not gotten the necessary attention from the European legislator and, as a consequence, has not been properly regulated. Furthermore, I have considered the need to better specify the concept of anonymous data and the consequences it can have on the application of data protection.

As far as the concept of anonymous data is concerned, a 'solution' was proposed and goes in a similar direction of the one adopted by Directive 95/46/EC, but putting more emphasis on the amount of time, expense and labour required to make a data identifiable.

I have then analysed the processing of genetic data, especially in the field of insurance. After discussing the pros and cons, I have concluded that this processing should be forbidden as a rule, but it could be accepted, as an exception, in the case of life insurance when a certain amount of coverage is involved and the genetic data refers to late onset single gene disorders. One important finding was that the non-discrimination principle should be used as another criterion, besides the other legal grounds for the processing of personal data, to evaluate if an intended processing of sensitive data in a specific case is legitimate or not.

The objective of the next three chapters is to compare the data protection systems of three EU Member States (France, UK and Italy), with an eye towards the possible improvements of the EU Data Protection Framework. The systematisation of this comparative exercise will be guided by the following scheme: five main aspects will be analysed, namely the role of the data protection authority, the concept of personal data, data subjects' rights, the processing of sensitive data and the processing by the case-studies (banking, credit information suppliers and insurance industries). Eventually, some of these countries will have further aspects to be analysed. These further aspects will be the object of a separate section at the end of each chapter.

It is important, however, to justify the choice of Italy, France and the United Kingdom for this comparative exercise. Firstly, these countries have implemented the EU directives in the field of data protection in different ways, as will be seen in the following chapters. In addition, the UK is a common law country (with a more liberal approach) while Italy and France have a continental system (with a more paternalistic/human rights approach), providing a different perspective for the analysis. Finally, in the fields covered by the three industries which are the case-studies, the application and interpretation of data protection rules by the national data protection authorities is quite different in the three countries.

---

guarantee the repayment of the debt. See http://www.aeras-infos.fr/sections/la_convention_en_3_q/view. Accessed 8 October 2010.

Chapter 3
Data Protection Systems in the European Union: The French Experience

France enacted its national data protection law in 1978,[1] becoming one of the first member states of the European Communities to adopt a system of General Data Protection Legislation.[2] However, the amendments required to implement Directive 95/46/EC only took place in 2004, with the adoption of Act of 6 August 2004 on data processing, data files and individual liberties.[3]

In this chapter the analysis will concentrate, besides the five common aspects of the three selected Member States, on the role of the data protection officer, because there is no similar provision in Directive 95/45/EC.

3.1 The Data Protection Authority: Enforcement Powers, Labels and General Authorisations

The Data Protection Authority in France is the *Commission Nationale de l'Informatique et des Libertés* (CNIL). It has powers of investigation and powers to apply sanctions to data controllers for data protection violations.[4] In comparison

---

[1] Act n° 78-17 of 6 January 1978 on Data Processing, Data Files and Individual Liberties, amended by the Act of 6 August 2004 relating to the protection of individuals with regard to the processing of personal data and by the Act of 12 May 2009 relating to the simplification and clarification of law and lightening of procedures.

[2] The German Federal Data Protection Act was adopted in February, 1977. A version of the Act in English is available at http://www.iuscomp.org/gla/statutes/BDSG.htm. Accessed 12 April 2011.

[3] Laffaire, Marie-Laure. Protection des données à caractere personnel. Paris: Éditions d'organisation, 2005. P. 19–20.

[4] Article 11(2)(f)(g) of Act n° 78-17. Amongst the Sanctions, the CNIL can apply a financial penalty, an injunction to stop the processing or even withdraw the authorisation given to the specific processing (Article 45, I). In a case where a "criminal court has definitely judged the same or related facts, the criminal court may order the deduction of the financial penalty from the fine that it imposes" (Article 47, 3rd paragraph).

M. Viola de Azevedo Cunha, *Market Integration Through Data Protection*, Law, Governance and Technology Series 9, DOI 10.1007/978-94-007-6085-1_3,

to the UK Information Commissioner—as will be seen in the next chapter -, the CNIL has broader powers over private and public entities and the refusal of those entities to give CNIL officers access to their facilities can potentially lead to criminal liability.[5] In that case, the CNIL would need to request a judicial order to continue the inspection.[6] If it has knowledge of any criminal offences regarding the processing of personal data, it has to inform the Public Prosecutor, who is the institution with powers to initiate criminal proceedings.[7] On the contrary, in the UK, as will be discussed, there are situations where the Information Commissioner has powers to start criminal proceedings (Sect. 4.1).

Moreover, all decisions taken by the CNIL[8] can be challenged through an appeal addressed to the Conseil d'État,[9] regarding lack of jurisdiction or acts considered ultra vires.[10] A decision related to penalties can be challenged on grounds of both fact and law.[11] It is important to notice that the jurisdiction of the CNIL does not curtail judicial jurisdiction,[12] it being up to the individual to decide to which one

[5]Article 21. The members of the commission shall receive no order from any authority in the exercise of their missions and powers.

The ministers, public authorities, executives of state-owned or private companies, heads of various groupings and more generally the holders and users of data processing and personal data filing systems may not oppose the actions of the commission or its members. They must rather take all useful steps to facilitate its task.

Except when they are bound by a duty of confidentiality, the persons interrogated in the context of verifications carried out by the commission in application of paragraph (f) of Sub-section 2° of Article 11 (onsite verification) shall be bound to supply the information requested by it for the performance of its missions.

[6]Bensoussan, Alain. Informatique et libertés. Paris: Éditions Francis Lefebvre, 2008. P. 713. See also Article 44 of the French Data Protection Act.

[7]Article 11(2)(e).

[8]The Conséil d'État has decided that the CNIL can be considered as a tribunal in the sense of article 6(1) of the European Convention on Human Rights. See decision n° 311,974 of 19 February 2008. Available at http://arianeinternet.conseil-etat.fr/arianeinternet/ViewRoot.asp?View=Html&DMode=Html&PushDirectUrl=1&Item=1&fond=DCE&texte=311974&Page=1&querytype=simple&NbEltPerPages=5&Pluriels=True. Accessed 8 October 2010.

[9]The Conseil d'État is the highest administrative court in France. See http://www.conseil-etat.fr/cde/fr/missions/. Accessed 7 October 2010.

[10]Bensoussan, Alain. Op. Cit. P. 700.

[11]Article 46, 3rd Paragraph.

[12]Mattatia, Fabrice. CNIL et tribunaux: concurrance ou complémentarité dans la répression des infractions à la loi informatique et libertes? RSC, Avril/Juin 2009. P. 327. "Les jurisprudences exposées montrent que les mêmes faits peuvent parfaitement être attaqués, soit devant les tribunaux en tant qu'infractions prévues au code penal, soit devant la CNIL en tant que violations de la loi informatique et libertes. Les victimes disposent donc de deux jurisdictions, que ne sont pas exclusives l'une de l'autre."

he/she will apply, as occurs in Italy.[13] In any case, the judicial decision will prevail over the CNIL's one.[14]

Furthermore, the CNIL has the power to "deliver a quality-label to products or procedures intended to protect individuals in respect to processing of personal data, once it has recognised them to be in conformity with the provisions"[15] of the Data Protection Act. The possibility of delivering quality-labels is an evolution of the provision contained in Directive 95/46/EC[16] with regard to the powers data protection authorities have to recognise codes of conduct adopted by the different sectors as complying with the data protection legislation.[17] The CNIL adopted in 8 September 2011 a "Délibération" regulating the procedure to deliver quality-labels.[18] However, the first quality-labels were only delivered in June 2012,[19] after many regrets from the CNIL itself, as declared by its president:

> We did not certify anything—and I regret that—for a simple reason: the decree of application of the law regarding certification is the only point that has not been treated yet (although I have discussed many times this subject with the government). We are very embarrassed for that: we realize that we have a role to play, but we are currently unable to analyse the requests we receive, and that we will have. I await impatiently the adoption of the decree.[20]

Apart from these powers, the CNIL authorises the processing of some types of personal data, such as that regarding sensitive data and any automatic processing "which may, due to its nature, importance or purposes, exclude persons from the benefit of a right, a service or a contract in the absence of any legislative or

---

[13]Laffaire, Marie-Laure. Protection des données à caractere personnel. Paris: Éditions d'organisation, 2005. P. 365. "Toutefois, sans avoir à passer par le recours à la CNIL, toute personne physique s'estimant vicitime d'une violation de la loi du 6 janvier 1978 peut saisir le juge selon le règles contentieuses habituelles de competénce, de forme, de procédure et de fond. L'intervention du juge n'est pas subordonée à aucune obligation de saisine préalable à la CNIL et l'intervention éventuelle de la Commission n'a pas aucune consequence sur les actes et delais procedureaux liés au contentieux."

[14]Mattatia, Fabrice. Op. cit. P. 317. "Pour une même infraction, une poursuite est désormais possible, soit devant la CNIL, soit devant les tribunaux, soit devant les deux em parallèle."

[15]Article 11(3)(c).

[16]See Article 27 of Directive 95/46/EC.

[17]Belleil, Arnaud. La regulation economique des données personnelles? In LEGICOM n° 42 – 2009/1. La régulation des données personnelles. Paris: Victoires Éditions, 2009. P. 149.

[18]Commission nationale de l'informatique et des libertés. Délibération no 2011-249 du 8 septembre 2011 portant modification de l'article 69 du règlement intérieur de la Commission nationale de l'informatique et des libertés et insérant un chapitre 4 bis intitulé « Procédure de labellisation ».

[19]"Lors de sa séance plénière du 14 juin 2012, la CNIL a délivré les cinq premiers labels: quatre pour les formations et un pour l'audit de traitement." Commission Nationale de L'Informatique et des Libertes. La CNIL délivre ses premiers labels. Available at http://www.cnil.fr/la-cnil/actualite/article/article/la-cnil-delivre-ses-premiers-labels/. Accessed 22 September 2012.

[20]Turk, Alex. 2009. Bilan et perspectives de la CNIL (Entretien). *Tracabilité et reséaux*. Hermes n° 53. CNRS-editions. P. 154. Unofficial translation by the author.

regulatory provision."[21] As in the Italian Data Protection Law (as will be seen in Chap. 5), the French Data Protection Authority has the power to deliver general authorisations (Autorisations Uniques) for the processings referred to above. It is worth noting that the CNIL, when adopting general authorisations, only requires data controllers to "send to the commission an undertaking that the processing complies with the description of the authorisation."[22]

As a rule, all processing operations have to be notified to the Data Protection Authority, exceptions being the ones involving sensitive data, State security and criminal offences, the public processing of NIR (national identification register), State biometrics, census and online services and any processing that may exclude persons from the benefit of a right, a service or a contract, all of which need a prior authorisation from the CNIL (article 22).[23] In this book I analyse only the general authorisations that have an impact on the insurance, banking and credit reporting industries. There are currently 29 general authorisations adopted by the CNIL; nonetheless, the ones which are relevant for our analysis are: AU-003 on the processing of personal data carried out by financial institutions for the fight against money laundering and the financing of terrorism, AU 005 on the processing of personal data for helping in the evaluation and selection of risks in terms of granting credit, AU-018 on the processing of personal data conducted by insurance companies for the purposes of searching for beneficiaries of life insurance policies that were not claimed after the death of the insured party and AU-024 on the processing of personal data carried out by the insurance industry for the fight against money-laundering and the financing of terrorism.[24] These General Authorisations will be analysed in Sect. 3.5.

Besides the general authorisations, there are other decisions from the CNIL that establish general rules for the processing of personal data which do not involve situations subject to an authorisation, the simplified standards (normes simplifies), which intend to simplify the obligation controllers have to notify the CNIL about any processing of personal data.[25] Some of these decisions also relate to the sectors under analysis.

---

[21]Article 25, I. According to Bensoussan, the processings which pose risk to individuals are identified according to: (a) the nature of the processing; (b) the use of a new technology; (c) the interconnection of databases; (c) the use of general identifiers. Bensoussan, Alain. Op. cit. P. 91–92.

[22]Article 25, II.

[23]Huet, Jérôme. La CNIL a-t-elle acompli les missions dévolues par le législateur?. In LEGICOM n° 42—2009/1. La régulation des données personnelles. Victoires Éditions: Paris, 2009. P. 18. "(...) les autorisations de la CNIL auxquelles sont subordonnées depuis la loi de 2004 certaines applications relevant du secteur privé (notamment biométrie, crédit scoring, fichiers de sélection, listes noires, traitements hors EU) (...)."

[24]There are other general authorisations which to a certain extent deal with issues that affect the industries under analysis, however, since they apply to very specific situations which go beyond the scope of this book, they will not be analysed here. See, for example, AU-021, AU-022, AU-023, AU-025.

[25]Article 24.

3.2 The Concept of Personal Data

The French Act defines personal data as "any information relating to a natural person who is or can be identified, directly or indirectly, by reference to an identification number or to one or more factors specific to him. In order to determine whether a person is identifiable, all the means that the controller or any other person uses or may have access to should be taken into consideration",[26] in other words, in France all possible means to identify a person can be considered independent of the amount of time, expense, and labour to be applied in this effort.[27] Nevertheless, the French Court of Cassation (Cour de Cassation), in a case involving information regarding the place of residence of a famous princess and a meeting with her husband in a restaurant, concluded that the "'Triviality' of some information was likely to exclude the invasion of privacy."[28] This approach can lead to the conclusion that the Court created another criterion for a data to be considered as personal data and to deserve protection, 'the non triviality', what seems to contradict both Directive 95/46/EC and the French Data Protection Act.

Moreover, although Article 2 does not include expressly deceased people in the definition of personal data, it can be inferred from Article 40 paragraph 5 that this category of persons is also included in the definition, since it recognises the right of heirs of the deceased person to demand of data controllers that they "take the death into account and update the data accordingly",[29] and from the fact that it did not include the words 'living individuals' as did the UK Data Protection Act 1998.[30] Nonetheless, in a famous case involving the book 'Le grand secret', which referred to a disease the former French President François Mitterrand had at the end of his life, the Court of Cassation decided that "the right to take legal action regarding the violation of private life ends with the death of the data subject, the only holder of this right."[31] Such decision limits the scope of personal data, since it limits the exercise of rights, by the heirs of the data subject, in terms of violations of privacy (and data protection).

---

[26] Article 2, 2nd paragraph of the French Act 78-15.

[27] Laffaire, Marie-Laure. Protection des données à caractere personnel. Paris: Éditions d'organisation, 2005. P. 43. The French Act, as the British one, did not adopt a definition of anonymous data, although in some of its provisions it refers to this kind of data. See, for instance, Article 25, §1 of the French Act 78-15.

[28] Mallet-Poujol, Nathalie. Protection de la vie privée et des données personnelles. Legamedia, Février 2006, http://www.educnet.education.fr/chrgt/guideViePrivee.pdf. Accessed 1 August 2011, 5. Unofficial translation by the author.

[29] Article 100 of the French Decree nº 2005-1,309 requires that "the heir of a deceased person who wishes to update the data concerning the deceased" proves "his capacity as heir by producing an attested affidavit or a family record book." In overseas regions such proof can be made through any means (Article 111, §9 of the same Decree).

[30] See Section 1(1) of the UK Data Protection Act 1998.

[31] Mallet-Poujol, Nathalie. Op. cit., 5. Unofficial translation by the author.

Furthermore, despite the fact that the Act does not include information regarding legal persons in the definition of personal data,[32] the French Authority in some of its decisions has been dealing with the processing of such data as it was amongst its competences.[33] In addition, some courts in France have already recognised the protection of privacy to legal entities.[34]

3.3 The Processing of Sensitive Data

Article 8 of the French Data Protection Act prohibits, as a rule, "the collection and processing of personal data that reveals, directly or indirectly, the racial and ethnic origins, the political, philosophical, religious opinions or trade union affiliation of persons, or which concern their health or sexual life", almost repeating the terms of article 8 of Directive 95/46/EC. Nonetheless, in section II of the same article it recognises as legitimate the processing of sensitive data when: (1) the data subject gives his express consent; (2) it is necessary for the protection of human life; (3) the processing is carried out by an association or any other non-profit religious, philosophical, political or trade union body; (4) it relates to personal data made public by the data subject; (5) it is necessary for the establishment, exercise or defence of a legal claim; (6) it is necessary for the purposes of preventive medicine, medical diagnosis, provision of healthcare or treatment, or for the management of healthcare services and carried out by a member of a medical profession or by someone who, due to his functions, is bound by a duty of confidence; (7) it refers to statistical processing carried out by the National Institute of Statistics and Economic Studies (INSEE) or any one of the statistical services of the Ministries; and, finally, (8) it is necessary for medical research.

Regarding the processing of what is called judicial data (personal data relating to offences, convictions and security measures), it can be put in place only by courts and legal entities that manage public services, the representatives of the law for the exercise of their functions granted by law[35] and by "the legal persons mentioned in

---

[32] Bensoussan, Alain, Informatiques et libertes. Paris: Éditions Francis Lefebvre, 2008. P. 19. "La protection de libertes fondamentales ne concerne que les personnes physiques. Les personnes morales sont exclues du regime de protection."

[33] In that sense, see Commission Nationale de L'Informatique et des Libertes. Autorisation Unique n° AU-003 and Autorisation Unique n° AU-024 of the French Data Protection Authority. http://www.cnil.fr/en-savoir-plus/deliberations/autorisations-uniques/. Accessed 4 January 2011.

[34] Lacoste, Jean-Marc, "Pour une pleine et entière reconnaissance du droit à la protection des données à caractère personnel" (PhD diss., Université de Toulouse, 2008), 188.

[35] The French Conseil Constitutionnel has decided that a Law authorising the creation and maintenance of databases by the private sector for the prevention of and fight against fraud is against the French Constitution. See decision n° 2004-499 DC of 29 July 2004. § 12. Available at

Articles L321-1 and L331-1 of the Intellectual Property Code, acting by virtue of the rights that they administer or on behalf of victims of infringements of the rights provided for in the same Code, and to ensure the defence of these rights."[36]

With regard to the processing of personal data for fighting fraud in the private sector, although it has been authorised by the CNIL, such data cannot be part of a database and are only permitted to be stored during the consideration of the incoherency of the act considered, or at the latest during the period necessary for the detection of a fraud.[37] By contrast, in the UK there are many databases for this purpose, where storage limits go beyond the necessary period for the detection of fraud.

Finally, as highlighted in Sect. 3.1 of this chapter, the French Data Protection Authority has the power to deliver general authorisations for the processing of sensitive data, which have to be previously authorised by the Data Protection Authority before it is put in place. The general authorisations which deal with the processing of sensitive data carried out by the case-studies will be analysed in the respective sections.

3.4 Data Subjects' Rights

The first data subject right is the one that imposes upon controllers the duty to inform data subjects when their data have been collected, at the latest at the time when data are first disclosed,[38] which will allow data subjects to exercise their other rights. To fulfil this obligation they have to inform the data subject of, for example, the purposes of the collection, who will be the addressees of the data collected, if such collection is compulsory or not and what the data subject's rights are.[39]

---

http://www.conseil-constitutionnel.fr/conseil-constitutionnel/francais/les-decisions/acces-par-date/decisions-depuis-1959/2004/2004-499-dc/decision-n-2004-499-dc-du-29-juillet-2004.904.html. Accessed 7 October 2010.

[36] Article 9, paragraph 4°.

[37] Bensoussan, Alain. Op. cit. P. 558–559.

[38] Article 32, III.

[39] Commission Nationale de L'Informatique et des Libertes. Guide banque-crédit : êtes-vous fichés? Available at http://www.cnil.fr/fileadmin/documents/La_CNIL/publications/CNIL_guide_banquecredit.pdf. Accessed 29 March 2011. P. 17. Following the adoption of the Law Murcef, the French Bank Federation adopted a charter where the banking sector agree to inform its clients about: "(. . .) the finalities of the treatments implemented by the financial institution, the recipients of information, the right to oppose to a data processing for commercial prospection purposes as well as about the methods of exercise of the right of access to information concerning themselves (. . .)." Fédération Bancaire Française (FBF). Charte relative aux conventions de compte de dépôt. Available at http://www.fbf.fr/web/internet/content_actualitebancaire.nsf/(WebPageList)/502AB0F373BE6762C1256DCD00490773/$File/AB_special.pdf. Accessed 29 March 2011. Unofficial translation by the author.

Moreover, the data controller has to reply to a request for access within a 2-month period.[40] Through this right to access data subjects can exercise their other rights to rectify, complete, update and even to erase their data if they were not regularly collected.[41]

Furthermore, data subjects have the right to know, and to object to, the logic involved in the automatic processing when an automated decision (as in the case of scoring) has legal effects on them, unless it adversely affects copyrights.[42] In the banking sector, for example, this right allows data subjects to know whether a bank registered "the trace of incidents of payment during the fulfilment of a preceding contract; the score which was attributed to them as well as the minimum and maximum possible grades and the comments that were included in their personal file."[43] The only possibility for a data controller to refuse a request of access is in the case where there is a misuse of such a right by the data subject (frequent and abusive requests of access).[44]

Another important right recognised by the French Law is the right to object to the processing of personal data for the purposes of canvassing, in particular for commercial ends. It is important to note that this right does not apply to processing which "satisfies a legal obligation or where an explicit provision of the decision that authorises the processing excludes" the exercise of this right.[45] Hence, to exercise such a right, individuals have to prove the existence of legitimate reasons (*motifs legitimes*) to object to a specific act of processing.[46] Nonetheless, this right can

---

[40]Article 94, 1st paragraph of Decree n° 2005-1309.

[41]Commission Nationale de L'Informatique et des Libertes. Guide banque-crédit : êtes-vous fichés? Op. cit. P. 18.

[42]Article 39, §5°.

[43]Commission Nationale de L'Informatique et des Libertes. Guide banque-crédit : êtes-vous fichés? P. 17. The information given to the data subject shall not violate intellectual property rights, as highlighted by Bensoussan, Alain. Op. cit. P. 65. "De manière expresse <<les informations communiqués à la personne concernée ne doivent pas porter atteinte du droit d'auteur, au sens des dispositions du livre 1er et du titre IV du livre III du Code de la propriété intellectuelle>> (L. 1978, art. 39, §5°). Dans ce cadre, le responsable du traitement est tenu de fournir le cheminement des opérations et de detailler les algorithmes mathematiques utilisés."

[44]Fédération Bancaire Française. Les min-guides. Repère n° 15. La protection de vos données personnelles. Available at http://www.fbf.fr/web/Internet2010/Content.nsf/DocumentsByIDWeb/87TFZB/$File/mini-guide_15_donnees_personnelles.pdf. Accessed 5 October 2010. P. 19. "C'est seulement si votre demande est manifestement abusive (demandes répétitives et fréquentes) que votre banque peut ne pas y donner suite (sous le contrôle, le cas échéant, de la CNIL)."

[45]Article 38.

[46]Pallez, Christophe. L'exercice du pouvoir de sanction est une revolution culturelle pour la CNIL. Les petites affiches, 29/9/2004, n° 195. P. 148.

be exercised without any justification concerning prospection for commercial,[47] political, cultural, philosophical or religious purposes.[48]

3.5 The Processing of Personal Data by the Case Studies

3.5.1 The Banking Sector

According to the CNIL, and to what I have been discussing in this book, financial institutions can only process information related to their relationship with their clients, as for example, data related to the bank accounts management and to lending contracts.[49] They cannot store, as a rule, the social security number of the data subject, or other sensitive data,[50] such as data related to political and religious opinions and trade union membership.[51]

Still regarding the storage of data, the Data Protection Authority has developed the so-called *droit à l'oubli numerique* (right to numerical oblivion),[52] i.e., the right

---

[47]Commission Nationale de L'Informatique et des Libertes. Guide banque-crédit : êtes-vous fichés? Op. cit. P. 18. See also Pallez, Christophe. L'exercice du pouvoir de sanction est une revolution culturelle pour la CNIL. Les petites affiches, 29/9/2004, n° 195. P. 15. "La CNIL a consideré três tôt que les personnes pouvaient s'opposer à la cession commerciale de leurs données à la cession commerciale de leurs données à des tiers sans avoir à justifier d'un motif quelconque (. . .)."

[48]Bensoussan, Alain. Op. cit. P. 177.

[49]Commission Nationale de L'Informatique et des Libertes. Guide banque-crédit : êtes-vous fichés? Op. cit. P. 3. "Aucun jugement de valeur, aucun commentaire subjectif ou désobligeant, aucune donnée sans lien avec l'activité bancaire ne peuvent être inscrits dans votre dossier client."

[50]Fédération Bancaire Française. Les min-guides. Repère n° 15. La protection de vos données personnelles. P. 7. "(. . .) en dehors de quelques exceptions prévues par la loi, la banque ne peut pas conserver d'informations ayant trait à vos origines raciales, ethniques, à vos opinions politiques, philosophiques ou religieuses, à votre appartenance syndicale ou encore à votre santé ou à votre vie sexuelle."

[51]Commission Nationale de L'Informatique et des Libertes. Guide banque-crédit : êtes-vous fichés? Op. cit. P. 2. "Que comporte votre dossier client?

- Des données d'identification : nom, prénoms, date et lieu de naissance, nationalité, adresse postale, numéro de client, coordonnées téléphoniques (facultatif), adresse électronique (facultatif);
- Des données liées à la gestion des produits et services souscrits ou demandes: situation professionnelle, situation familiale, revenus, score calcule pour l'obtention d'un crédit, note de risque attribuée au client, segment de clientèle (notamment pour vous adresser des offres commerciales adaptées), opérations effectuées sur vos comptes (pour éditer les releves de compte par exemple), litiges ou difficultés passés ou en cours (inscription dans un fichier de la Banque de France, saisie sur salaire, surendettement . . .), existence d'une mesure de protection (tutelle, curatelle), resume des entretiens avec votre chargé de clientèle."

[52]The right to oblivion is mainly recognised as "the right to have news concerning us forgotten after a reasonable amount of time". Paissan, Mauro. Privacy Protection and Right to Know. Striking a

to have personal information excluded from a database (or from the internet) after a certain (reasonable) period.[53] The CNIL, in comparison to the Italian data protection authority, establishes clear storage limits in its decisions.[54]

Another important issue relates to the exchange of customers' personal information between companies of the same economic group.[55] For the bank to transfer personal information it has to obtain the consent of the data subject (after having informed him/her clearly about the scope, addressees and purposes of the processing) and an authorisation from the CNIL to develop this kind of processing activity. Furthermore, there is also the possibility to transfer personal data to companies which are not part of an economic group, if such information has a connection with two contracts, one with the bank and the other with another company, as in the example of an insurance contract related to a loan or mortgage. However, in any case this third company cannot request (obtain) information not related to this new contract.[56]

It is worth noting that banks are authorised to request the presentation of an identity card at the moment of the opening of a bank account, in order to comply with their obligations in terms of vigilance, surveillance and the denunciation of

---

Difficult Balance. Spring Conference of European Data Protection Commissioners. 10–11 May 2007. Available at http://www.garanteprivacy.it/garante/doc.jsp?ID=1408388. Accessed 8 October 2010.

[53]About the right to numerical oblivion see Gentot, Michel. La protection des données personnelles à la croisée des chemins. In Tabatoni, Pierre. Société d'information et vie privée. Tome III. Available at http://www.asmp.fr/travaux/gpw/internetvieprivee/rapport3/chapitr1.pdf. Accessed 8 October 2010. P. 43; and Bensoussan, Alain. Op. cit. P. 38. "Le droit à l'oubli consiste à imposer aux responsables des traitements de ne plus conserver, au-delà de la finalité d'origine, les données à caractère personnel."

[54]Gentot, Michel. La CNIL et son experience de la regulation de l'information. In Mathieu, Michel (editor). La <<Société de l'Informations>>- Entre myths et réalités. Collection Médias, Sociétés et Relations Internationales. Nº 2. Bruylant: Bruxelles, 2008. P. 353. "Ainsi, pour la CNIL c'est en raison du <<droit à l'oubli>> que l'enterprise ne peut pas conserver de manière <<manifestement excessive>> des données."

[55]Commission Nationale de L'Informatique et des Libertes. Guide banque-crédit : êtes-vous fichés? Op. cit. P. 4. "(...) votre banque ou votre organisme de crédit peut être la filiale d'um group financier, comportant d'autres banques, sociétés de crédit, des compagnies d'assurance, etc. Sous certaines conditions, vos données peuvent être transmises aux autres sociétés du groupe afin de mieux gérer <<le risque client>> (ex.: possibilité qu'un client ne rembourse pas um crédit)."

[56]Commission Nationale de L'Informatique et des Libertes. Guide banque-crédit : êtes-vous fichés? Op. cit. P. 4. "Enfin, sachez que, lors d'une demande de prêt assortie d'une assurance, l'établissement de crédit communique à sa compagnie d'assurance, même si elle ne fait pas partie du même groupe, des informations telles que votre identité et vos coordonnées, la nature, le montant et la durée du prêt que vous avez demandé.

Ces informations permettent à la compagnie d'assurance de vous contacter afin d'obtenir d'autres informations (par exemple sur votre état de santé, sous certaines conditions, et sous pli confidentiel remis au médecin conseil de la compagnie d'assurance) en vue de se prononcer sur la demande d'assurance liée à votre demande de crédit.

En revanche, la compagnie d'assurance n'est pas fondée à obtenir des informations sans lien avec son activité, comme par exemple votre situation financière qui relève du secret bancaire."

illicit activities, such as drug trafficking, corruption, organised crime and financing of terrorism.[57] General Authorisation AU-003 of the CNIL deals exactly with the processing of personal data for the fight against money laundering and the financing of terrorism.[58] According to this authorisation, financial institutions can process personal data of their clients (and also data related to legal persons) for these purposes.[59] The Authorisation establishes the recipients of this information, the storage limits and the rules for the exercise of the right of access. Furthermore, two decisions of the CNIL authorise the operation by the financial sector of a system called DIANA, which has the aim of fighting fraud in banking cards.[60]

Furthermore, banks usually use scoring to take decisions relating to applications for credit. To calculate the score they make use of automatic systems that analyse personal data of the applicants, such as age, profession, family status and even nationality, as recognised by the French *Conseil d'État*, the highest administrative court in France.[61] Therefore, the rejection of an application for credit can be directly linked to the score the individual obtains. General Authorisation AU-005 deals with the processing of personal data for helping in the evaluation and selection of risks in terms of granting credit and, as a consequence, it addresses scoring systems. In this decision, the CNIL authorises financial institutions to create a score for their potential clients for the purposes mentioned above (evaluation and selection of risks), allowing the processing of data related not only to the credit-seeking applicant, but also to the members of his/her family who have an economic link with him/her and also information related to his/her grantors.[62] It is important to note that the results of the score can only be used for a specific application for credit. Nonetheless, in cases where the applicant is the customer of the financial institution to which the application was addressed, then data used for the scoring can be used to update the file of the respective client.[63] In case his/her application is declined and a scoring system was used, the data subject can request a meeting with an agent of the financial institution with powers to review the application, when he/she

---

[57]Ibid. P. 8.

[58]Commission Nationale de L'Informatique et des Libertes. Autorisation unique nº AU-003 – Délibération nº 2005-297 du 1er décembre 2005 portant autorisations unique de certains traitements de données à caractere personnel mis en œuvre dans des organismes financiers au titre de la lutte contre le blanchiment de capitaux et le financement du terrorisme.

[59]Article 1—Autorisation Unique AU-003.

[60]Déliberation nº 2007-324 du 25 octobre 2007 and Déliberation nº 2007-325 du 25 octobre 2007.

[61]Bensoussan, Alain. Op. cit. P. 547. "Le Conseil d'État a consideré qu'un traitement de scores relatifs à des décisions d'octroi ou de refus utilisant le critère du nationalité sont respectés les príncipes de proporcionalité, d'adequation et de pertinence (CE 30-10-2001 nº 204909, Association Française des Sociétpes Financières et autres c/ CNIL: RJDA 4/02 nº 463)."

[62]Data that can be processed include civil status, age, citizenship, economic situation and many others. See Commission Nationale de L'Informatique et des Libertes. Autorisation unique nº AU-005—Délibération nº 2008-198 du 9 juillet 2008 modifiant l'autorisation unique nº AU-005 relative à certains traitements mis en œuvre par les établissements de crédit pour aider à l'évaluation et à la sélection des risques em matière d'octroi de crédit.

[63]Commission Nationale de L'Informatique et des Libertes. Autorisation unique nº AU-005.

(data subject) will be able to make some observations regarding his/her financial situation.[64] Therefore, the French Data Protection Act interdicts any decision that may have a legal effect on an individual, including the ones taken in the context of entering into or performing a contract, based only on automated processing of personal data, and does not apply the derogation contained in Article 15(2)(a) of Directive 95/46/EC, which allows Member States to provide that a person can be subject to an exclusively automated decision when such decision "is taken in the course of the entering into or performance of a contract, provided the request for the entering into or the performance of the contract, lodged by the data subject, has been satisfied or that there are suitable measures to safeguard his legitimate interests, such as arrangements allowing him to put his point of view."

Moreover, Simplified Standards nº 12 and 13 concern the processing of personal data by financial institutions for the purposes of managing the accounts of their clients and the payment and lending operations related to them. It is important to note that the latter norm allows the processing of data related to the health status of the borrower when insurance is required in order to ensure the repayment of the debt.[65] All personal information processed according to simplified norm 13 can be stored for no more than 5 years after the conclusion of the contract and in cases where the contract is not concluded this information can be stored for no more than 6 months.[66]

3.5.2 The Credit Information Suppliers

As distinct from Italy and the UK, in France there is no credit bureau, the sole public register being the French Central Bank (La Banque de France), which is responsible for supplying credit institutions with credit information.[67] This means that there is no market for credit information, since the only supplier is the government, which creates constraints for the free movement of these services. Just to illustrate, a famous credit bureau requested authorisation from the CNIL to start a processing activity in France, but it was rejected on the grounds of risk to privacy and lack of legal basis,[68] this decision being confirmed by the *Conseil d'État*.[69] Until now,

---

[64]Commission Nationale de L'Informatique et des Libertes. Autorisation unique nº AU-005.

[65]Article 3(g). Regarding the processing of health data for the granting of credit, it is of importance the Aeras Convention, which regulates the granting of credit to people with high health risks. Available at http://www.aeras-infos.fr/sections/la_convention_en_3_q/view. Accessed 8 October 2010.

[66]See Article 4.

[67]Expert Group on Credit Histories. Report. May 2009. Op. cit. P. 57.

[68]Commission Nationale de L'Informatique et des Libertes. Délibération nº 2007-044 du 8 mars 2007.

[69]Conseil d'État. Décision nº 306173. Judgement of 30 December 2009. Available at http://arianeinternet.conseil-etat.fr/arianeinternet/ViewRoot.asp?View=Html&DMode=Html&PushDirectUrl=1&Item=1&fond=DCE&texte=306173&Page=1&querytype=simple&NbEltPerPages=5&Pluriels=True. Accessed 4 October 2010. It is important to notice that Experian, in its appeal to

the French Central Bank registers only negative information. However, Act n° 2010-737 of 1st July 2010 was approved establishing the creation of a new database, processing also positive information to be managed by the French Central Bank. This law also creates a committee, which delivered its first report about such a database on 2 August 2011.[70] Therefore, France will most-likely have, in the near future, a database with positive information, which will have as its main aims "to prevent the over-indebtedness and to ensure better information to lenders regarding the solvency of borrowers".[71]

Currently, the Central Bank manages four databases that are used by the banking/financial sector: Le Fichier Central des Chèques (FCC), Le Fichier National de Chèques Irreguliers (FNCI), Le Fichier National des Incidents de Remboursement des Crédits aux Particuliers (FICP) and Le Fichier bancaire des enterprises (FIBEN). The FCC collates information about interdictions of cheque drawers decided by a bank or a Court after a cheque is returned due to a lack of funds. This information can be kept in the database for no longer than 5 years and once the situation is rectified, it has to be deleted within 2 days.[72] There is also a subfile in the FCC, "volet carte bancaire - CB" which allows banks to access information regarding bankcards that were cancelled after an abusive use by the customer (lack of funds). Being different from the general FCC, the information stored in this subfile can be kept for only 2 years in the absence of rectification of the customer's situation. It is important to notice that the FCC and the CB can only be accessed simultaneously.

The second database managed by the Bank of France is the FNCI, which comprises oppositions to cheques for loss or robbery, the closing of accounts and banking or judicial prohibitions to write cheques.[73] In this database there are different storage limits in accordance with the reasons for which the information was registered.[74]

---

the Conseil d'État, did not challenge the issue of freedom to provide services, what prevented the Conseil d'État from analysing this subject.

[70]See Registre national des crédits: le Comité de préfiguration rend son rapport. Available at http://www.cnil.fr/la-cnil/actualite/article/article/registre-national-des-credits-le-comite-de-prefiguration-rend-son-rapport/. Accessed 23 September 2011.

[71]Article 49 of Law 2010-737. Unofficial translation by the author.

[72]Commission Nationale de L'Informatique et des Libertes. Guide banque-crédit : êtes-vous fichés? Available at http://www.cnil.fr/fileadmin/documents/La_CNIL/publications/CNIL_guide_banquecredit.pdf. P. 5.

[73]See http://www.cnil.fr/en-savoir-plus/fichiers-en-fiche/fichier/article/fnci-fichier-national-des-cheques-irreguliers-1/. Accessed 9 October 2010.

[74]"Jusqu'à ce que la personne recouvre le droit d'émettre des chèques (maximum 5 ans); 5 ans pour les chèques clôtures; 10 ans pour les chèques déclarés volés ou perdus ou 2 jours en l'absence de confirmation de la déclaration effectuée par téléphene." Commission Nationale de L'Informatique et des Libertes. Fichier em fiche. FNCI: Fichier National des Chèques Irréguliers. 23 mars 2010. Available at http://www.cnil.fr/en-savoir-plus/fichiers-en-fiche/fichier/article/fnci-fichier-national-des-cheques-irreguliers-1/. Accessed 15 April 2011.

The third database is the FICP, collating information regarding defaults, which remain in the register for 5 years, unless the repayment occurs before that period.[75]

Finally, the fourth database, created only in July 2011, is FIBEN, which stores information about companies, their administrators and individual entrepreneurs, having different storage limits according to the type of information stored.[76] In all four databases, data subjects will have to address a request to the data controller (French Central Bank) in order to exercise their rights of access and rectification. Nevertheless, they have to be informed by their banks that their personal data are being registered in the respective database. In case there is any inaccuracy regarding the information stored, data subjects will have to address a request to the respective financial institution—which will also be liable for damages suffered by them and not to the French Central Bank.

Moreover, there are other databases which are accessed by the banking industry which are managed by the French Ministry of Economy and Finance. The first one is FICOBA (Le fichier des Comptes Bancaires et assimilés), with information on the opening and closing of banking accounts, that remain stored for 3 years after the closing of the account.[77] The second one is TRACINFO (Le Fichier de Vigilance), which congregates information sent by financial institutions regarding signs of money laundering. Regarding the former, data subjects will exercise their rights of access in a direct way when dealing with identification data (name, surname, sex, birthday, city, department or country of birth and address), and in an indirect way through the CNIL when dealing with data linked to the nature and identification of the banking accounts (number, type, characteristics of the account, address of the institution which manages the account).[78]

---

[75]The storage limit will be of 8 years in the event of procedure of personal re-establishment and of 10 years maximum in the event of a recovery package or of recommendations of the commission of over-indebtedness. See Commission Nationale de L'Informatique et des Libertes. Guide banque-crédit : êtes-vous fichés? Available at http://www.cnil.fr/fileadmin/documents/La_CNIL/publications/CNIL_guide_banquecredit.pdf. Accessed 8 April 2011. P. 7.

[76]See http://www.cnil.fr/en-savoir-plus/fichiers-en-fiche/fichier/article/fiben/. Accessed 23 September 2012.

[77]Commission Nationale de L'Informatique et des Libertes. FICOBA: Fichier national des comptes bancaires et assimilés. 08 juin 2009. Available at http://www.cnil.fr/en-savoir-plus/fichiers-en-fiche/fichier/article/ficoba-fichier-national-des-comptes-bancaires-et-assimiles/. Accessed 8 April 2011.

[78]Commission Nationale de L'Informatique et des Libertes. Fiches pratiques. Fichier <<FICOBA>>: une nouvelle procédure de droit d'accès. Available at http://www.cnil.fr/en-savoir-plus/fiches-pratiques/fiche/article/fichier-ficoba-une-nouvelle-procedure-de-droit-dacces/. Accessed 8 April 2011. "Un arrêté du 13 décembre 2007, pris après avis de la CNIL, a redefini les procédures de droit d'accès aplicables à ce fichier. Le fichier FICOBA est désormais soumis à un droit d'accès mixte."

3.5.3 The Insurance Industry

In the insurance sector there is a database called AGIRA (Association pour la gestion des informations sur le risque automobile), which allows motor-insurance companies to verify past information regarding a potentially insured individual before the conclusion of a motor-insurance contract. This database stores the exchanges of information between insurance companies with the aim of "personalis(ing) premiums and contributions of motor-insurance and of detecting frauds regarding the omission of information about losses at the moment of the conclusion of the insurance contract."[79] Information regarding losses remain for 5 years in the database and information related to non-payment,[80] to inaccurate declaration of risk and to cancellation of the contract by the insured party remain for 2 years. Insured parties are informed about the possibility of having their personal data stored in this database through information included in the general conditions of the insurance contract.[81] In order to exercise their data subjects' rights, individuals have to address a request to AGIRA or to the insurance company which registered their information in the database.[82]

The processing of personal data carried out by AGIRA is authorised by Délibération n° 95-158 of 12 December 1995.[83] It is also recognised by general authorisation AU-18, which regulates the processing of personal data by insurance companies for the purposes of searching for beneficiaries of life insurance policies that were not claimed after the death of the insured party.[84]

Another important purpose for the processing of personal data carried out by the insurance industry is that regarding the fight against money-laundering and the financing of terrorism. In this respect, the CNIL adopted General Authorisation AU-024, allowing insurance companies to process the personal data of their clients for these purposes.[85]

---

[79]Commission Nationale de L'Informatique et des Libertes. AGIRA: Association pour la gestion des informations sur le risque automobile. 08 juin 2009. Available at http://www.cnil.fr/en-savoir-plus/fichiers-en-fiche/fichier/article/association-pour-la-gestion-des-informations-sur-le-risque-automobile/. Accessed 8 April 2011. Unofficial translation by the author.

[80]Once the debt is paid, information related to it has to be excluded from the AGIRA Database.

[81]Commission Nationale de L'Informatique et des Libertes. Fichier en fiche. AGIRA: Association pour la gestion des informations sur le risque automobile. 08 juin 2009. Op. cit.

[82]Ibid.

[83]Available at http://www.legifrance.gouv.fr/affichCnil.do?oldAction=rechExpCnil&id=CNILTEXT000017653157&fastReqId=857498319&fastPos=1. Accessed 19 October 2010.

[84]Commission Nationale de L'Informatique et des Libertes. Autorisation unique n° 18—Délibération n° 2008-579 du 18 décembre 2008 portant authorisation unique des traitements automatisés des enterprises d'assurance, des instituitions de prévoyance et de leurs unions, et des mutuelles et de leurs unions mis en œuvre aux fins de recherché des assures et des beneficiaries de contrats d'assurance sur la vie décédés.

[85]Commission Nationale de L'Informatique et des Libertes. Autorisation unique n° AU-024—Délibération n° 2009-429 du 2 juillet 2009 portant autorisation unique des traitements de données

Furthermore, an interesting decision of the CNIL that affects the insurance sector regulates the processing of information obtained from geolocation systems installed in vehicles.[86] Such processing has the aim of verifying policy-holders' adherence to duties with regard to driving periods, miles driven, and even the way they drive, in order to accurately calculate the premium of motor-insurance. Furthermore, the processing also has the aim of fighting the robbery of vehicles and of allowing an automatic emergency call by the geolocation device in case of an accident involving the insured vehicle.[87] The decision presents some rules concerning the consent of the data subject, storage limits, as well as the possibility of deactivating the geolocation system. As far as this latter issue is concerned, the CNIL is of the opinion that a system which allows a manual deactivation of the geolocation device could not be imposed, once the equipment has been acquired freely and the data subject was properly informed about the processing of data.

Moreover, Simplified Standard n° 16 relates to the processing of personal data by insurance, reinsurance and capitalization companies, and their brokers for the purposes of making and managing contracts, the execution of contracts, the development of statistics, and the selection of and compliance with legal obligations.[88] This norm presents the kinds of personal data that can be processed for all types of insurance coverage and some kinds of data which can be processed only for specific coverages (motor-insurance, insurance for damages, property insurance, life insurance, health insurance and civil liability insurance).[89] The storage limits vary from 2 to 30 years according to the type of contract.[90] The norm also highlights the fact that "only information likely to specify the risks incurred by the insured party, taking into consideration the legitimate professional interests of the insurer, can be used in the risk analysis".[91]

à caractere personnel mis en œuvre para les sociiétés du Group des assurance du Crédit mutuel dont la finalité est la lutte contre le blanchiment de capitaux et le financement du terrorisme.

[86]For a detailed analysis of geolocation systems in vehicles from a data protection perspective, see Doneda, Danilo; Viola de Azevedo Cunha, Mario. Notes About Vehicle Monitoring in Brazil and Europe from a Data Protection Perspective. In Firmino, Rodrigo J. et al. ICTs for Mobile and Ubiquitous Urban Infrastructures: Surveillance, Locative Media and Global Networks. IGI Publishing, 2011.

[87]Commission Nationale de L'Informatique et des Libertes. Délibération 2010-096 du 8 avril 2010 portant recommandation relative à la mise em œuvre, par les compagnies d'assurance et les constructeurs automobiles, de dispositifs de géolocalisation embarques dans les véhicules.

[88]Commission Nationale de L'Informatique et des Libertes. Norme simplifiée n° 16: Délibération n° 81-004 du 20 janvier 1981 concernant les traitements automatisés d'informations nominatives relatifs à la passation, la gestion et l'execution des contrats mis en œuvre par les organismes d'assurance, de capitalisation, de reassurances et d'assistance et par leurs intermediaries.

[89]See Article 3.

[90]See Article 4 of the Simplified Norm, Article 2,262 of the French Civil Code (Code Civil) and Article R. 341-4 of the French Insurance Code (Code des Assurances).

[91]Article 6. Unofficial translation by the author.

There is another database that is accessed by the Insurance Industry[92] and by financial institutions, according to the kind of contract they are negotiating with the data subject.[93] The SIV (Systéme d'immatriculation des véhicules), managed by the Ministry of Home Affairs, stores information about all vehicles, their owners, drivers and professionals working in activities related to the trade of vehicles.[94]

Finally, it is important to devote some attention to the use of genetic data by the insurance sector. In fact, the French insurance industry has adopted a moratorium since 1994[95] "pledging not to take into account the results of genetic tests conducted on insurance applicants, even if the individuals provided this information voluntarily."[96] Furthermore, the French Code of Public Health, in its Article L. 1,141-1, as amended by Law 2002-303 of 4 March 2002,[97] prohibits the use of genetic information by life and disability insurers[98]:

> Companies and organisations which propose coverage for disability and life risks, should not take into account the results of genetic tests of a person applying for these coverages, even if those information are transmitted to them by the person concerned or with her agreement. Moreover, they cannot pose any question related to genetic tests and their results, nor to ask a person to undergo a genetic test before the contract is concluded and throughout the duration of the contract.[99]

From that moment on, the use of genetic data by the private insurance sector is forbidden in France and, indeed, the CNIL has never adopted an authorisation regarding the processing of genetic data by the insurance sector: first there was a moratorium agreed by the industry and now there is a law forbidding such processing activity.[100]

---

[92]See Article L330-2, §8° of the French Traffic Code (Code de la route) and Article.

[93]See http://www.cnil.fr/en-savoir-plus/fichiers-en-fiche/fichier/article/siv-systeme-dimmatricul-ation-des-vehicules/. Accessed 9 October 2010.

[94]Arrêté du 10 février 2009 portant création d'un traitement automatisé de données à caractère personnel dénommé « système d'immatriculation des véhicules » ayant pour objet la gestion des pièces administratives du droit de circuler des véhicules. Available at http://www.legifrance.gouv.fr/affichTexte.do?cidTexte=JORFTEXT000020283692&dateTextee=. Accessed 9 October 2010.

[95]"(...) in April 1999, the French Conseil d'État recommended to the government to 'adopt a strict framework concerning the communication of [genetic test] results to third parties', specifying that 'the sensitivity of genetic data justifies prohibiting insurers from requesting that insurance candidates undergo genetic tests before the conclusion of a contract'". Yann, Joly. Life Insurers' Access to Genetic Information: A Way Out of the Stalemate? Health Law Review. Vol. 14, n° 3. Available at http://www.law.ualberta.ca/centres/hli/userfiles/2_Joly.pdf. Accessed 7 October 2010. P. 16.

[96]Ibid. P. 16.

[97]Loi no 2002-303 du 4 mars 2002 relative aux droits des malades et á la qualité du systéme de santé

[98]Laffarire, Marie-Laure. Protection des données à caractère personnel. Éditions d'organisation: Paris, 2005. P. 127.

[99]Unofficial translation by the author.

[100]Yann, Joly. Op. cit. P. 16. "The conclusion of the debate was foreseeable: With the Loi n° 2002-303 du 4 mars 2002 relative aux droits des malades et á la qualité du systéme de santé, the French

3.6 Other Relevant Issues

3.6.1 The Data Protection Officer

An interesting provision of the French Act is the 'new' Article 22, parag. 2°, III, as amended by the Act of 6 August 2004, which creates the institution of the data protection officer (*Correspondant à la protection des données personnelles*) who has to be independent and shall not receive any "instructions regarding the performance of his duties".[101] The nomination of a data protection officer (DPO), however, is not compulsory, but it allows data controllers to avoid many of the formalities required by the Data Protection Act. For example only the processing which is subject to an authorisation or an opinion from the CNIL has to be declared (registered).[102]

Amongst the duties of the DPO are the requirement to keep a record of all processing activities, of ensuring the application of the Data Protection Law (through advise and mediation, for example) and of working as a link between data controllers and the CNIL.[103]

Data controllers are authorised by Article 44 of Decree n° 2005-1309 to appoint a common data protection officer when they are members of an Economic Interest Group, a professional body or a body grouping data controllers, or even when it is a controlling or controlled company.[104]

In the French Act, distinct from the Regulation 45/2001 of the European Parliament and the Council of 18 December 2000, the nomination of a data protection officer is not compulsory.

3.7 Chapter Conclusion

In this chapter it could be seen that the French Data Protection Authority has powers that go beyond the ones provided for by Directive 95/46/EC, since it can deliver quality-labels, something that the EU Commission Proposal for a Regulation

government formally prohibited the use of genetic information by insurers. Pursuant to this law, '[n]o one can be made the object of discrimination because of his or her genetic characteristics'".

[101] Article 46, 2nd paragraph of Decree n° 2005-1309. See Commission Nationale de L'Informatique et des Libertes. Guide du Correspondant Informatique et Libertés. Available at http://www.cnil.fr/fileadmin/documents/Guides_pratiques/CNIL_Guide_correspondants.pdf. Accessed 28 March 2011. P. 3. "Le correspondant ne peut faire l'objet de sanctions de l'employer du fait de l'exercice des ses missions, sauf en cas de manquements graves dûment constatés et qui lui soient directment imputables. Afin d'assurer l'effectivité de cette protection, la CNIL devra être avertie de toute modification affectant sa fonction. Il ne pourra notamment être mis fin sans que la CNIL en connaisse les raisons."

[102] Ibid. P. 3.

[103] Ibid. P. 5–6.

[104] A good example of the appointment of a single data protection officer is the whole category of notaries in France.

on Data Protection[105] is adopting, as will be seen in Chap. 6. Furthermore, it was possible to conclude that despite some courts having extended privacy rights to legal persons and that the Data Protection Authority has been dealing with such entities in some of its decisions, the Data Protection Act covers only natural persons. Moreover, it became clear that there is a legal prohibition for the processing of genetic data for insurance purposes. Finally, the Data Protection Officer, something that does not exist in Directive 95/45/EC is a good example of a possible improvement in the EU DP Legislation.

[105]European Commission. Proposal for a Regulation of the European Parliament and of the Council on the protection of individuals with regard to the processing of personal data and on the free movement of such data (General Data Protection Regulation).

Chapter 4
Data Protection Systems in the European Union: The UK Experience

Apart from the common issues which will be equally analysed in Chaps. 3, 4 and 5, other issues will be the focus of analysis here: the scope of consent and data protection principles, because the way they are dealt with by the UK Data Protection Framework differ—to a larger or small extent—from the provisions contained in Directive 95/46/EC.

The United Kingdom (UK) adopted its first data protection legislation in 1984—the Data Protection Act 1984.[1] However, as a consequence of Directive 95/46/EC, it had to adopt a new piece of legislation which is currently in force, the Data Protection Act 1998 (hereinafter UK Act),[2] which will be the main focus of this chapter. The UK Act is divided into eight data protection principles. These principles are: (a) processing personal data fairly and lawfully; (b) processing personal data for specified purposes; (c) the amount of personal data one may hold (d) keeping personal data accurate and up to date; (e) retaining personal data; (f) the rights of individuals; (g) information security; (h) sending personal data outside the European Economic Area.[3]

As will be seen in the following sections, there are considerable differences between the approaches adopted in the UK and in the other selected EU Member States, not only in terms of legislation, but also regarding the interpretation of the rules and the practice, what leads to different outcomes when analysing similar issues.

---

[1] See http://www.opsi.gov.uk/RevisedStatutes/Acts/ukpga/1984/cukpga_19840035_en_1. Accessed 28 January 2010.

[2] Available at http://www.opsi.gov.uk/acts/acts1998/ukpga_19980029_en_1. Accessed 28 January 2010. See Information Commissioner's Office. Data Protection Act 1998: Legal Guidance. Available at http://www.ico.gov.uk/upload/documents/library/data_protection/detailed_specialist_guides/data_protection_act_legal_guidance.pdf. Accessed 5 February 2010. P. 6. "The Data Protection Act 1998 ("the Act") gives effect in the UK law to EC Directive 95/46/EC (the "Directive"). The Act replaces the Data Protection Act 1984 (the "1984 Act") and was brought into force on 1 March 2000."

[3] Information Commissioner's Office. The Guide to Data Protection. Op. cit. P. 41.

M. Viola de Azevedo Cunha, *Market Integration Through Data Protection*, Law, Governance and Technology Series 9, DOI 10.1007/978-94-007-6085-1_4,

4.1 The Data Protection Authority: The Role of the UK Information Commissioner

The Data Protection Act 1998 transformed the former Data Protection Registrar into the Data Protection Commissioner, which, subsequently to the entry into force of the Freedom of Information Act 2000, became the Information Commissioner (hereinafter ICO).[4] The ICO, in addition to the powers conferred by the Data Protection Act, also has powers conferred by the Freedom of Information Act, the Privacy and Electronic Communications Regulations and the Environmental Information Regulations.[5] Nonetheless, for the purposes of this work the powers that are relevant are the ones conferred by the Data Protection Act.

According to the UK Act the ICO has as its main duties to: (1) promote the following of good practice by data controllers and, in particular, promote the observance of the requirements of the Act by data controllers; (2) spread information on the Act and how it works; (3) encourage, where appropriate, the development of Codes of Practice for guidance as to good practice; (4) co-operate with foreign designated authorities in the manner prescribed by section 54 of the Act and by The Data Protection (Functions of Designated Authority) Order 2000 (S.I. No 186); (5) maintain a register of data controllers who are required to notify their processing; (6) provide annually before each House of Parliament a general report on the exercise of his/her functions under the Act; (7) lay before each House of Parliament any Code of Practice prepared pursuant to the Act; and (8) prosecute persons in respect of offences committed under the Act.[6]

Moreover, the ICO can also analyse requests for assessment presented by data subjects who believe that they are directly affected by any processing of personal data.[7] After receiving the request, if he/she considers that it "reasonably requires any information for the purpose of determining whether the data controller has complied or is complying with the data protection principles",[8] he/she can serve the data controller with an information notice "requiring the data controller to

---

[4] Schedule 5, Section 1(1) of the Data Protection Act 1998. Available at http://www.statutelaw.gov.uk/content.aspx?LegType=All+Primary&PageNumber=1&BrowseLetter=D&NavFrom=1&activeTextDocId=3190610&parentActiveTextDocId=3190610&showAllAttributes=0&hideCommentary=0&showProsp=0&suppressWarning=1. Accessed 12 February 2010.

[5] See Information Commissioner's Office. What the ICO covers. Available at http://www.ico.gov.uk/what_we_cover.aspx. Accessed 6 February 2010.

[6] "In England and Wales proceedings for a criminal offence under the Act can be commenced by the Commissioner or by or with the consent of the Director of Public Prosecutions." In Information Commissioner's Office. Data Protection Act 1998: Legal Guidance. Op. cit. P. 99. In Italy and France is the public prosecutor and not the data protection authority who has the power to prosecute persons for criminal violations of the data protection legislation.

[7] See Section 42 of the Data Protection Act 1998.

[8] Section 43(1) (a) and (b) of the Data Protection Act.

provide information relating to the request or to compliance with the principles"[9] in question. Furthermore, in cases where the Commissioner is convinced "that a data controller has contravened or is contravening any of the data protection principles", he/she also has the power to serve an enforcement notice upon a data controller.[10] Once the Commissioner serves an enforcement notice, the data controller will have to comply with its provisions within a specific period of time.[11] The data controller, however, will have the right to lodge an appeal against the notice. Until 18 January 2010 there was a specialised Tribunal, the Information Tribunal, which was competent to hear appeals against enforcement notices of the Information Commissioner. However, from 19 January 2010, as a consequence of the Transfer of Tribunal Functions Order 2010,[12] the functions of the Information Tribunal were transferred to the First-tier Tribunal and to the Upper Tribunal depending on the particular case. The jurisdiction of the respective tribunal will be decided according to Tribunal Procedure Rules. The general rule is that the appeal goes to the First-tier Tribunal, which is the immediate substitute for the Information Tribunal.[13] However, when the case involves the safeguard of national security or "raises complex or unusual issues",[14] after the decision of the President the General Regulatory Chamber, the case can be dealt with directly by the Upper Tribunal.[15] Appeals against decisions of the First-tier Tribunal will be heard by the Upper Tribunal[16] and against decisions by the latter by the relevant appellate court[17]—the Court of Appeal in England or Wales, the Court of Session in Scotland or the Court of Appeal in Northern Ireland.[18]

---

[9]Section 43(1) (b) second paragraph. See also Section 44 of the Data Protection Act, regarding special information notices.

[10]Information Commissioner's Office. Data Protection Act 1998: Legal Guidance. Op. cit. P. 89/90

[11]See Section 40 of the Data Protection Act 1998.

[12]http://www.opsi.gov.uk/si/si2010/pdf/uksi_20100022_en.pdf. Accessed 27 February 2010.

[13]See http://www.informationtribunal.gov.uk/. Accessed 27 February 2010

[14]Information Tribunal abolished as new service takes charge—The appeals process for freedom of information and data protection cases changes from today as the previous structure is absorbed into a wider tribunal's service. Available at http://out-law.com/default.aspx?page=10669. Accessed 27 February 2010. "Last year, however, the Tribunals Service told potential users of the new structure that some issues will be deemed serious enough to be heard immediately by that Upper Tribunal.

'For some information rights appeals, cases will be heard in the first instance in the Upper Tribunal,' said Tribunals Service officer Mike Watson in a letter to the Service's users last year 'This will occur where it is considered that the appeal raises complex or unusual issues and the importance of the case would merit it being dealt with in the higher Tribunal.'"

[15]Section 19 (2) and (3) of the The Tribunal Procedure (First-tier Tribunal) (General Regulatory Chamber) Rules 2009. Available at http://www.tribunals.gov.uk/Tribunals/Documents/Rules/GRCRulesConsolidated.pdf. Accessed 27 February 2010.

[16]Section 11(1) of the Tribunals, Courts and Enforcement Act 2007. Available at http://www.opsi.gov.uk/acts/acts2007/pdf/ukpga_20070015_en.pdf. Accessed 27 February 2010.

[17]Section 13(1) of the Tribunals, Courts and Enforcement Act 2007.

[18]Section 13(12) of the Tribunals, Courts and Enforcement Act 2007.

Returning to the UK Information Commissioner, in comparison to the Italian Data Protection Authority, it is not fully independent, as Directive 95/46/EC requires, since it is subordinated to a decision of the Secretary of State regarding the exercise of enforcement powers over the private sector.[19] As the Information Commissioner stated in the Memorandum submitted on Government amendments introduced in the House of Lords, with regard to the Coroners and Justice Bill, in July 2009:

> We work with organisations in a spirit of co-operation including agreeing the time, place and scope of any assessment. We intend to continue on this basis. However, there must be a fall-back position in which we can carry out checks on organisations whose activities pose a particular risk to individuals, but who will not co-operate with us voluntarily.[20]

In the same document the ICO referred to the report 'Surveillance, Citizens and the State' of the House of Lords Select Committee on the Constitution, in which the committee supported the need for an assessment notice power covering private sector organisations:

> [We] regret the decision not to legislate for a comparable [inspection] power with respect to private sector organisations. We recommend that the Government reconsider this matter. Organisations which refuse to allow the Commissioner to carry out inspections are likely to be those with something to hide.[21]

The Coroners and Justice Act 2009 was adopted but the issue of independence did not change much.[22] According to the act, which amended the Data Protection Act 1998:

> The Commissioner may serve a data controller within subsection (2) with a notice (in this Act referred to as an "assessment notice") for the purpose of enabling the Commissioner to determine whether the data controller has complied or is complying with the data protection principles.
>
> (2) A data controller is within this subsection if the data controller is—
>
> (a) A government department,
> (b) A public authority designated for the purposes of this section by an order made by the Secretary of State, or
> (c) A person of a description designated for the purposes of this section by such an order.[23]

---

[19]Charlesworth, Andrew. Op. cit. P. 968. "(. . .) the OIC should be granted an independent power of data audit and site inspection, with or without the consent of the data controller, rather than the limited powers currently held under the UK Data Protection Act of 1998."

[20]See http://www.ico.gov.uk/upload/documents/library/data_protection/detailed_specialist_guides/ico_commentary_on_lords_govt_amendment_130709.pdf. Accessed 12 February 2010.

[21]See http://www.ico.gov.uk/upload/documents/library/data_protection/detailed_specialist_guides/ico_commentary_on_lords_govt_amendment_130709.pdf. Accessed 12 February 2010.

[22]The Information Commissioner can, however, "apply to a circuit judge or, in Scotland, a sheriff for a warrant to enter and search premises and to seize evidence, where there are seasonable grounds for suspecting either a breach of the data protection principles or that an offence under the Act has been or is being committed." See The Information Commissioner's Office (ICO). Guide do Data Protection. Op. cit. P. 16.

[23]See the new Section 41A of the Data Protection Act 1998 as amended by the Coroners and Justice Act of 2009.

Therefore, the Information Commissioner will have full powers to serve assessment notices regarding a government department,[24] but regarding other public authorities or persons he/she will have to rely on an order made by the Secretary of State. Although the Commissioner could seek to extend his "powers to undertake compulsory audits in both the public and private sectors"[25] by making a recommendation that a description of specific persons be designated,[26] it will be up to the Secretary of State to decide whether or not to issue an order with this purpose.[27] The lack of full powers of supervision held by the Information Commissioner over the private sector leads, in my opinion, to non-compliance with the requirement of "complete independence"[28] imposed by article 28(1) and recital 62 of Directive 95/46/EC.

The European Court of Justice, in a ruling concerning the independence of the Data Protection Authorities in Germany, found that Germany was not in compliance with the Directive, because some data protection authorities were under direct or indirect influence of the State or Länder, highlighting that "the mere risk that the

[24]Linkomles, Laura. United Kingdom organisations now face fines up to £ 500,000. Privacy Laws & Business. Issue 103. February 2010. P. 14.

[25]Information Commissioner's Office (ICO). Consultation on the Assessment Notices Code of Practice. 10 February 2010. Available at http://www.ico.gov.uk/upload/documents/library/corporate/research_and_reports/consultation_assessment_notices_code_of_practice_20120209.pdf. Accessed 27 February 2010. P. 2.

[26]Section 41A(9) a of the Data Protection Act, as amended by the Coroners and Justice Act 2009.

[27]Information Commissioner's Office (ICO). Consultation on the Assessment Notices Code of Practice. 10 February 2010. P. 3–4. "Under section 51(7) of the Act the Information Commissioner may, with the consent of a data controller, assess their processing of personal information for the following of good practice. The Information Commissioner must inform the data controller of the results of the assessment; this in practice has been provided by way of a report.

Traditionally the extent of the Information Commissioner's audit activities has been limited to audits carried out with consent—'consensual audits'.

Under section 41A of the Act the Information Commissioner may serve certain categories of data controllers with a notice (in the Act referred to as an 'assessment notice') for the purpose of enabling him to determine whether the data controller has complied or is complying with the data protection principles. For the purpose of this Code these will be referred to as 'compulsory audits'.

Data controllers covered by section 41A include government departments, designated public authorities or designated persons. Any designations will be made by an order made by the Secretary of State."

[28]Mosca, Sophie. ECJ: Supervisory authorities must be completely independent. Europolitics. 09 March 2010. Available at http://www.europolitics.info/ecj-supervisory-authorities-must-be-completely-independent-art265573-10.html. Accessed 20 March 2010. "The court first identified the scope of the requirement of independence of the supervisory authorities, explaining that as a key element of data protection, they must enjoy independence that enables them to act without influence by the supervised bodies, but also without any direct or indirect external influence that could call into question the performance by those authorities of their task consisting of establishing a fair balance between the protection of the right to privacy and the free movement of personal data."

scrutinising authorities could exercise a political influence over the decisions of the supervisory authorities is enough to hinder the latter authorities' independent performance of their tasks."[29]

Despite the fact that the Information Commissioner lacks full powers regarding assessment notices in the private sector, he/she has focused its efforts on providing guidance in terms of good practice, aiming at helping organisations to comply with data protection legislation.[30] In this sense, he/she has adopted many documents which intend to help data controllers verify whether they comply with data protection principles and rules.[31] However, such documents do not have binding effect.[32]

Regarding the sectors under the supervision of the Financial Services Authority (FSE), the Information Commissioner signed in May 2008 a memorandum of understanding with the Financial Ombudsman Service Limited, where he recognises the possibility of dealing with complaints that "could also be considered by the ICO under its powers to investigate alleged breaches of the DPA (. . .) in accordance with its usual procedures and from making an award of compensation, where appropriate."[33] It is important to note that the UK Data Protection Act does not grant the Information Commissioner powers of awarding compensation.[34]

4.2 The Concept of Personal Data

Section 1(1) of the Data Protection Act 1998 defines personal data as data relating to "a living individual who can be identified—(a) from those data, or (b) from those data and other information which is in the possession of, or is likely to come into the possession of, the data controller." The Act also adds that "any expression of opinion about the individual and any indication of the intentions of the data controller or any other person in respect of the individual" are comprised by the

---

[29]European Court of Justice. Case C-518/07 Commission v Germany. Grand Chamber. 9 March 2010. Available at http://eur-lex.europa.eu/LexUriServ/LexUriServ.do?uri=CELEX:62007J0518:EN:HTML. Accessed 19 March 2010. §§ 25 and 36.

[30]See Section 51 of the Data Protection Act 1998.

[31]See http://www.ico.gov.uk/for_organisations/good_practice.aspx. Accessed 28 February 2010.

[32]Information Commissioner's Office. The Guide to Data Protection. Op. cit. P. 2. "The Guide is our interpretation of what the Data Protection Act requires and of how the data protection principles are intended to apply. It gives advice on good practice, but compliance with our recommendations is not mandatory where they go beyond the strict requirements of the Act. The Guide itself does not have the force of law."

[33]Memorandum of Understanding between the Information Commissioner's Office and the Financial Ombudsman Service Limited. Available at http://www.ico.gov.uk/upload/documents/library/memo_of_understanding/documents/mou_fos_limited.pdf. Accessed 13 March 2010.

[34]Information Commissioner's Office. The Guide to Data Protection. Op. cit. P. 13. "However, we have no power to award compensation to individuals—only the courts can do this".

definition of personal data. Such definition of personal data is different from the one contained in Article 2(a) of Directive 95/46/EC, which classifies personal data as "any information relating to an identified or identifiable natural person".

To verify whether there is or not a processing operation of personal data in the UK, it is important to understand what the Act means by "likely to come into possession". Although there is no clear criterion in the law to verify this "likely to come into possession",[35] the Information Commissioner takes the view that it is not necessary that the identifying data are or are likely to come under the physical control of the data controller to consider that such data are covered by the concept of personal data.[36] To illustrate, the Information Commissioner gives the example of the relationship between a data controller and a data processor, where the latter will receive data from third parties and will process such data in accordance with the instructions of the data controller. The controller will not have direct access to identifying data, although this data is in the possession of the data processor. Therefore, according to the Information Commissioner, in such a situation, the data controller could not argue that the identifying data is not in his possession or likely to come.[37]

I agree with the Information Commissioner to the extent that the data has not to be in the possession of the data controller, but in the given example, it seems to me that such data is likely to come into the possession, or at least is available, to the controller without much effort. In that case, I would say that the view of the Information Commissioner regarding "in the possession or likely to come into possession" follows the position adopted by Directive 95/46/EC when it refers to an "identifiable natural person".

It is important to notice that the UK Act, similar to the Italian Code—as will be seen in the next chapter—, did not adopt the idea of reasonableness contained in Directive 95/46/EC[38] as a limitation for the application of the data protection legislation.[39]

Another aspect of the definition of personal data in the UK is the extension of the concept to include "expressions of opinion or intention". According to the Information Commissioner, it means that any data controller would have to disclose not only the data it has about a specific data subject, but also its opinions about such person or its intention to offer or decline something to such a person. An example would be the case of the employer that has to disclose his/her opinions about his/her employees and also "any intention to offer or decline promotion on the basis of those opinions."[40] It would force, for example, insurance companies to disclose medical

---

[35]Information Commissioner's Office, Data Protection Act 1998: Legal Guidance, Op. cit.: 12.

[36]Ibid: 13.

[37]Ibid: 13.

[38]See Recital 26.

[39]It also did not include a definition of anonymous data.

[40]Information Commissioner's Office. Data Protection Act 1998: Legal Guidance. Op. cit.: 15. See also Information Commissioner's Office, The Guide to Data Protection.

opinions about an individual regarding his/her risks in terms of insurance, and also the impact these opinions would have in denying coverage, leading to a completely different outcome than the one adopted in Italy, where the advice given by medical doctors to their clients (insurance companies) does not have to be disclosed to data subjects.[41]

With regard to the scope of the concept of personal data, it is clear that data subjects will only be living individuals; deceased persons are not covered[42]—and also only natural persons and not legal entities.[43] As Peter Carey pointed out:

> There are two points to be made here (. . .). The first is that the data must relate to a living person—once a person has died her rights under the legislation cease. The second is that the definition applies only to individuals. A database containing names and addresses of limited companies is therefore not caught. However, where such a database includes names of officers or employees within the company (e.g., contact names) it will fall within the definition of personal data.[44]

The only exceptions, in the view of the UK Commissioner, would be the cases of small partnerships and of a sole trader, where the information about the business is indistinguishable from the partners' information.[45] Therefore, the processing of data related to an identified "deceased" person or to an identified "legal" person would not be included in this concept and would not be covered by the Data Protection Act 1998.[46] Nonetheless, the Consumer Credit Act 1974, as amended by the Consumer Credit Act 2006, grants some rights similar to the ones regarding

---

http://www.ico.gov.uk/upload/documents/library/data_protection/practical_application/the_guide_to_data_protection.pdf. Accessed 8 February 2011: 22.

[41]The Italian Data Protection Authority recognises that in such cases there are personal data not only in the identification part of the opinion, but also in the conclusions and evaluations of the medical expert of the insurance company, and, indeed, Article 7 of the Data Protection Code applies to the evaluation and conclusions of the expert. Nevertheless, it does not mean that full access has to be given: information related to counselling given by the expert to the insurance company concerning the decision of paying or not paying an indemnity or the strategy in a future legal claim are not included. In this sense, see Garante per la protezione dei dati personali, Provvedimento del 25 luglio 2007, http://www.garanteprivacy.it/garante/doc.jsp?ID=1434791. Accessed 22 December 2010.

[42]Information Commissioner's Office, Data Protection Act 1998: Legal Guidance, Op. cit.: 11. "The Act is only concerned with living individuals and so if the subject of the information is dead, then the information cannot be personal data." In the same sense, see Information Commissioner's Office. The Guide to Data Protection, Op. cit.: 26.

[43]Information Commissioner's Office. Data Protection Act 1998: Legal Guidance, Op. cit.: 16. "A data subject must be a living individual. Organisations, such as companies and other corporate and unincorporated bodies of persons cannot, therefore, be data subjects."

[44]Peter Carey, Data Protection in the UK (London, Blackstone Press, 2000), 12. See, also, Information Commissioner's Office, Data Protection Act 1998: Legal Guidance, Op. cit.: 11.

[45]Information Commissioner's Office, Data Protection Act 1998: Legal Guidance, Op. cit.: 11.

[46]Information Commissioner's Office, Data Protection Technical Guidance Determining what is personal data, http://www.ico.gov.uk/upload/documents/library/data_protection/detailed_specialist_guides/personal_data_flowchart_v1_with_preface001.pdf. Accessed 5 December 2010: 3.

data subjects—access, correction, erasure[47]—to partnerships[48] and unincorporated bodies of persons[49] when dealing as consumers with credit reference agencies. In these cases, however, the supervisory authority will not be the Information Commissioner but the Office of Fair Trading.[50]

Furthermore, the England and Wales Court of Appeal, in a ruling of 8 December 2003, in the famous case "Durant", gave a narrow interpretation to the concept of personal data, adding more limits for the application of the Act. According to the findings of the Court:

> (. . .) not all information retrieved from a computer search against an individual's name or unique identifier is personal data within the Act. Mere mention of the data subject in a document held by a data controller does not necessarily amount to his personal data. Whether it does so in any particular instance depends on where it falls in a continuum of relevance or proximity to the data subject as distinct, say, from transactions or matters in which he may have been involved to a greater or lesser degree. It seems to me that there are two notions that may be of assistance. The first is whether the information is biographical in a significant sense, that is, going beyond the recording of the putative data subject's involvement in a matter or an event that has no personal connotations, a life event in respect of which his privacy could not be said to be compromised. The second is one of focus. The information should have the putative data subject as its focus rather than some other person with whom he may have been involved or some transaction or event in which he may have figured or have had an interest, for example, as in this case, an investigation into some other person's or body's conduct that he may have instigated.[51]

In this case, there was also a discussion about the definition of "a relevant filing system" for the situations where personal data were not processed by automated means, but only by manual ones, and the Court of Appeal created some criteria to identify when the Act should apply to those instances of manual processing of personal data. Following the Court's criteria, a manual filing system would be a "relevant" one if: "(1) relate to individuals; (2) be a "set" or part of a "set" of information; (3) be structured by reference to individuals or criteria relating to individuals; and (4) be structured in such a way that specific information relating to a particular individual is readily accessible."[52]

---

[47] See Sections 158 and 169 of the Consumer Credit Act 1974. In the same sense see The Consumer Credit (Credit Reference Agency) Regulations 2000.

[48] 'Partnership' means "a partnership consisting of two or three persons not all of whom are bodies corporate" (Section 189(1)(a) of the Consumer Credit Act 1974 as amended by the Consumer Credit Act 2006).

[49] 'Unincorporated body of persons' means "an unincorporated body of persons which does not consist entirely of bodies corporate and is not a partnership" (Section 189(1)(b) of the Consumer Credit Act 1974 as amended by the Consumer Credit Act 2006).

[50] See sections 38–54 of the Consumer Credit Act 1974 as amended by the Consumer Credit Act 2006.

[51] England and Wales Court of Appeal. Durant Case. 8 December 2003. http://www.hmcourts-service.gov.uk/judgmentsfiles/j2136/durant-v-fsa.htm. Accessed 5 December 2010. § 28.

[52] England and Wales Court of Appeal. Durant Case. Paragraph 46.

Such scope defined by the Court of Appeal for both the concept of personal data and the "relevant filing system" contradicts the one provided for by Directive 95/46/EC.[53] The Directive does not impose any limits for the data to be considered as personal data,[54] being enough that it is related "to an identified or identifiable natural person".[55] Therefore, in applying the decision of the Court of Appeal, the UK is not complying with—or better—has not adequately implemented EU legislation, in this case the referred Directive.

Despite the fact that such decision is binding in terms of common law, the Information Commissioner, after the adoption by the Article 29 Working Party of its Opinion on the concept of personal data, published a document entitled "What is personal data?—A quick reference guide", which goes in a different direction than the one adopted by the Court of Appeal.[56] According to this document, the intention of the data controller in identifying the data subject is not the utmost issue as in the findings of the Court.

Nonetheless, the Court decision has a binding effect up to the moment when there is a new decision of the respective court or of a higher court which changes its view. As stated by the Information Commissioner

> The Commissioner can only give general guidance; the final decision in case of dispute is a question for the courts. (. . .) It is not possible for the Commissioner to state categorically whether or not certain types of information or files are caught by the Act although it is

---

[53]Nouwt, Sjaak, "Towards a Common European Approach to Data Protection: A Critical Analysis of Data Protection Perspectives of the Council of Europe and the European Union," in Gutwirth, Serge et al. (editors) Reinventing Data Protection? Springer: 2009. P. 283.

[54]Article 2 (a) of Directive 95/46/EC.

[55]See Article 29 Working Party, Opinion 4/2007 on the concept of personal data, Op. cit.: 13. "Concerning 'directly' identified or identifiable persons, the **name** of the person is indeed the most common identifier, and, in practice, the notion of 'identified person' implies most often a reference to the person's name." In the same sense are the findings of the European Court of Justice in the Lindqvist case. C-101. Judgement of 6 November 2003. http://curia.europa.eu/jurisp/cgi-bin/gettext.pl?lang=en&num=79968893C19010101&doc=T&ouvert=T&seance=ARRET. Accessed 5 January 2011. § 24.

[56]Information Commissioner's Office, What is personal data?—A quick reference guide, http://www.ico.gov.uk/upload/documents/library/data_protection/detailed_specialist_guides/160408_v1.0_determining_what_is_personal_data_-_quick_reference_guide.pdf. Accessed 5 December 2010. The Information Commissioner formulated eight questions to help data controllers in identifying if a certain data is personal data. If the answer for one of those questions is affirmative, it is likely that the processing into question involves personal data in the Commissioner's view. The questions are the following: (1) Can a living individual be identified from the data, or, from the data and other information in your possession, or likely to come into your possession? (2) Does the data 'relate to' the identifiable living individual, whether in personal or family life, business or profession? (3) Is the data 'obviously about' a particular individual? (4) Is the data 'linked to' an individual so that it provides particular information about that individual? (5) Is the data used, or is it to be used, to inform or influence actions or decisions affecting an identifiable individual? (6) Does the data have any biographical significance in relation to the individual? (7) Does the data focus or concentrate on the individual as its central theme rather than on some other person, or some object, transaction or event? (8) Does the data impact or have the potential to impact on an individual, whether in a personal, family, business or professional capacity?

> recognised that there are certain areas of business where the question of whether manual information falls within the definition will be of particular significance, e.g., personnel files.[57]

Therefore, the Durant case gives a binding interpretation of the concept of personal data under the Data Protection Act 1998. The Court of Appeal in Durant Case, in the views of other courts in the UK, recognises:

> (a) that not all information retrieved from a search against an individual's name or unique identifier is personal data within the 1998 Act, (b) that mere mention of an individual in a document held by a data controller does not mean that the document contains personal data in relation to that individual, (c) that whether information is capable of constituting personal data depends on where it falls in a continuum of relevance or proximity to the data subject, (d) that in answering that question it is relevant to consider whether the information is biographical in a significant sense; and whether it has the putative data subject as its focus and, finally, (e) that personal data is information that affects the privacy of the putative data subject, whether in his personal, business or professional capacity.[58]

It is clear, hence, that Directive 95/46/EC went further than the UK Data Protection Act 1998 regarding the definition of personal data, "by not including the words 'likely to come into the possession of', thus rendering an encrypted database personal data where the key exists anywhere in the world, however, unlikely it is that the key would come into the possession of the data controller."[59]

4.3 The Processing of Sensitive Data

Section 2 of the Data Protection Act 1998 defines sensitive data as information related to racial or ethnic origin, political opinions, religious beliefs or other beliefs of a similar nature,[60] membership of a trade union, physical or mental

---

[57]Information Commissioner's Office, Data Protection Act 1998: Legal Guidance, Op. cit.: 9.

[58]UK High Court of Justice. Terence William Smith and Lloyds TSB Bank Plc. Case No HV 03 C 02462. http://www.hmcourts-service.gov.uk/judgmentsfiles/j3127/smith-v-lloyds.htm. Accessed 16 December 2010. § 31.

[59]Carey, Peter. Data Protection: A Practical Guide to UK and EU Law, 2nd Edition. Oxford-New York: Oxford University Press, 2004. P. 15.

[60]Information Commissioner's Office. The Guide to Data Protection. Op. cit. P. 24. "Religion or ethnicity, or both, can often be inferred with varying degrees of certainty from dress or name. For example, many surnames are associated with a particular ethnicity or religion, or both, and may indicate the ethnicity and religion of the individuals concerned. However, it would be absurd to treat all such names as "sensitive personal data", which would mean that to hold such names on customer databases you had to satisfy a condition for processing sensitive personal data. Nevertheless, if you processed such names specifically because they indicated ethnicity or religion, for example to send marketing materials for products and services targeted at individuals of that ethnicity or religion, then you would be processing sensitive personal data."

health or condition, sexual life, commission or alleged commission of any offence, proceedings for any offence committed or alleged to have been committed and the disposal of such proceedings or the sentence of any court in such proceedings.

Nevertheless, for sensitive data to be processed at least one of the conditions in Schedule 2[61] of the Data Protection Act has to be met and also at least one of the conditions in Schedule 3.[62] In comparison to the Italian or French systems, there is no need for a previous authorisation from the ICO for a data controller to process sensitive data. If one of the conditions established in Schedule 3 is met (and, of course one of Schedule 2 at least), then the processing can be carried out. Moreover, according to paragraph 10 of Schedule 3, the Secretary of State can specify, by an order, other circumstances where sensitive data can be processed. A full list of the additional conditions for processing can be found in the Data Protection (Processing of Sensitive Personal Data) Order 2000 and subsequent orders.[63]

The analysis of the specific conditions which are relevant for our cases of study will be conducted in Sect. 4.5.

4.4 Data Subjects' Rights: The Rights of Preventing a Processing Likely to Cause Damage or Distress and the Obtaining of Records Under the Data Subject's Right to Access

Section 10 of the Data Protection Act 1998 recognises a 'new' right to data subjects not contemplated in Directive 95/46/EC: the right to prevent processing likely to cause damage or distress. According to this right, a data subject will be entitled, at

[61]Any processing of personal data has to meet at least one of the conditions in Schedule 2 of the Data Protection Act 1998. See Section 1(a) of Schedule 1 of the Data Protection Act 1998. The conditions that are relevant for our cases of study are the ones contained in Sections 1, 2, 3 and 6 of Schedule 2: "1. The data subject has given his consent to the processing.

2. The processing is necessary—
   (a) For the performance of a contract to which the data subject is a party, or
   (b) For the taking of steps at the request of the data subject with a view to entering into a contract.
3. The processing is necessary for compliance with any legal obligation to which the data controller is subject, other than an obligation imposed by contract. (...)

6.–(1) The processing is necessary for the purposes of legitimate interests pursued by the data controller or by the third party or parties to whom the data are disclosed, except where the processing is unwarranted in any particular case by the reason of prejudice to the rights and freedoms or the legitimate interests of the data subject."

[62]See Section 1(a) and (b) of Schedule 1 of the Data Protection Act 1998.

[63]Information Commissioner's Office. The Guide to Data Protection. Op. cit. P. 113.

any time, to require a data controller to cease or not to begin the processing of any personal data or the processing for a specific purpose or manner, if the processing "is causing or is likely to cause substantial damage or substantial distress to him or to another, and that damage or distress is or would be unwarranted."[64]

Although the reading of the provision gives the impression that this right is unrestricted, in practice it is significantly so.[65] To verify whether the exercise of this right is legitimate, the interests involved—of the individual and of the data controller—will need to be balanced.[66] In other words, it is necessary to decide which rights or interests should prevail.[67] The ICO in "The Guide to Data Protection" provides some examples of situations where the right to prevent processing likely to cause damage or distress cannot be exercised:

> A mobile phone company receives a written request from a customer requiring it to remove the customer's details from its database. This should be treated as an objection to processing. The customer explains that using his personal data for credit referencing is causing him distress and has led to him being refused a credit card. The mobile phone company does not have to comply with this notice because the credit referencing is necessary for putting into effect the contract that the customer signed (and the customer can be said to have consented to it). Consequently, the right to object to processing does not apply.[68]

Another interesting provision of the Act, which has impact on the industries under analysis in this work, is the one that prevents the obtaining of personal records under the data subject's right of access.[69] According to this prohibition, "a person must not, in connection with any contract for the provision of services to him by another person, require that other person or third party to supply him with a relevant

[64]Section 10(1) (a) and (b) of the Data Protection Act 1998.

[65]Information Commissioner's Office. The Guide to Data Protection. Op. cit. P. 137.

[66]"We take a wide view of the legitimate interests and we consider that it is in the interests of other creditors to make informed lending decisions. It is important to note here that the fact that the processing may be seen by some to prejudice a particular individual (for example, someone with an adverse entry on his credit reference file may not be able to obtain credit facilities) does not necessarily render the whole processing operation prejudicial to all individuals." Information Commissioner's Office. Credit agreements—Data sharing. http://www.ico.gov.uk/upload/documents/library/data_protection/practical_application/credit_%20agreements%20-%20data_%20sharing.pdf. Accessed 12 February 2010.

[67]In the view of the Information Commissioner this right could not be exercised if "any of the first four conditions of processing contained in Schedule 2 apply". Information Commissioner's Office. Data Protection Act 1998: Legal Guidance. Op. cit. P. 54.

[68]Information Commissioner's Office. The Guide to Data Protection. Op. cit. P. 138–139. The ICO, using again the example of the customer of a mobile phone company, states that the company, even in the case where the customer had cancelled his contract and had withdrew his consent to the company processing his personal data, "the company only has to comply with the objection (i.e., to stop processing the customer's personal data) if the processing is causing unwarranted and substantial damage or distress."

[69]See Section 56 of the Data Protection Act 1998.

record or to produce a relevant record to him".[70] This forbids, for example, banks and insurance companies from requiring that data subjects, making use of their right of access, consult information about themselves included in databases restricted to the general public and provide such information in order to enter into a contract.[71]

4.5 The Processing of Personal Data by the Case Studies

4.5.1 The Banking Sector

The lending sector adopted in November 2009 the so-called "The Lending Code",[72] aiming at "Setting standards for banks, building societies and credit card providers". In Section 3 (Credit Reference Agencies) the Code highlights some procedures to be followed in order to comply with data protection rules. The first regards the duty to inform customers whether they (lenders) will pass customers' details to credit reference agencies and the possible checks the subscribers of the credit reference agency can make with them. This duty to inform also covers the disclosure of default information to the credit reference agency. According to the Lending Code, even if the customer was informed at the time the account was open and has given his consent for the disclosure of information in case of default, the lender has to send him a "notice of the intention to disclose the information at least 28 days before the disclosure is made."[73] The Code also points out the need to obtain the consent of the customer in order to "share information about the day-to-day running of the customer's account, including positive data" and that "The Information Commissioner accepts that such permission may be made a condition of borrowing."[74]

Another deontological document adopted by the financial sector, which covers not only banks but also building societies, credit card companies and National Savings & Investments, is the so-called "Banking Code".[75] This code of practice

---

[70] Section 56(1) (c) of the Data Protection Act.

[71] Section 56(2) of the Data Protection Act. A table containing a list of what the Data Protection Act considers as "a relevant Record" is included in the Data Protection Act 1998 below paragraph 6 of Section 56.

[72] See http://www.lendingstandardsboard.org.uk/docs/lendingcode.pdf. Accessed 24 February 2010.

[73] Buildind Societies Association et al. Nov 2009. The lending code. Available at http://www.lendingstandardsboard.org.uk/docs/lendingcode.pdf. 6 Feb 2010. Items 3 and 36.

[74] Item 39 of The Lending Code.

[75] See http://www.bankingcode.org.uk/pdfdocs/BANKING%20CODE.pdf. Accessed 24 February 2010.

applies to current accounts, savings and deposit accounts, payment services, cards and PINs, loans and overdrafts.[76] Item 8.3 refers to an opt-in scheme for the transfer of personal data to third parties for marketing purposes[77] and item 11.1 informs the reader of situations where personal data can be disclosed to third parties. It includes the situations where there is a legal obligation, a duty to the public to reveal the information, the interests of the data controller mean it must provide the information (for example, in order to prevent fraud), the data subject asks the data controller to reveal the information, or where the data controller has the data subject's permission.[78]

Moreover, the Banking Code has a section devoted to the processing of personal data by credit reference agencies. According to this document, when negative personal information will be sent to credit reference agencies, the notice has to be sent before data are made available to credit reference agencies (at least 28 days' notice). The document also refers to the possibility of sending positive information and of using personal information to check identity for anti-money laundering and fraud purposes.[79]

As far as storage limits are concerned, the Information Commissioner recognises that "It is appropriate for the bank to retain this data for as long as the customer has an account with the bank. Even after the account has been closed, the bank may need to continue holding some of this information for legal or operational reasons."[80]

---

[76]Item 1.1.

[77]8.3. Unless you specifically give your permission or ask us to, we will not pass your name and address to any company, including other companies in our group, for marketing purposes. We will not ask you to give your permission in return for standard account services.

[78]11.1. We will treat all your personal information as private and confidential (even when you are no longer a customer). We will not reveal your name and address or details about your accounts to anyone, including other companies in our group, other than in the following four exceptional cases when we are allowed to do this by law.

- If we have to give the information by law.
- If there is a duty to the public to reveal the information.
- If our interests mean we must give the information (for example, to prevent fraud). However, we will not use this as a reason for giving information about you or your accounts (including your name and address) to anyone else, including other companies in our group for marketing purposes.
- If you ask us to reveal the information, or if we have your permission.

[79]Items 13.5–13.9.

[80]Information Commissioner's Office. The Guide to Data Protection. Op. cit. P. 75.

The financial industry in the UK,[81] as pointed out by the High Court of Justice in the McGuffick case,[82] adopted the "Information Sharing: Principles of Reciprocity", which establishes that:

> (...) data are shared ONLY for the prevention of over-commitment, bad debt, fraud and money laundering, and to support debt recovery and debtor tracing, with the aim of promoting responsible lending.[83]

It is possible to conclude, therefore, that despite the numerous documents dealing with the processing of personal data by the banking sector, there are no clear rules regarding delays or storage limits.

4.5.1.1 Fight Against Fraud

In the fight against financial fraud both the Banking and the Credit Reference sectors access a database controlled by a not-for-profit Membership association called CIFAS (Credit Industry Fraud Avoidance Scheme).[84] CIFAS has the following purposes:

> To protect the interests of CIFAS Members from the actions of criminals by pooling information on fraud and attempted fraud;
>
> To ensure that innocent members of the public who are the victims of fraud are not prejudiced by misuse of their identities and documentation;
>
> To expand crime prevention data-sharing to encompass both the private and public sectors in the public interest.[85]

---

[81]The finance industry in the UK established the Steering Committee on Reciprocity (SCOR) "to develop and maintain documented guidelines on the use and sharing of credit performance and related data." In Jargon Buster. Principles of Reciprocity. Available at http://www.annualcreditreport.co.uk/help/jargon/principles-of-reciprocity.htm. Accessed 12 March 2010.

[82]Phillip McGuffick v The Royal Bank of Scotland Plc. High Court of Justice, Queen's Bench Division, Commercial Court. Case n° 2009, Folio 910. 6 October 2009. Available at http://www.judiciary.gov.uk/docs/judgments_guidance/mcguffick-v-rbs.pdf. Accessed 12 March 2010. Paragraph 27.

[83]SCOR—Steering Committee on Reciprocity. Information Sharing: Principles of Reciprocity. November 2008. Available at http://www.experian.co.uk/www/pages/downloads/compliance/porVersion30.pdf. Accessed 12 March 2010.

[84]CIFAS represents both the private and public sectors and is dedicated to the identification of financial crime and the prevention of fraud and staff fraud. See http://www.cifas.org.uk/default.asp?edit_id=564-28. Accessed 15 February 2010. See Equifax Europe Limited and The Data Protection Registrar. Data Protection Tribunal. Appeal Decision (DA/90 25/49/7). Available at http://informationtribunal.gov.uk/Documents/decisions/equifax.pdf. Accessed 15 February 2010. § 32. "The Credit Industry Fraud Avoidance System ("CIFAS") was conceived by the Consumer Credit Trade Association in 1988 as an information exchange between licensed credit grantors and licensed credit reference agencies to facilitate the prevention of fraud and the dissemination of information on suspected fraud to its members. The preamble to CIFAS's rules states that the information is supplied solely for the prevention of fraudulent obtaining of credit or hire facilities and for associated law enforcement purposes."

[85]See http://www.cifas.org.uk/default.asp?edit_id=564-28. Accessed 15 February 2010.

CIFAS works by enabling its members to "exchange details of applications for products, services or employment, which are considered to be fraudulent, because the information provided by the applicant fails verification checks." They have also the ability to "exchange information about accounts and services which are being fraudulently misused or fraudulent insurance and other claims" and "information about innocent victims of fraud to protect them from further fraud."[86]

According to a ruling of the Data Protection Tribunal in Equifax Europe Limited versus The Data Protection Registrar:

> CIFAS deals with three main categories of suspected fraud. These may be summarised shortly as follows (1) False name, true address. Here "true address" does not necessarily mean the true address of the individual seeking credit under a false name. This category includes the so-called "empty house" fraud, where the address given is an empty house, usually one up for sale, where access can be obtained to collect mail and where address-based searches will provide information, if any, about the genuine former occupants. (2) Impersonation. The impersonation may be of a real or a fictitious person; typically the fraudulent person will pretend to be the person identified by stolen documents, such as driving licence or credit cards, in his possession. (3) True name, true address but false personal information. These cases include suppressing the fact of unemployment or falsely stating the type of employment or level of income. It was clear from the evidence we heard that address-based searches do not necessarily bring all these categories of fraud to light. Other categories of fraud, such as mortgage fraud, are not recorded.[87]

Moreover, when a member of CIFAS has a suspicion that it may have detected an act of fraud or attempted fraud, a CIFAS marker may be put on the applicant's credit reference file. This marker, however, does not authorise other members to simply reject an application for credit based on it.[88] CIFAS members are "required to conduct an investigation into the case and not just reject the application, as it may be a genuine application rather than one submitted by a fraudster."[89] It is worth noting that CIFAS guarantees the exercise of data subjects' right of access, and also rights of rectification and erasure. Nevertheless, regarding the right of access, CIFAS only discloses to individuals CIFAS data and not public information, payment history

[86]See Credit Industry Fraud Avoidance Scheme. How Does CIFAS work? Available at http://www.cifas.org.uk/default.asp?edit_id=953-28 Accessed 15 February 2010.

[87]Equifax Europe Limited and The Data Protection Registrar. Data Protection Tribunal. Appeal Decision (DA/90 25/49/7). Available at http://informationtribunal.gov.uk/Documents/decisions/equifax.pdf. Accessed 15 February 2010. § 33.

[88]Information Commissioner's Office. Credit Explained. Available at http://www.ico.gov.uk/upload/documents/library/data_protection/practical_application/credit_explained_leaflet_2005.pdf. Accessed 15 February 2010. P. 11.

[89]See How does CIFAS work? Available at http://www.cifas.org.uk/default.asp?edit_id=953-28. Accessed 15 February 2010. In the same sense see Information Commissioner's Office. Credit Explained. Op. cit. P. 11. "No one should be refused credit just because of a CIFAS marker, and these markers are not included in your credit score. A CIFAS marker simply means the lender should take extra care to make sure that the person applying for credit is who they claim to be and that the information they have given on their application form is correct. Only members of CIFAS see this information."

data or other fraud information, since it does not hold these kinds of information.[90] As far as other rights are concerned, CIFAS will only analyse a request from a data subject regarding the accuracy of his/her personal data after he/she presents a complaint to the specific CIFAS Member and such member issues a 'Final Response letter'.[91]

Nonetheless, there are no clear criteria to help CIFAS Members to decide whether to put a mark on the applicant credit reference file. This decision is left to the member's discretion, making the exercise of data subjects' rights more difficult, since they will not know the criteria under which the mark is placed on their credit reference file.

CIFAS—as an anti-fraud organisation[92]—is authorised not only to share data with public authorities, but also to process sensitive data.[93] It is important to note that one of the major credit reference agencies in the UK[94] is considered as an anti-fraud organisation and, as a result, is authorised to process sensitive data for the purposes of preventing fraud.[95] Furthermore, all the three major credit reference agencies in the UK have amongst their objectives crime prevention and prosecution of offenders.[96]

Finally, the Data Protection (Processing of Sensitive Personal Data) Order 2009 authorises banks and credit card companies to process information about a criminal conviction or caution "for the purpose of administering an account relating to the payment card (or for cancelling the payment card) used in the commission of one of the listed offences relating to indecent images of children and for which the data subject has been convicted or cautioned under the relevant legislation in England and Wales, Scotland or Northern Ireland."[97]

---

[90]See http://www.cifas.org.uk/default.asp?edit_id=693-59. Accessed 15 February 2010. "Please note CIFAS is not a credit reference agency and does not hold public information or payment history data."

[91]See http://www.cifas.org.uk/default.asp?edit_id=693-59. Accessed 15 February 2010. "CIFAS will not become involved in a dispute until the CIFAS Member has issued a Final Response letter. CIFAS will request a copy of this letter before looking into your case."

[92]See Section 2(a) of the The Serious Crime Act 2007 (Specified Anti-fraud Organisations) Order 2008.

[93]Section 7A of Schedule 3 of the Data Protection Act 1998.

[94]Experian Limited, which is one of the major credit reference agencies in the UK, was recognised by an order of the Secretary of State as an anti-fraud organisation for the purpose of data sharing for the prevention of fraud. See The Serious Crime Act 2007 (Specified Anti-fraud Organisations) Order 2008, Section 2(b). Available at http://www.statutelaw.gov.uk/content.aspx?LegType=All+Legislation&PageNumber=1&NavFrom=3&parentActiveTextDocId=3516442&ActiveTextDocId=3516442&filesize=4564. Accessed 28 February 2010.

[95]See Section 7A of Schedule 3 of the Data Protection Act.

[96]You can check the purposes for which credit reference agencies process personal data at http://www.ico.gov.uk/ESDWebPages/search.asp. Accessed 2 March 2010.

[97]Explanatory Note to the Data Protection (Processing of Sensitive Personal Data) Order 2009. Available at http://www.opsi.gov.uk/si/si2006/uksi_20062068_en.pdf. Accessed 2 March 2010.

4.5.2 The Credit Information Suppliers

In the UK, distinct from the Italian example—as will be seen in the next chapter—, there are only private credit bureaus, also called 'credit reference agencies', which provide credit information to the financial market.[98] There are three main credit reference agencies in the UK, Callcredit, Equifax and Experian, which collect information from many different sources: lenders, the electoral roll and other sources.

In a ruling in 1991, the Data Protection Tribunal identified most of the sources of information for credit reference agencies, which include electoral registration information,[99] court judgments, bankruptcies and related matters, the Scottish valuation roll, previous searches,[100] the Insight, the CIFAS (Credit Industry Fraud Avoidance Scheme—the UK's fraud prevention service), the Westrace, the Postal Address File (PAF), the telephone directory file and closed user groups.[101] In the "Credit Explained" document, the ICO identifies other sources of information, including individual voluntary arrangements (IVA), alias or association information, linked addresses, the Council of Mortgage Lender's repossession register and the GAIN (Gone Away Information Network).[102]

The processing of personal data by credit reference agencies is the one that has the most impact on an individual's ability to conclude a contract. In fact, the ICO adopted a series of documents providing guidance, for both individuals and companies, including the credit reference agencies, with regard to the processing of personal data by such institutions, aiming to help them to comply with data protection principles and rules. Moreover, the Data Protection Act 1998 at Section 9 regulates the exercise of data subjects' right of access when the data controller is a credit reference agency. Here the most relevant documents produced by the ICO will be analysed, showing that the approach in relation to this sector is more focused on the provision of guidance instead of on the enforcement of the law. This does not

---

[98] See Expert Group on Credit Histories. Op. cit. P. 12. Table 2.

[99] "Everyone who provides their details is included in the full register which is only available for certain statutory purposes (such as electoral purposes) and to credit reference agencies." Information Commissioner's Office. Use of Personal Information available on the Electoral Roll. Available at http://www.ico.gov.uk/upload/documents/library/data_protection/practical_application/use_of_personal_information_available_on_the_electoral_roll.pdf. Accessed 10 February 2010.

[100] Previous searches or search information refers to information regarding "When an organisation looks at your credit reference file (...). This will show the name of the organisation, the date it searched your file and the type of search." Information Commissioner's Office. Credit Explained. Op. cit. P. 9.

[101] Equifax Europe Limited and The Data Protection Register. Appeal Decision by the Data Protection Tribunal (DA/90 25/49/7). 28 June 1991. Available at http://www.informationtribunal.gov.uk/Documents/decisions/equifax.pdf. Accessed 9 February 2010.

[102] See http://www.ico.gov.uk/upload/documents/library/data_protection/practical_application/credit_explained_leaflet_2005.pdf. Accessed 9 February 2010.

mean that the former is more important than the latter. As highlighted by Andrew Charlesworth:

> (. . .) in the UK, the Office of the Information Commissioner ("OIC") has (in large part due to underfunding and understaffing) long taken the approach that a key part of the UK data privacy regime would be the promotion of the use of sectoral policies and codes of practice, rather than a rigid scheme of enforcement. It is noticeable when discussing the activities of national data protection agencies with representatives of international business that the UK OIC is frequently praised for its constructive and pragmatic approach to the application of data protection laws. This is not to say that the UK OIC is lax in its enforcement of the law, or that UK national transposition of the DPD resulted in significantly weaker national legislation. Rather, the process of consultation and discussion related to the development of sectoral policies and codes of practice has meant that the staff of the OIC are well placed to advise on effective privacy protection mechanisms, and are knowledgeable about the practical difficulties which face national and international business.[103]

The first document addressed to the banking sector and to the credit reference industry is the "Data Protection Technical Guidance: Filing defaults with credit reference agencies".[104] The document identifies three reasons for information being filed by lenders[105] with credit reference agencies: to help lenders make responsible lending decisions; to help lenders trace and collect overdue debts; and, occasionally, prevent fraud and money laundering.[106] The document presents a series of obligations that both banks and credit reference agencies have to comply with, regarding the registering of information, delays, storage limits, etc.

One important point highlighted by the document is the fact that lenders offering the same product type should use the same standards in filing defaults. Not doing that would "increase the likelihood that default records for different product types will not be able to predict bad debt equally."[107] Imagine those differences from a cross border perspective; it would make it even more difficult to offer credit from one member state to another, because lenders would not have the right tools to analyse the risk, since different standards of filling defaults are used even within one specific member state.[108]

---

[103] Charlesworth, Andrew. Op. cit. P. 966.

[104] http://www.ico.gov.uk/upload/documents/library/data_protection/detailed_specialist_guides/default_tgn_version_v3%20%20doc.pdf. Accessed 9 February 2010.

[105] 'Lenders' is used in the text with the meaning of Banks and other institutions which provide credit.

[106] International Finance Corporation (IFC)—World Bank Group. Op. cit. P. 45. "The range of potential value-added services is quite extensive and includes, but it is not limited to: Marketing services; Credit scoring; Application processing; Portfolio monitoring; Fraud detection; Collections."

[107] Information Commissioner's Office. Data Protection Technical Guidance: Filling defaults with credit reference agencies. http://www.ico.gov.uk/what_we_cover/data_protection/guidance/technical_guidance_notes.aspx. Accessed 10 February 2010. P. 4.

[108] Expert Group on Credit Histories. Op. cit. P. 45. "Divergences between member states do not just lie in the type of information that their credit registers process. A number of other credit reporting features render difficult the comparison of data across borders.

The definition of default, according to the Technical Guidance, corresponds "to a situation when 'the lender in a standard business relationship with the individual decides the relationship has broken down'."[109] Although the definition is quite broad and the decision is left to the lender's discretion, the document presents some 'indicators of a default', which include:

- The account has been referred to a collection agency or in-house debt collection department.
- The account has been referred for legal action.
- The account has been included in a bankruptcy, IVA, or similar.
- The asset financed has been repossessed or instructions for repossession have been given.
- The lender takes or has taken steps to cut off the service provided (or would do so if they were not prevented on social rather than commercial grounds or by other regulations, codes of practice or statute).
- The customer has not made satisfactory proposals in response to a demand for repayment.
- The customer has given a clear indication, for example, by handing back an asset, that they do not intend to meet their contractual obligations.
- The lender has evidence that an account has been opened or used for fraudulent purposes by the applicant.[110]

Although this guidance is not a binding document, it reflects the view of the ICO, and will probably be applied when analysing an individual complaint. As far as delays are concerned, the recommendation made by the guidelines is that lenders can only register it when there are at least three consecutive months in arrears.[111]

Another important recommendation of the Technical Guidance refers to the need to maintain data quality. Every change in the situation of the customer, whether through the payment of a debit or an agreed rescheduling with the lender, has to be reported to the credit reference agency.[112] Specially for the purpose of granting credit, it is important that the data stored reflect the data subject's

Different definitions are used in the different member states, for instance, as to what is to be considered payment defaults and delinquencies. For example, in some countries, such as Romania, late payments are registered after 30 days, in others, e.g. Belgium or Lithuania after 3 months/90 days. In some countries, definitions are clarified by law, in others, guidance on the criteria to use (e.g., to determine whether the client is in default) is given to reporting creditors. As such, a consumer classified as 'in default' in one member state may not necessarily be classified—under the same circumstances—'in default' in another member state."

[109]Information Commissioner's Office. Data Protection Technical Guidance: Filling defaults with credit reference agencies. P. 5.

[110]Ibid. P. 5.

[111]The document also points out that "accounts should be filed as being a default where those payments due have not been received for 6 months." Information Commissioner's Office. Data Protection Technical Guidance: Filling defaults with credit reference agencies. P. 6.

[112]Ibid. P. 10.

current circumstances, and, hence, "steps should be taken to ensure that the data are kept to date, or when the data are used, account should be taken of the fact that circumstances may have changed."[113]

In terms of time limits for storage, the document considers 6 years as the maximum period for keeping data in the file,[114] after which this specific data has to be removed.[115] In the same vein is the document on "Credit agreements—Data Sharing" which suggests that account information should be held by the credit reference agencies for a period of 6 years after the account was last active.[116] Such storage limit was agreed between the ICO and the Credit Reference Agencies.[117]

Returning to the Technical Guidance, it recommends that before filling a default lenders should send to their customers a notice of their intention to fill it:

> Lenders should tell their customers about filing information with a credit reference agency as part of the account opening procedure, in line with the requirements of the 'fair processing code'.[118]

In the notice of intention[119] lenders should give to their customers at least 28 days before effectively filling a default.[120] Finally, the Technical guidance

---

[113]Information Commissioner's Office. Data Protection Act 1998: Legal Guidance. Op. cit. P. 38.

[114]"The Act does not prescribe the period for which information is retained by credit reference agencies. However we understand that the Crowther Report on Consumer Credit 1971 expressed support for the view that a statutory time limit should be considered and suggested a period of 6 years should be adopted. At the time this was already the practice common to some of the major credit reference agencies." Information Commissioner's Office. Credit agreements—Data sharing. Available at http://www.ico.gov.uk/upload/documents/library/data_protection/practical_application/credit_%20agreements%20-%20data_%20sharing.pdf. Accessed 10 February 2010.

[115]Information Commissioner's Office. Data Protection Technical Guidance: Filling defaults with credit reference agencies. Op. cit. P. 19.

[116]Information Commissioner's Office. Credit agreements—Data sharing. Op. cit. "Account information is held by the credit reference agencies for a period of 6 years after the account was last active. It appears to be the case that in addition to current credit commitments the preceding 6 years of an individual's credit history is taken into account by credit grantors when applications for credit facilities are assessed. As a consequence this historical information would appear to be relevant to the purpose of credit referencing and by holding this information the agencies would not appear to be in breach of the fifth principle."

[117]Information Commissioner's Office. The Guide to Data Protection. Op. cit. P. 78.

[118]Information Commissioner's Office. Data Protection Technical Guidance: Filling defaults with credit reference agencies. Op. cit. P. 1.

[119]The Information Commissioner recognises that there are situations where there is no need for a notice, for example in cases "involving fraud; where the lender has been notified under the terms of a bankruptcy or IVA; where there has been successful court action or repossession; or, where a customer has made no attempt to resolve their arrears." Ibid. P. 14.

[120]In the same sense is Section 13.7 of the Banking Code. British Bankers' Association et al. The banking code. Available at http://www.bankingcode.org.uk/pdfdocs/BANKING%20CODE.pdf. Accessed 10 February 2010. P. 23. "13.7 In these cases, we will give you at least 28 days' notice that we plan to give information about the debts you owe us to credit reference agencies. At the same time, we will explain to you the role of credit reference agencies and the effect the information they provide can have on your ability to get credit."

briefly analyses the liability of credit reference agencies regarding the accuracy of information received from a lender. According to this document, to have a defence against an action, credit reference agencies will have to prove that they took "reasonable steps to make sure the data is accurate and, as soon as they become aware of the challenge, take steps to mark the file accordingly."[121]

Another relevant document produced by the ICO tries to explain to individuals how their personal data is processed for credit purposes ("Credit Explained").[122] Many issues are discussed in the document, including credit scoring, access to third party information, storage limits and exercise of data subjects' rights. The document presents a full list containing all the different kinds of information and their respective storage limits. For almost all kind of data, the maximum storage period is 6 years.[123] However, there are some types of data with different storage limits[124] or even without any limit, as in the case of CIFAS[125] and the Electoral roll. It is important to notice that the Data Protection Act brings no storage limits,[126] providing only that "data cannot be kept for longer than it is necessary".[127]

With regard to the exercise of data subjects' rights, the ICO in "The Guide to Data Protection" explains how credit reference agencies should proceed if an individual challenges the accuracy of data held about him/her:

> When an individual tells a credit reference agency its record of a particular account is wrong, the agency will usually have to contact the lender concerned to confirm that the record is accurate. If the lender satisfies the credit reference agency that the record is correct then the agency can retain it. However, if the agency is not satisfied that the record is accurate, it should amend or remove it. The credit reference agency will mark the record as being in dispute while the lender looks into the matter but it must tell the individual whether it has amended or removed the record within 28 days of receiving the challenge.[128]

---

[121]Information Commissioner's Office. Data Protection Technical Guidance: Filling defaults with credit reference agencies. Op. cit. P. 15.

[122]http://www.ico.gov.uk/upload/documents/library/data_protection/practical_application/credit_explained_leaflet_2005.pdf. Accessed 10 February 2010.

[123]It includes Bankruptcy (unless it lasts longer than this); Individual voluntary agreements (IVA); Administration order; County court judgement; High court judgement/decree; Closed account; Defaults; Linked Addresses; Council of Mortgage Lenders and GAIN (Gone Away Information Network); Document on "Credit Explained". P. 12–13.

[124]For Arrangement to pay information it will depend on the terms of the arrangements; for Association information it will remain in the database until the link ends and the dissociation is requested to the Credit Reference Agency; for live account, the information is collected until the account is closed and then is kept for 6 years; Searches will be kept for 1 or 2 years depending on the credit reference agency (Experian and Equifax—1 year; Callcredit—2 years); for Alias information it will depend on the data subject circumstances. Information Commissioner's Office. Credit Explained. Op. cit. P. 13.

[125]However, according to the ICO, if there is evidence of fraud the data can be kept in the credit reference database. Information Commissioner's Office. Credit Explained. Op. cit. P. 13.

[126]See footnote 114.

[127]Schedule 1, Part I, Section 4 of the Data Protection Act.

[128]Information Commissioner's Office. The Guide to Data Protection. Op. cit. P. 69.

Regarding the right to access, credit reference agencies "must provide a copy of the information within 7 days of a written request and on a payment of a £2 fee."[129] As far as credit scoring is concerned, although the ICO recognises that lenders using credit scores have to explain to their customers why they are refused credit and also that individuals have the right of not being subject only to an automated decision,[130] it accepts that lenders are not obliged to give details about how their credit scoring works.[131] This position complies with Section 8(5) of the UK Act, since it interprets Section 7(1) (d) as not requiring "the provision of information as to the logic involved in any decision-taking if, and to the extent that, the information constitutes a trade secret."

4.5.2.1 Access to Information Related to Third Parties

In the UK when someone applies for credit banks and other lenders usually look at the applicant credit reference file and, if such person has a financial link—a joint account with someone else for example—they may also look at that second person's credit reference file.[132] Furthermore, during the period where the Data Protection Act 1984 was in force, some credit reference agencies, when receiving a request from a lender, searched for information about third parties with an address link with the applicant for credit. In this kind of search—by address—all individuals "recorded as living at the address searched at any time" would have their personal data disclosed.[133] Such behaviour, however, was limited by the Data Protection Tribunal in many cases. According to the Tribunal opinion, these kinds of search

[129] Ibid. P. 133.

[130] See Section 12 of the Data Protection Act 1998.

[131] Information Commissioner's Office. Credit Explained. Op. cit. P. 3.

[132] Ibid. P. 2.

[133] Equifax Europe Limited and The Data Protection Registrar. Appeal Decision (DA/90 25/49/7). Data Protection Tribunal. Available at http://informationtribunal.gov.uk/Documents/decisions/equifax.pdf. Accessed 24 February 2010. §25. In the same sense see CCN Systems Limited and The Data Protection Registrar. Appeal Decision (Cases Refs. DA/90 25/49/9 and DA/90 25/49/9). Data Protection Tribunal. Available at http://www.informationtribunal.gov.uk/Documents/decisions/ccn_systems.pdf. Accessed 24 February 2010. § 31. "Since the information generated by a credit enquiry is obtained by reference to an address, which may be the applicant for credit's present address or a previous address or, sometimes, another address which bears some similarity to one of these addressed, it is inherently likely to contain information about other individuals—'third parties'. These individuals may be members of the applicant's family and share the same surname and, possibly, initials, or members of the family with different surnames, or persons living with the applicant for credit, or friends, or tenants or dogers, or estranged spouses. They may have financial links with the applicant for credit, as is sometimes the case with spouses and children, but they may well be completely financially independent of the applicant. However, they may have nothing with the applicant for credit, but simply persons who have at some time lived at the same address as the applicant, at different times—'non concurrent'—as in the example of Simon Jones we gave in paragraph 8 above."

would only be legitimate and fair "if they were revised so as only to retrieve information about persons who were reasonably believed to be closely financially linked with the subject of the search".[134] Therefore, credit reference agencies could only extract personal information about any other individual different from the applicant for credit if such individual is:

> Recorded as residing at the same present or previous address as the data subject concurrently with the subject, who (a) (i) has the same surname, and forenames or initials where these are recorded, as the subject, or (ii) has a name sufficiently similar to that of the subject for it to be reasonable to believe that he or she is the subject, or (b) (i) has the same surname as the subject, or (ii) has a surname sufficiently similar to that of the subject for it to be reasonable to believe that it is the same surname, and where in either case it is reasonable to believe that he or she has been living as a member of the same family as the subject in a single household, or (c) does not have the same surname as the subject but in respect of whom, on the basis of information obtained before extraction, it is reasonable to believe (i) is the subject or (ii) has been living as a member of the same family as the subject in a single household.[135]

4.5.3 The Insurance Industry

Insurance companies use different kinds of personal data obtained from many different sources. In processing personal data they have to comply with data protection rules that are both in the Data Protection Act 1998 and in the Data Protection (Processing of Sensitive Personal Data) Order 2000, which have provisions that apply specifically to insurance activities. Let us start with the processing of sensitive data, since it is of particular relevance to the insurance industry.

4.5.3.1 Sensitive Data in the Insurance Sector

The Secretary of State adopted "The Data Protection (Processing of Sensitive Personal Data) Order 2000" with the aim of regulating other circumstances in which sensitive personal data may be processed. Amongst its provisions there are some which apply exclusively to insurance. Sections 5 and 6 of the Schedule to the

---

[134]Infolink Limited and The Data Protection Registrar. Appeal Decision (DA/90 25/49/6). Data Protection Tribunal. Available at http://informationtribunal.gov.uk/Documents/decisions/infolink.pdf. Accessed 24 February 2010. § 77. In the same sense see Credit and Data Marketing Services Limited and The Data Protection Registrar. Appeal Decision. Data Protection Tribunal. Available at http://informationtribunal.gov.uk/Documents/decisions/credit_data.pdf. Accessed 24 February 2010. § 55. "In essence, our finding is that the extraction of 'third party information'—information about persons who have no financial link with the applicant for credit—is unfair within the first data protection principle."

[135]Infolink Limited and The Data Protection Registrar. Appeal Decision Conclusion. Data Protection Tribunal. § 3(2).

Order[136] allow the processing of sensitive data for insurance purposes, including data related to the parent, grandparent, great grandparent or sibling of a specific data subject who is an insured person or is seeking insurance coverage. Therefore, the Order allows not only the processing of sensitive data of a specific data subject but also information related to third parties without the express consent of the third party. Nevertheless, "The data controller must not process these data to make decisions or take actions with respect to the relatives, nor if he is aware of the relative withholding his consent to the processing."[137]

The ICO, again, brings good examples of situations where personal data (and even sensitive data) of third persons is used by insurance companies:

> (...) in a common scenario where negotiations are taking place between an individual and an insurance company with a view to entering into a contract of insurance, various disclosures have to be made which may include sensitive personal data about a third party to enable the insurer to assess the risk and calculate the premium. Examples could be a group insurance policy for holiday insurance where medical details of individuals who are not party to the negotiations are disclosed, or car insurance where conviction details of named drivers would have to be revealed by the proposer. No contract exists at this stage and the insurance company may decide not to accept the risk and enter into a contract of insurance.[138]

Regarding the processing of medical data, which is one of the most sensitive types of information used by Insurance companies, the data is collected from different sources: (a) direct from the applicant him or herself; (b) from the applicant's general practitioner or other doctor, through a general practitioner's report (GPR); (c) from an independent medical practitioner who examines the

---

[136]"5. (1) The processing—(a) is necessary for the purpose of—(i) carrying on insurance business, or (ii) making determinations in connection with eligibility for, and benefits payable under, an occupational pension scheme as defined in section 1 of the Pension Schemes Act 1993[2]; (b) is of sensitive personal data consisting of information falling within section 2(e) of the Act relating to a data subject who is the parent, grandparent, great grandparent or sibling of—(i) in the case of paragraph (a)(i), the insured person, or (ii) in the case of paragraph (a)(ii), the member of the scheme; (c) is necessary in a case where the data controller cannot reasonably be expected to obtain the explicit consent of that data subject and the data controller is not aware of the data subject withholding his consent; and (d) does not support measures or decisions with respect to that data subject.(2) In this paragraph—(a) "insurance business" means insurance business, as defined in section 95 of the Insurance Companies Act 1982[3], falling within Classes I, III or IV of Schedule 1 (classes of long term business) or Classes 1 or 2 of Schedule 2 (classes of general business) to that Act, and (b) "insured" and "member" includes an individual who is seeking to become an insured person or member of the scheme respectively. 6. The processing—(a) is of sensitive personal data in relation to any particular data subject that are subject to processing which was already under way immediately before the coming into force of this Order; (b) is necessary for the purpose of—(i) carrying on insurance business, as defined in section 95 of the Insurance Companies Act 1982, falling within Classes I, III or IV of Schedule 1 to that Act; or (ii) establishing or administering an occupational pension scheme as defined in section 1 of the Pension Schemes Act 1993;"

[137]See the Explanatory Note to the The Data Protection (Processing of Sensitive Personal Data) Order 2000. Available at http://www.opsi.gov.uk/si/si2000/20000417.htm. Accessed 2 March 2010.

[138]Information Commissioner's Office. Data Protection Act 1998: Legal Guidance. Op. cit. P. 23.

applicant specifically for the purpose of assessing medical risk factors; (d) from a medical examination by their general practitioner; and/or (e) through the results of a health screening or blood test.[139]

In fact, the Insurance Industry—together with the British Medical Association—adopted in 2008 joint guidelines regarding the processing of medical information for insurance purposes. Basically, there are two moments in the life of the insurance contract where insurers need to use medical data. The first is to analyse the risk of the potential insured parties and to classify them according to their risks or to deny the coverage. The second moment is when assessing insurance claims, as in the situation "when the payout on a claim is triggered by an insured person having a particular medical condition".[140]

It seems, however, that the most 'sensitive issue' is the collection of medical data from the applicant's general practitioner or other doctor, through a general practitioner's report (GPR). According to the joint guidelines, some doctors had manifested their concerns about this process. They say that many of their patients decide not to share information with them or simply do not visit their doctor, putting their health into risk, because "They may believe that it will jeopardise their employment prospects, their chances of getting insurance at standard rates or of obtaining insurance cover at all."[141]

With this scenario in mind, the document gives guidance to insurers on how to comply with the data protection principles and rules. The first point addressed by the guidelines is the finality principle. The document states that "Insurance companies only need information that is relevant to the type of insurance, and should make unambiguously clear to doctors what information they require".[142] It also highlights that:

> The full records are not necessary and will very probably include information that is not relevant to the insurance being applied for. Insurance companies only need information that is relevant to the policy. Disclosure or other processing of information that is released without the consent of the applicant or insured person is likely to breach the Data Protection Act 1998, and may compromise a doctor's registration.[143]

Other important aspects of the processing of sensitive data are addressed in the guidelines with particular focus on the general practitioner reports, the consent of data subjects and the exercise of their rights of access and rectification. According to the document, doctors cannot disclose information about their patients without

---

[139]Association of British Insurers; British Medical Association. July 2008. Medical information and insurance. Joint ABI BMA guidelines. Available at http://www.abi.org.uk/Information/CodesandGuidanceNotes/527.pdf. 14 Mar 2010. P. 4.

[140]Ibid. P. 4.

[141]Ibid. P. 6.

[142]Ibid. P. 5.

[143]Ibid. P. 7.

their consent—in the case of sensitive data the UK Act requires express consent.[144] Moreover, insurance companies are advised to inform applicants (and also insureds) of their rights under the Data Protection Act.[145] If an individual manifests his/her intention to exercise his/her right of access and to see the General Practitioner Report before it is sent to the insurance company, the latter will have to inform the doctor and explain to him/her the rights of his/her patient. According to the guidelines the individual has 21 days from the notification received from the insurance company to see the report and exercise his/her other rights. If the individual has access to the report and decides to withdraw his/her consent, then the report cannot be sent to the insurance company. Nevertheless, if the individual finds any inaccuracy in the report, the doctor will amend it in cases where he/she agrees or will have to append a note to the report regarding the disputed information, in case he/she disagrees.

Furthermore, if the individual does not exercise his/her rights of access or rectification, then the report can be sent after the delay of 21 days from the notification.[146] As far as sexually transmitted infections (STI) are concerned, the document advises "that insurers should not request, and doctors should not reveal, information about an isolated incident of an STI that has no long-term health implications, or even multiple episodes of non-serious STIs, again where there are no long-term health implications."[147]

Although the Joint Guidelines are supposed to deal only with medical information, other kinds of sensitive information are included, such as information related to habits (lifestyle) and information related to third parties, including family history information. Concerning the former, the document recognises that the individual is the only one who has accurate information about his/her lifestyle. However, it accepts that "Medical conditions that have arisen as a result of a patient's lifestyle choice are legitimate areas for doctors to comment on with, of course, appropriate consent."[148]

---

[144]Ibid. P. 7. "The GMC [General Medical Council] requires doctors to: 'Obtain, or have seen, written consent to the disclosure from the patient or a person properly authorised to act on the patient's behalf.'"

[145]Ibid. P. 8. "The administrative requirements of the Act fall mainly upon insurance companies. Companies must inform applicants of their rights under the Act:

- to withhold permission for the company to seek a medical report (that is, to refuse consent to the release of information)
- to have access to the medical report after completion by the doctor either before it is sent to the company or up to 6 months after it is sent
- if seeing the report before it is sent, to instruct the doctor not to send the report; and
- to request the amendment of inaccuracies in the report.

The applicant must be notified in writing of these rights."

[146]Ibid. P. 8.

[147]Ibid. P. 10.

[148]Ibid. P. 11.

Regarding family (medical) history information, despite the fact that there are some ethical and practical difficulties for doctors in disclosing this kind of information, the joint guidelines suggest that once a patient had undergone tests because of his family history, the doctor should include the results of such test in the report to the insurance company:

> Doctors should, however, report the results of any tests or investigations they have undertaken on applicants because of their family history, whilst bearing in mind the limited moratorium on the use of genetic information in insurance (see section 6.4). This information may be useful in confirming or counteracting information about family history provided by the patient. For example if the applicant had mentioned a family history of breast cancer, it may be helpful for the doctor to report that the applicant had undergone tests, such as BRCA testing, which revealed a reduced risk of developing cancer (subject to the restrictions under 6.4 regarding disclosure of genetic test results). Under no circumstances should doctors reveal information about an insurance applicant's family if the information did not come from the applicant him or herself.[149]

Finally, the guidelines also refer to medical information related to third parties, not necessarily linked to the insured's health. That is the case of travel insurance, where the insurance company needs to confirm the health status of another person (not insured) to confirm that the illness of the third party "was sudden and unexpected and occurred at the time the insured person claimed."[150] Of course in this case, all the requirements regarding the processing of sensitive data provided for by both the Data Protection Act 1998 and the Order 2000 will apply.

4.5.3.2 Fight Against Fraud

The Association of British Insurers estimates that the amount of undetected insurance fraud totals 1.9 billion pounds a year, what represents an increase of 44 pounds on the average costs of every individual policyholder.[151] The insurance industry has taken many initiatives to fight against fraud,[152] the most significant ones

149 Ibid. P. 12.

150 Ibid. P. 14.

151 Association of British Insurers. Research Brief: General Insurance claims fraud. July 2009. Available at http://www.abi.org.uk/Media/Releases/2009/07/40569.pdf. Accessed 8 February 2010.

152 Information Commissioner's Office. Data Protection Good Practice Note—When can I disclose information to a private investigator? Available at http://www.ico.gov.uk/upload/documents/library/data_protection/practical_application/disclosures_to_private_investigators_v1.0.pdf. Accessed 3 March 2010. "Private investigators undertake a wide variety of work that includes helping insurers to investigate fraud and lenders to trace debtors."

being the Insurance Fraud Bureau (IFB),[153] the Motor Insurance Database (MID),[154] the Motor Insurers Anti Fraud and Theft Register (MIAFTR)[155] and the Claims and Underwriting Exchange (CUE).[156]

The MID, in comparison to the other three initiatives, was set up in order to assist the insurance industry in combating uninsured driving[157] and "therefore reducing the cost to the industry of compensating victims of accidents involving uninsured motorists."[158] Besides this role, it is also used to help "the UK comply with the fourth EU Motor Insurance Directive, which requires that insurance details of all vehicles in each member state can be easily identified by a national information centre"[159] and the police to try to reduce the number of uninsured drivers. The database contains information regarding the insurance situation of all vehicles registered in the UK, including:

> (...) the vehicle registration mark (VRM), duration of insurance, the name of the Insurer, the policy number, as well as the name, address and age of the policyholder and details of any named drivers on the policy. Other information relating to the type of insurance cover may be included (Class of Use, Permitted Drivers), along with an indication of whether the policy allows the policyholder to Drive Other Vehicles. The make and model of the vehicle is usually included, depending on whether the insurance company has specified this information.[160]

With regard to the use of the database for fighting uninsured driving, it is quite clear that there is a legal basis to legitimise such use. However, the database is also

---

[153] See http://www.insurancefraudbureau.org/. Accessed 8 February 2010.

[154] See http://www.mib.org.uk/Motor+Insurance+Database/en/Motor+Insurance+Database+Information/Default.htm. Accessed 8 February 2010.

[155] See http://www.miaftr-hpi.info/index.asp. Accessed 24 February 2010.

[156] See http://www.cueuk.org/default.aspx. Accessed 9 February 2010. The insurance industry is also a member of CIFAS, however, different from the other initiatives, CIFAS covers not only the insurance sector but also banking, credit cards, asset finance, retail credit, mail order, savings and investments, telecommunications, factoring, and share dealing, and for that reason we will analyse its implication in terms of data protection in the section devoted to the banking sector. See http://www.cifas.org.uk/. Accessed 8 February 2010.

[157] "The Road Safety Act became law in November 2006, and introduced a new offence which is aimed at overcoming the problem of vehicles not specifically covered by any insurance policy (even a blanket policy) being used by drivers who claim cover under their "driving other vehicles" extension." In http://www.mib.org.uk/Motor+Insurance+Database/en/Continuous+Insurance+Enforcement/default.htm. Accessed 9 February 2010. See also Section 22(1) of the Road Safety Act 2006. http://www.opsi.gov.uk/acts/acts2006/ukpga_20060049_en_1. Accessed 9 February 2010.

[158] See http://www.mib.org.uk/Motor+Insurance+Database/en/default.htm. Accessed 9 February 2010.

[159] See http://www.mib.org.uk/Motor+Insurance+Database/en/default.htm. Accessed 9 February 2010.

[160] See http://www.mib.org.uk/Motor+Insurance+Database/en/MID+Faqs/What+information+does+the+MID+hold.htm. Accessed 9 February 2010.

used for fighting insurance fraud.[161] In the latter case, the exemption[162] regarding the processing of personal data for the detection or prevention of crime will apply.[163] In terms of compliance with the UK Act as a whole, individuals have access to the database, free of charge, to check whether their own vehicles are there,[164] but if they want to have access to all data held by MID about them or their vehicles,[165] they will have to pay a fee.[166]

As previously stated, all rights provided for by Part I of the Act apply to the processing operations carried out by MID. Nevertheless, in the case of any inaccuracy, the data subject will have to contact his/her insurance company to exercise his/her right of rectification.[167] This provision, in my opinion, does not comply with the Data Protection Act, since MID is a data controller and as such has

[161]"Government organisations can use the information on the MID for reasons of fraud prevention. Insurance fraud is an increasingly problematic issue and the MID data helps the Insurance Fraud Bureau (IFB) detect motor insurance fraud by comparing the MID data with data held on other databases to identify fraudsters and launch legal offensives against such criminals." http://www.mib.org.uk/Motor+Insurance+Database/en/MID+Faqs/Who+can+access–the+MID.htm. Accessed 9 February 2010.

[162]Section 29(1) (b) of the 1998 Data Protection Act.

[163]"Investigation of fraud: Data controllers need to exercise a great deal of care to ensure that their fraud prevention initiatives do not conflict with the general requirement to be open and transparent when processing personal information. Under Section 29 DPA, data processed for the purposes of the prevention or detection of fraud may be exempt from the First Principle (fair obtaining and lawful processing). Section 29(3) exempts such data from disclosure, if the investigation is likely to be prejudiced. But section 29 is applied on a case by case basis e.g., when the data controller is contemplating legal action against an alleged offender, and where it would be detrimental to that particular legal action if the normal rules of transparency were to apply.

We believe that the ability of organisations to detect and prevent fraud would be enhanced if the section 29(3) exemption were to be applied more broadly, for example, to allow the interrogation of databases to identify and trace patterns for organised crime." Thomas, Richard; Walport, Mark. Data Sharing Review—Consultation paper on the use and sharing of personal information in the public and private sector. Available at http://www.justice.gov.uk/docs/Association-of-British-Insurers-Data-Sharing-Response.pdf. Accessed 9 February 2010.

[164]See http://www.mib.org.uk/Motor–Insurance+Database/en/MID+Faqs/Can+I+have+access+to+MID.htm. Accessed 9 February 2010.

[165]"A search of the MID can only be conducted using the full Vehicle Registration Mark (VRM). It is not possible to search on a name, or address, or policy number or even a partial VRM." In http://www.mib.org.uk/Motor+Insurance+Database/en/Motor+Insurance+Database+Information/MID+Enquiries/default.htm. Accessed 9 February 2010.

[166]"Your rights—With limited exceptions you have the right to request a copy of the personal information the MIB holds about you and to have any inaccuracies corrected. (We charge £10 per information request.) Please address your request, with an appropriate fee, to the Compliance Manager, Linford Wood House, 6–12 Capital Drive, Milton Keynes, MK14 6XT (cheques should be made payable to the Motor Insurers' Bureau)." In http://www.mib.org.uk/Company+Information/en/_SiteNotices/PrivacyPolicy.htm. Accessed 9 February 2010.

[167]"The information held on the database is supplied by motor insurance companies and reflects the information that has been supplied to them by the policyholder. If the information retrieved is found to be incorrect or the data is missing, the insurance company should be notified so that they can make the correction to their own files and the MID." In

to allow individuals to exercise their rights, even if it has to contact the insurance companies before rectifying or erasing a specific part of the data. Finally, as far as storage periods are concerned, the data related to a specific insurance policy is kept in the database for 7 years after its expiration.[168]

The other initiatives of the Insurance industry were developed with the aim of fighting insurance fraud. The CUE "is a central database of motor, home and personal injury/industrial illness incidents reported to insurance companies, which may or may not give rise to a claim", having as its main purposes "preventing multiple claims fraud and the misrepresentation of claims histories."[169] Since it stores personal information,[170] individuals can exercise directly through the data controller—Insurance Database Services Limited (IDSL)—their data subjects' rights.[171]

The MIAFTR contains details of all vehicles written–off or reported stolen and "It helps identify fraudsters, for example by detecting those who insure their vehicle with several insurers at the same time and then try to claim from each following an accident, or having reported the vehicle as 'stolen'."[172] It is important to note that neither the Claims and Underwriting Exchange nor the Motor Insurers Anti Fraud and Theft Register have a clear data protection policy, both in terms of the exercise of data subjects' rights and regarding storage limits.

In a ruling of October 2009 the Court of Appeal[173]:

> (. . .) held that retaining information for police operational needs in the fight against crime and for other purposes was justified and did not infringe the data protection principles ('the

http://www.mib.org.uk/Motor+Insurance+Database/en/Motor+Insurance+Database+Information/MID+Enquiries/default.htm. Accessed 9 February 2010.

[168]"The data protection act stipulates that we should keep the data no longer than necessary. The fourth EU Motor Insurance Directive stipulates that policies need to be identified for up to 7 years after expiry, to aid tracing of insurance following an accident, at which point we securely dispose of all old data on a rolling, annual basis." In http://www.mib.org.uk/Motor+Insurance+Database/en/MID+Faqs/How+long+is+data+held.htm. Accessed 9 February 2010.

[169]http://www.cueuk.org/default.aspx. Accessed 9 February 2010. This database is also used for underwriting purposes. See http://www.cueuk.org/default.aspx. Accessed 9 February 2010.

[170]"The information contained in the database will comprise that supplied by the policyholder or claimant on their application or claim form, together with other information relating to the incident or claim. It does not hold sensitive information or details relating to the amount of premium paid." http://www.cueuk.org/default.aspx. Accessed 9 February 2010.

[171]A fee of 10 pounds will be charge for the exercise of the right to access.

[172]Association of British Insurers. ABI News Release. Stripped, searched and found—national database exposes its first fraudster http://www.abi.org.uk/Media/Releases/2005/05/Stripped_searched_and_found_-_national_database_exposes_its_first_fraudster.aspx. Accessed 9 February 2010.

[173]Chief Constable of Humberside Police v Information Commissioner (2009) EWCA Civ 1079. England and Wales Court of Appeal (Civil Division). Available at http://www.bailii.org/ew/cases/EWCA/Civ/2009/1079.html. Accessed 9 February 2010.

DPP') under the DPA 1998, especially principles 3 (personal data shall not be excessive in relation to the purpose for which they are procured) and five (personal data shall not be kept for longer than is necessary).[174]

According to this decision, the police can store personal data related to "convictions, however old and however minor" since this information "can be of value in the fight against crime and thus the retention of that information should not be denied to the police."[175] Following this reasoning, in the case of databases created with the aim of fighting crime, including insurance and financial fraud, the outcome would presumably be the same and personal data kept in those databases would remain there for data subjects' whole life. The ICO have applied to the Supreme Court for leave to appeal,[176] however, the permission to appeal was refused by the Supreme Court, on the grounds that the Information Commissioner did not raise an arguable point of law of general public importance.[177]

Finally, the last initiative is the IFB, which was launched in 2006, precisely in order to combat fraud. "The IFB collates and combines data contained with industry claims and policy databases (Claims and Underwriting Exchange [CUE, managed by Insurance Database Services Ltd], the Motor Insurers Database [MID], and the Motor Insurers Anti Fraud and Theft Register [MIAFTR])."[178] It is considered by the Serious Crime Act 2007[179] as an anti-fraud organisation and for that reason it is

---

[174]UK Court of Appeal Judgment on Police Database. Cyber Law Blog. Available at http://cyberlaw.org.uk/2009/10/27/uk-court-of-appeal-judgment-on-police-database/. Accessed 9 February 2010.

[175]Chief Constable of Humberside Police v Information Commissioner (2009) EWCA Civ 1079. England and Wales Court of Appeal (Civil Division). §43.

[176]Information Commissioner's Office. Police cases: ICO's response to the Court of Appeal's judgement. 13 November 2009. Available at http://www.ico.gov.uk/upload/documents/pressreleases/2009/statement_police_cases_appeal_131109.pdf. Accessed 24 February 2010. "We have carefully considered the judgement of the Court of Appeal and believe it raises important issues not just for these and the many other individuals about whom very minor and aged conviction details are held but also about how the Data Protection Act 1998 is interpreted in practice. It also engages serious questions about the applicability of Article 8 of the European Convention on Human Rights to conviction data held by the police. We have applied to the Supreme Court for leave to appeal and we hope that the application will be successful so that these issues can be examined by the Supreme Court."

[177]The decision is available at http://www.unlock.org.uk/userfiles/file/employment/docs_supreme%20court%20judgment%20refuse%20appeal.pdf. Accessed 16 June 2011.

[178]Insurance Fraud Bureau—Background Facts. http://www.insurancefraudbureau.org/files/misc_pdfs/ifb_background_information.pdf. Accessed 9 February 2010.

[179]"An anti-fraud organisation is defined in the SCA as 'any unincorporated association, body corporate or other person which enables or facilitates any sharing of information to prevent fraud or a particular kind of fraud or which has any of these functions as its purpose or one of its purposes'. An anti-fraud organisation becomes specified by an order made by the Secretary of State. At present there are six specified anti-fraud organisations: CIFAS; Experian Limited; Insurance Fraud Investigators Group; N Hunter Limited; the Insurance Fraud Bureau; and the Telecommunications United Kingdom Fraud Forum Limited." UK Home Office. Data Sharing for the Prevention of Fraud—Code of practice for public authorities disclosing information to a specified anti-fraud

authorised to receive information from public authorities with the aim of preventing fraud.[180] Although the IFB is recognised by law as an anti-fraud organisation, it has to fully comply with the data protection rules and any exemption it intends to apply will be considered on a case by case basis.[181] According to the meaning of Section 7A(2) of Schedule 3 of the Data Protection Act, all those initiatives can be considered as anti-fraud organisations and, therefore, are authorised to process sensitive data.

A similar database in Italy is "the databank of losses on the compulsory insurance scheme for motor vehicles registered in Italy" controlled by the Insurance Supervisory Authority (ISVAP), which is the public supervisory body of the insurance sector. Moreover, in comparison to Italy, where the database has a specific regulation with provisions regarding the processing of personal data, in the UK there is no specific legal statute regulating the processing of personal data by these databases and there is no clear policy concerning data subjects' rights. This would be important, since the outcome of the information processed by such databases is quite sensitive because it identifies potential frauds and fraudsters.

Besides these self-developed initiatives, the insurance market uses information stored in other databases. A good example is the database controlled by the Driver and Vehicle Licensing Agency (DVLA), a public body responsible for the licensing of vehicles and drivers in the UK, which "holds a register containing details of all vehicles licensed for use on the Road. This register also contains the name and

organisation under sections 68–72 of the Serious Crime Act 2007. http://www.crimereduction.homeoffice.gov.uk/organisedcrime/organisedcrime07c.pdf. Accessed 9 February 2010. See also The Serious Crime Act 2007 (Specified Anti-fraud Organisations) Order 2008, Section 2(e).

[180]"Section 68 of the SCA provides for public authorities to disclose information for the purposes of preventing fraud, or a particular kind of fraud, as a member of a specified anti-fraud organisation or otherwise in accordance with any arrangements made with such an organisation." UK Home Office. Data Sharing for the Prevention of Fraud—Code of practice for public authorities disclosing information to a specified anti-fraud organisation under sections 68–72 of the Serious Crime Act 2007.

[181]"Fraud prevention is a key priority for the public and private sectors alike. The powers under the Serious Crime Act 2007 allow public sector information to be exchanged with the private sector so that fraud can be detected, targeted and prevented on a much wider scale. However, the powers under the Act must be considered in the context of any Data Protection Act requirements. Specifically, information must be shared in a manner that is proportionate, and any organisations using this information sharing gateway must take steps to ensure that they only share such data as is necessary for the prevention of fraud. Where multiple partners engage in information sharing, being transparent and enabling individuals to exercise their rights to know how their information is being used is crucial. Equally, the importance of security when sharing personal information has never been as prominent as in recent months, and this must remain a major priority for any organisation wishing to share personal information." Foreword by the Information Commissioner. UK Home Office. Data Sharing for the Prevention of Fraud—Code of practice for public authorities disclosing information to a specified anti-fraud organisation under sections 68–72 of the Serious Crime Act 2007.

address of the registered keeper of each vehicle."[182] Although subject to the Data Protection Act 1998, the DVLA has the practice of disclosing information related to vehicles and their owners to the police or to a local authority to investigate criminal offences or non-criminal parking offences.[183] Furthermore, the DVLA also discloses information stored in its database "to anyone who can prove that they have 'reasonable cause' to have it."[184] The ICO has considered, amongst others, the investigation of suspected insurance fraud as a reasonable cause which justifies the disclosure of information contained in the DVLA to insurance companies presenting a request.[185]

4.5.3.3 The Processing of Genetic Data

The UK Government and the Insurance Industry agreed in March 2005 on a Concordat and Moratorium on Genetics and Insurance.[186] Although this document

---

[182]Information Commissioner's Office. Use and disclosure of vehicle information. Available at http://www.ico.gov.uk/upload/documents/library/data_protection/practical_application/its_your_information_dvla_vehicle_information_final.pdf. Accessed 14 February 2010. The DVLA holds also a drivers' register, however, the disclosure of information regarding drivers is more restricted than the one of vehicles. Driving and Vehicle Licensing Agency. Release of information from DVLA records. Available at http://www.dft.gov.uk/dvla/data/relinfo.aspx. Accessed 14 February 2010. "DVLA's driver register. Disclosure of driver information is more limited than vehicle information. However, the Agency can share driver data with other government departments or public sector bodies who can demonstrate a statutory provision to permit sharing and meet the Data Protection Act requirements. The legislation will state for what purpose the information can be requested and how it may be used.

Driver information may be shared, with the consent of the driver, with other organisations such as car hire companies or employers wishing to confirm employees' entitlement to drive. The organisations must show a demonstrable and relevant need to obtain that information."

[183]Road and Vehicles (Registration and Licensing) Regulations 2002. Available at http://www.opsi.gov.uk/si/si2002/20022742.htm#27. Accessed 9 February 2010. Section 27.

[184]Information Commissioner's Office. Use and disclosure of vehicle information. Op. cit. See also Section 27(1) e of the Road and Vehicles (Registration and Licensing) Regulations 2002; and Information Commissioner's Office. Compliance Advice—Implications of the Use and Disclosure of Vehicle Keepers Information. Available at http://www.ico.gov.uk/upload/documents/library/data_protection/practical_application/vehicle_keepers_information_-_implications_on_use_and_disclosures.pdf. Accessed 14 February 2010.

[185]Information Commissioner's Office. Use and disclosure of vehicle information. Op. cit. The DVLA, by its turn, considers that an insurance company has a reasonable cause not only for the investigation of a suspected insurance fraud but also when acting for a policy holder to trace other parties involved in a road traffic accident or incident. Besides, the DVLA helps reducing crime by enabling finance companies to trace vehicle keepers who have fraudulently obtained a leasing or loan agreement on a vehicle. Driving and Vehicle Licensing Agency. Reasonable cause for data release. Available at http://www.dft.gov.uk/dvla/data/rc.aspx. Accessed 14 February 2010.

[186]The moratorium has been extended until 2017, after an agreement reached by the Association of British Insurers and the British Department of Health. Association of British Insurers. ABI News Release. Tuesday, 05 April 2011 Ref: 17/11. Insurance Genetics Moratorium extended to 2017. Available at http://www.abi.org.uk/Media/Releases/2011/04/Insurance_Genetics_Moratorium_extended_to_2017.aspx. Accessed 12 June 2011.

is, in theory, non-binding, some aspects, including the moratorium, are in practice considered binding to the members of the Association of British Insurers, which have to subscribe to its Code of Practice as a precondition to affiliation.[187] As a rule, insurers will not use information from predictive genetic tests to underwrite travel insurance, private medical insurance, or any other one-off or annual policy, or for long-term care. However, regarding life, critical illness and income protection, insurers will have access to predictive genetic tests only when two requirements are fulfilled[188]: (1) the Genetics and Insurance Committee (GAIC)[189] has approved the test and (2) the policies have to be over £500.000 (for life insurance), £300.000 (for critical illness insurance) or the paying annual benefits have to be over £30.000 for income protection insurance.[190] Until now, the only predictive test approved by the GAIC was the one that identifies the gene for Huntington's disease.[191]

Still, according to this document, "Insurers are permitted to seek, with customers' consent, access to certain family medical history, diagnostic (but not predictive) genetic test results, and to reports from GPs in order to accurately price the additional risk from any health problems an applicant discloses."[192] This is a clear authorisation for the use of family medical history information and other related genetic information apart from the predictive genetic tests.

Following the moratorium, the Association of British Insurers (ABI) adopted an updated Code of Practice for Genetic Tests in June 2008. Compliance with provisions of the Code is a mandatory requirement of ABI membership.[193] The Code considers another possible use of genetic information which is not stated by the Concordat and Memorandum on Genetics and Insurance, when:

> An applicant may choose to disclose a predictive genetic test result that is in his favour in order to over-ride family history information. Insurers must publish information about the way they will use such test results to inform the underwriting decision. For example, a favourable (negative) result may be taken into account if it is relevant and could prevent a

---

[187]The Association of British Insurers represents the interests of 400 insurance companies which provide around 90% of domestic insurance services sold in the UK. See http://www.abi.org.uk/About_The_ABI/role.aspx. Accessed 6 February 2010.

[188]"Insurers may only take into account adverse results of those predictive genetic tests that the government's advisory body, GAIC, has decided are technically, clinically and actuarially relevant." Association of British Insurers. ABI Code of Practice for Genetic Tests. June 2008. Available at http://www.abi.org.uk/Information/Codes_and_Guidance_Notes/41697.pdf. Accessed 6 February 2010.

[189]GAIC is a non-statutory advisory and non-departmental public body of the Department of Health of the UK. See http://www.dh.gov.uk/ab/Archive/GAIC/index.htm?ssSourceSiteId=en. Accessed 16 June 2010.

[190]Item 20 (i)(ii) of the Concordat and Moratorium on Genetics and Insurance.

[191]See Genetics and Insurance Committee, October 2000: Huntington's Disease (GAIC/01.1). Available at http://www.dh.gov.uk/dr_consum_dh/groups/dh_digitalassets/@dh/@ab/documents/digitalasset/dh_087703.pdf. Accessed 6 February 2010.

[192]Item 16(vi) of the Concordat and Moratorium on Genetics and Insurance.

[193]See http://www.abi.org.uk/Information/Codes_and_Guidance_Notes/41697.pdf. Accessed 20 February 2010.

> loading that would otherwise have been applied because of the applicant's family history. An adverse (positive) result may only be taken into account if it is favourable to the applicant (see Principle 4).[194]

From the provision above, it is possible to conclude that it will only apply to situations where the insurance policy is under the financial limit established in the Concordat and Memorandum on Genetics and Insurance and when there is a positive result. It is not clear from the Code of Practice whether all kinds of genetic predictive tests can be used or not. This provision, however, presents some risks in terms of disclosure of genetic information, because individuals who have a family medical history presenting a genetic disease will probably be compelled to disclose their positive genetic tests in order to conclude an insurance contract

It is important to note that besides those rules provided for by the Concordat and Memorandum, the insurance company will have to comply with the requirements contained in the Data Protection Act regarding the processing of sensitive data (and of personal data as a whole) and in the Data Protection (Processing of Sensitive Personal Data) Order 2000.

4.6 Other Relevant Issues

4.6.1 Data Protection Principles: The Necessity Test and Data Minimisation

The ICO is of the view that many of the conditions for the processing of personal data set out in Schedules 2 and 3 of the Data Protection Act present the requirement of necessity for the purposes of the processing. In that sense, the Information Commissioner argues that data controllers will have to succeed in a "necessity test"[195] in order to justify the use of specific personal data (when consent is not involved) or, in the words of the Information Commissioner[196]:

> (...) data controllers must be able to show that it would not be possible to achieve their purposes with a reasonable degree of ease without the processing of personal data. Where

[194]Item 10.2 of the ABI Code of Practice for Genetic Tests.

[195]The Commissioner presents some criteria to be followed by data controllers in order to verify whether the processing is necessary: (a) purposes for which the data are being processed are valid; (b) such purposes can only be achieved by the processing of personal data and; (c) the processing is proportionate to the aim pursued. See Information Commissioner's Office. Data Protection Act 1998: Legal Guidance. Op. cit. P. 30.

[196]Information Commissioner's Office. Use and Disclosure of health data. Guidance on the application of the Data Protection Act 1998. Op. cit. P. 4. "The Commissioner takes the view that when considering the issue of necessity, data controllers must consider objectively whether:

Such purposes can be achieved only by the processing of personal data; and

The processing is proportionate to the aim pursued."

> the data controllers are able to achieve, with a reasonable degree of ease, a purpose using data from which the personal identifiers have been removed, this is the course of action that they must pursue. This may require the use of Privacy Enhancing Technologies (PET's) (...)[197]

Moreover, the Act also requires that data controllers use the minimum amount of personal data they need in order to fulfil the requirements of the processing,[198] which reflects the already mentioned 'data minimisation principle'.[199] On the one hand, personal data that is not necessary for the intended purpose should not be processed,[200] and, on the other hand, data controllers should not process personal data if it is insufficient for the intended purposes.[201] In the words of Peter Carey, "processing will not be necessary for contractual performance where the contract could be performed in some other way without the need for such processing."[202] The view taken by the ICO is slightly different from the one taken by the Italian Data Protection Authority, since the latter imposes the compliance with the necessity principle even when consent is involved.

4.6.2 *The Scope of Consent*

The idea of consent in the UK, which has a common law system, is quite different from the one of a continental system such as Italy or France. In the Common Law system, "the courts have not generally found that consent is rendered invalid by having conditions attached, providing that those conditions are not unduly onerous."[203] Based on this approach the ICO developed three conditions for the consent to be valid: (a) consent must be informed; (b) the person giving the consent must have some degree of choice; (c) there must be some indication that

---

[197] Privacy Enhancing Technologies or just PET's is a term "used to refer to an IT design philosophy which seeks to deploy new technology in ways which enhance rather than undermine privacy. From this standpoint, the use of techniques such as encryption, password control and other measures designed to ensure that data are guarded with appropriate security can all be regarded as privacy enhancing Technologies." Information Commissioner's Office. Use and Disclosure of health data. Guidance on the application of the Data Protection Act 1998. May 2002. P. 5.

[198] Information Commissioner's Office. The Guide to Data Protection. Op. cit. P. 60.

[199] This is the view of the UK Information Commissioner. In Ibid. P. 59.

[200] See Runnymede Borough Council (CCRO) and Others v The Data Protection Register. Data Protection Tribunal [Cases DA/90 24/49/3; DA/90 24/49/4; DA/90 24/49/5]. October 1990. Available at http://informationtribunal.gov.uk/Documents/decisions/community_charge_last.pdf. Accessed 3 March 2010. P. 7–8.

[201] Information Commissioner's Office. The Guide to Data Protection. Op. cit. P. 61.

[202] Carey, Peter. Data Protection in the UK. Op. Cit. P. 40.

[203] Information Commissioner's Office. Use and Disclosure of health data. Guidance on the application of the Data Protection Act 1998. May 2002. Available at http://www.ico.gov.uk/upload/documents/library/data_protection/practical_application/health_data_-_use_and_disclosure001.pdf. Accessed 11 February 2010. P. 15.

the data subject has given his or her consent.[204] Regarding the first condition, the data subject must know the purposes for which data are being collected and the potential disclosures of such data. As far as the second condition is concerned, the Information Commissioner is of the view that consent can be to a certain extent conditioned.[205] Finally, the idea of having an indication that the data subject gave his/her consent does not mean that it has to be written, it can be oral or even implied.[206]

Nonetheless, the approach adopted by common law courts and, as a consequence, by the ICO, in regard to consent, provides less protection for individuals than Directive 95/46/EC does, according to the interpretation of the Article 29 working party. The directive defines consent as "any freely given specific and informed indication of wishes by which the data subject signifies his agreement to personal data relating to him being processed",[207] and the Working Party has specified that for something to be "freely given" it cannot be subject to any condition, even a small one.[208] Where there is any condition, the legal basis for the processing of personal data, according to the Directive, will have to be another one but not consent itself.[209]

---

[204]Ibid. P. 15.

[205]Ibid. P. 15. "'Consent' given under duress or coercion is not consent at all. By contrast consent which is entirely optional and may be withheld without any consequences is clearly valid. Between these two extremes is consent which is more or less conditional upon agreement to some other term or condition. It would not necessarily be unfair that a patient should be asked to consent to the disclosure of data by, for example, a GP to a Health Authority for administrative purposes as a condition of receiving treatment from that GP. By contrast it could be argued that a requirement to consent to the disclosure of data to a medical student as a condition of receipt of treatment in a NHS hospital was unfair."

[206]Ibid. P. 15.

[207]Article 2(h) of Directive 95/46/EC.

[208]Article 29 Data Protection Working Party. Working Document 1/2009 on pre-trial discovery for cross border civil litigation. Adopted on 11 February 2009. Available at http://ec.europa.eu/justice_home/fsj/privacy/docs/wpdocs/2009/wp158_en.pdf. Accessed 24 February 2010. P. 8–9. "Consent—Whilst consent is a ground for processing under Article 7, the Working Party considers that it is unlikely that in most cases consent would provide a good basis for processing. Article 2(h) defines data subject's consent as 'any freely given specific and informed indication of his [the data subject's] wishes by which the data subject signifies his agreement to personal data relating to him being processed'. The main argument underlying the US jurisprudence since the Aérospatiale case is that if a company has chosen to do business in the United States or involving US counterparts it has to follow the US Rules on Civil Procedure. However, very often the data subjects such as customers and employees of this company do not have this choice or have not been involved in the decision to do business in or relating to the United States. (...) Similarly, valid consent means that the data subject must have a real opportunity to withhold his consent without suffering any penalty, or to withdraw it subsequently if he changes his mind. This can particularly be relevant if it is employee consent that is being sought. As the Article 29 Working Party states in its paper on the interpretation of Article 26(1): 'relying on consent may... prove to be a 'false good solution', simple at first glance but in reality complex and cumbersome'."

[209]Information Commissioner's Office. Use and Disclosure of health data. Guidance on the application of the Data Protection Act 1998. Op. cit. P. 15. "The EU Directive, for instance, defines consent as: '... any freely given specific and informed indication of his wishes by which the data

Furthermore, a distinction has to be made between consent for the purposes of processing 'normal' (Schedule 2 of the Act) and sensitive data (Schedule 3 of the Act). The former accepts implied consent and the latter only explicit consent.[210]

Finally, it is worth noting that also in the UK consent is not the only legal basis for the processing of personal data. "All conditions provide an equally valid basis for processing. Merely because consent is the first condition to appear in both Schedules 2 and 3, this does not mean that data controllers should consider consent first."[211] As I stated in section 2.1, for the industries under analysis consent is not a relevant legal ground for the processing, since, in general, they process personal data "for the performance of a contract to which the data subject is party or in order to take steps at the request of the data subject prior to entering into a contract; or (. . .) for compliance with a legal obligation to which the controller is subject".[212]

4.6.3 The Data Protection Officer

An interesting provision of the UK Act is the one that confers powers to the Secretary of State to formulate a provision, by order, that allows data controllers to "appoint a person to act as a data protection supervisor responsible in particular for monitoring in an independent manner the data controller's compliance with the provisions" of the Act.[213] This provision resembles Article 24(1) of Regulation 45/2001 regarding the appointment of Data Protection Officers to EU Institutions (see 1.3.2 supra), with no similar equivalent in Directive 95/46/EC. Until now, however, the Secretary of State has not exercised these powers.

4.7 Chapter Conclusion

In this chapter it was possible to conclude that the fact that the Information Commissioner lacks full powers of supervision over the private sector leads to non-compliance with the requirement of "complete independence" imposed by

---

subject signifies his agreement to personal data relating to him being processed.' On one reading this definition suggests that the giving of consent may not legitimately be made a condition of receiving a service such as health care since to impose conditions might mean that consent had not been 'freely given'. Were a data controller to seek to rely upon consent as a condition of processing medical data (rather than one of the other possible conditions suggested in Chap. 2) such a strict reading of the definition in the Directive might invalidate the consent that had apparently been obtained."

[210] Carey, Peter. Data Protection in the UK. Op. Cit. P. 39.

[211] Information Commissioner's Office. Data Protection Act 1998: Legal Guidance. Op. cit. P. 29.

[212] Article 7(b) (c) of Directive 95/46/EC.

[213] See Section 23 of the Data Protection Act 1998.

article 28(1) and recital 62 of Directive 95/46/EC. Moreover, the approach adopted by UK Courts regarding the scope of the concept of personal data made the UK not adequately implement EU legislation, in this case the referred Directive. Furthermore, it could be seen that the UK, like France, has included in its legislation the data protection officer, with no similar provision in the EU Directive. Finally, in what concerns one of the case-studies, namely insurance, it showed that the processing of genetic data is only allowed for late onset single gene disorder over a certain amount of coverage, what could be a possible solution for the processing of genetic data for insurance purposes.

Chapter 5
Data Protection Systems in the European Union: The Italian Experience

Following the same logic of the previous chapters, this one will focus on five specific issues: data protection authority, concept of personal data, data subjects' rights, processing of sensitive data and processing of personal data by the case-studies. Furthermore, it will dedicate some attention to other issues which deserve a different treatment than the one provided in Directive 95/46/EC, namely, the necessity principle and the use of codes of conduct.

Italy was the penultimate EU Member state—before the enlargements in 2004 and 2007—to adopt data protection legislation, through Act n 675 of 31 December 1996.[1] Only the Greek legislator came later. This Act was repealed and substituted by the Legislative Decree n 196 of 30 June 2003, called the Personal Data Protection Code (*Codice in materia di protezione dei Dati Personali* or just *Codice Privacy*), which currently regulates the matter.[2]

The Italian Codice is divided into three main parts, one concerning the principles applicable to the processing of personal data, the second related to sectorial rules and the third on the protection of individuals or legal persons.[3] It is important to highlight the adoption of the necessity and data minimisation principles by the Italian system, which force data controllers to adopt measures for ensuring that personal items of data will only be used when the finality of the processing can be achieved exclusively through them.[4] Moreover, it is worth noting that the Italian Data Protection Authority is of the opinion that anonymous data used for statistical purposes are exempt from the Data Protection Legislation.[5]

---

[1]DONEDA, Danilo. Um código para a proteção de dados na Itália. Revista Trimestral de Direito Civil, Rio de Janeiro, v. 16, out/dez. 2003. P. 121.

[2]Ibid. P. 123.

[3]Ibid. P. 124.

[4]Ibid. P. 127.

[5]See Garante per la protezione dei dati personali. Resolution n 9 of the Italian Data Protection Authority on balancing of interests: data collection by CRAs without consent (Adopted on 16 November 2004), where it expressly recognises that anonymous data that are processed for

M. Viola de Azevedo Cunha, *Market Integration Through Data Protection*,
Law, Governance and Technology Series 9, DOI 10.1007/978-94-007-6085-1_5,

5.1 The Data Protection Authority

Another important issue in the Italian system is the structure of the Data Protection Authority, named *Garante per la protezione dei dati personali*—hereinafter Garante,[6] which works as a real supervisor—and sometimes as an ad hoc legislator—, having amongst its powers one to adopt general authorisations for the processing of sensitive data and also to approve of and making enforceable codes of practice adopted by different sectors—public and private.[7] The possibility "to approve of and making enforceable" ensures that such codes of conduct comply with data protection rules, since for them to be approved by the Data Protection Authority it is necessary that they are in compliance with the Data Protection Legislation.

The Garante also has powers to "order that data banks and filing systems be accessed and audits on the spot be performed as regards premises where the processing takes place or investigations are anyhow to be carried out with a view to checking compliance with personal data protection regulations", the only exceptions being inquiries which are "carried out at a person's home or in another private dwelling place and/or the relevant appurtenances", where the inquiries can only "be carried out with the data controller's or data processor's informed consent" or with a court order.[8]

5.2 The Concept of Personal Data[9]

Article 4(1)(b) of the Italian Data Protection Code establishes that "personal data shall mean any information relating to natural or legal persons, bodies or associations that are or can be identified, even indirectly, by reference to any other information including a personal identification number" and article (1)(i) stresses that "data subject shall mean any natural or legal person, body or association that is the subject of personal data".[10]

statistical purposes fall outside the scope of application of the Data Protection Code. Available at http://www.garanteprivacy.it/garante/doc.jsp?ID=1671380. Accessed 27 January 2010.

[6]Doneda, Danilo. Ob. cit. P. 131.

[7]Ibid. P. 131.

[8]Article 158(1) and (3) of the Italian Data Protection Code. Official translation available at http://www.garanteprivacy.it/garante/document?ID=311066. Accessed 10 November 2010.

[9]Some parts of the discussions about the concept of personal data carried out in Chaps. 3, 4 and 5 were published in a previous work. Viola de Azevedo Cunha, Mario. Review of the Data Protection Directive: Is There Need (and Room) For a New Concept of Personal Data? In Serge Gutwirth et al. (editors). European Data Protection: In Good Health? Springer, 2012.

[10]Garante per la protezione dei dati personali. Relazione 2004—L'attuazione del Codice nel quadro della Costituzione per l'Europa. http://www.garanteprivacy.it/garante/document?ID=1093820. Accessed 15 December 2010. P. 61. "Nella nozione di dato personale rientra 'ogni informazione relativa a persona fisica, persona giuridica, ente o associazione, identificati o identificabili,

This definition goes beyond that of Directive 95/46/EC[11] firstly, because it includes both natural and legal persons[12]—the Directive only considers natural persons[13]—and secondly, because it does not specify any factor to which the information should be related,[14] as does the Directive when it establishes that an identifiable person "is one that can be identified, directly or indirectly, in particular by reference to an identification number or to one or more factors specific to his physical, physiological, mental, economic, cultural or social identity".[15] Furthermore, the Italian Code also applies to data related to deceased persons.[16] It is important to notice, however, that some Italian courts have been deciding that only data that is objective can be considered as personal data. This is the case, for instance, of a decision adopted by the Court of Rome in a case where an employee requested access to the evaluation forms filled in by his employer. The Court refused the request on the grounds that "The indicated evaluation, as a consequence of its subjectivity", could not be considered as personal data.[17]

In relation to anonymous data, the Italian Code, although presenting a definition of anonymous data in its Article 4(1)(n), does not take into account the idea of

---

anche indirettamente, mediante riferimento a qualsiasi altra informazione, ivi compreso un numero di identificazione personale' (art. 4, comma 1, lett. b), del Codice). Il Garante ha pertanto accolto un ricorso (Provv. 23 luglio 2004) avente ad oggetto l'accesso ai dati relativi alle registrazioni telefoniche degli ordini di negoziazione effettuati dal ricorrente, secondo le disposizioni di cui al regolamento Consob n. 11522/1998. Anche in tali fattispecie viene infatti effettuato un trattamento di dati personali (qui la voce del cliente) e sono pertanto proponibili le istanze ex art. 7 del Codice."

[11]See article 2(a) of Directive 95/46/EC

[12]BIANCA, Cesare Massimo; BUSNELLI, Francesco Donato. Op. cit. P. 25. "Nonostante l'art. 2, comma 1 del Codice non specifichi più espressamente, come invece faceva l'art. 1, comma 1 della l. n . 675 del 1996, che la tutela dei dati personale è prevista anche a favore delle persone giuridiche, dal tenore complessivo del Codice emerge chiaramente che alche questi vedono protetti i propri dati personali: già la definizione del dato personale (art. 4, comma 1, lett. b) del Codice) e quella dell'interessato (art. 4, comma 1, lett. i) del Codice) prevedono espressamente persone giuridiche, enti e associazioni come soggetti destinatari della protezione delle informazioni che li riguardano."

[13]See Article 2(a) of Directive 95/46/EC.

[14]BIANCA, Cesare Massimo; BUSNELLI, Francesco Donato. Op. cit. P. 52. "Cio trova peraltro conferma nell'assoluta mancanza di ogni ulteriore determinazione in ordine alla personalità del dato nella formula utilizzata dal legislatore, la quale richiede soltanto che l'informazione sia riferibile, direttamente, ad um soggetto determinato o determinabile. In quest'ottica sembra si debba considerare superata una lettura dell'analoga disposizione della direttiva comunitaria n. 95/46/CE (art. 2, a), la quale nell'indicazione che il riferimento del dato al soggetto può avvenire anche attraverso <<elementi specifici caratteristici della sua identità fisica, fisiologica, psichica, economica, culturale o sociale>>, vedeva nei primi informazioni strettamente legale alla persona fisica, mentre in quelle relativi all'identità economica, culturale e sociale notizie relative ad interessi meno legali alla persona fisica e come tali suscettibili di essere valutati anche in chiave transpersonale: per quanto tale chiavi di lettura avesse l'apprezzabile intento di fondare l'estensione della tutela anche in favore delle persone giuridiche, le quali avrebbero interessi omologhi a quelli delle persone fisiche relativamente alle informazioni della seconda categoria, essa non appare condivisibile né sul piano comunitario, né su quello del diritto interno."

[15]See Article 2(a) of Directive 95/46/EC.

[16]Article 9(3) of the Italian Personal Data Protection Code.

[17]Tribunale di Roma, Sent. 2/6/00, http://www.ictlex.net/?p=784. Accessed 1 August 2011.

reasonableness contained in the Directive.[18] According to the Italian Code "'anonymous data' shall mean any data that either in origin or on account of its having been processed cannot be associated with any identified or identifiable data subject".[19]

It can be seen, therefore, that there are slight differences in the concept of personal data adopted by the selected member states, which can have important consequences, especially given a cross-border perspective. Just to illustrate, a database containing information related to legal persons could be processed in a member state outside of data protection rules but in others such rules would apply, the same for data relating to deceased people.

5.3 Data Subjects' Rights

Following the same line of reasoning as the General Data Protection Directive,[20] the Italian Codice establishes a series of data subjects' rights concerning the processing of personal data, and regulates the way to exercise such rights and the mechanisms to enforce them. Article 7 of the Codice lists most of the rights of data subjects. In its first and second paragraphs it recognises the right to access and define the way in which the data subject has to be informed about the processing of his personal information. Paragraph 3 incorporates the rights of updating, rectification, integration,[21] erasure, anonymisation and blocking[22] of the data,[23] and also the right of certification to the effect that the exercise of the other rights "have been

[18]Cesare Massimo Bianca and Francesco Donato Busnelli, Op. cit.: 54.

[19]The Italian Code of Conduct and Professional Practice applying to processing of personal data for statistical and scientific purposes lists in its article 4(1) some means that can be considered as reasonable for identifying a data subject. www.garanteprivacy.it/garante/doc.jsp?ID=1115480. Accessed 23 December 2010.

[20]Directive 95/46/EC.

[21]Integration means to add information to clarify the interpretation of data included in a specific database.

[22]"(...) il blocco del trattamento deriva l'obbligo, per il titolare, di sospendere ogni altra operazione di trattamento diversa dalla mera conservazione delle informazione già raccolte e, in particolare, di astenersi dal diffondere ulteriormente i dati, anche in modo indiretto; pertanto, ad esempio, ove il blocco sia stato adottato asseguto dell'avvenuta divulgazione di alcune informazione a mezzo di un articolo giornalistico, l'obbligo di astensione dall'ulteriore diffusione dei dati può anche comportare il divieto, per il quotidiano e la società editrice, di pubblicare il testo del provvedimento cautelare adottato del Garante (Gar. 16.2.2000, Boll. N. 11/12, p. 21—Mass. 87)." Acciai, Riccardo. Il codice della privacy—Annotato con la giurisprudenza e le decisione del Garante. Maggioli: 2007. P. 55.

[23]"L'art. 7, 2° comma, del Codice fornisce un elenco dettagliato delle informazione che l'interessato ha diritto di ottenere con riguardo al trattamento in corso. Alcune di questi informazione erano già presente nella formulazione del <<vecchio>> art. 13 della legge n° 675/1996: ad esempio, le finalità e le modalità del trattamento, la logica applicata al trattamento medesimo, gli estremi identificativi del titolare e del responsabile. Altre informazione, invece, sono di nuovo come: l'origine dei dati personali e l'indicazione—anche per categoria—dei soggetti ai quali i dati personale possono essere comunicati o che possono venirne a conoscenza. Attraverso tali

notified (...) to the entities to whom or which the data were communicated or disseminated".[24] The response to the request of the data subjects has to be provided by the data controller within 15 days of receiving the request.[25] Furthermore, the Codice states that personal data should be "kept in a form which permits identification of the data subject for no longer than is necessary for the purposes for which the data were collected or subsequently processed".[26]

In relation to the exercise of such rights, article 8(1) establishes that these rights "may be exercised by making a request to the data controller or processor without formalities, also by the agency of a person in charge of the processing", and that "A suitable response shall be provided to said request without delay", in no longer than 15 days.[27] If the request of the data subject concerning the exercise of his/her rights is rejected by the controller, they can choose between lodging a complaint to the Garante[28] or filing a lawsuit, however, allowing for one 'jurisdiction' prevents the use of the other (article 145).[29]

5.4 The Processing of Sensitive Data

The Italian Data Protection Code, different from Directive 95/46/EC, adopted the term "sensitive data" to refer to "personal data allowing the disclosure of racial or ethnic origin, religious, philosophical or other beliefs, political opinions, membership of parties, trade unions, associations or organizations of a religious, philosophical, political or trade-unionist character, as well as personal

informazione viene ampliato in maniera significativa lo spettro di notizie che l'interessato può ottenere in merito ai trattamenti che lo riguardano." Cuffaro, Vincenzo et al. (editor). Op. cit. P. 75

[24]Concerning the notification about the exercise of the rights mentioned in letters a and b of Article 7(3) to all entities that were communicated or to which personal data was disseminated, the same provision states that such notification can be disregarded if "this requirement proves impossible or involves a manifestly disproportionate effort compared with the right that is to be protected."

[25]See Article 146(2).

[26]See Article 11(1)(a).

[27]"Il ricorso del Garante per fare valere i diritti di cui all'art. 7, può essere proposto soltanto dopo che la relativa richiesta sia stata presentata al titolare o al responsabile del trattamento e non sia stata adottata nessuna misura decorsi quindici giorni, ovvero sia stato opposto un esplicito diniego, anche soltanto parziale." Panetta, Rocco. Op. cit. P. 425.

[28]To present a complain to the Garante, the data subject has first to try to exercise his/her rights directly with the data controller and only if it is rejected or if he/she does not receive a reply within 15 days it can go to the Garante. There is one exemption to this rule that is the case of risk of imminent and irreparable harm to the person (Article 146 (1)). See also Panetta, Rocco. Op. cit. P. 426.

[29]"I diritto dell'interessato possono essere fatti valere sia di fronti all'autorità giudiziaria, sia mediante ricorso al Garante. Si tratta di due percorsi alternative che si escludono reciprocamente, perché se l'interessato sceglie di ricorrere al Garante non può poi adire anche l'autorità giudiziaria e viceversa." Panetta, Rocco. Op. cit. P.425.

data disclosing health and sex life".[30] Within this definition data related to criminal records was not included, nor was that relating to offence-related administrative sanctions and the relevant current charges, or the status of being either defendant or the subject of investigations, which were classified as "judicial data",[31] despite the evident "sensitive" nature of this kind of personal data.[32]

In what concerns the processing of sensitive and judicial data, the Codice divided the regulation of the topic into two different groups of provisions: the first group, comprising articles 20, 21 and 22, applies only to public bodies, and, the second, comprising articles 26 and 27, applies to private bodies and profit-seeking public bodies. Although this study will focus on the second group of provisions, the provisions of the first group will be briefly described.

Article 20 establishes that sensitive data can only be processed by public bodies if it is expressly authorised by a law specifying the categories of data and operations that may be, respectively, processed and performed, "as well as the substantial public interest to be pursued". Nonetheless, when there is no express provision in the law, if it is demonstrated that the activities "pursue a substantial public interest" the Garante can be requested to provide an authorisation for the processing.[33] The same applies to the processing of judicial data, as provided for by article 21(1). Both sensitive and judicial data have to be "indispensable"[34] for the processing, what some authors call the "indispensability principle".[35]

In relation to private bodies (and profit-seeking public bodies), article 26 establishes two requirements for the processing of sensitive data[36]: (a) written consent; and, (b) prior authorisation of the Garante.[37] However, in the case of judicial data, its processing can only be carried out when "expressly authorised by law or an order by the Garante specifying the reasons in the substantial public interest underlying such processing, categories of processed data and the operations that may be performed".[38]

It is important to notice that the Garante does not need to give authorisations for the processing of sensitive or judicial data on a case-by-case basis; it can

[30]See Article 4(1)(d).

[31]See Article 4(1)(e).

[32]"I dati definiti sensibili, pertanto, si caratterizzano per la particolare capacità di incidere sulla riservatezza dell'individuo cui si riferiscono e di determinare rischi di discriminazione sociale." Panetta, Rocco. Op. cit. P. 1071.

[33]Article 20(3).

[34]Article 22 (3)—Public bodies may process exclusively such sensitive and judicial data as are indispensable for them to discharge institutional tasks that cannot be performed, on a case by case basis, by processing anonymous data or else personal data of a different nature.

[35]Panetta, Rocco. Op. cit. P. 1103.

[36]Ibid. P. 1072.

[37]Sartor, Giovanni; Viola de Azevedo Cunha, Mario. The Italian Google-Case: Privacy, Freedom of Speech and Responsibility of Providers for User-Generated Contents. International Journal of Law and Information Technology. Oxford University Press (2010). P. 7.

[38]Article 27(1).

adopt general authorisations that cover different processing operations and sectors.[39] Currently, there are eleven general authorisations in force: (a) 1/2012 Concerning Processing of Sensitive Data in the Employment Context; (b) 2/2012 Concerning Processing of Data Suitable for Disclosing Health or Sex Life; (c) 3/2012 concerning the processing of sensitive data by associations and foundations; (d) 4/2012 Concerning Processing of Sensitive Data by Self-Employed Professionals; (e) 5/2012 Concerning Processing of Sensitive Data by Various Categories of Data Controller; (f) 6/2012 Concerning Processing of Sensitive Data by Private Detectives; (g) 7/2012 concerning the processing of judicial data by private bodies, profit-seeking and non profit-seeking public bodies; (h) for the processing of genetic data; (i) for the processing of judicial data related to the activity of mediation aiming at the conciliation of civil and commercial disputes; (j) for the processing of sensitive data related to the activity of mediation aiming at the conciliation of civil and commercial disputes; and, (k) for the processing of personal data for scientific research purposes.

These general authorisations will be analysed in this section according to the specific sectors chosen in this book (Insurance, Banking and Credit information suppliers sectors). Concerning the authorisation for the processing of genetic data it will be discussed separately, in a specific sub-section (5.4.1).

General Authorisation n° 1/2012[40] regulates the processing of sensitive data in labour relationships, but in item 3(f) it states that the processing activities of sensitive data "must be indispensable (…) in order to fulfil obligations resulting from insurance contracts against risks related to employers' liability for occupational health and safety and occupational diseases, or against any damage caused to third parties in the exercise of labour or professional activities." In other words, in such a situation the employer can process sensitive data and transfer it to an insurance company, following the safeguards of this General Authorisation. Such authorisation also allows employers to communicate and disseminate sensitive information to "health care organisations, private health insurance funds (…) insofar as this is closely relevant to the obligations, tasks, and purposes referred to under point 3" (item 7).[41]

---

[39] Article 40 (General Authorisations) 1. The provisions of this Code referring to an authorisation to be granted by the Garante shall also be implemented by issuing authorisations applying to specific categories of data controller or processing, which shall be published in the Official Journal of the Italian Republic.

[40] Available at http://www.garanteprivacy.it/garante/doc.jsp?ID=1822566. Accessed 7 April 2012

[41] 3. Purposes of the Processing

The processing of sensitive data must be indispensable

(a) in order to perform or enforce performance of specific obligations, or else to discharge specific tasks as provided for by Community legislation, laws, regulations or collective agreements, also related to individual businesses, particularly with a view to setting up, managing and terminating employment relationships or else in order to apply provisions related to social security and assistance, including social allowances, occupational or population hygiene and safety, taxation, trade unions, health care, and public order and security;

General Authorisation nº 2/2012[42] deals with the processing of health data and data related to sex life.[43] Its item 1.2(e) allows insurance companies and financial institutions, including credit bureaus, to process sensitive data related to health and sex life only to the extent they are necessary for the supply of a specific good or service requested by the data subject.[44] The authorisation also considers as lawful

---

(b) for account-keeping purposes or the payment of salaries, allowances, premia, other kinds of remuneration, gifts or fringe benefits, also irrespective of the cases referred to under a), in accordance with the law and for specific, legitimate purposes;
(c) for the protection of either the data subject's or a third party's life or bodily integrity;
(d) for the establishment or defence of a legal claim, also by third parties, before judicial authorities, administrative authorities, and in arbitration or settlement proceedings in the cases provided for by laws, Community legislation, regulations or collective agreements, on condition that the data are only processed for said purposes and for no longer than is absolutely necessary to achieve these purposes. If the data are suitable for disclosing health and sex life, the said claim shall have to be of an equal level compared with the data subject's one or must consist in a personal right and/or another fundamental, inviolable right or freedom;
(e) in order to exercise the right of access to administrative records in compliance with the relevant laws and regulations;
(f) in order to fulfil obligations resulting from insurance contracts against risks related to employers' liability for occupational health and safety and occupational diseases, or against any damage caused to third parties in the exercise of labour or professional activities;
(g) with a view to affirmative action policies;
(h) in order to pursue specific, legitimate purposes as set out in the by-laws of associations, organisations, federations or confederations representing employers' categories or else in collective agreements with regard to the support provided by trade unions to employers. Official translation available at http://www.garanteprivacy.it/garante/doc.jsp?ID=1699433. Accessed 14 August 2011.

[42] Available at http://www.garanteprivacy.it/garante/doc.jsp?ID=1822577. Accessed 7 April 2012.

[43] Another provision that could have an indirect impact on insurance is the one that allows the processing of health and sex life data for defensive investigations, since in some situations insurance companies use this service. See item 1.3(a) of the General Authorisation 2/2011-1.3. This authorisation shall also be granted in case the processing of data suitable for disclosing health and sex life is necessary.

(a) to carry out the investigations by defence counsel as per Act no. 397 of 07.12.2000 or else to establish or defend a legal claim also by third parties, including administrative proceedings and arbitration or settlement proceedings in the cases referred to in laws, Community legislation, regulations or collective agreements, providing the said claim either is of an equal level compared with the data subject's one or consists in a personal right or another fundamental, inviolable right or freedom and the data are processed exclusively for said purposes and for no longer than is absolutely necessary therefor;" The same can be said about General Authorisations nº 4 (item 3(b)) and 6/2011 (item 2(b)), since both of them apply to investigative activities.

[44] 1.2. This authorisation shall also be granted:

(e) to natural and legal persons, businesses, bodies, associations and other entities with regard to such data—including, if necessary, those concerning sex life—and operations as are indispensable to fulfil obligations, including pre-contractual obligations, resulting from a relationship that entails the supply of goods and/or services to the data subject. Where the said relationship concerns credit institutions and/or insurance companies, or if it has to do with securities, only such data

the transfer of health data to private health insurance funds by third parties (included in the authorisation) in the line of its item 1.[45]

The most important General Authorisations for insurance companies, banks and credit information suppliers are n° 5 and n° 7/2012.[46] The first applies fully to insurance companies and banks, as is stated in item 1(a): "any undertaking authorised to carry out banking, credit or insurance activities and the relevant associations". Besides, according to item 1(e) and (f), it is possible to conclude that also credit information suppliers are covered by this general authorisation.[47] It is worth noting that this authorisation allows the processing of sensitive data, excluding data related to sex life, where processing is regulated by General Authorisation 2/2012, and permitted only when it "is indispensable in order to fulfil the obligations, including pre-contractual obligations, undertaken by the entities referred to under 1) within the relevant sectors of activity, with a view to supplying specific goods or services that have been requested by a data subject."[48]

Authorisation n° 7/2012 regulates the processing of judicial data and, in what concerns this work, allows it for the purposes of "the assessment of responsibility in relation to losses or events relating to the human life" or of "the correct risk assessment for the development of the insurance activity in relation to an unlawful act linked to such activity."[49] With regard to the latter purpose, if an insurance company decides to create a database to process this kind of information, it will

---

and operations shall be considered to be indispensable as are required to supply specific products or services pursuant to a request by the data subject. The relationship may also concern the supply of visual, hearing or walking aids;

[45] 5. Data Communication and Dissemination

Subject to the provisions made for genetic data in the aforementioned authorisation as adopted in pursuance of Section 90 of the DP Code, data suitable for disclosing health may be communicated—exclusively to the extent that they are relevant to the obligations, tasks and purposes referred to under (1)—to public and private bodies including private health insurance funds, businesses carrying out activities that are closely related either to the exercise of health care professions or to the supply of goods and services to the data subject, credit institutions and insurance companies, voluntary associations or organisations, and the data subject's family members.

[46] These general authorizations are available at http://www.garanteprivacy.it/garante/doc.jsp?ID=1822608 and http://www.garanteprivacy.it/garante/doc.jsp?ID=1822640. Accessed 7 April 2012.

[47] 1. Scope of the Authorisation

(e) undertakings carrying out, on their own behalf, activities that are closely related and instrumental to those mentioned above as regards risk assessment, factoring, processing of a large amount of records, data transmission, packing and/or sorting of mail, and management of tax collectors' offices [esattorie] or treasury departments [tesorerie];

(f) undertakings in the tourism, hostelling or transport sectors, travel agencies, and tour operators. Official translation available at http://www.garanteprivacy.it/garante/doc.jsp?ID=1703161. Accessed 14 August 2011.

[48] See item 2.

[49] Chapter 4—Banking and Insurance Companies and Other Types of Processing

1. Scope of Application and Purposes of the Processing.

This authorisation shall be granted, without any request being necessary, to:

have to send a detailed report to the Garante specifying all types of data processing it intends to carry out.[50] In contrast to the UK, as was seen in Chap. 4 (Sect. 4.5.4), the Italian database aiming at fighting insurance fraud is managed by the Insurance Supervisory Authority (ISVAP), which is a governmental body, and not by the Insurance Industry Association.[51]

It is clear, therefore, that the provisions contained in the Italian Codice regarding the processing of sensitive data have a wider scope than the ones of Directive 95/46/EC. Firstly, because it applies both to private and public bodies. Secondly, it requires either an authorisation from the Data Protection Authority or a legal authorisation for a processing of sensitive data to take place. Finally, it includes the "indispensability principle" as a requirement for the processing.

5.4.1 *The Processing of Genetic Data*

In contrast to Directive 95/46/EC, the Codice has a specific provision concerning the processing of genetic data,[52] even though it does not contain any definition of

---

(a) businesses authorised and/or intending to be authorised to carry out banking, crediting, insurance or pension fund-related activities, also in case of their compulsory winding-up, with a view to establishing:

1. moral qualifications of partners and holders of executive and/or elective offices, as provided for by the relevant laws and regulations;
2. personal qualifications and grounds for disqualification exclusively where this is provided for by law;
3. liability for accidents and/or events relating to human life;
4. the existence of a concrete danger affecting appropriate discharge of insurance functions, as regards offences that are directly related to said functions. In the latter cases, the controller must provide the Garante with a detailed report on processing arrangements insofar as the processing concerns data contained in a specific database pursuant to Section 4(1), letter p), of the Code. Official translation available at http://www.garanteprivacy.it/garante/doc.jsp?ID=1705708. Accessed 14 August 2011.

[50]See Item 1.4 of Title 4.

[51]It is important to mention the existence of a specific authorisation for an insurance company to process sensitive data related to religious beliefs. This company is a catholic insurance cooperative which process this kind of data in order to identify whether a person is catholic, because its statute allows only Catholics to become associates and to have better conditions when contracting an insurance coverage. The data will not be used to evaluate the risk but for the sole fact to confirm that a person is catholic and, thus, able to become an associate of the insurance cooperative. See Garante per la protezione dei dati personali. Autorizzazione al trattamento di dati sensibili da parte della Società cattolica di assicurazione—16 dicembre 2009. Available at http://www.garanteprivacy.it/garante/doc.jsp?ID=1692886. Accessed 18 March 2010.

[52]"Diversamente da quanto avveniva nella legge n. 675/1996, dove si registrava l'assenza di una disciplina specifica per il trattamento dei dati genetici, con il <<Codice>> il legislatore ha

genetic data or genetic test.[53] Paragraphs 1 and 2 of article 90 establish that the processing of genetic data can only be carried out if there is an ad-hoc authorisation granted for the data protection authority.[54]

According to this article, the processing of genetic data can only be carried out in the cases provided for by ad-hoc authorisations of the Garante and when the right to object to the processing is granted to the data subject. Following such provision, the Garante adopted in 2007 a General Authorisation regarding the processing of genetic data, replacing previous documents about the subject[55] and regulating all processing concerning genetic data.[56] Such authorisation was replaced by a new authorisation adopted on June 24, 2011,[57] which kept the same wording.[58]

---

dedicato a questo settore un intero Capo, il V, sebbene composto dal solo art. 90." CUFFARO, Vincenzo et al. (editors). Op. cit. P. 437.

[53]"1- Preliminarmente occorre rilevare come nel testo legislativo in commento no esista una precisa definizione di <<dato genetico>> né, tantomeno, fino a poco tempo fa, alcun riferimento in proposito poteva essere ricavato da altre fonti del nostro ordinamento, per cui poteva, fino ad oggi, affermarsi che la normative in tema di dati genetici non avesse carattere definitivo, ma che fosse costituita, per lo più, di disposizione di principio, volte a vietare le discriminazioni basate sui caratteri genetici." Bianca, Cesare Massimo; Busnelli, Francesco Donato. Op. cit. P. 1345 Nowadays this problem is solved with the adoption of the General Authorisation for the Processing of Genetic Data.

[54]Article 90 (Processing of Genetic Data and Bone Marrow Donors)

1. Processing of genetic data, regardless of the entity processing them, shall be allowed exclusively in the cases provided for in ad-hoc authorisations granted by the Garante, after having consulted with the Minister for Health who shall seek, to that end, the opinion of the Higher Health Care Council.
2. The authorisation referred to in paragraph 1 shall also specify the additional items of information that should be contained in the information notice pursuant to Section 13, with particular regard to the purposes sought and the results to be achieved also in connection with the unexpected information that may be made known on account of the processing as well as with the data subject's right to object to the processing on legitimate grounds.

[55]See Garante per la protezione dei dati personali. General authorisation no. 2/2005 concerning the processing of data suitable for disclosing health and sex life, which expressly refers (point 1.4) to authorisation no. 2/2002 (point 2, letter b)).

[56]In General Authorisation nº 2/98 the Garante have already regulated the processing of genetic data. Monducci, Juri; Pasetti, Giulia. Il trattamento dei dati sanitari e genetici. In Monducci, Juri; Sartor, Giovanni (editors). Op. cit. P. 275. "Prima del D.Lgs. 135/99 il Garante, nell'autorizzazione generale n. 2/98, aveva già consentito il trattamento dei dati genetici solo agli esercenti le professioni sanitarie, agli organismi sanitari pubblici e privati, alle organizzazione di volontariato, nonché a soggetti pubblici e privati per finalità di ricerca scientifica; e, sulla scorta dei pericoli connessi, aveva espressamente vietato il loro trattamento, oltre che alle comunità di recupero e di accoglienza, alle case di cura e di riposo e alle organizzazioni religiose, ad ogni soggetto che volesse procedervi per finalità contrattuali, precontrattuali o per l'attività sportiva."

[57]Such authorisation was again replaced, keeping the same wording, by a new one adopted on 13 December 2012.

[58]Garante per la protezione dei dati personali. Autorizzazione generale al trattamento dei dati genetici—24 giugno 2011. Available at http://www.garanteprivacy.it/garante/doc.jsp?ID=1822650. Accessed 8 August 2011.

In this provision the Garante defines 'genetic data' as "any data that, regardless of its type, concerns an individual's genotypic characteristics, or the pattern of inheritance of such characteristics within a related group of individuals"[59] and 'genetic test' as "the analysis, for clinical purposes, of a specific gene, or of a product and/or function thereof or of other DNA constituents and/or a chromosome, in order to carry out a diagnosis or confirm a clinical suspicion in an individual already affected by disease (diagnostic test), or else in order to detect or rule out a mutation associated with a genetic disease that might develop in a healthy individual (presymptomatic test), or in order to assess an individual's liability to develop common diseases (predictive test)".[60]

The authorisation also states that any other processing operations of genetic data that are not explicitly permitted in its text are considered unlawful, especially the operations concerning "employers' activities" and the activities of insurance companies.[61] It is clear from the analysis of the above-mentioned general authorisation that the processing of genetic data cannot be performed either by employers or insurance companies,[62] or by banks, public registers or credit bureaus. The former have a specific provision excluding them,[63] and the latter are not included in the scope of the authorisation as sectors to which an authorisation for the processing should be granted.[64]

---

[59]Some authors criticise the definition adopted by the Garante, saying that it would have been better to adopt the definition used by Recommendation n° R(97)5 of Council of Europe. In that sense, see Bianca, Cesare Massimo; Busnelli, Francesco Donato. Op. cit. P. 1355. "(. . .) ciò suggerirebbe di privilegiare la definizione di dato genetico che si ricava alla raccomandazione che, in quanto più articolata e, quindi, più efficace del bene protetto."

[60]The General Authorisation presents many other definitions, such as 'biological sample', 'pharmacogenetic test', 'individual variability test', 'genetic screening', 'genetic counselling' and 'genetic information'. See Article 1 of the General Authorisation for the Processing of Genetic Data. Op. cit.

[61]"Whereas any other processing operations concerning genetic data that are not referred to herein shall be regarded as unlawful except for those mentioned above, including employers' activities aimed at establishing employees' and/or job candidates' professional eligibility, irrespective of whether such activities are grounded on the data subjects' consent, and the activities carried out by insurance companies" (Recital of the General Authorisation for the Processing of Genetic Data).

[62]"L'authority di vigilanza avverte, però, che una <<personalizzazione esasperata della costruzione tariffaria, conseguente all'accesso indiscriminato alle informazione fornite attraverso i testi genetici, potrebbe condurre alla quantificazione di livelli di premio talmente elevate da precludere la possibilità di usufruire della copertura assicurativa proprio a quei soggetti che più necessitano di tale servizio>>, stravolgendo la logica tipica dell'assicurazione che vuole che il rischio sia ripartito su una platea larga di soggetti." Ibid. P. 1153.

[63]"Considerato che, fuori dei casi appena indicati, ulteriori trattamenti di dati genetici non ricompresi nella presente autorizzazione non risultano allo stato leciti, anche in riferimento all'attività dei datori di lavoro volta a determinare l'attitudine professionale di lavoratori o di candidati all'instaurazione di un rapporto di lavoro, anche se basata sul consenso dell'interessato, nonché all'attività delle imprese di assicurazione." Last recital of the General Authorisation for the Processing of Genetic Data. Op. cit.

[64]Article 2 (a) to (h).

Moreover, the authorisation establishes: (a) purposes of the processing; (b) processing mechanisms—which include collection, storage and security measures—; (c) information notices (genetic counselling and information activities); (d) consent; (e) processing operations in a specific sector; (f) retention of data and samples; (g) data communication and dissemination; and, (h) requests of authorisation.

Despite the fact that the authorisation deals with data and sample retention, it does not establish any specific time limit for this retention, saying only that it has to "be retained for no longer than is absolutely necessary to fulfil the obligations and/or discharge the tasks mentioned in point 3 hereof,[65] or else to pursue the purposes

---

[65]Point 3 of the General Authorisation for the Processing of Genetic Data establishes the purposes for which the processing of genetic data can be carried out:

"3. Purposes of the Processing

Such genetic data may be processed as are closely relevant to the purposes mentioned below, where they may not be achieved, on a case by case basis, by processing either anonymous data or personal data of a different nature:

(a) health care, with particular regard to genetic diseases, and protection of the data subject's genetic identity, with the data subject's consent, except for the provisions made in sections 26 and 82 of the Code for the case where a data subject is unable to provide his/her consent because legally incapable, physically impaired, or mentally disabled;
(b) health care, with particular regard to genetic diseases, and protection of the genetic identity of a third party belonging to the same genetic line as the data subject, where consent has not or may not be provided because of legal incapacity and/or physical impairment or mental disability; this shall apply to such genetic data as have already been collected, if the processing is indispensable to allow the third party in question to make informed reproductive choices or is justified by the availability of preventive care and/or treatment in respect of the said third party;
(c) scientific and statistical research with a view to protecting the community's health in the medical, biomedical and epidemiological sectors, providing that the availability of exclusively anonymous data on population samples does not allow the research purposes to be achieved, whereby the said research shall be carried out with the data subject's consent except for the statistical surveys and/or scientific researches provided for by law.

Within the framework of the purposes mentioned under a. and b. above, this authorisation shall also be granted exclusively for the purpose of allowing the authorised entities to fulfil specific obligations and/or ensure that such obligations are fulfilled, or to discharge specific tasks set out in Community legislation, laws and/or regulations with particular regard to public health and hygiene, prevention of occupational diseases, diagnosis and treatment including organ and tissue transplantation, rehabilitation from physical and mental disability and/or impairment, protection of mental health, and pharmaceutical assistance pursuant to the law. The processing operations may also concern the filling out of health records, certifications and other health care documents.

This authorisation shall also be granted if the processing of genetic data is indispensable:

(a) for defence counsel to carry out the investigations referred to in Act no. 397 of 7 December 2000, also by the agency of alternates, technical experts and/or authorised private detectives, or else to establish or defend a legal claim, whether related to a third party or not, also without the data subject's consent—except where the processing requires the performance of genetic tests. The foregoing provisions shall apply on condition the claim to be established or defended is not overridden by the data subject's one or consists in a personal right or another fundamental, inviolable right or freedom, and if the data are only processed for these purposes and for no longer than is absolutely necessary to achieve such purposes. The processing must be carried

referred to therein for which they were collected or subsequently used". Therefore, according to this provision the decision should be made by the data controller through case-by-case analysis. This does not appear to be the best solution, since the use of genetic data, as recognised not only in the general authorisation but also in many international documents to which the authorisation makes reference, represents a serious risk for discrimination.[66]

5.5 The Processing of Personal Data by the Case Studies

5.5.1 The Banking Sector

Banks, as already stated, process a huge amount of personal data in order to conduct their business. However, for the processing to be lawful and according to the data protection legislation, banks have to comply not only with the Italian Data Protection Code and the General Authorisations for the Processing of Sensitive or Judicial Data but also with the Code of conduct and professional practice applying to information systems managed by private entities with regard to consumer credit, reliability, and timeliness of payments.[67] Regarding the latter, the analysis will be made in the next section, when analysing the processing of personal data by

out in compliance with the general authorisations issued by the Garante for the processing of sensitive data by self-employed professionals and private detectives (authorisation no. 4/2005 and no. 6/2005, respectively). The processing may also concern the information related to medical history and/or the data subject's family members.

(b) To fulfil specific obligations or ensure that specific obligations are fulfilled, or to discharge specific tasks as set out expressly in Community instruments, laws and/or regulations applying to social security and welfare, occupational and/or population safety and hygiene, also without the data subject's consent, in compliance with the limitations laid down in the Garante's general authorisation for the processing of sensitive data in the employment context (authorisation no. 1/2005) and without prejudice to the provisions contained in the code of practice referred to in section 111 of the Code. The processing may also concern the information related to medical history and/or the data subject's family members.

(c) To establish consanguinity with a view to family reunion in respect of non-EU nationals, stateless persons, and refugees pursuant to legislative decree no. 286 of 25 July 1998. In particular, the processing of genetic data that is carried out in spite of the availability of alternative procedures entailing no processing of such data shall not be regarded as indispensable."

[66]"Negli Stati Uniti, infatti, si sono verificati casi in cui molte persone hanno deciso di non sottoporsi a test genetici, pur necessari per la tutela della loro salute, nel timore che le informazioni potessero giungere a conoscenza di datori di lavoro e assicuratori. Queste persone hanno compiuto una <<scelta tragica>>, al fine di evitare di perdere il posto di lavoro o la possibilità di stipulare un contratto di assicurazione, sacrificando cosi la propria salute." Panetta, Rocco. Op. cit. P. 1130.

[67]The Code of Conduct was subscribed by ABI—Associazione bancaria italiana, FEDERCASSE—Federazione italiana delle banche di credito cooperative, ASSOFIN—

credit information suppliers, which also applies to banks. As far as the General Authorisations are concerned, they are analysed in the section regarding the processing of sensitive data in the Italian System (5.4).

In addition to these rules, the Italian Data Protection Authority, based on the experience on complaints and questions, adopted on 25 October 2007 Guidelines for the Processing of Customers' Data in the Banking Sector,[68] aiming "at providing general guidance on the processing of customers' personal data performed by banks in order to ensure compliance with data protection principles under Italy's data protection Code."[69] Although these guidelines do not constitute a binding document, compliance with them will avoid the misapplication and misinterpretation of the data protection rules and principles, since they represent the official interpretation of the data protection authority.

The Guidelines are divided into five sections: (1) Foreword (purpose and scope); (2) Compliance with Personal Data Protection Principles; (3) Communicating Personal Data Protection Rules and Banking Secrecy; (4) Safeguarding the Bank's interests; and, (5) Exercise of the Rights Set out in Section 7 of the Data Protection Code (Access, Rectification, etc.).

The purpose of the guidelines is providing guidance to the banking sector. However, the document applies not only to banks but also to "the corresponding activities carried out by the post office (...) insofar as they are compatible with specific sector-related features".[70] Concerning compliance with data protection principles, the guidelines point out that only personal data that are relevant and not excessive may be processed by banks for lawful purposes.[71]

Associazione italiana del credito al consumo e immobiliare and ASSILEA—Associazione italiana leasing, which are the trade associations of the financial sector in Italy.

[68]Available at http://www.garanteprivacy.it/garante/doc.jsp?ID=1478096. Accessed 27 January 2010.

[69]See item 1.1.

[70]See items 1.1 and 1.2.

[71]The Guidelines present the main requirements the Italian Data Protection Code imposes to banks for the processing to be lawful. According to the Guidelines "the data protection Code requires the data to be processed:

only by the persons in charge of the processing (and/or the data processors, where appointed) within the framework of the authority conferred on them;

in compliance with data minimization and data quality principles as regards data accuracy and updating (sections 3 and 11);

by informing data subjects appropriately beforehand;

by only requesting the data subjects' consent if no other precondition for the processing can be fulfilled by having also regard to the nature of the data (sections 23, 24, 26, and 43);

in compliance with the requirements laid down in the (general) authorisations issued by the Garante as for sensitive or judicial data (sections 26 and 27);

by taking suitable security measures in order to prevent certain events (in particular, unauthorised accesses and/or use of the data), for which a bank might be regarded as liable under both civil and criminal law (sections 15, 31 et seq., 167, and 169)."

Still regarding the lawfulness of the processing, the Guidelines analyse some specific issues of relevant importance: (a) customer identifying information; (b) phone based-services and recorded calls; and, (c) payments performed via direct debiting (RID). With regard to customer information, banks have the onus to require the identity card of the customers and, in some situations, to photocopy this document, in order to confirm the identity of a specific person. The Garante considers that in these situations, "since the data are processed pursuant to legal requirements and/or to fulfil contractual obligations and/or comply with specific requests made by the customers", the processing is legitimate.[72] Nevertheless, banks have to inform their customers about the processing which will be conducted "at least once for all". In a decision of 27 October 2005, the Garante defined the criteria to be followed in order to verify whether it is necessary to identify the customer and to photocopy his/her ID.[73]

Moving to phone based-services and recorded calls, it is common practice in the banking sector to record the content of the calls when receiving orders or instructions from customers. In this case, the bank has to inform its customers about the recording, according to article 13 of the Codice, "either when stipulating the relevant contract or at the onset of the first phone call."[74] Moreover, "The recordings and such personal data as are related thereto, where stored, are to be secured via measures aimed at preventing them from being accessed, modified or used by unauthorised entities" and the contents of conversations "may not be stored for longer than is necessary to achieve the purposes of the recording."[75]

In relation to payments performed via direct debit, the Garante calls attention to the need to establish appropriate controls in order to allow the payer's bank, in cooperation with the creditor's bank, to check—beforehand—whether there is any mismatch or inaccuracy in the data informed by its customer. This would allow them, when necessary, to contact the respective customer "before the direct debt instruction is performed in order to ensure that the data are accurate and prevent debiting an account that is not the one specified by the payer."[76]

The third section of the Guidelines deals with communication of personal data to third parties, which, considering its importance, will be discussed in more detail in a specific subsection (5.5.1.1).

The guidelines also deal with 'cheque clearance', which is the procedure where banks verify whether there are sufficient funds available to debit the amount of the

[72]See item 2.2, last paragraph.

[73]See Garante per la protezione dei dati personali. Quando identificare e fotocopiare i documenti di riconoscimento dei clienti. Available at http://www.garanteprivacy.it/garante/doc.jsp?ID=1189435. Accessed 27 January 2010.

[74]See item 2.3.

[75]The Garante also highlights the right of access of data subjects regarding the content of the recordings. See item 2.3, last paragraph.

[76]Item 2.4, last paragraph.

cheque to the drawer's account,[77] and with the sale of banking offices.[78] Regarding the former, there is no important issue, since banks will have to fully comply with data protection rules and principles—especially data minimisation, data quality, proportionality and finality principles—and also with the information notices made available to their customers.

Moreover, the Guidelines point out that banks have the right to process personal data in order to safeguard their interests in judicial proceedings involving their customers. Nonetheless, only data that are relevant for the defence of the bank or for establishing judicial proceedings can be processed.[79]

Furthermore, the guidelines address data subjects' rights, in particular the right of access, both to personal information and to third parties' data. As a general rule, all kinds of personal information processed under the bank-customer relationship, including recorded calls, are covered by the right of access. It is important to notice that this right of access, according to the Data Protection Code, is to be exercised free of charge, unless "an especially considerable effort is required on account of the complexity and/or scope of the request."[80] A distinction is made between the exercise of the right of access to personal information and the right to access banking documents (regulated under Section 118 Consolidated Banking Statute). The latter, distinct from the former, gives to individuals—subject to the payment of a fee—"the right to obtain a copy of banking documents and instruments regardless of whether they contain personal data to the data subject". Data related to third parties can, according to the Consolidate Banking Statute, be disclosed to the specific customer if contained in the documents requested.

Finally, in terms of access to personal data related to a deceased person, as discussed in item 5.2 above, such right can be exercised by "anyone with a vested interest therein, or else acting to protect the data subject, or else on account of family-related reasons deserving to be upheld", who will have access to personal data related only to the deceased person.[81]

---

[77]See item 3.4.

[78]This processing will be analysed in the next topic (5.5.1.1).

[79]"This means that, for instance, it is unnecessary to produce the whole bank statements containing personal data (relating e.g. to third parties) that are irrelevant for the purpose of defending the claim in question" (item 4, 3rd paragraph).

[80]Article 10(7) states that a fee can be charged if it is not confirmed that personal data concerning the data subject exist in the 'hands' of the controller.

[81]"For instance, it is not allowed to communicate the name of the payee of the balance of the deceased person's account because this information does not relate to the deceased consumer, but to a third party—of course this does not apply if the account was held jointly by the applicant for access and the deceased person. By the same token, it is not permitted to grant a request for access to the personal data relating to a deceased person if the request is aimed at becoming apprised specifically of the name of the person deceased had entrusted with performing certain banking transactions" (Item 5.3, last paragraph).

5.5.1.1 Communication of Personal Information (to Third Parties)

According to the Italian Data Protection Code, the communication of customer's data to third parties is permitted only if two requirements are fulfilled: the customer gave his consent or if one of the conditions set up by article 24 of the Codice for the processing of data without the consent of the subject are met.[82] Based on these conditions, the Guidelines divide the analysis of communication of personal data to third parties into unauthorised (meaning impermissible or illegal) and authorised or required communication. The former lists the situations where data would be illegally communicated. Examples of the latter cases include a person receiving a document concerning the spouse, a family member who received a call intended for a given consumer,[83] professionals and/or other entities having contact with the data subject on account of employment relations and so on.[84] In those cases, the bank will be under civil and criminal liability under articles 15 and 167 of the Italian Data Protection Code.

Regarding the authorised (or required) communication of personal data, the Guidelines distinguish in particular the following: (1) personal data to the Centrale d'allarme Interbancaria (Bank Alert System); (2) cheque clearance; and (3) the

[82]"Except where the data are communicated because this is instrumental to the activities requested and/or the services provided—in which case the data subject's consent is unnecessary under section 24(1)b, of the DP Code—banks and the staff in charge of performing banking operations must keep confidential all the data at issue" (item 3.1, 2nd paragraph).

[83]In a case where the father of a bank account holder was contacted by the municipal police regarding the debit of his son with the bank the Garante considered that there was a violation of the Data Protection Code and a consequent unlawful communication of personal data. See Garante per la protezione dei dati personali. Opinion of 28 May 2009 (Dati bancari: illecita comunicazione). Available at http://www.garanteprivacy.it/garante/doc.jsp?ID=1624734. Accessed 27 January 2010. "VISTO il reclamo pervenuto in data 16 gennaio 2008, con cui XY, rappresentato dall'avv. Conte, ha lamentato l'illecita comunicazione al padre WZ, di informazioni bancarie a sé riferite da parte della filiale di KW di Intesa SanPaolo. Tale comunicazione sarebbe avvenuta il 16 agosto 2006 a seguito della convocazione di WZ presso l'istituto bancario—per il tramite della polizia municipale del comune di residenza –, il quale, "messo a conoscenza di una grave situazione debitoria in capo al figlio, con tanto di indicazioni di cifre di scoperto e del dettaglio di tutti i movimenti del CC in oggetto", provvedeva a pagare i titoli in scadenza (cfr. reclamo, p. 2) (...) RILEVATO che alla luce della documentazione in atti e delle dichiarazioni rese dalle parti, ai sensi e per gli effetti di cui all'art. 168 del Codice, il comportamento tenuto dal personale della banca, ancorché i fatti si fossero svolti secondo la versione dalla stessa resa, ha determinato un trattamento di dati personali non conforme a correttezza (art. 11, comma 1 lett. a) del Codice) e che non risulta essere stato previamente autorizzato dall'interessato (art. 23 del Codice), ben potendo la banca, una volta acquisito il recapito telefonico ricercato, mettersi in contatto, in assenza del padre, con XY, informarlo circa la presentazione all'incasso dei titoli e delle conseguenze derivanti dal loro mancato pagamento e, quindi, rimettere ad un'autonoma scelta dello stesso le successive iniziative da assumere (cfr. Provv. 8 marzo 2007, in www.garanteprivacy.it, doc. web n. 1390910; Provv. 25 ottobre 2007, Linee guida per trattamenti dati relativi al rapporto banca-clientela, doc. web n. 1457247, punto 3.2);"

[84]See item 3.2.

transfer of customer's data in the case of the sale of banking offices.[85] The Guidelines recognise that the communication of customer's data without his/her consent is permitted when provided for by the law, as for example, for the purpose of anti-money laundering legislation, counter-terrorism legislation, child pornography legislation, legislation for the detection and countering of taxation offences, rules relating to the Centralised system for low-level risk assessment,[86] requests for access to bank documents according to the Consolidated Bank Act and communication to judicial authorities and creditors in connection with enforcement proceedings in compliance with the law. An example of this last situation is illustrated by a case in which a bank disclosed the number of a new bank account of one of its customers to his creditor, and the Garante considered that there was an unlawful processing and imposed some measures to be adopted by the bank in order to avoid future unlawful disclosure of personal data.[87] The guidelines also recognise the possibility of sending 'positive' personal information to credit bureaus in accordance with Resolution nº 9 of 16 November 2004.[88]

The other lawful communication of personal data to third parties without the consent of the data subject refers to the Bank Alert System, and is regulated by law. The interesting aspect here is the observation made by the Garante that efforts should be made in order to keep data accurate and complete, ' in particular with a view to preventing inclusion in the BAS of data related to identity theft victims; at all events data should be rectified and/or deleted timely, also following exercise of the

---

[85]This means the transfer of customer's data to the new owner of the Bank.

[86]The Centralised system for low-level risk assessment will be analysed in topic 3.1.9.1.

[87]Garante per la protezione dei dati personali. Opinion of 23 July 2009 (Dati bancari: accesso non autorizzato e misure di sicurezza). Available at http://www.garanteprivacy.it/garante/doc.jsp?ID=1640294. Accessed 27 January 2010. "In data 21 marzo 2007 veniva notificato alla segnalante un pignoramento presso terzi sul nuovo conto corrente. Non potendo, a detta della segnalante, il creditore oppignorante essere a conoscenza dell'esistenza del nuovo conto corrente, tale informazione sarebbe stata frutto di 'una violazione della privacy da parte degli addetti alla filiale di Pomigliano D'Arco del San Paolo Banco di Napoli S.p.A., unici che hanno potuto fornire [al creditore] le notizie di cui si è avvalso per la notificazione del precisato atto' (cfr. segnalazione cit.). (. . .) ritenuto illecito il trattamento di dati personali effettuato presso Banco di Napoli S.p.A. da un proprio incaricato (punto 3), ai sensi dell'art. 154, comma 1, lett. c), del Codice, prescrive a Banco di Napoli S.p.A. di adottare, immediatamente e comunque non oltre il 30 settembre 2009, idonee misure organizzative e idonee misure di sicurezza tese sia a garantire la scrupolosa vigilanza sull'operato degli incaricati, sia a sensibilizzare gli stessi incaricati al rispetto delle istruzioni ricevute in occasione di iniziative formative (prescritte dalla regola 19.6 dell'Allegato B) al Codice) (punto 3)".

[88]"With regard to the processing of personal data, including data related to credit relationships evolving "flawlessly" [positive information], the private entities managing the aforementioned information systems must obtain the data subjects' free, informed consent—possibly by the agency of the participating entities -, which must be given specifically in connection with the individual processing operations pursuant to both the Code (Section 23) and the aforementioned code of conduct and professional practice. Available at http://www.garanteprivacy.it/garante/doc.jsp?ID=1671380. Accessed 27 January 2010.

data subject's rights of access", i.e., even if there is a legal authorisation/requirement for the transfer of personal data, the processing has to comply with data protection principles.[89]

Finally, still with regard to the sale of banking offices (involving transfer of personal data of the clients) the Garante affirmed that in this case there is "an exemption from the obligation for the assignee bank to provide information notices to the customers concerned". In the Garante's opinion, banks can make use of the simplified arrangements set up in section 58 of the Consolidated Bank Statute to make customers aware of the processing of their personal data which is being carried out.

5.5.2 The Credit Information Suppliers

There are two different types of credit information suppliers in Italy: (1) Public Registers[90]; and, (2) Credit Bureaus.[91] The databases controlled by them will be analysed in the following sub-sections.

---

[89]See item 3.3,

[90]JENTZSCH, Nicola. Op. cit. P. 84. "Italy: The country has a public credit registry at the central bank, which was established in 1962 as a Central Credit Register (Centrale dei Rischi) with a focus on monitoring systemic risk. There is a high threshold of 77.500 Euro. It registers bank loans and informs participants about the aggregate indebtedness (Banca d'Italia 2005). But there are other information sharing mechanisms in the country: Centrale Rischi Finanziaria (CRIF) and Consorzio per la Tutela del Credito (CTC). Whereas CRIF is a for-profit institution, CTC is non-profit and collects only negative information. Otherwise, the Italian system is one of positive and negative information sharing. CRIF connects 440 financial institutions (CRIF 2005) and manages over 30 million credit files. The company has expanded European-wide in the 1990s and has even entered the U.S. market. Across the Atlantic, in Mexico, it pairs up with the TransUnion. CTC is a creation of the association of Italian financial service providers, particular car finance. The database is more focused on non-banking institutions, whereas CRIF focuses on the banking industry. A third player in the market is Experian Information Services S.p.a. in Rome—this credit bureau of Experian in Italy was founded in 1995. In 2004, the company acquired 100% ownership of Equifax Italy SRL. The latter was founded in 2000 when Equifax acquired the company SEK but then exited the market as the competition apparently made it unattractive." There is another type of "credit supplier" in Italy, that is something "in between" the public register and the credit bureau, that is the controller of the "Sistema centralizzato di rivelavazione dei rischi di importo contenuto" (Centralised system for low-level risk assessment). This system, that is controlled by Interbancaria per l'Automazione (SAI-SSB) S.p.A., however, is being incorporated by the Centralised risk service managed by the Italian Central Bank, according to Decree n. 374 of 22 September 2008 of the Minister of Economy and Finance.

[91]Credit Reference Agency, Credit Reporting Agency or Firm and Credit Registry are synonyms of Credit Bureau. See Ferretti, Federico. Op. cit. P. 3.

5.5.2.1 Public Registers

In relation to credit information, the public register[92] in Italy is the Italian Central Bank (Banca d'Italia), which manages a centralised risk service called "Centrale dei Rischi" (Centralised Risk Database).[93] The objective of this database is to make available to the participants (banks and other financial institutions) useful information for credit risk analysis and management, and such information can only be used for these purposes and for a legal claim defence.[94] This database is not regulated by the Code of Conduct of the private credit information suppliers (Recital n. 6 of the Code of Conduct) but by Circolare n. 139 of 11 February 1991[95] and by Deliberazione of 29 March 1994.[96] However, the Italian Data Protection Code has full application also to this database.

Data subjects have the right to access the information stored in this database and can exercise their right by presenting a request to the financial institution with which

---

[92]Ferretti, Federico. Op. Cit. P. 4.

[93]There is another centralised database managed by the Italian Central Bank, called "Centrale d'allarme interbancaria" (Bank Alert System), regulated by Legislative decree no. 507/1999, which is a computerised register of bank cheques and postal orders as well as of debit cards. About the application of Data Protection rules to this "register" see Garante per la protezione dei dati personali. Guidelines for the Processing of Customers' Data in the Banking Sector—25 October 2007—As published in Italy's Official Journal no. 273 dated 23 November 2007. Item 3.4. Available at http://www.garanteprivacy.it/garante/doc.jsp?ID=1478096. Accessed 29 March 2009. "Based on the cases addressed by the Garante, it appears that the entities reporting information to the BAS should take special care in establishing whether the personal data at issue are accurate and complete, in particular with a view to preventing inclusion in the BAS of data related to identity theft victims; at all events, the data should be rectified and/or deleted timely, also following exercise of the data subjects' rights of access. The same applies to the individuals correctly reporting theft and/or loss of cheques, who at times are the subject of alerts entered because those cheques have been used unlawfully (e.g. in the case of bounced cheques, or cheques issued without authorisation, etc.).

The entities entering alerts in the BAS should process the data lawfully, i.e. in compliance with the sector-specific legislation applying to the register, as well as fairly (pursuant to section 11(1) a of the DP Code).

It should be pointed out that alerts may also be entered lawfully if a cheque is "withdrawn" by the negotiating bank, since the offence is committed at the time the cheque is issued if the cheque was issued without authorisation, whilst it is committed at the time the cheque is presented for payment in the case of cheque bouncing.

As regards bounced cheques, it should be recalled that no alerts may be entered in the BAS if the debtor timely complies with the requirements listed in section 8 of the relevant Act (386/1990). Additionally, an alert concerning the drawer/maker may not be entered if the bank preferring the information failed to send out a withdrawal notice beforehand, given that an alert may only be entered after at least 10 days from the receipt of the said notice."

[94]Section 1, items 2 and 3 of Circolare n. 139.

[95]These regulations are in accordance with Legislative Decree n. 385 of 1 September 1993 (Testo unico bancario) that is the general rule for the whole banking and financial system in Italy.

[96]There is also another system called "Centrale di Allarme Interbancaria", which stores information about drawers of cheques emitted without authorization or funds. See http://www.bancaditalia.it/sispaga/servpag/cai/info_norma/foglio_informativo.pdf. Accessed 3 November 2010.

they have a credit relationship, which will have to render a notice to data subjects (or to their representatives) of the total and partial position of risk that identifies from the informative flows received from the Banca d'Italia and of joint bank accounts which they possess. If they want to have access to information concerning all financial institutions that included information about themselves and to all credit co-obligations different from joint accounts, they have to address a request to the office of the Italian Central Bank where they have their residence.[97]

The participants have to update information they send to the 'Centrale dei rischi' on a monthly basis and, if any debt is remedied, they have to send this information to the database within 3 days of the payment of the debt.[98] Concerning the other data subjects' rights, such as rectification, erasure and blocking, the request has to be sent to the financial institution that sent the respective personal data to the Centrale dei rischi,[99] despite the fact that the Banca d'Italia is the controller of this database.[100]

Furthermore, Circolare n. 139 establishes that only information concerning credit transactions of more than 30.000€ can be registered at the Centrale dei Rischi.[101] However, with the incorporation of the 'Sistema centralizzato di rivelavazione dei rischi di importo contenuto' (Centralised system for low-level risk assessment) by the Centrale dei rischi, it will also process information related to low-level risks and not only to risks over 30.000€.[102] It is also important to note that this database processes both positive and negative data.

Until recently the Italian Central Bank was not considered liable for damages regarding information of data subjects stored in its Centralised Risk Database. Nevertheless, in a recent ruling, the Italian Supreme Court of Cassation (Corte Suprema di Cassazione) considered that the Italian Data Protection code applies to the Italian Central Bank and that it is therefore liable both for the rectification or erasure of erroneous data and for civil damages as a consequence of a fault of one of its employees in the receipt or processing of personal data.[103]

---

[97] Section 1, item 3 of the Circolare.

[98] Section 2, item 5 of the Circolare. The period of data retention, however, is not clearly defined in the Circolare n. 139, which establishes some limits for the access to information by banks and financial institutions, without defining a specific time-limit for storage personal information (See Section 1, item 9.1).

[99] Section 2, item 5 of the Circolare.

[100] Garante per la protezione dei dati personali. Provvedimento del 19 dicembre 2008. Available at http://www.garanteprivacy.it/garante/doc.jsp?ID=1582849. Accessed 29 March 2009.

[101] Chapter 2, Sect. 2.1, item 5.

[102] See Decree n. 374 of 22 September 2008 of the Italian Minister of Economy and Finance.

[103] Corte Suprema di Cassazione Italiana. Prima Sezione. Sentenza n. 7958 de 1° aprile 2009. Available at http://www.cortedicassazione.it/Notizie/GiurisprudenzaCivile/SezioniUnite/SchedaNews.asp?ID=2442. Accessed 22 January 2010. "Dall'esame del complesso delle norme innazi richiamate si trae, dunque, Il convincimento che la Banca d'Italia, in relazione al trattamento dei dati personali effetuato dalla Centrale Rischi, non è estranea all'applicazione del codice in esame, essendo esclusi soltanto alcuni rimedi altrimenti a disposizione dell'interessato (...), mentre resta applicabile, ovviamente, la tutela giurisdizionale (...). Peraltro, che la Banca d'Italia non possa sottrarsi alla disciplina comune in tema di responsabilità civile nel tratamento dei dati discende

Finally, it is important to highlight that, although the court recognised the submission of the Central Bank to data protection rules and its liability for damages as a consequence of the misuse and misprocessing of personal data, the court also confirmed the view adopted by the Italian Data Protection Authority that there is no possibility of lodging a complaint to the Garante[104] against Banca d'Italia[105] according to article 8(2)(d) of the Italian Data Protection Code.[106]

5.5.2.2 Credit Bureaus

This kind of credit information suppliers—which is controlled by private entities[107]—is regulated by the Codice, which states in its article 117 that the Garante should encourage the adoption of a code of conduct for the processing of personal data carried out by these institutions.[108]

---

dall'ovvia considerazione che, per errore di uno degli 'incaricati' (definiti come <<Le persone fisiche autorizzate a compiere operazioni di trattamento dal titolare o dal responsabile>>), la segnalazione da parte del responsabile potrebbe essere recepita e trattata in modo non corretto."

[104]Garante per la Protezione dei Dati Personali. Provvedimento Del 26 luglio 2006. Available at http://www.garanteprivacy.it/garante/doc.jsp?ID=1332498. Accessed 22 January 2010. "RITENUTO che il ricorso è inammissibile nei confronti della Banca d'Italia in quanto il trattamento dei dati effettuato da tale Istituto per la gestione della predetta Centrale dei rischi rientra tra quelli rispetto ai quali, ai sensi dell'art. 8, comma 2, lett. d), del Codice, non possono essere esercitati i diritti di cui all'art. 7, né può essere proposto ricorso al Garante al sensi dell'art. 145 del Codice".

[105]Corte Suprema di Cassazione Italiana. Prima Sezione. Sentenza n. 7953 de 1° aprile 2009. "Si che appare tutto irrilevante la pronuncia del Garante richiamata dalla Banca d'Italia in sede di memória, con la quale è stato ritenuto inammissibile Il ricorso nei confronti della Banca d'Italia <<in quanto il trattamento dei dati effettuato da tale Istituto per la gestione della Centrale dei rischi rientra tra quelli rispetto ai quali, ai sensi dell'art. 8, comma 2, lett. d), del Codice, non possono essere esercitati i diritti di cui all'art. 7, ne può essere proposto ricorso al Garante ai sensi dell'art. 145 del Codice>>."

[106]Article 8 (Exercise of Rights)

2. The rights referred to in Section 7 may not be exercised by making a request to the data controller or processor, or else by lodging a complaint in pursuance of Section 145, if the personal data are processed:

d) by a public body other than a profit-seeking public body, where this is expressly required by a law for purposes exclusively related to currency and financial policy, the system of payments, control of brokers and credit and financial markets and protection of their stability;

[107]Ferretti, Federico. Op. Cit. P. 4.

[108]Section 117—(Reliability and Timeliness in Payment-Related Matters)

1. The Garante shall encourage, pursuant to Section 12, adoption of a code of conduct and professional practice for the processing of personal data that is carried out within the framework of information systems owned by private entities, where they are used to grant consumer credits or else concern data subjects' reliability and timeliness in performing payments, by also laying down specific arrangements to facilitate communication of accurate, up-to-date personal data in compliance with data subjects' rights.

After significant debate involving all interested parties (consumers, financial institutions and credit information suppliers), the code of conduct was approved and included in Annex A.5 of the Codice, putting an end to the discussion about the veracity of these databases.[109] I will analyse here some provisions of the code of conduct to demonstrate that it supplements the law according to the specifics of the processing. As will be seen in the following paragraphs, the Code of Conduct establishes the recipients of information, the kinds of information that can be stored, the storage limits, the purposes of the collections, and rules regarding data subjects' rights and sanctions.[110]

According to the Code of Conduct, credit bureaus can contain "in particular: (1) negative credit information, only concerning credit relationships affected by defaults; and, (2) positive and negative credit information concerning credit applications/relationships irrespective of the existence of defaults as recorded in the system at the time they occurred".[111] Furthermore, "Banks, financial brokers and any other private entity that, in exercise of commercial and/or professional activities, grants an extension for the payment related to the supply of goods and/or services",[112] called by the Code as "participants", can have access to the information stored in such databases.[113] Nonetheless, personal data can only be processed by the controller and participants "for the purpose of protecting credit and limiting the relevant risks, and in particular, to assess data subjects' financial status and creditworthiness or anyhow their reliability and timeliness of payment" and, in any case, they cannot access data "in a manner allowing bulk queries and/or acquisition of lists of data regarding credit applications/relationships in respect to entities other than those applying for and/or participating in a credit relationship with the relevant participant".[114] Therefore, in line with the finality principle already discussed in Chap. 1 (Sect. 1.3.1.1), the access

[109]"Mentre le centrali rischi pubbliche travano la loro regulamentazione nel <<Texto Unico Banche>>, nelle delibere del Comitato interministeriale per il credito e il risparmio e nelle circolare della Banca d'Italia, quelle private difettavano, prima dell'adozione del Codice, di una disciplina vincolante, tanto da generare numerosi contenziosi davanti al Garante." Cuffaro, Vincenzo et al. (editors). Op. cit. P. 834.

[110]"Si tratta di un sistema che si sviluppa attraverso differenti livelli. Un primo livello è rimesso all'operatività dei principi generali che regolano ogni tipologia di trattamento e che qui vengono oppontamente specificati; un secondo livello è legato alla selezione ed individuazione dei dati che possono essere trattati; un terzo livello riguarda le regole attinenti alla raccolta, alla registrazione ed all'utilizzazione dei dai; un quarto livello concerne i diritti dell'interessato; un ulteriore riguarda le misure sanzionatorie." Panetta, Rocco. Op. cit. P. 1857.

[111]Article 1(c) (1) and (2).

[112]Article 1(e) (1), (2) and (3).

[113]"Furthermore, it shall not be allowed for third parties to access a credit information system except for the requests made by judicial and police authorities for purposes of justice, or else by other public institutions, authorities, administrative agencies and bodies exclusively in the cases referred to in laws, regulations and/or Community legislation as well as in compliance with the relevant provisions." (Article 7(4)).

[114]Article 7(3).

to personal data has to be linked to a specific provision of credit by the recipient of such information (participant) to the respective data subject.[115]

In what concerns the kinds of personal data to be processed, only objective personal data related to a credit application/relationship reported to a credit information system can be processed[116]; any processing of sensitive or judicial data is expressly forbidden.[117]

---

[115]Ferretti, Federico. Op. Cit. P. 215. "(...) the new Law [code of conduct] sets out the limits to the use of consumer credit data, providing that they may only be processed for the purpose of protecting credit and limiting the risks of non-repayment by assessing the financial status of the data subjects and their creditworthiness. No other purposes may be pursued, especially in connection with marketing activities and/or promotion, advertising and/or direct selling of products or services."

[116]Article 3(2).

[117]Concerning the processing of data from public sources, see Article 10 of the Code of Conduct and the observations of the Garante in its "Relazione 2007":

Article 10 (Processing Data from Public Sources)

1. If the manager of a credit information system processes, whether directly or by the agency of subsidiary and/or related companies, personal data from public registers, lists, records or publicly available documents, in whatever manner, or if it provides participants with services to access the data from said sources, manager and participants shall be responsible for ensuring compliance with the principles reported below subject to the limitations and arrangements set out in the law as for availability and publicity of the data in question as well as to the provisions referred to in Section 61(1) of the Code:

(a) the personal data from public registers, lists, records or publicly available documents, if recorded, must be contained in personal data banks that are separate from and not connected with the credit information system;
(b) if a participant accesses personal data contained both in a credit information system and in any of the data banks referred to in letter a), the manager shall take suitable technical and organisational measures to ensure that the data from the credit information system can be separated and distinguished from those originating from other data banks, also by adding appropriate notices, so as to do away with any and all ambiguities as to the different nature and sources of the accessed data;
(c) if a credit application is not granted, the participant shall inform the data subject as to whether it has also consulted negative data contained in the data banks as per letter a) in order to investigate the credit application, and it shall specify the public source(s) of said data at the data subject's request.

Relazione 2007—16 luglio 2008—Parte II—L'atività del Garante

"17.6. Brevi cenni sulla casistica

(...) Negli ultimi mesi, peraltro, diversi provvedimenti hanno riguardato non l'archivio *del sic* propriamente ditto, ma quegli ulteriori e distinti archive dove gli operatori del settore conservano altri tipi di informazioni, quale le banche dati contenenti le informazioni ricavate dai tribunali e dai registri immobiliari. Si tratta di dati tratti da pubbl chi registri che, in via generali, possono essere utilizzati senza il consenso degli interessati. Sono informazioni cui non si applica il codice di deontologia previsto per il settore del credito al consume, avendo la legge previsto la redazione dello specifico codice deontologico di cui all'art. 61 del Codice.

Nei casi sottoposto all'esame dell'Autorità sono emersi, in particolare, profile connessi alla completezza ed esattezza dele informazioni rese disponibili. Ciò, con particolare riferimento all'utilizzo di espressioni (quali "atto colpito da annotamento") che, in presenza dell'intervenuta cancellazione di un'ipoteca, risultavano equivoche e fuorvianti (v., fra gli altri, Provv. 21 febbraio 2008 [doc. web n. 1501246]). L'attenzione alla qualità dei dati ha, del resto, un ruolo fondamentale nella realtà economica contemporanea atteso che le informazione

Regarding the availability of the information stored, the Code makes a distinction between "negative credit information systems" and "positive and negative credit information systems".[118] The former can make available the information "after 120 days as of the relevant payment deadlines or in case the debtor defaulted on at least four monthly instalments and these were not remedied"[119] and the latter can make available the information related to consumers[120] "after 6 months of the monthly update referred to in paragraph 8,[121] or in case he/she defaulted on at least two consecutive monthly instalments, or if the delay has to do with either the last or the last but one instalment." In the second case referred to, "the data shall be made available after the monthly update concerning the second consecutive default."[122] In other situations, the data can be made available "after at least 30 days following the monthly update referred to in paragraph 8, or in case the debtor defaults on one instalment."[123]

It is important to notice that in case of payment delays the participants have to notify their clients (data subjects) that their data will be recorded in credit information databases and that such information can only be made available to the other participants after 15 days from this notification.[124] Moreover, when a credit application is not granted, the participants have to inform data subjects whether they consulted personal data related to negative credit information in one or more bureaus, providing them with all the details concerning the system, the source of information and the controller.[125]

---

inesatte o incomplete possono rappresentare in maniera distorta l'identità e, in particolare, il profile impreditoriale degli interessati." Available at http://www.garanteprivacy.it/garante/doc.jsp?ID=1549689. Accessed 21 January 2009.

[118]International Finance Corporation (IFC)—World Bank Group. Op. cit. P. 12. "A report that includes positive information allows the lender to more accurately assess the creditworthiness of a borrower. A database with negative-only information, excludes high-risk borrowers that have accumulated significant debt exposure without yet defaulting on any loans. In such instances, even a small shock to the borrower's income could lead to cascading defaults on all of the accounts."

[119]Article 4(6) (a).

[120]"consumer" shall mean a natural person who, in connection with a credit application/relationship, acts for purposes that cannot be related to his/her professional and/or business activity, if any (Article 1(f) of the Code of Conduct.

[121]8. Subject to the provisions made in paragraph 6, the data recorded in a credit information system shall be updated regularly at monthly intervals by the participant that has communicated them.

[122]Article 4(6) (b)1.

[123]Article 4(6) (a).

[124]Article 4(7).

[125]Article 5(6).

Another important issue relates to data retention periods.[126] Article 6 establishes the rules concerning data retention. Data related to credit applications can be stored for 120 days, from the day of the submission of the application, or if the credit application is not granted or is waived, it can be stored for no longer than 30 days as of the monthly update. Negative credit information related to payment delays that are remedied may be retained for up to 12 months, if it relates to delays not in excess of two instalments/months, and up to 24 months if it relates to delays in excess of two instalments/months. Negative credit information related to defaults that are not remedied can be retained for 36 months subsequent to the expiry of the contractual agreement.[127] In turn, positive credit information related to a relationship that was concluded by extinguishing all monetary obligations can be stored for no longer than 24 months as of the date of termination and/or expiry of the contractual agreement, or else as of the first update performed in the month following the aforementioned dates.[128]

Also important is the so-called "Automated Credit Scoring Techniques and Systems". Article 9 establishes the criteria for using such systems or techniques, which include: (a) the purposes of the "credit scoring"; (b) the addressees; (c) the updating of the statistic models and/or factors; and, (d) the duty to inform the data subject about the logic of the system and the data obtained through automated means.[129]

---

[126]Paragraph 9 of Article 6 states that "The provisions of this Article shall not apply to retention by a participant, for internal use, of contractual and/or accounting records containing the personal data related to a credit application/relationship."

[127]"(. . .) if other events occur that are material to the payment, said information may be retained for no longer than 36 months as of the date on which the information had last to be updated or the relevant relationship was terminated." (Article 6(5))

[128]"(. . .)In light of the requirement whereby the data should be complete in respect of the purposes to be achieved (see Section 11(1), letter d), of the Code), the aforementioned positive credit information may be retained further in the system if the latter contains negative credit information related to delays and/or defaults that have not been remedied with regard to other credit relationships concerning the same data subject. In the latter case, the positive credit information shall be removed from the system upon expiry of the term set out in paragraph 5 as to retention of the negative information recorded in the system in respect of any other credit relationships concerning said data subject." (Article 6(6)).

[129]Ferretti, Federico. Op. Cit. P. 220–221. "When the personal data contained in a credit information system are also processed by means of credit scoring techniques, both CRAs and lenders are made responsible for ensuring that:

(i) such techniques may solely be used for investigating a credit application and/or managing a credit relationship already set up;(. . .)
(ii) in the event credit is not granted, the relevant lender has to inform the applicant as to whether it has consulted or made use of credit scoring techniques. Upon express request of the consumer, then, the lender shall provide him/her with those same data and explain both the logic underlying the operation of the scoring system and the main factors that have been taken into account in processing the application."

Therefore, personal data can only be processed using "Automated Credit Scoring Techniques and Systems" for investigating a credit application and/or managing the credit relationships already set up, and the results of such processing can only be made available to the participant that received the credit application or that has a credit relationship with the respective data subject, which has to comply with his duty to inform the data subject if the credit application is not granted.[130]

Finally, and probably the most relevant issue concerning the Code of Conduct, is the section dealing with the sanctions for non-compliance with the rules provided for by this Code. Article 13 (7) recognises the competence of the Garante to "supervise over compliance with the provisions" of the Code of Conduct, "subject to the power provided for by the Code [Codice] concerning investigations and controls", without prejudice to the sanctions provided for by the Code of Conduct.[131] The powers conferred to the Garante, the fact that the Code of Conduct has to be "approved" by the Garante, and also its publication into Annex A of the Italian Data Protection Code, give to the Code of Conduct the status of a real source of law,[132] and not of a self-regulatory regime.

5.5.3 *The Insurance Industry*

Besides the general provisions that have full application to insurance activities, the Italian Codice has a specific provision concerning the insurance market. Article 120[133] recognises the database of losses related to the compulsory insurance

[130]See also Article 7(2)(c) of the Codice

Article 7 (Right to Access Personal Data and Other Rights)

2. A data subject shall have the right to be informed

c) of the logic applied to the processing, if the latter is carried out with the help of electronic means.

[131]See Article 12 of the Code of Conduct:

Article 12 (Sanctions)

1. Without prejudice to such sanctions as are provided for by the administrative, civil, and criminal laws in force, managers and participants shall jointly lay down, also by the agency of the associations underwriting this code, suitable mechanisms to impose sanctions that are proportionate to the seriousness of the relevant breaches, in particular as regards the trade associations underwriting this code as well as the body referred to in Article 13(7), after informing the Garante thereof. Such measures shall include an official warning, suspension or withdrawal of the authorisation to access the credit information system, and—in the most serious cases—publication of the news concerning the breach(es) in one or more dailies or magazines with nationwide circulation at the offender's expense.

[132]"Se il carattere giuridico di uma fonte trova sicura conferma nella coercibilità, oltre che nell'originalità delle regole poste, parebbe che quest'ultimo codice possa a tutti gli effetti essere considerato una fonte giuridica." Cuffaro, Vincenzo et al. Il codice dei trattamento dei dati personali. G. Giappichelli: Torino, 2007. P. 836.

[133]Article 120 (Car Accidents).

scheme for motor vehicles registered in Italy, and attributes to the Supervisory Authority of the insurance market—Istituto per la vigilanza sulle assicurazioni private e di interesse collettivo (ISVAP)—the powers "to lay down procedural and operational mechanisms."[134] This database aims at preventing and combating fraud in connection with the above-mentioned insurance scheme.[135] The Italian Private Insurance Code in its article 135[136] also recognises this database and the competence of ISVAP to regulate its use.

The ISVAP, through the use of its attributions and in cooperation with the Italian Data Protection Authority,[137] adopted Provision nº 2179 of 10 March 2003, which regulates procedural and operational mechanisms of the databank of losses on the

---

1. The Istituto per la vigilanza sulle assicurazioni private e di interesse collettivo (ISVAP) [Supervisory Body for Private Insurance] shall lay down procedural and operational mechanisms applying to the car accidents data bank that was set up to prevent and fight fraud in connection with the compulsory insurance for motor vehicles registered in Italy; further, the arrangements for accessing the information collected in said data bank as regards judicial authorities and public administrative agencies that are competent over prevention of and fight against fraud in the compulsory insurance sector as well as limitations on and arrangements for access to said information by insurance companies shall be set out.
2. Personal data may be processed and communicated to the entities referred to in paragraph 1 in order to discharge the tasks referred to in said paragraph.
3. To the matters that are not regulated by this Section there shall apply the provisions contained in Section 135 of the Private Insurance Code.

[134] Bravo, Fabio. Il trattamento dei dati nel settore bancario, finanziario ed assicurativo. In Monducci, Juri; Sartor, Giovanni (editors). Op. cit. P. 357. "Più rigoroso è stato l'approccio legislativo concernente il sistema informativo che attiene alla banca dati dell'ISVAP. Diversamente da quanto previsto per il sistema finanziario, in materia assicurativa la regolamentazione è stata fatta poggiare su di una fonte diversa, capace di garantire una maggior terzietà nel procedimento di formazione della norma."

[135] Such provision goes in the same direction of Recommendation Rec(2002) 9 of the CoE Committee of Ministers, on the protection of personal data collected and processed for insurance purposes.

[136] Art. 135. Banca dati sinistri

1. Allo scopo di rendere più efficace la prevenzione e il contrasto di comportamenti fraudolenti nel settore delle assicurazioni obbligatorie per i veicoli a motore immatricolati in Italia, è istituita presso l'ISVAP una banca dati dei sinistri ad essi relativi.
2. Le imprese sono tenute a comunicare i dati riguardanti i sinistri dei propri assicurati, secondo le modalità stabilite con regolamento adottato dall'ISVAP. I dati relativi alle imprese di assicurazione che operano nel territorio della Repubblica in regime di libera prestazione dei servizi o in regime di stabilimento sono richiesti dall'ISVAP alle rispettive autorità di vigilanza degli Stati membri interessati.
3. Le procedure di organizzazione e di funzionamento, nonché le condizioni e le limitazioni di accesso alla banca dati sono stabilite dall'ISVAP, con regolamento, secondo quanto previsto dall'articolo 120 del codice in materia di protezione dei dati personali.

[137] See Garante per la Protezione dei dati Personali; Istituto per la vigilanza sulle assicurazioni private e di interesse collettivo Join communication of 10 March 2003 (Communicato Congiunto del 10 marzo 2003). Available at http://www.garanteprivacy.it/garante/doc.jsp?ID=34907. Accessed 28 January 2009.

compulsory insurance scheme for motor vehicles registered in Italy, including the limits and kinds of access to the information stored. More recently, ISVAP adopted a new provision, Regulation n° 31 of 1 June 2009, which expressly abrogated Provision n° 2179, aiming at making the database more effective.[138]

In this regulation, the ISVAP states that the database has as its only purpose the prevention of and fight against fraud in this specific compulsory insurance sector.[139] Article 6 of this regulation and its Annex 1 define the kinds of data to be included in the database and article 8 regulates its functioning. Data included in the database can be stored for no more than 5 years (from the end of the loss liquidation).[140] After that period, data concerning losses are transferred to another IT platform managed by ISVAP and cannot be accessed by insurance companies. However, following a judicial request in a criminal case—or a request from data subjects—ISVAP gives access to information included in this other computer platform.[141] It is worth noting that after 5 years in this 'new' platform, data related to losses have to be anonymised.[142]

According to articles 9, 10 and 11, the Police, the Judiciary and insurance[143] companies have access to this database, within the limits established in these articles. Data subjects also have right of access, mainly for the exercise of the rights provided for by the Data Protection Code.[144] As mentioned at the beginning of this section, the Italian Data Protection Code applies fully to insurance activities which give rise to complaints from data subjects.

A bill of law which proposes the creation of a public agency in charge of investigating cases of insurance fraud, with powers to connect information contained in different databases controlled by public authorities, including the one managed by ISVAP, is now under discussion at the Italian Parliament.[145]

---

[138] See ISVAP. Communicato Stampa del 18 Febbraio 2009. Available at http://www.isvap.it/isvap_cms/docs/F20481/isvcs0218.pdf. Accessed 28 October 2010.

[139] Article 4.1.

[140] Article 8(4).

[141] Article 8(5).

[142] Article 8(6).

[143] According to Articles 9 and 11, also the UCI (Ufficio Centrale Italiano) and the CONSAP (Concessionaria servizi assicurativi pubblici S.p.a.) have access to this database. The UCI is "the body which has been set up by insurance undertakings authorized to conduct the business of motor vehicle insurance against civil liability and has been licensed to perform the functions of national insurers' bureau in the territory of the Italian Republic and the other tasks envisaged by Community and Italian law." CONSAP or Concessionaire for Public Insurance Services Ltd, in its turn, is in charge to manage the national guarantee fund. See http://www.isvap.it/isvap_cms/docs/F5091/decreto_7_settembre_2005_%20english_version.pdf. Accessed 30 October 2010.

[144] Article 15.

[145] See Senato della Repubblica Italiana. Schede di Lettura: Disegno di legge A.S. n. 2809 "Istituzione di un sistema di prevenzione delle frodi nel settore dell'assicurazione della responsabilità civile derivante dalla circolazione dei veicoli a motore". Luglio 2011. N° 303. Available at http://www.senato.it/documenti/repository/dossier/studi/2011/Dossier_303.pdf. Accessed 8 August 2011.

5.5.3.1 Insurance Chain (Catena Assicurativa)

Since before the adoption of the Italian Data Protection Code, in the period when the previous data protection law (Act 675/96) was in force, the insurance industry had asked the Garante to analyse the possibility of a new format for notifications to be given to data subjects[146] taking into account the multiple number of actors that integrate the insurance chain (insurer, reinsurer and co-insurer, for example). The insurance company, which is the one link in the chain that may have direct contact with data subjects, could notify them on behalf of the whole chain, which would make this notification simpler and less bureaucratic.

The Garante, recognising the specificity of the insurance contract and the existence of the so-called "insurance chain" (catena assicurativa), adopted a decision on 26 April 2007 exempting the obligation to present various notifications within the "insurance chain". In this decision, it recognised the plurality of actors that take part in the insurance sector and the potential benefits a simplification in the notification would bring to data subjects. In addition, it considered in its decision some important aspects and established limits for the "new notification" to be carried out by insurance companies in the name of the whole "insurance chain".

In relation to data collected directly from data subjects, insurance companies have to inform (by means of the notification) the data subject of the purposes of the collection and the potential recipients of the data or the kinds of potential recipients, such as reinsurers and co-insurers.[147] Moreover, insurance companies will have to maintain on their web sites an up-to-date list of the possible recipients of the data.[148]

The decision also addresses issues regarding the consent of data subjects, observing that consent is not necessary when data are used for the performance of contracts or when they are used for the other purposes listed in article 24 of the

[146]See Garante per la protezione dei dati personali. Relazione 2000. Available at http://www.garanteprivacy.it/garante/doc.jsp?ID=1335443. Accessed 26 March 2009. "Come per le banche, l'Autorità è in procinto di completare, in collaborazione con la competente associazione di categoria, l'A.N.I.A., alcuni approfondimenti per addivenire ad una modulistica-tipo ancora più semplificata per l'informativa ed il consenso, che tenga conto della molteplicità di trattamenti di dati personali, anche sanitari, posti in essere dalle compagnie assicurative e da un complesso di soggetti coinvolti nella c.d. catena assicurativa (a partire dagli agenti e dalla variegata rete di intermediari assicurativi per finire ai periti, ai legali ed alle autofficine)."

[147]"L'informativa, pur dovendo illustrare la (talora inevitabile) intensità dei flussi comunicativi, deve consentire all'interessato di rendersi conto con chiarezza dei medesimi; a tal fine essa deve indicare con precisione (evitando formulazioni generiche o dal significato oscuro, tenuto conto del destinatario della comunicazione) le finalità in concreto perseguite dalla compagnia di assicurazione, indicando altresì i soggetti o le tipologie di soggetti ai quali i dati possono essere comunicati (in qualità di autonomi titolari del trattamento) o che, considerando anche quanto sopra indicato al punto 2.2., possono venirne a conoscenza in qualità di 'responsabili del trattamento.'"

[148]"Un elenco aggiornato di tali soggetti deve essere comunque reso disponibile, anche on-line sul sito web delle compagnie di assicurazione, per agevolare l'esercizio del diritto d'accesso da parte dell'interessato (art. 13, comma 1, lett. f) del Codice)."

Codice.[149] However, written consent is required for processing sensitive data, and has to refer to all specific acts of data processing, which have to be clearly listed in the notification,[150] observing the finality principle and avoiding any generalisation.

Finally, the notification has to inform in a clear way about the situations where the processing of non-sensitive data can be carried out in the interest of the reinsurer, even without the consent of the data subject.[151]

5.5.3.2 Legal Opinions of Insurance Companies' Medical Experts (Perizie Medico-Legale)

Many complaints to the Garante concern access to personal information included in opinions elaborated by medical experts of insurance companies.[152] Many individuals request insurance companies, on the basis of articles 7 and 8(4) of the Codice, to provide access to information contained in the above-mentioned opinions, including the conclusions of the medical expert, which represent his own interpretation of the facts and, for this reason, are subjective. Insurance companies usually reject the requests of the data subjects based on two arguments: (1) the conclusions and evaluations of the medical expert are not personal data of the insured party and for that reason access should not to be given; and, (2) the access has to be

[149] "In riferimento ad una larga parte dei trattamenti effettuati nell'ambito della c.d. catena assicurativa, il consenso dell'interessato non è richiesto dal momento che i dati sono necessari (per instaurare o) per dare esecuzione a un contratto di assicurazione (art. 24, comma 1, lett. b), del Codice), oppure in quanto gli stessi sono trattati sulla base di uno dei presupposti equipollenti di cui all'art. 24 del Codice (e, ovviamente, in tutti i casi in cui il 'titolare del trattamento' si avvalga in conformità al Codice di un 'responsabile' cui trasmetta i dati personali)."

[150] "Qualora il consenso dell'interessato sia necessario (talora in forma scritta, come accade per il trattamento dei dati sensibili), l'operatività della formula di consenso può essere limitata ai soli trattamenti effettuati dall'assicurazione stipulante (compresa la comunicazione ai terzi indicati nell'informativa), oppure estendersi, in relazione al medesimo rischio assicurato, anche ai trattamenti ulteriori effettuati da altri 'titolari' appartenenti alla c.d. catena assicurativa.

In quest'ultima evenienza, dal momento che il consenso deve essere prestato in forma specifica, esso deve riferirsi agli specifici trattamenti effettuati dal distinto titolare del trattamento, chiaramente individuabile nell'informativa resa (in tal senso cfr. Provv. 28 maggio 1997, cit.)."

[151] "(. . .) individua, ai sensi dell'art. 24, comma 1, lett. g), del Codice, nei termini di cui in motivazione (punto 6), i casi nei quali il trattamento dei dati personali di natura non sensibile possono essere effettuati per perseguire un legittimo interesse dei riassicuratori anche senza il consenso degli interessati."

[152] BRAVO, Fabio. Op. cit. P. 383. "Dalla casistica emergente dai ricorsi, tuttavia, le attenzioni più forti si sono registrate in ordine alle possibilità di esercizio del diritto di accesso alle perizie medico-legali elaborate dai medici fiduciari delle compagine di assicurazione, al fine di valutare l'eventuale sussistenza del nesso causale, di determinare la caratteristica e l'entità delle lesioni lamentate o, comunque, dei danni riportati alla persona, in funzione della successiva eventuale liquidazione, ovvero in funzione della predisposizione di elementi in vista della difesa giudiziale."

postponed according to Article 8(2)(e) of the Codice,[153] because the disclosure of such information will prejudice the defence of the insurance company in a future possible legal claim.

In regard to the first argument, the Garante has affirmed that there are personal data not only in the identification part of the opinion, but also in the conclusions and evaluations of the medical expert of the insurance company. Thereby, article 7 of the Codice applies to the evaluation and conclusions of the expert.[154] It is worth noting that this does not mean that full access has to be given: information related to advice given by the expert to the insurance company concerning the decision of paying or not an indemnification or the strategy in a future legal claim is not included.[155]

Concerning the second argument, the Garante has been deciding on a case-by-case basis,[156] it being up to the insurance company to prove that the disclosure of

---

[153] Article 8

2. The rights referred to in Section 7 may not be exercised by making a request to the data controller or processor, or else by lodging a complaint in pursuance of Section 145, if the personal data are processed:

e) In pursuance of Section 24(1), letter f), as regards the period during which performance of the investigations by defence counsel or establishment of the legal claim might be actually and concretely prejudiced;

[154] Garante per la protezione dei dati personali. Provvedimento del 25 luglio 2007. Available at http://www.garanteprivacy.it/garante/doc.jsp?ID=1434791. Accessed 22 January 2009. "Le perizie medico-legale redatte in âmbito assicurativo (come quela richiesta da parte del ricorrente) comprendono dati personali dell'interessato non solo nella parte in cui sono riportati dati identificativi, ma anche in quella che comprende valutazioni e giudizi del perito fiduciario. Si tratta di informazioni riferente all'interessato da considerare 'dati personali' secondo la definizione di cui all'art.4, comma 1, lettera d), del Codice, e che ricadono pertanto nell'ambito di applicazione del medesimo Codice." In the same direction, see Garante per la protezione dei dati personali. Bollettino del n. 10/ottobre 1997. Available at http://www.garanteprivacy.it/garante/doc.jsp?ID=47726. Accessed 22 January 2009. P. 97. "Esaminando il ricorso, l'Autorità ha ricordatto che nelle perizie medico legali si ritrovano, normalmente, tre categorie di dati:

(a) dati identificativi di tipo anagrafico;
(b) dati referiti allo stato di salute, con particolare riferimento all'anamnesi;
(c) la valutazione peritale vera e propria che risulta dalla visita medica cui viene sottoposto l'assicurato da parte del medico fiduciario dell'assicurazione, la parte della perizia cioè nella quale il medico esprime appunto un giudizio sui rapporto tra sinistro denunciato e patologie lamentate per lê quali l'interessato chiede il risarcimento nonché, spesso, valutazioni e giudizi sull'eventuale grado di genuinità delle istanze presentate all'assicurazione."

[155] Garante per la protezione dei dati personali. Provvedimento del 25 luglio 2007. Available at http://www.garanteprivacy.it/garante/doc.jsp?ID=1434791. Accessed 22 January 2009. "L'esercizio del diritto di accesso di cui al citato art. 7 del Codice riguarda peraltro le sole informazioni di carattere personale e non anche, secondo quanto disposto dall'art. 8, comma, 4 <<l'indicazione di condotte da tenersi o di decisioni in via di assunzione da parte del titolare del trattamento>>, o possibili considerazioni a carattere difensivo o di strategia contrattuale o processuale eventualmente espresse in sede di consulenza."

[156] Garante per la protezione dei dati personali. Bollettino del n. 20/maggio 2001. Available at http://www.garanteprivacy.it/garante/doc.jsp?ID=39272. Accessed 28 November 2009. P. 20. "La valutazione dell'esistenza di un effettivo pregiudizio ai sensi del citato art. 14, comma 1, lettera e), deve essere effettuata caso per caso e sulla base di concreti elementi forniti dal titolare del trattamento o comunque risultanti dagli atti."

information will really reduce its right of defence.[157] The mere fact that a legal claim is still pending is not enough to justify the postponing of the disclosure of information in the opinion of the Garante.[158] Thus, if the insurance company proves that the disclosure will harm its defence in a legal proceeding, the disclosure will be postponed.[159] If not, access will be given to the data subject.[160] Hence, the insurer

---

[157]Garante per la protezione dei dati personali. Bollettino del n. 10/ottobre 1997. Available at http://www.garanteprivacy.it/garante/doc.jsp?ID=47726. Accessed 28 January 2009. P. 97. "Il Garante ha precisato che il titolare del trattamento (nel caso, l'assicurazione) che vuole avvalersi del differimento non deve però limitarsi a far riferimento alla norma che lo prevede, ma deve fornire adeguate motivazioni che diano ragione del pregiudizio effetivo cui si andrebbe incontro in caso di immediato accesso ai dati."

[158]Garante per la protezione dei dati personali. Provvedimento del 25 luglio 2007. Available at http://www.garanteprivacy.it/garante/doc.jsp?ID=1434791. Accessed 28 January 2009. "Nel caso in esame, è stata comprovata la ricorrenza di uno dei presupposti già riconosciuti idonei—in altri casi—da questa Autorità a giustificare un differimento del diritto di accesso. Cio, non in ragione del mero fatto che presso un ufficio giudiziario pende un giudizio civile, ma per effetto di uma specifica situazione nel corso della quale si può determinare un condizionamento o un'alterazione nell'esercizio del diritto alla prova rispetto ad um determinato mezzo istruttorio (v. Provv. 17 maggio 2001, in Bollettino del Garante n. 20/2001, p. 20)." See also BRAVO, Fabio. Op. cit. P. 385. "Sembra in ogni caso consolidato, al contempo, l'orientamento fondato, sull'art. 14, commal, lett. e), della legge 675/1996 che consente ai titolari di trattamento di poter in casi particolari differire temporaneamente l'accesso ai daí contenuti nelle perizie, limitatamente al periodo in cui potrebbe derivare, negli stessi, un effetivo pregiudizio per lo svolgimento delle indagini o per far valere o difendere um diritto in sede giudiziaria. L'Autorità si è nuovamente espressa sull'argomento chiarendo che è, tuttavia, necessario dimostrate in concreto e realmente l'efettiva esistenza del pregiudizio, con uma valutazione da condurre caso per caso (Provv. 19 giugno 2002, in Bolletino n. 29; Provv.ti 16 ottobre 2002 e 11 dicembre 2002)."

[159]Garante per la protezione dei dati personali. Provvedimento del 25 luglio 2007. Available at http://www.garanteprivacy.it/garante/doc.jsp?ID=1434791. Accessed 21 January 2009. "Nel caso di specie sussiste quindi, effettivamente, la documentata esigenza di non pregiudicare l'esercizio del diritto di difesa del titolare del trattamento rispetto al completamento della menzionata consulenza tecnica d'ufficio attualmente in corso di svolgimento e appare pertanto legittimo l'invocato differimento temporane del diritto di accesso." In the same sense see Bollettino del n. 89/dicembre 2007. Available at http://www.garanteprivacy.it/garante/doc.jsp?ID=1497600. Accessed 28 March 2009. P. 0. "RILEVATO che, nel caso in esame, sussiste la documentata esigenza di non pregiudicare l'esercizio del diritto di difesa del titolare del trattamento nell'attuale fase precontenziosa che, in ragione delle iniziative intraprese dall'interessato, risulta allo stato preludere all'instaurazione di una controversia giudiziaria. Ciò, in relazione agli specifici profili messi in luce dalla compagnia di assicurazione e, in particolare, agli elementi contenuti nella perizia del medico legale incaricato dalla compagnia costituenti informazioni riservate di carattere tecnico-valutativo rivolte alla stessa e rientranti nell'ambito di un più ampio servizio di consulenza prestato;

RILEVATO che, alla luce degli elementi di valutazione forniti dal titolare del trattamento, appare allo stato legittimamente invocato il differimento temporaneo del diritto di accesso."

[160]Garante per la protezione dei dati personali. Provvedimento del 27 ottobre 2005. Available at http://www.garanteprivacy.it/garante/doc.jsp?ID=1213613 Accessed 28 January 2008. "RILEVATO che in ordine ai predetti dati di tipo valutativo la società resistente ha menzionato, semplicemente, la possibilità offerta ai ricorrente di dirimere in sede arbitrale le contestazioni preliminari in atto, e non ha documentato, come dovuto, i pressuposti per differire temporaneamente il diritto di accesso durante il periodo in cui dall'accesso potrebbe derivarne um pregiudizio

has the burden to prove the risk to its right of defence. Such approach goes in a different direction than the one adopted by the Court of Rome regarding requests of access to the evaluation forms filled by employer. In that case, as discussed previously (5.2), the Court considered that evaluations are subjective and, as a consequence, should not be considered as personal data. If we take this approach for the medical expert's evaluation, we would have a different outcome and the insurance company would not have to disclose the information contained in this document to the respective insured.

5.5.3.3 Access to Information of Deceased People

The final issue that will be analysed here deals with the request for access to information relating to deceased people, mainly to information concerning the beneficiaries of a life insurance policy. Article 9(3) of the Codice recognises the rights provided for by article 7 of the Codice regarding personal data related to deceased people, which are to be exercised by "any entity that is interested therein or else acts to protect a data subject or family-related reasons deserving protection." On the basis of this provision, some people have requested access to information contained in life insurance policies of deceased relatives with the intent of discovering who the beneficiaries of such life insurance policies are.

The Garante has already recognised in many opportunities that the right to access to personal data (even sensitive ones) grants to heirs[161] and to widowers[162] access

documentato, effettivo e concreto per l'esercizio di um diritto in sede giudiziaria (art. 8, comma 2, lett e), del Codice).

RITENUTO che il ricorso deve essere quindi accolto per questa parte, e che va pertanto ordinato alla resistente di comunicare al ricorrente, entro il 28 dicembre 2005, in modo dettagliato ed intelligibile (artt. 9 e 10 del Codice), anche i dati personali di tipo valutativo che lo riguardano contenuti nella predetta perizia e non ancora comunicati, dando conferma a questa Autorità dell'avvenuto adempimento entro lo stesso termine."

[161]Garante per la protezione dei dati personali. Provvedimento del 12 febbraio 2009. Available at http://www.garanteprivacy.it/garante/doc.jsp?ID=1598386. Accessed 28 March 2009. "hanno chiesto a Poste Italiane S.p.A. di ottenere la comunicazione dei dati personali riguardanti la nonna defunta, di cui gli stessi sono eredi, in relazione ai rapporti contrattuali intrattenuti dalla defunta con l'ufficio postale di Norcia; ciò, con particolare riferimento ad alcuni libretti di risparmio e buoni postali di cui la stessa risultava intestataria; (...) rilevato che è legittimato ad accedere ai dati personali di una persona defunta, ai sensi dell'art. 9, comma 3, del Codice, anche 'chi ha un interesse proprio, o agisce a tutela dell'interessato o per ragioni familiari meritevoli di protezione': posizione nella quale, senza dubbio, si trovano i due ricorrenti."

[162]Garante per la protezione dei dati personali. Provvedimento del 10 novembre 2004. Available at http//www.garanteprivacy.it/garante/doc.jsp?ID=1103284. Accessed 21 January 2009. "Ai sensi dell'art. 9, comma 3, del Codice, i diritti di cui al medesimo art. 7, tra cui il diritto di accesso, se 'riferiti ai dati personali concernenti persone decedute', possono essere esercitati da 'chi ha um interesse próprio, o agisce a tutela o per ragioni meritevol di protezione'. In base a tale disposizione l'interessata, nella qualità di erede del difunto marito, ha quindi titolo ad accedere ai dati pesonali dello stesso."

to personal data regarding the deceased. Nevertheless, such access concerns only personal data related to the deceased and not to third parties. Therefore, the access to information contained in the life insurance policy is limited to data on the deceased person and not data relating to anyone else. With this interpretation, the Garante does not allow access to information related to the beneficiaries of the insurance policy but only to data concerning the deceased himself.[163]

5.6 Other Relevant Issues

5.6.1 Data Protection Principles: Necessity, Data Minimisation and Privacy by Design

An important issue that arises with the Italian Data Protection Code is the application of the principles that impose limits to the processing of personal data. Giovanni Buttarelli identified what he calls 'three top principles' amongst which he highlights the importance of the necessity principle.[164] The others two principles are the finality[165] and proportionality principles. The finality principle[166] is included in article 11(1)(b) of the Code and reproduces article 6(1)(b) of Directive 95/45/EC. As far as the proportionality principle is concerned, it also reproduces

---

[163]Garante per la protezione dei dati personali. Newsletter n. 186 del 6–12 ottobre 2003. Available at http://www.garanteprivacy.it/garante/doc.jsp?ID=346897. Accessed 28 March 2009. "Il diritto di accesso ai dati di un defunto non riguarda informazioni relative a terzi, come ad esempio i beneficiari di polizze assicurative.

Questa la sostanza del provvedimento emesso dall'Autorità dopo aver esaminato il ricorso dell'erede legittimo di una donna che, poco prima di morire, aveva stipulato con una società di assicurazioni una polizza a favore di un terzo le cui generalità non erano note al ricorrente. Il Garante, infatti, pur riconoscendo all'erede legittimo il diritto ad accedere a tutte le informazioni personali che riguardano la defunta, non ha consentito alla società assicuratrice di comunicare il nome del beneficiario della polizza."

[164]"Con il principio di necessità, il legislatore ha in sostanza codificato nella protezioni dei dati il principio della precauzione che si affaccia in altre contesti normativi." Butarelli, Giovanni. In Bianca, Cesare Massimo; Busnelli, Francesco Donato. Op. cit. P. 33.

[165]"Il principio di finalità impone al titolare, con il primo atto di esercizio della propria libertà informative, di circoscrivere i contorni dell'attività di trattamento e di creare così un limite a priori rispetto agli atti successive (Navarretta 1999, 330) (. . .)." In Panetta, Rocco. Op. cit. P. 859.

[166]"I dati devono essere raccolti e registrati (. . .) per scopi <<determinati, espliciti e legittimi>>, secondo una triplice qualificazione che costituisce una specificazione, sai pur solo parziale e non certo esaustiva, del principio di finalità." Cuffraro, Vincenzo et al. Il codice del trattamento dei dati personali. G. Giappichelli Editore: Torino, 2007. P. 84.

provisions contained in the Directive.[167] Therefore, my considerations on finality and proportionality in the EU Data Protection Framework[168] also apply to the Italian legislation.[169]

I need to analyse here the necessity principle, that complements both the finality[170] and proportionality,[171] since Italian law expressly recognises this principle, which is not the case in Directive 95/46/EC.[172] One can argue that we can infer this principle from article 6(1)(b) of Directive 95/46/EC, but this provision does not state that data have to be necessary for the processing, it only requires that data are "collected for specified, explicit and legitimate purposes", what underlines the idea of 'finality'. Therefore, the idea of necessity is still missing. In the Italian Codice this principle plays a fundamental role as the guide for all of the data protection system,[173] acting not only as a limit for the processing of personal data as a whole.[174]

---

[167] See article 6(1)(c) of Directive 95/46/EC.

[168] See 1.3.1.1 supra.

[169] "Uno dei principi fondamentali della Convenzione 108/1981 (e della direttiva 95/46) è, però, quello dell'utilizzazione dei dati per "scopi compatibili", pertanto, la raccomandazione specifica che i dati raccolti per una delle finalità previste non possono essere trattati per fini diversi: ad esempio, dati relativi allo stato di salute raccolti per la stipula di una polizza sanitaria non devono essere utilizzati per le esigenze di un'altro tipo di contratto ad esempio, una polizza sulla vita, a meno che il diritto interno stabilisca la compatibilità di tali trattamenti." BIANCA, Cesare Massimo; BUSNELLI, Francesco Donato. Op. cit. P. 1157.

[170] "Il principio di necessità si intreccia com quello di finalità e costituisce un rinforzamento della tutela dell'interessato. Se il principio di finalità, coordinato com i requisiti di pertinenza, completezza e non eccedenza, circoscrive l'ambito quantitativo e qualitativo all'interno del quale i dati si possono considerare raccolti e trattati in modo lecito, il principio di necessita si presenta come un filtro all'utilizzabilità dei dati legittimamente raccolti." In PANETTA, Rocco. Op. cit. P. 860.

[171] "(...) il principio di necessità sul trattamento dei dati personali implica il concetto della <<proporzione>> dell'atto che si intendi porre in essere rispetto ad un fine prefissato, cosi da recare il minor sacrificio possibile a quanti ne subiscono gli effetti." Cuffrano, Vincenzo et al. Op. cit. P. 26.

[172] See article 6 of Directive 95/46/EC.

[173] "Il Codice in material di protezione dei dati personali, informato ai canoni di semplificazione, armonizzazione ed efficacia, è ispirato al principio di necessità. Lo scopo è di controllare la circolazione dei dati personali in maniera più efficiente, limitando il pericolo di intrusione esterna al minimo indispensabile e impedendo il riferimento di informazioni sulla vita dell'utente non necessarie con gli scopi dichiarati o in contrasto con le finalità della raccolta. Questo principio permette di garantire il mantenimento di un livello elevato di protezione dei dati raccolti in occasione di contratti dei consumatori." Panetta, Rocco. Op. cit. P. 393.

[174] "L'espressa previsione del principio di necessita è stata, giustamente, salutata come una delle più rilevanti novità apportate dal codice della privacy e come segno di una linea di politica legislativa particolarmente impegnativa." Rodotà, Stefano. Relazione 2004, Garante Privacy—Discorso del president. Op. cit. P. 6.

In fact, the Italian Codice presents another facet of such principle,[175] the principle of minimisation: "Information systems and software shall be configured by minimizing the use of personal data and identification data".[176] According to this idea data controllers should use and collect as little personal data as possible.[177] Consequently, the fact that a method makes the processing easier does not mean that this method is necessary.[178] The European Data Protection Supervisor argues that this principle, in terms of obligations of controllers, already exists in Directive 95/46/EC, but celebrates the explicit inclusion of this principle in the EU Commission Proposal for a General Data Protection Regulation:

> The principle of 'data minimisation' is explicity mentioned in Article 5(c). According to this provision personal data should be limited to the minimum necessary and should only be processed if the purposes of the processing could not be fulfilled by other means. Although, in terms of substance, this obligation already exists under the current rules, the EDPS welcomes the visibility to it given by the addition in Article 5(c).[179]

Actually, the way this principle is designed in Italian Law, by requiring the choice of technologies minimising the use of personal data, reflects the idea of 'privacy by design',[180] a concept initially developed by the Privacy Commissioner

---

[175]"(...) la <<necessità>> a cui fa riferimento l'art 3 del Codice fornisce il criterio non solamente per individuare il limite al quale devono soggiacere le attività dei soggetti pubblici e private incidenti sul diritto, di rango fondamentale alla protezione dei dati personali, ma anche per <<l'accettazione istituzionale delle tecnologie dell'informazione e della comunicazione>>." Cuffrano, Vincenzo et al. Op. cit. P. 27. In the same sense, see Niger, Sergio. Il diritto alla protezione dei dati personali. In Monducci, Juri; Sartor, Giovanni (editors). Op. cit. P.13. "Il presente articolo delinea, infatti, il principio di necessità nel trattamento dei dati personale. Secondo tale principio i sistemi informativi ed i software, fin dalla loro configurazione, devono essere predisposti in modo da assicurare che i dati personali o identificativi siano utilizzati solo se indispensabili per il conseguimento delle finalità consentite, e non anche quando gli stessi obiettivi possano essere realizzati attraverso l'uso di dati anonimi o che consentano una più circoscritta identificazione degli interessati. Il principio di necessità si pone come integrazione e completamento, in relazione alla configurazione stessa dell'ambiente in cui i dati sono trattati, del principio di pertinenza e non eccedenza dei dati trattati, già previsto dall'art. 9 della L. 675/96."

[176]Official translation available at http://www.garanteprivacy.it/garante/document?ID=311066. Accessed 10 November 2010.

[177]"Questa disposizione intendi arginare la tendenza all'impiego di qualsiasi innovazione tecnologica per realizzare trattamento di dati personali sempre più avanzati e, pertanto, sempre più invasive." Rodotà, Stefano. Relazione 2004. Garante Privacy—Discorso del presidente. Op. cit. P. 5.

[178]"Principio di necessità (art 3), che prevedi la configurazione dei sistemi informativi in modo da ridurre al minimo l'utilizzazione dei dati personali, escludendone il trattamento quando le finalità perseguite possono essere realizzate mediante dati anonimi o sistemi che permettano di identificare l'interessato solo in caso di necessità." Bianca, Cesare Massimo; Busnelli, Francesco Donato. Op. cit. P. LXIII.

[179]European Data Protection Supervisor. 2012. Op. cit. P. 20.

[180]Costa, Luiz; Poullet, Yves. Privacy and the regulation of 2012. Computer Law & Security Review. Volume 28, Issue 3, June 2012. P. 260.

of Ontario (Canada), Dr. Ann Cavoukin, during the 90s, with the aim of dealing with issues that arose as a consequence of the developments in information and communication technologies and in large scale databases. According to the notion of 'privacy by design', data protection principles should be applied to: (1) IT systems; (2) accountable business practices; and (3) physical design and infrastructure.[181] In the definition of the European Data Protection Supervisor, "Privacy by design aims at building privacy and data protection up front, into the design specifications and architecture of information and communication systems and technologies, in order to facilitate compliance with privacy and data protection principles."[182] The application of 'privacy by design' to the development of systems for the processing of personal data would reduce the risks of violation of privacy and would ensure the adequacy of these systems to data protection norms and principles, since they would be structured and developed taking into account the requirements imposed by such principles and norms for a processing to be legitimate.[183]

5.6.2 *Codes of Conduct*

Another important aspect of the Italian system is the adoption of 'codes of conduct' by different sectors (private and public). In the line of article 27 of Directive 95/46/EC,[184] the Italian Codice in its article 12(1) encourages "the drawing up

[181]Cavoukian, Ann. "What is Privacy by Design?". Available at http://www.privacybydesign.ca/. Accessed 21 January 2010.

[182]European Data Protection Supervisor. Glossary. Available at http://www.edps.europa.eu/EDPSWEB/edps/Home/EDPS/Dataprotection/Glossary/pid/84. Accessed 21 January 2010.

[183]In this sense is the position adopted by the European Data Protection Supervisor in its Opinion on a notification for Prior Checking received from the Data Protection Officer of the European Commission on "the implementation of flexitime—specific to DG INFSO". European Data Protection Supervisor. Opinion on a notification for prior checking received from the data protection officer of the European commission on "the implementation of flexitime—specific to DG INFSO". Available at http://www.edps.europa.eu/EDPSWEB/webdav/site/mySite/shared/Documents/Supervision/Priorchecks/Opinions/2007/07-10-19_Commissionflexitime_INFSO_EN.pdf. 25 Jan 2010. Available at http://www.edps.europa.eu/EDPSWEB/webdav/site/mySite/shared/Documents/Supervision/Priorchecks/Opinions/2007/071019_Commission_flexitime_INFSO_EN.pdf. Accessed 21 January 2010.

[184]"La direttiva 24 ottobre 1995, n. 46—la cosiddetta 'Direttiva madre' (di seguito anche, semplicemente, Direttiva), da cui è derivata la legge n. 675/1996 prevede che gli Stati membri (oltre che la Commissione) incoraggino l'elaborazione di codici di condotta, al fine di 'contribuire, in funzione delle specifica settoriali alla corretta applicazione delle disposizione nazionali di attuazione' della Direttiva madre (art. 27)." Panetta, Rocco. Op. cit. P. 211. See also, Cuffaro, Vincenzo et al. Op. cit. P. 816. "Il 1o comma dell'art. 27, riprendendo il considerando sopra citato, obbliga Stati e Commissione ad incoraggiare l'elaborazione di codice che contribuiscano, ciascuno secondo le caratteristiche specifiche dei trattamenti effettuati nei singolo settori, alla <<corretta applicazione delle disposizione nazionali di attuazione della presente direttiva>>".

of codes of conduct and professional practice for specific sectors".[185] The Codice stated in paragraph 2 of article 12 that the Italian Data Protection Authority would be in charge of publishing these codes in the Official Journal of the Italian Republic. These codes will be included in Annex A of the Codice, based on a decree of the Minister of Justice.[186]

Accordingly, the codes of conduct and professional practice in the field of data protection will be part of the Italian Data Protection Legislation[187] and not only self-regulatory documents, since they have binding effects and are enforceable[188] by the Data Protection Authority, becoming a new source of law in the Italian legal system, as was seen when the "code of conduct and professional practice applying to information systems managed by private entities with regard to consumer credit, reliability, and timeliness of payments" was analysed. Currently there are six Codes of Conduct and/or professional practice in the Annex A of the Italian Data Protection Code; these consider the processing of personal data for the exercise of journalistic activities, for historical purposes, for statistical purposes within the framework of the SISTAN [national statistical system], for statistical and scientific purposes, for the functioning of information systems managed by private entities with regard to consumer credit, reliability, and timeliness of payments and for the defence investigations.[189]

5.7 Chapter Conclusion

In this chapter it was possible to conclude that the Garante works—to a certain extent—as ad hoc legislator, since it has amongst its powers the one to adopt general authorisations for the processing of sensitive data and also to approve of and making

---

[185] Article 12 (Codes of Conduct and Professional Practice)

1. The Garante shall encourage, within the framework of the categories concerned and in conformity with the principle of representation, by having regard to the guidelines set out in Council of Europe recommendations on the processing of personal data, the drawing up of codes of conduct and professional practice for specific sectors, verify their compliance with laws and regulations by also taking account of the considerations made by the entities concerned, and contribute to adoption of and compliance with such codes.

[186] The procedure for the adoption of codes of conduct is regulated by Regulation no 2/2006 of the Italian Data Protection Authority. Available at http://www.garanteprivacy.it/garante/doc.jsp?ID=1320030. Accessed 29 March 2011.

[187] "La novità posta dalla legge n. 675/1996 consiste piuttosto sul fatto che una leggi rinvii per l'attuazione dei propri precetti a una fonte normativa di <<creazione>> privata: i codici di deontologia." Cuffaro, Vincenzo et al. Op. cit. P. 102.

[188] Bravo, Fabio; Monducci, Juri. Le condizioni di liceità del trattamento dei dati. In Monducci, Juri; Sartor, Giovanni (editors). Op. cit. P. 51. "Le predette peculiarità hanno indotto la dottrina a ritenere 'che ci si trovi in presenza di una nuova modalità di normativa atipica, avente ad oggetto una sorta di codificazione dei codici di deontologia.'"

[189] See http://www.garanteprivacy.it/garante/navig/jsp/index.jsp?folderpath=Normativa%2FItaliana%2FCodici+deontologici. Accessed 13 January 2010.

enforceable codes of practice adopted by different sectors. Actually, as we have seen, these codes of practice are considered by the doctrine as a new source of law. Moreover, another conclusion reached is that the concept of personal data in Italy is broader than the one contained in Directive 95/46/EC, including both natural and legal persons and also deceased people. Furthermore, the processing of sensitive data deserves a higher level of protection in Italy. Firstly, because it applies both to private and public bodies. Secondly, it requires either an authorisation from the Data Protection Authority or a legal authorisation for a processing of sensitive data to take place. Thirdly, it includes the "indispensability principle" as a requirement for the processing. Finally, it also explicitly comprises the processing of genetic data, which is the focus of an entire General Authorisation adopted by the Garante.

Chapter 6
The Differences Between the Selected Member States and the Recommendations for a Further Harmonisation in the Post Lisbon Era

The entry into force of the Lisbon Treaty brought many changes to the EU legal framework and some of them have a direct impact on data protection.

From an institutional point of view, the abolition of the pillar structure will allow a greater involvement of the European Parliament in all areas, including activities previously covered under the former third pillar. According to Article 87 (2) of the Treaty on the Functioning of the European Union, the Council and the Parliament may adopt, on the basis of the ordinary legislative procedure, measures relating to "the collection, storage, processing, analysis and exchange of relevant information" between the police authorities of member states. In this regard, the recent decision of the European Parliament rejecting the SWIFT agreement with the U.S. on the transfer of banking data to U.S. authorities in the fight against terrorism shows that the Parliament will not be afraid to exercise its new veto power.[1]

Furthermore, the entry into force of the Lisbon Treaty also marked a turning point in relation to the protection of the right to privacy and personal data. These two fundamental rights are expressly recognised by Articles 7 and 8 of the Charter of Fundamental Rights. The Lisbon Treaty included an express reference to the Charter in Article 6 of the Treaty on European Union. According to Article 6 (1) TEU "The Union recognises the rights, freedoms and principles set out in the Charter of Fundamental Rights of the European Union of 7 December 2000, as adapted at Strasbourg, on 12 December 2007, which shall have the same legal value as the Treaties". Thus, despite the fact that the text of the Charter has not been included in the Treaty of Lisbon, it has become a binding document. Moreover, Article 51 (1) of the Charter establishes that it has to be taken into account by European institutions when carrying out their legislative activities.

Finally, a new legal basis for the regulation of the processing of personal data was introduced by the Lisbon Treaty. Article 39 of the Treaty on European Union

[1] European Parliament. SWIFT: MEPs to Vote on Backing or Sacking EU/US Data Sharing Deal. http://www.europarl.europa.eu/news/public/story_page/019-68537-039-02-07-902-20100205STO68536-2010-08-02-2010/default_en.htm. Accessed 19 February 2010.

M. Viola de Azevedo Cunha, *Market Integration Through Data Protection*, Law, Governance and Technology Series 9, DOI 10.1007/978-94-007-6085-1_6,

requires the adoption of a more comprehensive instrument for data protection.[2] Nevertheless, Declaration 21 on the protection of personal data in the fields of judicial and police cooperation in criminal matters, annexed to the final act of the intergovernmental conference which adopted the Treaty of Lisbon, recognises that

> specific rules on the protection of personal data and the free movement of such data in the fields of judicial cooperation in criminal matters and police cooperation, based on Article 16 of the Treaty on the Functioning of the European Union may prove necessary because of the specific nature of these fields.[3]

In the same sense is the abovementioned Article 39 of the Treaty on European Union (TEU), with regard to the areas of Common Foreign and Security Policy, which authorises the Council to

> adopt a decision laying down the rules relating to the protection of individuals with regard to the processing of personal data by the Member States when carrying out activities which fall within the scope of this Chapter, and the rules relating to the free movement of such data.[4]

It is worth noting that "the Digital Agenda for Europe and, more generally, the Europe 2020 strategy promote the consolidation of the 'single market' dimension of data protection and the reduction of administrative burdens on companies."[5]

This is, hence, a great opportunity for the adoption of single concepts and legal instruments which would provide general rules for all types of processing of personal data within the EU. In fact, it is not by chance that the European Commission recently put forward two proposals for new EU legislation in the field of data protection: for a Regulation of the European Parliament and of the Council on the protection of individuals with regard to the processing of personal data and on the free movement of such data (General Data Protection Regulation) and for the Directive of the European Parliament and of the Council on the protection of individuals with regard to the processing of personal data by competent authorities for the purposes of prevention, investigation, detection or prosecution of criminal offences or the execution of criminal penalties, and the free movement of such data.[6]

---

[2]In this sense, see European Commission. Draft communication from the commission to the European parliament, the council, the economic and social committee and the committee of the regions [COM(2010) 609 final]. http://ec.europa.eu/justice/news/consultingpublic/0006/com_2010_609_en.pdf. 22 Jan 2011.

[3]Available at http://eur-lex.europa.eu/LexUriServ/LexUriServ.do?uri=OJ:C:2010:083:0335:0360:EN:PDF. Accessed 3 August 2011.

[4]This article is included in Chapter 2 of the Treaty, entitled 'Specific Provisions on the Common Foreign and Security Policy'.

[5]European Economic and Social Committee. Opinion on proposal for a regulation of the European Parliament and of the Council on the protection of individuals with regard to the processing of personal data on the free movement of such data (General Data Protection Regulation). SOC/45. 23 May 2012. 2012. P. 6.

[6]Available at http://ec.europa.eu/justice/newsroom/data-protection/news/120125_en.htm. Accessed 7 April 2012.

The analysis carried out in this book, regarding the different sources of legislation that integrate the European Data Protection Framework and the data protection legislation of the selected Member states, with a special emphasis on insurance, bank and credit reporting industries, shows that there are some aspects differently developed at a national level, which create barriers for the creation of an integrated market for these industries. As noted by the European Data Protection Supervisor:

> practice has shown that under the current Directive 95/46/EC, there are still numerous differences between the legislation of Member States which hamper the EU Single Market. Further harmonisation is clearly needed.[7]

Consequently, this is the right moment for discussing the necessary changes in the EU Data Protection Legal Framework.[8] Here I will make some recommendations that impact on all processing of personal data, taking on board the 'improvements' currently incorporated by the EU Commission Proposal for a General Data Protection Regulation.[9] However, they are made from the perspective of the selected industries, i.e., they are concentrated on the three sectors that were analysed in this book: insurance, banking, and credit reporting. Although these recommendations are not exhaustive, since they are limited by the scope of this book, they intend to contribute to the debate about the review of the General Data Protection Directive in the post Lisbon Treaty era. The next sections will concentrate on the following topics: concept of personal data, consent, the data protection officer, the mutual recognition system and codes of conduct.

6.1 A 'New' Concept of Personal Data

The first object of my recommendation is the very concept of personal data, which is one of the main foundations of EU legislation regarding data protection.[10] As could be seen in the previous chapters, there are significant differences in relation to this concept among the selected member states. In Italy and France, it includes deceased persons, which does not happen in the UK where just "living individuals" are covered by the Data Protection Act of 1998. This difference creates a situation where

---

[7]European Data Protection Supervisor. Op. Cit. 2012. P. 3.

[8]European Commission. Draft Communication to the European Parliament, The Council, The Economic and Social Committee and The Committee of the Regions on a comprehensive approach on personal data protection in the European Union. Op. cit. P. 10.

[9]The DG INFSO "is of the view that taken as a whole the draft DP Regulation would have significant negative effects on the development of the digital economy and jeopardise the Commission's Digital Agenda." Information Society and Media Directorate General (INFSO). Reply to the interservice consultation launched by DG JUST on the draft proposal of a DP Regulation and a draft proposal of a Police and Criminal Justice DP Directive. 22 December 2011. P. 4.

[10]Ibid. P. 5. "The concept of 'personal data' is one of the key concepts for the protection of individuals by the current EU data protection instruments (. . .)."

a processing activity such as the one regarding the beneficiaries of a life insurance policy, just to give an example, will not be supervised by the Data Protection Authority, because the concept of personal data does not consider information related to deceased people as personal data. The same conclusion was reached by Andrew Charlesworth, during the period of the EU 15:

> The extent to which the existing legal framework for data protection lacks basic consistency is demonstrated neatly by the fact that of the 15 Member States, four protect the personal data of 'natural' and 'legal' persons in their data protection laws, while the remaining 11 protect only the personal data of 'natural' persons.[11]

Moreover, as previously shown (4.2), the UK Act has reduced the scope of the concept of personal data by adding the expression "likely to come into possession", as a requirement for the information to be considered as personal data. Furthermore, the England and Wales Court of Appeal has tightened even more the scope of the concept as discussed above (4.2). As a consequence, the UK Data Protection Framework does not fully comply with Directive 95/46/EC.

These different approaches concerning the concept of personal data can lead to a barrier for the free movement of services, since it would cause providers of certain activities to deal with different rules in different member states and possibly create problems for the free movement of services, because in some states a processing carried out could involve information considered as personal data and, in others, the same information would not be considered as such. This is of particular importance in a cross-border scenario, as in the EU, where the trade between member states intensifies the flow of personal data, making it necessary to establish a uniform trade environment in order to guarantee the protection of personal data within the bloc, avoiding different levels of protection between member states.[12]

Another aspect for the review of the EU Data Protection Legal Framework is the extension of the concept of personal data to also include information related to legal persons. Among the analysed member states, only Italy has adopted such a position, making all processing of data related to individuals or legal persons subject to the Data Protection Legislation.[13] The European Economic and Social Committee in its Opinion on the Proposal for a General Data Protection Regulation, although understanding the reasons behind the non inclusion of legal persons in the scope of the proposed regulation, "calls the Commission to turn its attention to data concerning legal persons as well, particularly those which have legal personality."[14]

It could be argued that physical, physiological, and mental data are only related to natural persons; nonetheless, the other kinds of data mentioned in the Directive

---

[11]Charlesworth, Andrew. Op. Cit. P. 939.

[12]Doneda, Danilo and Viola de Azevedo Cunha, Mario. Data Protection as a Trade Resource in Mercosur. Op. cit. P. 366.

[13]Austria and Switzerland have adopted the same approach. See Bygrave, Lee A. and Schartum, Dag Wiese, "Consent, Proportionality and Collective Power" in Reinventing Data Protection?, ed. Serge Gutwirth et al. (Springer, 2009), 168.

[14]European Economic and Social Committee. Op. cit. P. 10.

can obviously belong to legal persons. This need to extent the concept of personal to incorporate legal persons becomes even more evident when we talk about cases of small partnerships and of a sole trader, where the information about the business is indistinguishable from the partners' information. For such reasons, it seems that the Italian Legislator adopted a better solution, since problems concerning the processing of these data can affect both legal and natural persons.

Furthermore, in many member states the protection given by the Data Protection Legislation to natural persons is usually extended to legal persons through other pieces of legislations, as for example the UK Consumer Credit Act 1974 (as amended by the Consumer Credit Act 2006), which grants the rights of access, correction and erasure to partnerships and unincorporated bodies of persons, giving supervisory powers to the Office of Fair Trading (OFI) and not to the Information Commissioner (ICO). This is a further argument for adopting a general concept of personal data which includes legal persons: to avoid different interpretations/positions of different supervisory authorities dealing with similar cases. It can be a case, for example, where the ICO and the OFI will analyse complaints dealing with the same processing activity, one from a data subject and the other from a legal entity, and will have different outcomes, one considering the processing fair and the other unfair. The existence of different pieces of legislation affecting the same processing of data—or the same databases—create an extra burden on controllers. This situation becomes even more complicated in a cross-border scenario as, for example, in the e-justice initiative aiming at interconnecting national insolvency registers.[15] These differences in the concept of personal data could create considerable problems for the intended interconnection of databases. Moreover, as highlighted in the analysis of the French Data Protection Framework (3.2), in some situations it is difficult for the supervisory authority not to deal with processing activities involving data related to legal entities, as did the CNIL in some of its general authorisations.

It can be seen, hence, that there are slight differences in the concept of personal data adopted by the selected member states, which can have important consequences, especially in a cross-border perspective. Just to illustrate, a database containing information related to legal persons could be processed in a member state without the incidence of data protection rules but in others such rules would apply. This different approach can configurate a barrier for the provision of specific cross-border services, because a provider A of a certain service in a Member State which processes data of legal persons will be subject to data protection rules and a provider B in a different Member State processing the same information will not. Therefore, it can be a barrier for the provider A to provide services in the country of the provider B, because he will have the additional burden to comply with data protection rules, what the provider B will not.

[15]See, for instance, Giovanni Buttarelli, Speaking points of the Assistant European Data Protection Supervisor on the Council Working Group on e-Justice and interconnection of insolvency registers, 15 July 2009. http://www.edps.europa.eu/EDPSWEB/webdav/shared/Documents/EDPS/Publications/Speeches/2009/09-07-15_eJustice_insolvency_EN.pdf. Accessed 4 January 2011.

A possible solution seems to be the enlargement of the concept of personal data contained in the Directive, in order to compulsorily comprise information related to legal persons, since there is no sense in such a distinction, because both kinds of data are processed in the same way and for the same purposes. It is worth noting that the European Court of Human Rights in the Société Colas Est Case[16] extended to legal persons the protection of one sphere of privacy ensured by Article 8 of the European Convention on Human Rights.[17] The e-Privacy Directive (2002/58/EC), adopted a similar position, extending some of its provisions to legal persons.[18]

The EU Commission Proposal for a General Data Protection Regulation lost the opportunity to harmonise the concept of personal data as suggested here. According to Article 4 (2) of the Proposal "'personal data' means any information relating to a data subject" and "data subject means an identified natural personal or a natural person who can be identified, directly or indirectly, by means reasonably likely to be used by the controller or by any other natural or legal person (. . .)."[19] That is to say that the concept of personal data adopted by the Proposal does not bring a solution for the current discrepancies in the concept of personal data adopted by different Member States.

Finally, and equally important, is the 'identifiability' of the data subject. None of the selected member states has incorporated reasonableness as a limit for the identification of the data subject. As discussed in Chap. 2 (2.1), it is important to establish clear criteria as to whether a data subject is identifiable or not. A criterion that fulfils the objectives of the expression 'means likely reasonably to be used' contained in Recital 26 of Directive 95/46/EC is the one that uses the amount of time, expenses and labour to verify whether an individual can be identified from a specific processing of data and whether such data can be considered as personal data. In the same sense, a definition of anonymous data, taking into account the reasonableness of the identification of the data subject, should also be incorporated.

---

[16]European Court of Human Rights. Société Colas Est v. France case. Application nº 37971/97 (16/04/2002). http://cmiskp.echr.coe.int/tkp197/view.asp?item=1&portal=hbkm&action=html&highlight=37971/97&sessionid=64275468&skin=hudoc-en. Accessed 4 January 2011.

[17]De Hert, Paul and Gutwirth, Serge, "Data Protection in the Case Law of Strasbourg and Luxemburg: Constitutionalisation in Action." Reinventing Data Protection?, Gutwirth, Serge et al. (editors). Springer, 2009. P. 17. "The Court has even gone so far as to recognise privacy protection to firms and business activities, which is non-mandatory feature of data protection regulation (which optionally allows Members States to recognise data protection rights not only to natural persons but also to legal persons)."

[18]Article 29 Working Party, Opinion 4/2007 on the concept of personal data, Op. cit.: 23. "Some provisions of the e-privacy Directive 2002/58/EC extend to legal persons. Article 1 thereof provides that '2. The provisions of this Directive particularise and complement Directive 94/46/EC for the purposes mentioned in paragraph 1. Moreover, they provide for protection of the legitimate interests of subscribers who are legal persons.' Accordingly, Articles 12 and 13 extend the application of some provisions concerning directories of subscribers and unsolicited communication also to legal persons."

[19]Article 4 (1).

The EU Proposal, although including in the definition of personal data the idea of reasonableness contained in Recital 26 of Directive 95/46/EC, does not present clear criteria for considering a data subject identifiable as proposed in this book.

Therefore, my contribution in that regard would be to broaden the concept of personal data to cover both legal and deceased persons and to incorporate clear criteria for the identification of the data subject, taking into account the time, expense, and labour involved in this process, and the adoption of a definition of anonymous data following these same parameters.[20]

6.2 Should We Still Rely on Consent?

The second theme that deserves attention is consent as a legal ground for the processing of personal data. From the comparison between the approaches adopted by the selected member states, especially in the industries under analysis, it can be seen that in most situations consent is a condition for the provision of a service.

Alaisdair R Maclean builds a possible definition of consent, although she recognises there is no consensus in that regard:

> Depending on context, consent may be seen as an agreement, a decision, a shared decision, a choice or permission (or waiver of a right). There is also disagreement over whether consent is a state of mind, an act of communication or both. Furthermore, while consent has traditionally been seen as an event, recent discussions have conceptualised consent as a process. It is, however, widely agreed that consent works by transforming a morally or legally impermissible act into a permissible one: if I give you my consent—and that consent is effective—I give you permission to do something to me or to something over which I exercise control.[21]

This same author presents what she believes are the prerequisites for consent to be effective:

> These are: understanding of what is being proposed (in the legal context this is expressed as information rather than understanding, which may be because it is practically easier to give someone information than it is to ensure that they understand it); the mental capacity to use the information and make a decision (legal competence); and the freedom to make a 'voluntary' decision, which is a decision not caused by the unjust influence of others through coercion, deception, or manipulation.[22]

---

[20]European Data Protection Supervisor. Opinion of 18 January 2011 on the Communication from the Commission to the European Parliament, the Council, the Economic and Social Committee and the Committee of the Regions—"A comprehensive approach on personal data protection in the European Union", http://www.edps.europa.eu/EDPSWEB/webdav/site/mySite/shared/Documents/Consultation/Opinions/2011/11-01-14_Personal_Data_Protection_EN.pdf. Accessed 9 January 2011: 13.

[21]Maclean, Alasdair R. The doctrine of informed consent: does it exist and has it crossed the Atlantic? Legal Studies, Vol. 24 (2004). P. 391.

[22]Ibid. P. 392.

Baroness Onora O'Neill, in the field of bioethics, questions the validity of informed consent as a clear free exercise of autonomy:

> Countless examples reveal the limits of consent. I may consent to a diagnostic genetic test, but if I have not been told or have not understood the implications of receiving a 'positive' result, I will not have consented to receiving the bad news. I may consent to an operation, yet for whatever reason not see its consequences—even its likely consequences—as something to which I have consented. I may go along with proposals for treatment and care that strike me as far from desirable because I am too weary or despairing or unconfident to do otherwise, or because I falsely believe that there are no other options or that I have to do what my doctor appears to want.[23]

David Lazer and Viktor Mayer-Schönberger discussing the importance of knowing the purpose of data collection for the validity of consent have a similar opinion:

> purpose plays an important role in how individuals decide to share their personal information or not. A person may not be willing to share medical information even with her doctor if it is just for the doctor's personal curiosity. If, however, the doctor explains that the personal information will be used in her treatment, the person may want to share her information with her doctor, and perhaps even other medical specialists. Individuals can only make an informed decision whether to share their personal information with somebody else if they know the exact purpose the information will be used for.[24]

There are many situations where there is no contract involved, so that consent is required as a condition for getting a certain consideration.[25] Even in those situations, the bargaining power of the data subject is very reduced, since he/she has only two options: either he/she gives his/her consent or he/she does not get the consideration offered.[26] Daniel Solove recognised the fragility of consent as a legal ground for the processing of personal data:

> The choices given to people over their information are hardly choices at all. People must relinquish personal data to gain employment, procure insurance, obtain a credit card, or otherwise participate like a normal citizen in today's economy. Consent is virtually meaningless in many contexts. When people give consent, they must often consent to a total surrender of control over their information.[27]

---

[23]O'Neill, Onora. Informed Consent and Genetic Information. Studies in History and Philosophy of Biological and Biomedical Sciences, Vol. 32, No. 4 (2001). P. 693.

[24]Lazer, David; Mayer-Schönberger, Viktor. Statutory Frameworks for Regulating Information Flows: Drawing Lessons for the DNA Data Banks from other Government Data Systems. Journal of Law, Medicine & Ethics, Vol. 34 (2006). P. 367.

[25]Article 29 Working Party. Opinion 15/2011 on the definition of consent. Op. cit. P. 14. "While a situation of subordination is often the main reason preventing consent to be free, other contextual elements can influence the decision of the data subject. They can have for instance a financial dimension, or an emotional or a practical dimension. The fact that the collection of data is performed by a public authority can also have some influence on the data subject. It can however be difficult to draw the line between a simple incentive and something that has a real influence on the freedom of the data subject to exercise a choice.

[26]For the sense the word consideration is used in this book, see footnote 99 of Chap. 1.

[27]Solove, Daniel J. The digital person. Op. cit. P. 60. Solove in another article quotes an example presented by Paul M. Schartz, which demonstrates the fragility of consent. In Solove, Daniel J.

The same author argues that "Consent is virtually meaningless in many contexts. When people give consent, they must often consent to a total surrender of control over their information",[28] and gives the example of opt-out systems, which, in his view "often provide individuals with an all-or-nothing choice: either agree to all forms of information collection and use or to none whatsoever. Such a limited set of choices does not permit individuals to express their preferences accurately."[29]

It is important to notice, however, that even when the consent is expressly given, this does not mean that the data subject had consciousness about what he/she was consenting to or that he/she had the possibility not to consent, as advocated by Baroness O'Neill. Edgar A. Whitley confirms the relevance of this problem:

> For informed consent to be meaningful, it is generally acknowledged that the individual giving the consent should understand what they are giving consent to (. . .). Informed consent is also meaningless if the individual has no choice about providing the consent ('Hobson's consent'). This lack of choice can arise in cases where data is collected for statutory purposes (such as data relating to your income tax obligations). In other cases, individuals may find that they have to provide data and consent to its use in order to gain access to electronic sources and services.[30]

It is true that Directive 95/46/EC excludes consent as a legal ground for the processing of personal data when it "is necessary for the performance of a contract to which the data subject is party or in order to take steps at the request of the data subject prior to entering into a contract; or (. . .) is necessary for compliance with a legal obligation to which the controller is subject." It is also true that the consent by itself "is not presented as a completely sufficient basis for legitimating processing. In any case—even in a case of unambiguous consent—it may be possible to declare the processing illegitimate if that processing is disproportionate."[31] However, this requirement still exists when sensitive data is involved, which, as observed in the previous chapters of this book, is often the case in the processing of personal data carried out by the industries under analysis. Charlesworth highlights the fact that:

> The construction of the Directive means that there is a significant role for data subject consent with respect to the fair and lawful processing of their data, both 'non-sensitive' and 'sensitive'. While there are other grounds under which fair and lawful processing may

---

Identity Theft, Privacy, and the Architecture of Vulnerability. Hastings Law Journal, Vol. 54 (2003–2003). P. 1234/1235. "Schartz notes how consent screens on a website asking users to relinquish control over information often do so on a 'take-it-or-leave-it basis' resulting in the 'fiction' that people have 'expressed informed consent to [the website's] data processing practices.'"

[28] Solove, Daniel J. Privacy and Power: Computer Databases and Metaphors for Information Privacy. Standford Law Review, Vol. 53 (2000–2001). P. 1427.

[29] Ibid. P. 1459.

[30] Whitley, Edgard A. Informational privacy, consent and the "control" of personal data. Information Security Technical Report, Vol. 14 (2009). P. 156.

[31] Rouvroy, Antoinette, Poullet, Yves. The right to informational self-determination and the value of self-development: Reassessing the importance of privacy for democracy. In *Reinventing data protection?* ed. Serge Gutwirth et al. Dordrecht: Springer. P. 73.

> take place, for example, the 'balance of interests' ground, which allows processing which is necessary for the legitimate interests of the data controller where the processing does not cause undue prejudice to the fundamental rights and freedoms of the data subject, consent is often the ground on which data controllers would prefer to justify their processing.[32]

Furthermore, Members States seem not to have reached an agreement on the way consent should be obtained:

> For example, it appears that Italy requires that consent must be 'freely expressed', 'specific', and 'documented in writing', which may cause difficulties with consent which has purportedly been given online. In Germany the standard for consent appears to be based on the 'opt-in' model, where the data subject must make some positive indication of consent, such as ticking a check box, while in the UK, it appears that implied consent, such as where the data subject has failed to tick an opt-out box, or where a customer, having been notified of new data processing purposes, continues to use the facilities provided by a company, will suffice, at least for the processing of non-sensitive data.[33]

Many are the examples of situations where consent is used as a legal ground for the processing of personal data but the data subject has no choice. For instance:

> The personal information required for account registration and identity verification varies between services, and potentially requires a wide range of personal and financial information (e.g., name, age, gender, email address, bank details, username and password). The user has very little control or choice over whether to provide the requested information if they wish to register with that service, although the type of personal and financial information required varies according to the nature of the service and according to the age of the user.[34]

Therefore, and considering the problems consent faces as a legal basis for the processing of personal data, it should only remain as such for the situations in which there is no consideration involved and when the requirements for a free consent are present: awareness of the implications of a specific data processing and the availability of acceptable alternatives regarding the manifestation of the consent, as discussed in Chap. 1.[35] In these cases there will not be any conditions limiting the freedom of choice of the data subject.[36] In all the other situations where the bargaining power of the data subject is compromised a different legal basis has to be used.

The EU Commission proposal for a General Data Protection Regulation seems to have adopted a similar approach, when "excluding the validity of the consent where

---

[32]Charlesworth, Andrew. Op. cit. P. 942.

[33]Charlesworth, Andrew. Op. cit. P. 943.

[34]Bryce, Jo and Klang, Mathias. Young people, disclosure of personal information and online privacy: Control, choice and consequences. Information Security Technical report, Vol. 14 (2009). P. 163.

[35]See item 1.3.1.1.

[36]Article 29 Working Party. Opinion 15/2011 on the definition of consent. Op. cit. P. 12. "Consent can only be valid if the data subject is able to exercise a real choice, and there is no risk of deception, intimidation, coercion or significant negative consequences if he/she does not consent. If the consequences of consenting undermine individuals' freedom of choice, consent would not be free."

there is a significant imbalance between the position of the data subject and the controller.[37] This is what can be inferred from Article 7 (4) of the EU Commission Proposal:

> Consent shall not provide a legal basis for the processing, where there is a significant imbalance between the position of the data subject and the controller.

However, the reading of the provision leads to the conclusion that all situations where there is an imbalance, even when a refusal to give consent does not trigger any negative effect or does not involve any consideration, of what seems to be inappropriate. As argued by DG INFSO:

> DG INFSO agrees that in many situations of imbalance (such as in an employer/employee relation), individuals' consent will not be freely given (individuals may feel coerced to accept). However, there may be the case when a refusal to accept does not rigger any negative consequence (e.g., acceptance/refusal to have a picture loaded in the intranet). Therefore, it seems inappropriate for the draft DP Regulation to completely exclude the use of consent in these situations.[38]

Nevertheless, to ensure the possibility of data subjects to exercise, to a certain extent, their autonomy with regard to the processing of their personal data in cases where consent is not a legal basis for the processing, I would suggest enlarging the scope of the right to object contained in article 14 of Directive 95/46/EC, to make it similar to the right to prevent a processing likely to cause damage or distress adopted in the UK. Actually, recital 38 of the EU Commission Proposal ensures the exercise of this 'new' right by affirming that "The data subject should have the right to object the processing, on grounds relating to their particular situation".[39] Furthermore, I would strengthen the principle of data minimisation, as does the EU Commission Proposal, by explicitly incorporating this principle both in Recital 30 and in article 5(c), which, in my view, would put a heavier burden on data controllers to only process data which are really necessary for the achievement of the intended

---

[37] European Data Protection Supervisor. Op. cit. 2012. P. 21.

[38] Information Society and Media Directorate General (INFSO). Reply to the interservice consultation launched by DG JUST on the draft proposal of a DP Regulation and a draft proposal of a Police and Criminal Justice DP Directive. 22 December 2011. P. 8.

[39] See also article 19 of the EU Commission Proposal for a General Data Protection Regulation: Article 19—Right to object.

1. The data subject shall have the right to object, on grounds relating to their particular situation, at any time to the processing of personal data which is based on points (c), (e) and (f) of Article 6 (1), unless the controller demonstrates compelling legitimate grounds for the processing which override the interests or fundamental rights and freedoms of the data subject.
2. Where personal data are processed for direct marketing purposes, the data subject shall have the right to object free of charge to the processing of their personal data for such marketing. This right shall be explicitly offered to the data subject in an intelligible manner and shall be clearly distinguishable from other information.
3. Where an objection is upheld pursuant to paragraphs 1 and 2, the controller shall no longer use or otherwise process the personal data concerned.

result, adopting all technological means for such a purpose. This would impose upon data controllers the need to apply the idea of the 'Privacy by Design'[40] in all systems developed with the aim of processing personal data[41]:

> It should convey the requirement that ICT should not only maintain security but also should be designed and constructed in a way to avoid or minimize the amount of personal data processed.[42]

Such approach of expressly requiring the application of the principle of privacy by design was adopted by the EU Commission Proposal in its article 23.[43]

Specifically regarding the processing of sensitive data, I would recommend the inclusion of the requirement to obtain a prior authorisation from the National Data Protection Authority, as in the case of Italy and France, before starting any

---

[40]Article 29 Working Party; Working Party on Police and Justice. Op. cit. P. 13. "They should be obliged to take technological data protection into account already at the planning stage of information-technological procedures and systems. Providers of such services as well as controllers should demonstrate that they have taken all measures required to comply with these requirements."

[41]In the same sense see Linkomles, Laura. European Union to Strengthen Privacy Framework. Privacy Laws & Business. Issue 103. February 2010. P. 7. "The European Digital Rights Initiative (EDRi) calls for more transparency and data minimisation. The group says: <<A revision of the directive should include stronger principles ensuring the minimisation of the collection and processing of personal data. The criterion should be 'adequate, relevant and not excessive in relation to the purposes for which they are collected and/or further processed' has proven to be an inadequate threshold for judging legitimate versus illegitimate collection of personal data. Firstly, this standard should be made more strict, by allowing only the collection of data which is 'strictly necessary' for the purposes. Secondly, the 'legitimate interest' test under which most of these purposes are evaluated, should be interpreted so as to minimise the collection and processing of personal data."

[42]Article 29 Working Party; Working Party on Police and Justice. Op. cit. P. 13.

[43]Article 23—**Data protection by design and by default**

1. Having regard to the state of the art and the cost of implementation, the controller shall, both at the time of the determination of the means for processing and at the time of the processing itself, implement appropriate technical and organizational measures and procedures in such a way that the processing will meet the requirements of this Regulation and ensure the protection of the rights of the data subject.
2. The controller shall implement mechanisms for ensuring that, by default, only those personal data are processed which are necessary for each specific purpose of the processing and are especially not collected or retained beyond the minimum necessary for those purposes, both in terms of the amount of the data and the time of their storage. In particular, those mechanisms shall ensure that by default personal data are not made accessible to an indefinite number of individuals.
3. The Commission shall be empowered to adopt delegated acts in accordance with Article 86 for the purpose of specifying any further criteria and requirements for appropriate measures and mechanisms referred to in paragraph 1 and 2, in particular for data protection by design requirements applicable across sectors, products and services.
4. The Commission may lay down technical standards for the requirements laid down in paragraph 1 and 2. Those implementing acts shall be adopted in accordance with the examination procedure referred to in Article 87 (2).

processing involving this kind of data, since Directive 95/46/EC does not include in article 8 (2) this requirement for the processing of sensitive data to be legitimate. It is important to notice that the new legal instrument should also include provisions regarding the processing of genetic data, establishing the limits of such use by the private sector as indicated in Chap. 2 of this book (Sect. 2.2.3).

6.3 The Compulsoriness of the Data Protection Officer

With the entry into force of the Lisbon treaty and with the abolishment of the pillar structure, there is a clear need for the adoption of a coordinated and uniform approach to data protection for all former pillar issues, as highlighted at the beginning of this chapter. In that sense, an interesting point is the mechanism adopted by some member states,[44] the so-called Data Protection Officer, which goes in the same direction of Regulation 45/2001.[45] This mechanism helps data protection authorities to enforce the rules and to maximise their activities, since they will only have to communicate with a specific person, limiting some bureaucratic burdens. Furthermore, the nomination of the Data Protection Officer by a specific sector usually reduces the formalities this sector has to comply with in terms of data protection rules and also some duties of the national data protection authority, such as the one of keeping a register of data controllers.[46] Therefore, the inclusion in the Directive of a provision regarding the nomination of Data Protection Officers, as a compulsory requirement for large companies and corporations (and governmental bodies), and as a non-compulsory one for small and medium enterprises, with the possibility of indicating a single DPO for a whole sector, would be an important contribution to facilitating the tasks of the national data protection authorities.[47] In this same line, the new EU Commission proposal creates an obligation in its article 35 for controllers (and processors) which employ 250 or more or whose core activities "consist of processing operations which, by virtue of their nature, their scope and/or their purposes, require regular and systematic monitoring of data subjects" to nominate a DPO.[48] It also creates the possibility for groups of

---

[44] Laffaire, Marie-Laure. Op. cit. P. 195. "Ce système a déjà été adopté et consacré par plusieurs autres états membres: le Luxembourg, l'Allemagne, les Pays-bas, la Suède, la Finlande et la Belgique. Dans certains cas ce détaché est obligatoire, dans d'autres il est facultatif."

[45] See Article 41 of Regulation 45/2001.

[46] See, for instance, the French Data Protection Act.

[47] European Commission. Draft Communication to the European Parliament, the Council, the Economic and Social Committee and the Committee of the Regions on a comprehensive approach on personal data protection in the European Union. Available at http://ec.europa.eu/justice/news/consulting_public/0006/com_2010_609_en.pdf. Accessed 29 March 2011. P. 12.

[48] Article 35.

undertakings to designate a single DPO for the whole group and for associations or other bodies representing categories of controllers or processors; for these latter this possibility only exists when the controllers or processors they represent are not included in the cases referred to paragraph 1 of Article 35 of the Proposal. As advocated by the European Data Protection Supervisor:

> the DPO, performing his duties and tasks independently, is a key element of the proposed new legal framework since he would have not only to inform and advise the controller or the processor of their obligations but also to monitor internally the application of the Regulation and finally to act as the contact point of the supervisory authority.[49]

However, I agree with INFSO that the obligation to designate a DPO should exist only for large companies and corporations, and that the threshold established by the proposed Regulation—250 employees—could impose an excessive burden on small or medium sized companies.[50]

6.4 Towards a Mutual Recognition System for Data Protection

Another interesting system adopted by some member states is the one that allows data protection authorities to deliver quality labels to certify that personal data are processed in compliance with data protection rules and standards.[51] It seems, however, that in the review of the Data Protection Directive a step towards a mutual recognition mechanism should be adopted. Instead of only stimulating the adoption of quality labels at a national level, a true mechanism of mutual recognition in the data protection sphere should be created. Through mutual recognition, once a state recognises that a processing activity complies with data protection rules, the other states have to accept this decision.[52] In the words of Patrick Griffin, "mutual recognition can be defined as reciprocal agreement among jurisdictions to accept the others' regulatory standards that govern the creation and conduct of companies and business."[53]

---

[49]European Data Protection Supervisor. Op. Cit. 2012. P. 34.

[50]Information Society and Media Directorate General (INFSO). Op. cit. 2011. P. 15.

[51]Belleil, Arnaud. La regulation economique des données personnelles? In LEGICOM nº 42—2009/1. La régulation des données personnelles. Victoires Éditions: Paris, 2009. P. 149. "En Europe le chantier n'est pas partout au point mort. Une riche expérience a été acquise par l'autorité de protection du Schwelsig Holstein (Allemagne), véritable précurseurs européen en matière de délivrance de label protection des données personnelles (Datenschutz-Gütesiegel)."

[52]About the importance of the principle of mutual recognition for an integration process see Schmidt, Susanne K. Mutual Recognition as a new mode of governance, in Journal of European Public Policy 14:5 August 2007. P. 671.

[53]Griffin, Patrick B. Delaware Effect: Keeping the Tiger in Its Cage—The European Experience on Mutual Recognition in Financial Services. 7 Colum. J. Eur. L. 337 (2001). P. 337.

The lack of a mutual recognition system creates undue constraints to data controllers, since "Where a data controller is established in several Member States, each of those establishments must comply with the obligations laid down by the relevant national law."[54]

The adoption of a mutual recognition mechanism would avoid, for example, the decision taken by the French Data Protection Authority against the request presented by Experian to initiate the specific processing of personal data that was already carried out in many EU member states and would foster the integration of markets and reduce legal uncertainty.[55]

Andrew Charlesworth suggests a mechanism, with which I agree, based on the 'country of registration', according to which controllers could designate one Member State "where they are formally registered for data protections purposes".

It could be argued, however, that the possibility of choosing a specific Member State could lead to 'mutual recognition tourism', i.e., companies concentrating their activities (or registering for data protection purposes) in member states that they know have a more flexible approach to data protection, which could result in a "race to the bottom" regarding the level and quality of data protection. The same author points out that:

> While it might be argued that this would lead to a 'race to the bottom', with data controllers choosing to register in the Member State with the least onerous data protection rules, if the Member State concerned has a satisfactory implementation of the Directive, as ascertained by the Commission (and, where necessary, the European Court of Justice), then the baseline of EU protection will still be maintained. Such a mechanism would encourage Member States to harmonize more effectively, because the imposition of national rules not required by the Directive, or which are significantly more onerous than the norm, will simply lead to data controllers registering elsewhere.[56]

The EU Commission proposal "introduces a consistency mechanism for ensuring unity of application in relation to processing operations which may concern data

---

[54]Charlesworth, Andrew. Op. cit. P. 949.

[55]Linkomles, Laura. European Union to Strengthen Privacy Framework. Privacy Laws & Business. Issue 103. February 2010. P. 7. "On applicable law, the group supports the suggestions by Francis Aldhouse, the former UK Deputy Information Commissioner, who advocates the system of mutual recognition: <<Applying their experience since 1995, national data protection authorities have, through the Article 29 Working Party and other means, generated great consensus on the application of the law. With the increased understanding and confidence between national governments and regulators, the time is now right to amend the Directive and adopt the practice of home-country regulation. The system of mutual recognition, which is well precedented in the European Union, would allow users of personal information operating in more than one European state to be subject only to the law and regulation of one of those states. Those providing information services from outside Europe in more than one European state would similarly be subject to the jurisdiction of a single European regulator. None of these changes would prejudice the rights of individuals to secure a remedy in their home jurisdiction."

[56]Charlesworth, Andrew. Op. cit. P. 955.

subjects in several Member States".[57] However, such mechanism does not go so far as the mutual recognition system proposed in this chapter, since it leaves for the EU Commission the final decision regarding a measure intended to produce legal effects adopted by a national supervisory authority, creating a hierarchy between the EU Commission and such authorities,[58] instead of stimulating a procedure where the authorities themselves would recognise the decisions taken by each single national supervisory authority.[59] Furthermore, the EU Commission proposal also creates a 'one-stop shop rule' for jurisdiction and competence of Data Protection Authorities, which empowers the DPA of the Member State where the controller has its main establishment to supervise the processing activities of the respective controller in all Member States.[60] But again, this mechanism does not create a mutual recognition system, instead, it puts a heavy burden on DPAs, which will have to supervise processing activities in different Member States.

Therefore, the best option for ensuring consistency and fostering harmonisation would be the adoption of a mutual recognitions system, based on the country of registration instead of the approach adopted by the EU Commission proposal, which impose a very heavy burden on DPAs to supervise processing activities out of their Member State of origin.

6.5 Codes of Conduct as a Supplement of the Data Protection Legislation

Finally, the last recommendation regards the industries analysed in this book. As observed in the previous chapters, there are significant differences in the data protection rules affecting these industries in the different member states, such as regarding storage limits, the kinds of data that can be processed, and the extension of data subjects' rights, amongst others. For example, in some states both negative and positive information can be processed for credit purposes and in others just

---

[57]European Commission. Explanatory Memorandum to the Proposal for a Regulation of the European Parliament and of the Council on the protection of individual with regard to the processing of personal data and on the free movement of such data (General Data Protection Regulation). COM (2012) 11 final. Published 25 January 2012. Available at http://ec.europa.eu/justice/data-protection/document/review2012/com_2012_11_en.pdf. Accessed 7 April 2012. P. 13.

[58]Costa, Luiz; Poullet, Yves. Op. cit. P. 261. "We underline the strange role played by the Commission according to Articles 59, 60 and 61, which enact that in a last resort the Commission may adopt an opinion to ensure 'correct and consistent application of this Regulation'. Such opinion must be taken into 'utmost account' by the supervisory authority otherwise it may see its measure suspended."

[59]See Article 62.

[60]ARTICLE 29 Data Protection Working Party. Opinion 01/2012 on the data protection reform proposal. WP 191. Adopted on 23 March 2012. P. 18.

negative information. Moreover, there are states where some kinds of information, such as judicial data, can be processed by credit registers and where information stored by credit bureaus can be exchanged with other sectors outside of the financial industry. Furthermore, the storage limits vary significantly from one member state to another, resulting in some providers having more access to the personal data of their customers than others. All these differences[61] create a clear barrier for the offering of cross-border services by these companies and for the integration of these markets, especially without a system of mutual recognition, since they have to face not only the differences of interpretation of the law, but also of the different standards developed by the respective sectors in the different member states.

It would be impossible to include in the Directive provisions specific to all the different sectors. Nevertheless, the strategy applied in Italy seems to be a good one: the adoption of codes of conduct for certain sectors, establishing rules focused on the characteristics of those sectors. Such codes of conduct, which play an important role in the supplementation of the law, take into account the specificities of the processing carried out by a certain sector, and would not be normal self-regulatory regimes. Instead, they would have binding effects and could be enforced by the national data protection authorities as in the Italian case. Accordingly, Article 27 of Directive 95/46/EC should be amended to include an obligation for the member states to work together with some specific sectors, which include the financial one, to develop codes of conduct with binding effects. This approach should also be taken with regard to either European Codes of Conduct or National Codes of Conduct. The first could work as important instruments, collating all existing national codes of conduct, reducing further the remaining differences,[62] and the latter, combined with a mutual recognition system, could work as an important tool for market integration.

It is true that the current EU framework allows the Commission and the Member States to encourage the drawing up of Codes of Conduct,[63] however, it does not create enforcement powers either to the Commission or to Member States over the rules of the Codes of Conduct they approve.[64] Furthermore, as highlighted by Andrew Charlesworth:

> It seems that the major stumbling block to this type of development is the fact that, despite the Directive providing for the drawing up of Codes of Conduct at the national level, and providing an oversight mechanism for conformity of EU-level Codes with national legislation, it provides neither the Commission nor the Member States with the power to approve EU-wide Codes of Conduct for particular sectors or enterprises, or any administrative mechanism by which this might occur. This has led to the growth of often

[61]See, for instance, Article 29 Working Party. Contribution to the public consultation of DG MARKET on the report of the Expert Group on Credit Histories. Op. cit. P. 6.

[62]European Commission. Draft Communication to the European Parliament, the Council, the Economic and Social Committee and the Committee of the Regions on a comprehensive approach on personal data protection in the European Union. Op. cit. P. 12.

[63]See article 27 of Directive 95/46/EC.

[64]Actually, who analyses the 'Community Codes' is the Article 29 Working Party, whose decisions do not have a binding effect. See Article 27 (3) of Directive 95/46/EC.

> incompatible national codes of practice for particular sectors. In contrast, EU-wide Codes of Conduct could be used as harmonizing tools, by virtue of Commission or Member State approval permitting mutual recognition of a Code across the Member States.[65]

The EU Commission Proposal clarifies "the content of the codes and the procedures and providing for the empowerment of the Commission to decide on the general validity of codes of conduct", in a way similar to the one suggested in this book.[66] Nevertheless, it does not empower the Commission or the National Data Protection Authorities with supervisory or enforcement powers over the rules contained in these codes of conduct, failing to confer binding effects to them.[67]

Therefore, the recommendation made in this section goes further than the new proposal for a general data protection regulation, recently put forward by the European Commission.

6.6 Chapter Conclusion

The recommendations made in this chapter have as their aim to offer a contribution to the debates on the review of the current Data Protection Framework in the European Union, with a view of reducing the barriers for the free flow of information and to help to foster the creation of a single market of services, with emphasis on the case-studies analysed in this book.

I hope that the recommendations made in this book will be duly taken into account in the final text of the regulation.

---

[65]Charlesworth, Andrew. Op. cit. P. 967.

[66]European Commission. Explanatory Memorandum to the Proposal for a Regulation of the European Parliament and of the Council on the protection of individual with regard to the processing of personal data and on the free movement of such data (General Data Protection Regulation). Op. cit. P. 11.

[67]See article 38 of the EU Commission Proposal for a General Data Protection Regulation.

Conclusion

As a consequence of the revolution caused by the information technologies, governments and private companies process personal data on a very large scale. Air companies collect and transfer passenger data to law enforcement authorities around the world, Internet Service Providers store traffic data and telecom companies keep track of all calls made and received by a specific phone number, mobile phones and geo-location devices allow the identification of the exact location of a certain individual, and CCTV cameras record images of millions of people around the world every day. This 'revolution' poses new threats to information privacy that need to be countered through data protection.

I have concentrated my research on this informational aspect, with special attention to the impact of different data protection rules on the integration of insurance and financial markets in a regional bloc, and have tried to show how important it is to harmonise those rules between the bloc's member states.

In carrying out this analysis, I firstly came to the conclusion that the European model of data protection is the prevailing one. Even US companies are adhering to the 'Safe Harbour Scheme' in order to be recognised by the EU as complying with data protection rules. Thus my analysis has been focused on the European Framework. I have also shown that at the European level there are different legal frameworks that apply to personal data, CoE Convention 108/81, Directive 95/46/EC, Council Framework Decision 2008/977/JHA and so on. This diversity makes the task of interpreting the law more complex.

I have then addressed the case studies of this book—insurance, banks and credit information suppliers—and the way the European Framework is responding to new threats posed not only by the development of new technologies but also by this 'new' globalised world without boundaries, where the flow of information has become a fundamental tool for business activities.

In this regard, I observed that different kinds of data, such as the genetic ones, are now largely used by companies in order to better know their clients. However, this type of information has not received the necessary attention from the European

M. Viola de Azevedo Cunha, *Market Integration Through Data Protection*,
Law, Governance and Technology Series 9, DOI 10.1007/978-94-007-6085-1,

legislator and, as a consequence, has not been properly regulated. Furthermore, I have considered the need to better specify the concept of anonymous data and the consequences it can have on the application of data protection.

Regarding the first issue, I have identified some criteria for checking whether the further use of data complies with data protection rules and standards. As far as the concept of anonymous data is concerned, a 'solution' was proposed and goes in a similar direction to the one adopted by Directive 95/46/EC, but putting more emphasis on the amount of time, expense and labour required to make a data identifiable.

I have then analysed the processing of genetic data, especially in the field of insurance. After discussing the pros and cons, I have concluded that this processing should be forbidden as a rule, but it could be accepted, as an exception, in the case of life insurance when a certain amount of coverage is involved and the genetic data refers to late onset single gene disorders.

After analysing the legal framework at the EU level, I have concentrated on the different experiences of three selected EU member states (France, Italy and the UK) in terms of the implementation of data protection law. I have shown that there are considerable disparities in the way each member state approaches data protection, starting from the sole definition of personal data, through the role of data protection authorities and data subjects' rights. Differences are even greater in the specific sectors that were analysed in this book.

Taking into account this scenario and the changes imposed by the Lisbon Treaty, both in terms of decision making processes and of data protection itself, I have proposed some changes in the current EU data protection framework, in order to stimulate not only further harmonisation within the EU/EEA area, but also (and perhaps, more importantly) to promote a better integration of the analysed markets without reducing the level of protection of individuals.

My main suggestions relate to the concept of personal data, which should be extended to legal and deceased persons; to the role of consent as a legal ground for the processing of personal data, which should be sufficient only when no consideration is involved; to strengthening the data minimisation principle in combination with the idea of Privacy by Design; to the creation of a legal obligation for companies to nominate a data protection officer as provided for by Regulation 45/2001 for EU institutions and bodies. Moreover, I have suggested the creation of a mutual recognition system, to avoid that a processing being carried out in one member state could be considered as illegitimate in another one. Finally, I have recommended the incorporation of the idea of codes of conducts, supplementing general data protection laws for sector-specific regulation, as a new source of law, with binding effects and giving powers to data protection authorities to enforce them.

I believe that an appropriate framework for data protection can play an important role in the process of market integration. For providing better services to their customers, companies have to know them, and their main asset in that case is information.[1] In the financial and insurance sectors, as highlighted in other parts of this book, the use of information is even more important, becoming a true raw material of these activities.

I have already pointed out the fact that the lack of convergence of data protection laws in a transnational scenario, as the one of the European Union, "leads to additional costs, administrative and organizational problems, or may even lead, though in practice only occasionally, to a total prohibition" of data flow or data transfer amongst the countries involved and, of course, "creates uncertainty for those who are dependent on the free flow of personal data."[2] Therefore, the establishment of a more harmonised level of data protection norms within the European Union could reduce such differences and facilitate cross-border services,[3] helping to achieve one of the main objectives of the Union: market integration. Nevertheless, that is not the only reason for data protection to be considered as an important tool for integration.

Providers of products and services, while needing to use personal information of their customers, must ensure that information is accurate and regularly updated. Inaccuracy of data is a barrier for market integration, because it leads providers of services and goods to make decisions based on wrong premises. Banks and insurance companies wrongly reject risks based upon inaccurate information.

At this point the principle of data quality comes into the picture. As already highlighted, this principle requires that personal data be kept accurate and up-to-date. To ensure compliance with the data quality principle, data protection laws created a mechanism for the enforcement of data subjects' rights. It is through the exercise of these rights that data subjects can control the quality of their data stored by providers, ensuring that decisions which affect them will be based on accurate information. Hence, the implementation of a common level of data protection within the European Union, which ensures similar data protection rights for data subjects in all member states, helps to reduce the barriers for the integration of a specific market. The establishment of a more harmonised legislative environment would

[1] Soriano, Paul. Lire, Écrire, Parler, Penser dans la société de l'information. Descartes & Cie: Paris, 1999. P. 114. "Pour mieux servir (ou mieux paître) le consomateur, l'entreprise s'éclate, en réseau, virtuelle, débarassée des organigrammes et autres status paralysants (. . .). Désormais, son actif pricipal, immatériel, est constitué par de l'intelligence, de l'information, des logiciels et des bases des données."

[2] Nugter, A.C.M. Transborder Flow of Personal Data within the EC: A comparative analysis of the privacy statutes of the Federal Republic of Germany, France, the United Kingdom and The Netherlands and their impact on the private sector. Deventer: Kluwer Law and Taxation Publishers, 1990. P. 320.

[3] "A questo proposito, peraltro, non solo la dottrina sul tema, ma gli stessi <<considerando>> della direttiva comunitaria rendono consapevoli della complessità della materia anche in considerazione dell'esigenza di contemperare interessi contraposti, ad un capo dei quail sta quello alla circolazione delle informazione ed all'altro queli relative al rispetto della persona." In Bianca, Cesare Massimo; Busnelli, Francesco Donato. Op. cit. P. 14.

facilitate the supply of cross-border services (and goods) and ensure the quality of the information providers use to make their decisions regarding a specific customer.

Accordingly, it is possible to conclude by reaffirming that data protection is an important integrative tool because it allows the free flow of personal information amongst member states; creates a good atmosphere for the free movement of services (and goods), reduces the costs for the supply of services and goods in a cross-border perspective, and increases the competitiveness of member states' markets as a whole, protecting at the same time individuals' privacy concerning the use of their personal data. As pointed out by the European Data Protection Supervisor, "Data protection fosters trust, and trust is an essential component of the well functioning of our society."[4]

References

Books, Book Chapters, Articles, Working Papers and Other Academic Publications

Acciai, Riccardo. 2007. *Il codice della privacy—Annotato con la giurisprudenza e le decisione del garante*. Santarcangelo di Romagna: Maggioli.

Agre, Philip E., and Marc Rotenberg (eds.). 1998. *Technology and privacy: The new landscape*. Cambridge: MIT Press.

Bagenstos, Samuel R. 2003. "Rational discrimination", accommodation, and the politics of (disability) civil rights. *Virginia Law Review* 89(5): 825–923.

Baker, Tom. 2001. Containing the promise of insurance: Adverse selection and risk classification. University of Connecticut School of Law articles working paper series. Available at: http://lsr.nellco.org/cgi/viewcontent.cgi?article=1002&context=uconn/ucwps. 1 Feb 2008.

Basedow, Jürgen, et al. (eds.). 2009. *Principles of European Insurance Contract Law (PEICL)*, 69. Munich: Sellier European Law Publishers.

Batellaan, Pieter, and Fons Coomans. 1999. The international basis for intercultural education including anti-racist and human rights education: A selection of articles from relevant documents, adopted by the governments of member states of the United Nations, UNESCO, the Organisation on Security and Co-operation in Europe, and the Council of Europe, 2nd ed. International Association for Intercultural Education (IAIE) in co-operation with UNESCO: International Bureau of Education (IBE) and the Council of Europe. Available at http://arno.unimaas.nl/show.cgi?fid=113. 13 Apr 2009.

Belleil, Arnaud. 2009. La regulation economique des données personnelles? In *LEGICOM n° 42–2009/1. La régulation des données personnelles*. Paris: Victoires Éditions.

Bennett, Louise. 2009. Reflections on privacy, identity and consent in on-line services. *Information Security Technical Report* 14: 120.

Bennett, Colin, and Charles D. Raddb. 2006. *The governance of privacy—Policy instruments in global perspective*. Cambridge: MIT Press.

Bensoussan, Alain. 2008. *Informatique et libertes*. Paris: Éditions Francis Lefebvre.

---

[4]European Data Protection Supervisor. Opinion on the Communication from the Commission to the European Parliament, the Council and the Economic and Social Committee and the Committee of the Regions—"A comprehensive approach on personal data protection in the European Union". Op. cit. P. 6.

Bianca, Cesare Massimo, and Francesco Donato Busnelli. 2007. La protezione dei dati personali. Cedam: Torino, LXXIX.

Botta, Marco, and Mario Viola de Azevedo Cunha. 2010. La protezione dei dati personali nelle relazioni tra UE e USA: Le negoziazioni sui trasferimento dei PNR. *Diritto Dell'Informazione e Dell'Informatica* 26(2): 315–341.

Brandeis, Louis, and Samuel Warren. 1890. The right to privacy. *Harvard Law Review* IV(5): 193–220. http://groups.csail.mit.edu/mac/classes/6.805/articles/privacy/Privacy_brand_warr2.html. 5 Jan 2010.

Bryce, Jo, and Mathias Klang. 2009. Young people, disclosure of personal information and online privacy: Control, choice and consequences. *Information Security Technical Report* 14(3): 160–166.

Burley, Justine. 2007. An abstract approach to the regulation of human genetics: Law, morality and social policy. In *The regulatory challenge of biotechnology*, ed. H. Somsen. Cheltenham: Edward Elgar Publishing.

Buster, Jargon. 2010. Principles of reciprocity. Available at http://www.annualcreditreport.co.uk/help/jargon/principles-of-reciprocity.htm. 12 Mar 2010.

Buttarelli, Giovanni. 2009. Speaking points of the assistant European data protection supervisor on the council working group on e-justice and interconnection of insolvency registers. 15 July. http://www.edps.europa.eu/EDPSWEB/webdav/shared/Documents/EDPS/Publications/Speeches/2009/09-07-15_eJustice_insolvency_EN.pdf. 4 Jan 2011.

Bygrave, Lee A., and Dag Wiese Schartum. 2009. Consent, proportionality and collective power. In *Reinventing data protection?* ed. Serge Gutwirth et al. Dordrecht, Heidelberg, New York, London: Springer.

Capron, A.M. 2000. Genetics and insurance: Accessing and using private information. In *Social philosophy & policy: The right to privacy, vol. 17, Number 2*, ed. Ellen Frankel Paul. Bowling Green: Bowling Green State University.

Carey, Peter. 2000. *Data protection in the UK*. London: Blackstone Press.

Carey, Peter. 2004. *Data protection: A practical guide to UK and EU law*, 2nd ed. New York: Oxford University Press.

Cate, Fred H., et al. 2003. *Financial privacy, consumer prosperity and the public good*. Washington: Brookings Joint Center for Regulatory Studies.

Cavoukian, Ann. What is privacy by design? Available at http://www.privacybydesign.ca/. 21 Jan 2010.

Charlesworth, Andrew. 2002–2003. Information privacy law in the European Union: E pluribus unum or ex uno plures? *Hastings Law Journal* 54: 931–969.

Clayton, Richard. 2010. The Phorm 'Webwise' system. http://www.cl.cam.ac.uk/~rnc1/080518-phorm.pdf. Accessed 7 Nov 2010.

Costa, Luiz, and Yves Poullet. 2012. Privacy and the regulation of 2012. *Computer Law & Security Review* 28(3): 251–378.

Cuffaro, Vincenzo, et al. 2007. *Il codice del trattamento dei dati personali*. Torino: G. Giappichelli Editore.

De Hert, Paul, and Serge Gutwirth. 2009. Data protection in the case law of Strasbourg and Luxemburg: Constitutionalisation in action. In *Reinventing data protection?* ed. Serge Gutwirth et al. Dordrecht, Heidelberg, New York, London: Springer.

DeCew, Judith Wagner. 1997. *In pursuit of privacy—Law, ethics, and the rise of technology*. Ithaca and London: Cornell University Press.

DeCew, Judith. 2006. Privacy. Stanford encyclopedia of philosophy. Available at http://plato.stanford.edu/entries/privacy/. 13 Mar 2010.

Digital Civil Rights in Europe. 2010. SWIFT agreement adopted by the European parliament. 14 July. Available at http://www.edri.org/edrigram/number8.14/swift-20-adopted-european-parliament. Accessed 12 Sept 2012.

Dolgin, Janet L. 2001. Ideologies of discrimination: Personhood and the 'genetic group'. *Studies in History and Philosophy of Biological and Biomedical Sciences* 32(4). Great Britain: Elsevier.

Doneda, Danilo. 2003. Um código para a proteção de dados na Itália. *Revista Trimestral de Direito Civil*. Rio de Janeiro. v. 16, out/dez.

Doneda, Danilo, and Mario Viola de Azevedo Cunha. 2009. Risk and personal information: The finality principle and data protection in the Brazilian Legal System. *RBRSi*, Rio de Janeiro, Brazil, 3(3): 133–150. Available at http://www.rbrs-i.com/img/upload/RBRSi%203-3%20Danilo%20Doneda.pdf. Accessed 21 Jan 2010.

Doneda, Danilo, and Mario Viola de Azevedo Cunha. 2010. Data protection as a trade resource in Mercosur: A data protection framework as an integrative tool. In *The law of Mercosur*, ed. Filho Franca, Toscato Marcílio, et al. Oxford: Hart Publishing.

Etzioni, Amitai. 2006. A communitarian approach: A viewpoint on the study of the legal and ethical policy considerations raised by DNA tests and databases. *The Journal of Law, Medicine & Ethics* 34: 214–221.

Ferretti, Federico. 2008. *The law and consumer credit information in the European community—The regulation of credit information systems*. London: Routledge-Cavendish.

Financial Times. German court ruling on data law sends out shock waves. Available at http://www.ft.com/cms/s/0/c6191de8-2663-11df-aff3-00144feabdc0.html?nclick_check=1. 18 Mar 2010.

Firmino, Rodrigo J. et al. 2011. *ICTs for mobile and ubiquitous urban infrastructures: Surveillance, locative media and global networks*. Hershey: IGI Publishing.

Francioni, Francesco. 2007. The international legal framework. In *Biotechnologies and international human rights*, ed. Francesco Francioni. Oxford/Portland: Hart Publishing.

Gediel, José Antônio Peres, and Adriana Espíndola Corrêa. 2008. Proteção jurídica de dados pessoais: A intimidade sitiada entre o estado e o mercado. *Revista da Faculdade de Direito da UFPR* 47: 141–153.

Gelpi, Rosa-Maria, and François Julien-Labruyère. 1994. *Histoire du crédit à La consommation—Doctrines et pratiques*. Paris: Éditions la découverte.

Gentot, Michel. 2008. La CNIL et son experience de la regulation de l'information. In *La <<Société de l'Informations>>—Entre myths et réalités. Collection medias, societes et relations internationales. N° 2*, ed. Michel Mathieu. Bruxelles: Bruylant.

Gentot, Michel. 2010. La protection des données personnelles à la croisée des chemins. In *Société d'information et vie privée. Tome III*, ed. Pierre Tabatoni. Available at http://www.asmp.fr/travaux/gpw/internetvieprivee/rapport3/chapitr1.pdf. 8 Oct 2010.

Godard, Béatrice, Yann Joly, and Bartha Maria Knoppers. 2004. A comparative international overview. In *Genetics and life insurance—Medical underwriting and social policy*, ed. Mark A. Rothstein. Cambridge: The MIT Press.

Griffin, Patrick B. 2001. Delaware effect: Keeping the tiger in its cage—The European experience on mutual recognition in financial services. *Columbia Journal of European Law* 7: 337.

Grodzinsky, Frances S., and Herman T. Tavani. 2005. P2P networks and the Verizon v. RIAA case: Implications for personal privacy and intellectual property. *Ethics and Information Technology* 7. Springer.

Hijmans, Hielke, and Alfonso Scirocco. 2009. Shortcomings in EU data protection in the third and the second pillars. Can the Lisbon treaty be expected to help? In *Common Market Law Review 46*. Netherlands: Kluwer Law International.

Huet, Jérôme. 2009. La CNIL a-t-elle acompli les missions dévolues par le législateur?. *LEGICOM n° 42–2009/1*. La régulation des données personnelles. Victoires Éditions: Paris.

Hurley, Deborah, and Viktor Mayer-Schönberger. 2000. Information policy and governance, in Joseph S. Nye and John D. Donahue (eds), *Governance in a Globalizing World* (Brookings 2000), 330.

Jentzsch, Nicola. 2007. *Financial privacy: An international comparison of credit reporting systems*, 2nd ed. Berlin: Springer.

Juth, Niklas, Marian Radetzki, and Marcus Radetzki. 2003. *Genes and insurance—Ethical, legal and economic issues*. Cambridge: Cambridge University Press.

Kass, Nancy E. 1997. The implications of genetic testing for health and life insurance. In *Genetic secrets: Protecting privacy and confidentiality in the genetic era*, ed. Mark A. Rothstein. New Haven/London: Yale University Press.

Kuner, C. 2003. *European data protection law and online business*. New York: Oxford University Press.

Kuner, C. 2007. *European data protection law—Corporate compliance and regulation*, 2nd ed. Oxford: Oxford University Press.

La Rochefoucauld, François. 2007. *La Rochefould Collected Maxims and other reflections – New translations with parallel French text*. Trans. E.H. Blackmore, A.M. Blackmore, and Francine Giguère. Oxford World's Classics. New York: Oxford University Press.

Lacoste, Jean-Marc. 2008. Pour une pleine et entière reconnaissance du droit à la protection des données à caractère personnel. Thesis presented with a view to obtaining the degree of Doctor of Laws of the Université de Toulouse (unpublished).

Laffaire, Marie-Laure. 2005. *Protection des données à caractere personnel*. Paris: Éditions d'organisation.

Lazer, David, and Viktor Mayer-Schönberger. 2006. Statutory frameworks for regulating information flows: Drawing lessons for the DNA data banks from other government data systems. *The Journal of Law, Medicine & Ethics* 34(2): 366–374.

Leemens, Trudo. 2003. Genetics and insurance discrimination: Comparative legislative, regulatory and policy developments and Canadian options. Health Law Journal Special Edition. Available at http://www.law.ualberta.ca/centres/hli/userfiles/Lemmens.pdf. 13 Jan 2011.

Lenox, Bryce A. 1997–1998. Genetic discrimination in insurance and employment: Spoiled fruits of the human genome project. *University of Dayton Law Review* 23: 209–211.

Lessig, Lawrence. 1999. *Code and other laws of cyberspace*. New York: Basic Books.

Lewicki, Bruno. 2003. *A privacidade da pessoa humana no ambiente de trabalho*. Rio de Janeiro: Renovar.

Liedtke, Patrick M. 2007. What's insurance to a modern economy. *The Geneva Papers on Risk and Insurance* 32: 211–221.

Linkomles, Laura. 2010a. United Kingdom organisations now face fines up to £ 500,000. *Privacy Laws & Business* Issue 103, Feb 2010.

Linkomles, Laura. 2010b. European Union to strengthen privacy framework. *Privacy Laws & Business* Issue 103, Feb 2010.

Maclean, Alasdair R. 2004. The doctrine of informed consent: Does it exist and has it crossed the Atlantic? *Legal Studies* 24(3): 386–413.

Mallet-Poujol, Nathalie. 2006. Protection de la vie privée et des données personnelles. Legamedia, Février. Available at http://www.educnet.education.fr/chrgt/guideViePrivee.pdf. Accessed 1 Aug 2011.

Martini, Luca. 2006. *Il diritto internazionale e comunitário della bioetica*. Torino: G. Giappichelli Editore.

Mattatia, Fabrice. 2009. CNIL et tribunaux: Concurrance ou complémentarité dans la répression des infractions à la loi informatique et libertes? RSC, Avril/Juin.

Mayer-Shönberger, Viktor. Apr 2007. Useful void: The art of forgetting in the age of ubiquitous computing. Faculty research working paper series, John F. Kennedy School of Government—Harvard University. RWP07-022.

Meyer, Roberta B. 2004. The insurer perspective. In *Genetics and life insurance—Medical underwriting and social policy*, ed. Mark A. Rothstein. Cambridge: The MIT Press.

Moraes, Maria Celina Bodin de. 2003a. *Danos à pessoa humana: Uma leitura civil constitucional*, 1st ed. Rio de Janeiro: Renovar.

Moraes, Maria Celina Bodin de. 2003b. O conceito de dignidade humana: Substrato axiológico e conteúdo normativo. In *Constituição, direitos fundamentais e direito privado*, ed. Ingo Sarlet. Porto Alegre: Editora Livraria do Advogado.

Moraes, Maria Celina Bodin de. 2006. *Princípios do direito civil contemporâneo*. Rio de Janeiro: Renovar.

Mosca, Sophie. 2010. ECJ: Supervisory authorities must be completely independent. Europolitics. 09 March. Available at http://www.europolitics.info/ecj-supervisory-authorities-must-be-completely-independent-art265573-10.html. 20 Mar 2010.

Mörth, Erika. 2004. Introduction. In *Soft law in governance and regulation: An interdisciplinary analysis*, ed. Erika Mörth. Cheltenham: Edward Elgar Publishing.

Murray, Thomas H. 1997. Genetic exceptionalism and 'future diaries': Is genetic information different from other medical information? In *Genetic secrets: Protecting privacy and confidentiality in the genetic era*, ed. Mark A. Rothstein. New Heaven/London: Yale University Press.

Niger, Sergio. 2004. Il diritto alla protezione dei dati personali. In *Il codice in materia di protezione dei dati personali*, ed. Juri Monducci and Giovanni Sartor. Padova: Cedam.

Nouwt, Sjaak. 2009. Towards a common European approach to data protection: A critical analysis of data protection perspectives of the council of Europe and the European Union. In *Reinventing data protection?* ed. Serge Gutwirth et al. Dordrecht, Heidelberg, New York, London: Springer.

Nugter, A.C.M. 1990. *Transborder flow of personal data within the EC: A comparative analysis of the privacy statutes of the Federal Republic of Germany, France, the United Kingdom and The Netherlands and their impact on the private sector*. Deventer: Kluwer Law and Taxation Publishers.

Ohm, Paul. Broken promises of privacy: Responding to the surprising failure of anonymization (13 Aug 2009). University of Colorado Law School legal studies research paper No. 09-12. http://ssrn.com/abstract=1450006. Accessed 7 Nov 2010.

O'Neill, Onora. 1998. Insurance and genetics: The current state of play. In *Law and human genetics—Regulating a revolution*, ed. Roger Brownsword et al. Oxford: Hart Publishing.

O'Neill, Onora. 2001. Informed consent and genetic information. *Studies in History and Philosophy of Biological and Biomedical Sciences* 32(4): 689–704.

Paissan, Mauro. 2007. Privacy protection and right to know. Striking a difficult balance. In *Spring conference of European data protection commissioners*. 10–11 May 2007. Available at http://www.garanteprivacy.it/garante/doc.jsp?ID=1408388. 8 Oct 2010.

Pallez, Christophe. L'exercice du pouvoir de sanction est une revolution culturelle pour la CNIL. Les petites affiches, n° 195, 29 Sept 2004.

Posner, Richard A. 1979. The 1978 James McCormick Mitchell lecture: Privacy, secrecy, and reputation. *Buffalo Law Review* 28(1): 1–55.

Poullet, Yves. 2009. La loi des données à caractère personnel: Un enjeu fondamental pour nos sociétés et nos démocraties ? In *LEGICOM n° 42–2009/1. La régulation des données personnelles*. Paris: Victoires Éditions.

Reden, Armgard von. Data protection activities in the private sector. Speech at the 21st international conference on privacy and personal data protection. Available at http://www.pcpd.org.hk/english/infocentre/files/von-reden-paper.doc. 15 Mar 2009.

Robinson, Neil, Hans Graux, Maarten Botterman, and Lorenzo Valeri. 2009. *Review of the European data protection directive*. Santa Monica, Arlington, Pittsburgh, Cambridge: RAND. Available at http://www.ico.gov.uk/upload/documents/library/data_protection/detailed_specialist_guides/review_of_eu_dp_directive.pdf. 23 Feb 2010.

Rodotà, Stefano. 2004. Transformações do corpo. *Revista Trimestral de Direito Civil* 19, jul/set. Rio de Janeiro: Renovar.

Rodotà, Stefano. 2006a. *La vita e le regole—Tra diritto e non diritto*. Milano: Feltrinelli.

Rodotà, Stefano. 2006b. In *Libera circolazione e protezione dei dati personali. Tomo I*, ed. Rocco Panetta. Milano: Giuffrè Editore.

Rodotà, Stefano. 2006c. Relazione de 2004 dal attività svolta dal garante per la protezione dei dati personali—Discorso del presidente da garante. Available at http://www.garanteprivacy.it/garante/navig/jsp/index.jsp?folderpath=Attivit%E0+dell%27Autorit%E0%2FRelazioni+annuali+al+Parlamento%2F2004%2FVersione+PDF. 23 Dec 2006.

Rodotà, Stefano. 2008. *A vida na sociedade da vigilância: Privacidade hoje*. Rio de Janeiro: Renovar.

Rothstein, Mark A. 1997. Genetic secrets: A policy framework. In *Genetic secrets: Protecting privacy and confidentiality in the genetic era*, ed. Mark A. Rothstein. New Heaven: Yale University Press.

Rothstein, Mark A., and Carlton A. Horung. 2004. Public attitudes. In *Genetics and life insurance* ed. Mark A. Rothstein. London: MIT Press.
Rouvroy, Antoinette, and Yves Poullet. 2009. The right to informational self-determination and the value of self-development: Reassessing the importance of privacy for democracy. In *Reinventing data protection?* ed. Serge Gutwirth et al. Dordrecht: Springer.
Sarmento e Castro, Catarina. 2005. *Direito da informatica, privacidade e dados pessoais*. Coimbra: Almedina.
Sartor, Giovanni. 2004. Prefazione. In *Il codice in materia di protezione dei dati personali*, ed. Juri Monducci and Giovanni Sartor. Padova: Cedam.
Sartor, Giovanni, and Mario Viola de Azevedo Cunha. 2010. The Italian Google-case: Privacy, freedom of speech and responsibility of providers for user-generated contents. *International Journal of Law and Information Technology*. 18(4): 356–378. Oxford, New York: Oxford University Press.
Schauer, Frederick. 2003. *Profiles, probabilities and stereotypes*. Cambridge: Belknap Press of Harvard University Press.
Schmidt, Susanne K. 2007. Mutual recognition as a new mode of governance. *Journal of European Public Policy* 14(5): 667–681.
Schwartz, Paul M. 1997. European data protection law and medical privacy. In *Genetic secrets: Protecting privacy and confidentiality in the genetic era*, ed. Mark A. Rothstein. New Heaven: Yale University Press.
Scolik, Hélio. O prêmio Nobel de economia de 2001 e a informação assimétrica. Available at http://www.vemconcursos.com/opiniao/index.phtml?page_ordem=assunto&page_id=274&page_print=1. 11 Mar 2007.
Simitis, Spiros. 1998. From the general rules of data protection to a specific regulation of the use of employee data: Policies and constraints of the European Union. *Comparative Labor Law & Policy* 19: 351.
Slobogin, Christopher. 2007. *Privacy at risk—The new government surveillance and the fourth amendment*. Chicago: University of Chicago Press.
Sofsky, Wolfgang. 2008. *Privacy – A Manifesto*. Trans. Steven Rendall. Princeton & Oxford: Princeton University Press.
Solove, Daniel. 2000–2001. Privacy and power: Computer databases and metaphors for information privacy. *Stanford Law Review* 53: 1393–1462.
Solove, Daniel. 2002. Conceptualizing privacy. *California Law Review* 90: 1087.
Solove, Daniel. 2003. Identity theft, privacy, and the architecture of vulnerability. *Hastings Law Journal* 54: 1227.
Solove, Daniel. 2004. *The digital person: Technology and privacy in the information age*. New York: New York University Press.
Solove, Daniel. 2006. A taxonomy of privacy. *University of Pennsylvania Law Review* 154(3): 477.
Solove, Daniel. 2007. I've got nothing to hide and others misunderstandings of privacy. *San Diego Law Review* 44: 745. Available at https://ssrn.com/abstract=998565. 4 Sept 2008.
Solove, Daniel. 2008. *Understanding privacy*. Cambridge: Harvard University Press.
Solove, Daniel J., and Chris Jay Hoofnagle. 2006. A model regime of privacy protection. *University of Illinois Law Review* 2: 357.
Somsen, H. 2007. *The regulatory challenge of biotechnology*. Cheltenham: Edward Elgar Publishing.
Soriano, Paul. 1999. *Lire, écrire, parler, penser dans la societe de l'information*. Paris: Descartes & Cie.
Spoto, Giuseppe. 2006. I diritti dei consumatore. In *Libera circolazione e protezione dei dati personali. Tomo I*, ed. Rocco Panetta. Milano: Giuffrè Editore.
Staples, Willian G. (ed.). 2007. *Encyclopedia of privacy, vol. 2*. Westport: Greenwood Press.
Stein, Michael Ashley. 2004. Review: Generalizing disability. *Michigan Law Review* 102(6): 1373. Survey of Books Relating to the Law (May, 2004).
Sweeney, Latanya. Foundations of privacy protection from a computer science perspective. http://dataprivacylab.org/projects/disclosurecontrol/paper1.pdf. Accessed 22 Feb 2011.

Tene, Omer. 2011. Privacy: The new generations. *International Data Privacy Law* 1(1): 15–27.

Thomas, Richard, and Mark Walport. 2010. Data sharing review—Consultation paper on the use and sharing of personal information in the public and private sector. Available at http://www.justice.gov.uk/docs/Association-of-British-Insurers-Data-Sharing-Response.pdf. 9 Feb 2010.

Turk, Alex. 2009. Bilan et perspectives de la CNIL (Entretien). *Traçabilité et reséaux.* Hermes n° 53. CNRS-editions.

Uhlmann, Wendy R., and Sharon F. Terry. 1997. Perspectives of consumers and genetics professionals. In *Genetic secrets: Protecting privacy and confidentiality in the genetic era*, ed. Mark A. Rothstein. New Heaven: Yale University Press.

Viola de Azevedo Cunha, Mario. 2009. *Privacidade e seguro: A coleta e utilização de dados pessoais nos ramos de pessoas e de saúde. Cadernos de seguro—Teses n. 33.* Rio de Janeiro: Funenseg.

Viola de Azevedo Cunha, Mario. 2010. Data protection and insurance: The limits on the collection and use of personal data on insurance contracts in EU law. *Global Jurist* 10(1): 1934–2640. Topics, Article 6.

Viola de Azevedo Cunha, Mario. 2012. Review of the data protection directive: Is there need (and room) for a new concept of personal data? In *European data protection: In good health?* ed. Serge Gutwirth et al. New York: Springer.

Viola de Azevedo Cunha, Mario, Danilo Doneda, and Norberto Andrade. 2010. La re-identificazione dei dati anonimi e il trattamento dei dati personali per ulteriori finalità: Sfide alla privacy. *Ciberspazio e Diritto* 11(4): 641–655.

Viola de Azevedo Cunha, Mario, Luisa Marin, and Giovanni Sartor. 2012. *Peer-to-peer privacy violations and ISP liability: Data protection in the user-generated web. Data privacy law*. New York: Oxford University Press.

Walden, Ian. 2002. Anonymising personal data. *International Journal of Law and Information Technology* 20(2): 224–237. Oxford University Press.

Webster, Mandy. 2006. *Data protection in the financial services industry*. Aldershot: Gower Publishing Limited.

Westin, Alan. 1968. *Privacy and freedom*. New York: Atheneum.

Whitley, Edgard A. 2009. Informational privacy, consent and the "control" of personal data. *Information Security Technical Report* 14(3): 154–159.

Whitman, James Q. 2003–2004. The two western cultures of privacy: Dignity versus liberty. *The Yale Law Journal* 113: 1151.

Winn, Jane K. 2008. Can a duty of information security become special protection for sensitive data under US law? In *Défis du droit de la protection de la vie privée—Perspectives du droit Européen et Nord-Américain. Cahiers du centre du recherche informatique et droit*, ed. Maria Verónica Pérez and Pablo Palazzi. Bruxelles: Bruylant, 31.

Wong, Rebbecca. 2005. Privacy: Charting its developments and prospects. In *Human rights in the digital age*, ed. Mathias Klang and Andrew Murray. London: Glasshouse Press.

Yann, Joly. Life insurers' access to genetic information: A way out of the stalemate? *Health Law Review* 14(3). Available at http://www.law.ualberta.ca/centres/hli/userfiles/2_Joly.pdf. 7 Oct 2010.

Institutional Documents

Article 29 Working Party on Data Protection. Opinion 10/2001 on the need for a balanced approach in the fight against terrorism. Adopted on 14 Dec 2001. Available at http://ec.europa.eu/justice_home/fsj/privacy/docs/wpdocs/2001/wp53en.pdf. 22 Jan 2010.

Article 29 Working Party on Data Protection. Opinion 4/2007 on the concept of personal data. Adopted on 20 June 2007. Available at http://ec.europa.eu/justice_home/fsj/privacy/docs/wpdocs/2007/wp136_en.pdf. 10 May 2008.

Article 29 Working Party on Data Protection. Working document 1/2009 on pre-trial discovery for cross border civil litigation. Adopted on 11 Feb 2009. Available at http://ec.europa.eu/justice_home/fsj/privacy/docs/wpdocs/2009/wp158_en.pdf. 24 Feb 2010.

Article 29 Working Party on Data Protection. Contribution of the article 29 working party to the public consultation of DG MARKET on the report of the expert group on credit histories. Adopted on 1 Dec 2009. Available at http://ec.europa.eu/justice_home/fsj/privacy/docs/wpdocs/2009/wp164_en.pdf. 26 Feb 2010.

Article 29 Working Party on Data Protection. Working document on the processing of personal data relating to health in electronic health records (HER). Adopted on 15 Feb 2007. Available at http://ec.europa.eu/justice_home/fsj/privacy/docs/wpdocs/2007/wp131_en.pdf.

Article 29 Working Party on Data Protection. Working document on genetic data. Adopted on 17 March 2004. Available at http://ec.europa.eu/justice_home/fsj/privacy/docs/wpdocs/2004/wp91_en.pdf. 10 May 2008.

Article 29 Working Party on Data Protection. Working document on biometrics. Adopted on 1 Aug 2003. Available at http://ec.europa.eu/justice_home/fsj/privacy/docs/wpdocs/2003/wp80_en.pdf.

Article 29 Working Party on Data Protection. Working document on blacklists. Adopted on 3 Oct 2002. Available at http://ec.europa.eu/justice_home/fsj/privacy/docs/wpdocs/2002/wp65_en.pdf. 9 May 2008.

Article 29 Working Party on Data Protection. Opinion 1/2008 on data protection issues related to search engines. Adopted on 4 Apr 2008. Available at http://ec.europa.eu/justice/policies/privacy/docs/wpdocs/2008/wp148_en.pdf. 22 Jan 2011.

Article 29 Working Party on Data Protection. Opinion 4/2010 on the European code of conduct of FEDMA for the use of personal data in direct marketing. Adopted on 13 July 2010. Available at http://ec.europa.eu/justice/policies/privacy/docs/wpdocs/2010/wp174_en.pdf. 19 Oct 2010.

Article 29 Working Party on Data Protection. Opinion 15/2011 on the definition of consent. Adopted on 13 July 2011. Available at http://ec.europa.eu/justice/policies/privacy/docs/wpdocs/2011/wp187_en.pdf. Accessed 6 Aug 2011.

Article 29 Working Party on Data Protection. Opinion 01/2012 on the data protection reform proposal. WP 191. Adopted on 23 Mar 2012.

Article 29 Working Party; Working Party on Police and Justice. The future of privacy: Joint contribution to the consultation of the European Commission on the legal framework for the fundamental right to protection of personal data. Adopted on 1 Dec 2009. Available at http://ec.europa.eu/justice/policies/privacy/docs/wpdocs/2009/wp168_en.pdf. 21 Oct 2010.

Association of British Insurers. ABI news release. Stripped, searched and found—National database exposes its first fraudster http://www.abi.org.uk/Media/Releases/2005/05/Stripped_searched_and_found_-_national_database_exposes_its_first_fraudster.aspx. 9 Feb 2010.

Association of British Insurers. Research brief: General insurance claims fraud. July 2009. Available at http://www.abi.org.uk/Media/Releases/2009/07/40569.pdf. 8 Feb 2010.

Association of British Insurers. June 2008. ABI code of practice for genetic tests. Available at http://www.abi.org.uk/Information/Codes_and_Guidance_Notes/41697.pdf. 6 Feb 2010.

Association of British Insurers. June 2008. Code of practice for genetic tests. Available at http://www.abi.org.uk/Information/Codes_and_Guidance_Notes/41697.pdf. 23 Feb 2010.

Association of British Insurers. ABI news release. Tuesday, 5 Apr 2011 Ref: 17/11. Insurance genetics moratorium extended to 2017. Available at http://www.abi.org.uk/Media/Releases/2011/04/Insurance_Genetics_Moratorium_extended_to_2017.aspx. 12 June 2011.

Association of British Insurers; British Medical Association. July 2008. Medical information and insurance. Joint ABI BMA guidelines. Available at http://www.abi.org.uk/Information/Codes_and_Guidance_Notes/527.pdf. 14 Mar 2010.

Association of British Insurers; Government of the United Kingdom. Mar 2005. Concordat and moratorium on genetics and insurance. Available at http://www.dh.gov.uk/prod_consum_dh/groups/dh_digitalassets/@dh/@en/documents/digitalasset/dh_4106050.pdf. 23 Feb 2010.

British Bankers' Association et al. The banking code. Available at http://www.bankingcode.org.uk/pdfdocs/BANKING%20CODE.pdf. 10 Feb 2010.

Buildind Societies Association et al. Nov 2009. The lending code. Available at http://www.lendingstandardsboard.org.uk/docs/lendingcode.pdf. 6 Feb 2010.

Comissão Nacional de Proteção de Dados de Portugal. Parecer nº 22/20. Available at http://www.cnpd.pt/bin/decisoes/2001/htm/par/par022-01.htm. 25 Jan 2010.

Commission Nationale de L'Informatique et des Libertes. 2009. L'impressionnante profusion des initiatives tendant à la révision de la directive de 1995 sur la protection des données. Published on 30 March. Available at http://www.cnil.fr/index.php?id=2538&tx_ttnews%5btt_news%5d=432&tx_ttnews%5bbackPid%5d=1&cHash=c8572d9b47. 16 June 2011.

Commission Nationale de L'Informatique et des Libertes. Guide du correspondant informatique et libertés. P. 3. Available at http://www.cnil.fr/fileadmin/documents/Guides_pratiques/CNIL_Guide_correspondants.pdf. 22 Jan 2011.

Commission Nationale de L'Informatique et des Libertes. Guide banque-crédit: Etes-vous fichés? Available at http://www.cnil.fr/fileadmin/documents/La_CNIL/publications/CNIL_guide_banquecredit.pdf. 22 Jan 2011.

Commission Nationale de L'Informatique et des Libertes. 2010. Fichier em fiche. FNCI: Fichier national des cheques irreguliers. 23 Mars. Available at http://www.cnil.fr/en-savoir-plus/fichiers-en-fiche/fichier/article/fnci-fichier-national-des-cheques-irreguliers-1/. 22 Jan 2011.

Commission Nationale de L'Informatique et des Libertes. 2009. Les grands fichiers. FICOBA: Fichier national des comptes bancaires et assimilés. 08 Juin. Available at http://www.cnil.fr/en-savoir-plus/fichiers-en-fiche/fichier/article/ficoba-fichier-national-des-comptes-bancaires-et-assimiles/. 22 Jan 2011.

Commission Nationale de L'Informatique et des Libertes. Fiches pratiques. Fichier <<FICOBA>>: Une nouvelle procédure de droit d'accès. Available at http://www.cnil.fr/en-savoir-plus/fiches-pratiques/fiche/article/fichier-ficoba-une-nouvelle-procedure-de-droit-dacces/?tx_ttnews%5BbackPid%5D=91&cHash=ee8f0fae36. 22 Jan 2011.

Commission Nationale de L'Informatique et des Libertes. 2009. Fichier en fiche. AGIRA: Association pour la gestion des informations sur le risque automobile. 08 Juin. Available at http://www.cnil.fr/en-savoir-plus/fichiers-en-fiche/fichier/article/association-pour-la-gestion-des-informations-sur-le-risque-automobile/. 22 Jan 2011.

Commission Nationale de L'Informatique et des Libertes. Délibération no 2011-249 du 8 septembre 2011 portant modification de l'article 69 du règlement intérieur de la Commission nationale de l'informatique et des libertés et insérant un chapitre IV bis intitulé « Procédure de labellisation ».

Commission Nationale de L'Informatique et des Libertes. La CNIL délivre ses premiers labels. Available at http://www.cnil.fr/la-cnil/actualite/article/article/la-cnil-delivre-ses-premiers-labels/. Accessed 22 Sept 2012.

Council of Europe. Committee of ministers recommendation no. R (97) 5 on the protection of medical data. 13 Feb 1997. Available at www.coe.int. 17 Nov 2009.

Council of the European Union. Council conclusions on an information management strategy for EU internal security. 2979th Justice and Home Affairs council meeting Brussels, 30 Nov 2009. Available at http://www.consilium.europa.eu/uedocs/NewsWord/en/jha/111549.doc. 5 Mar 2010.

Credit Industry Fraud Avoidance Scheme. How does CIFAS work? Available at http://www.cifas.org.uk/default.asp?edit_id=953-28. 15 Feb 2010.

Driving and Vehicle Licensing Agency. Request of information. Available at www.dft.gov.uk/dvla/foi/Disclosure/ReleaseofInfo.aspx. 23 Feb 2010.

Driving and Vehicle Licensing Agency. Release of information from DVLA records. Available at http://www.dft.gov.uk/dvla/data/relinfo.aspx. 14 Feb 2010.

Driving and Vehicle Licensing Agency. Reasonable cause for data release. Available at http://www.dft.gov.uk/dvla/data/rc.aspx. 14 Feb 2010.

Eurogappp. Genetics and public and professional policy in Europe. Available at http://ec.europa.eu/research/biosociety/pdf/bmh4_ct98_0550_partb.pdf. 5 Mar 2008.

European Commission. 1995. Press release: IP/95/822. Council definitively adopts directive on protection of personal data. July 25. Available at http://www.ieee-security.org/Cipher/ConfReports/ECprivdirective.html. 5 Mar 2010.

European Commission. Communication from the commission to the European parliament and the council—An area of freedom, security and justice serving the citizen (COM(2009)0262 final). Available at http://eur-lex.europa.eu/LexUriServ/LexUriServ.do?uri=CELEX:52009DC0262:EN:HTML. 5 Mar 2010.

European Commission. Draft communication from the commission to the European parliament, the council, the economic and social committee and the committee of the regions [COM(2010) 609 final]. http://ec.europa.eu/justice/news/consulting_public/0006/com_2010_609_en.pdf. 22 Jan 2011.

European Commission. 2011. Communication from the commission—Guidelines on the application of council directive 2004/113/EC to insurance, in the light of the judgment of the court of justice of the European Union in Case C-236/09 (TestAchats). C(2011) 9497 final. Brussels, 22 Dec 2011. Available at http://ec.europa.eu/justice/gender-equality/files/com_2011_9497_en.pdf. Accessed 17 Sept 2012.

European Commission. 2012. Explanatory memorandum to the proposal for a regulation of the European parliament and of the council on the protection of individuals with regard to the processing of personal data and on the free movement of such data (General Data Protection Regulation). COM (2012) 11 final. Published 25 January. Available at http://ec.europa.eu/justice/data-protection/document/review2012/com_2012_11_en.pdf. 7 Apr 2012.

European Commission. 2012. Proposal for a regulation of the European parliament and of the council on the protection of individuals with regard to the processing of personal data and on the free movement of such data (General Data Protection Regulation). COM (2012) 11 final. Published 25 Jan 2012. Available at http://ec.europa.eu/justice/data-protection/document/review2012/com_2012_11_en.pdf. 7 Apr 2012.

European Commission. 2012/484/EU: Commission implementing decision of 21 August 2012 pursuant to directive 95/46/EC of the European parliament and of the council on the adequate protection of personal data by the Eastern Republic of Uruguay with regard to automated processing of personal data (notified under document C(2012) 5704). Available at http://eur-lex.europa.eu/LexUriServ/LexUriServ.do?uri=OJ:L:2012:227:0011:01:EN HTML. Accessed 12 Sept 2012.

European Commission. Proposal for a directive on the protection of individuals with regard to the processing of personal data by competent authorities for the purposes of prevention, investigation, detection or prosecution of criminal offences or the execution of criminal penalties, and the free movement of such data ('the proposed directive').

European Data Protection Supervisor. Opinion on the proposal for a directive of the European parliament and of the council on the retention of data processed in connection with the provision of public electronic communication services and amending directive 2002/58/EC (COM92005) 439 final).

European Data Protection Supervisor. Opinion on the proposal for a regulation of the European parliament and of the council on European statistics (COM(2007) 625 final). Adopted on 20 May 2008. Available at http://www.edps.europa.eu/EDPSWEB/webdav/site/mySite/shared/Documents/Consultation/Opinions/2008/08-05-20_Statistics_EN.pdf. 25 Jan 2010.

European Data Protection Supervisor. Opinion of 5 September 2007 on the proposal for a regulation of the European Parliament and of the council on community statistics on public health and health and safety at work (COM(2007) 46 final). http://www.edps.europa.eu/EDPSWEB/webdav/site/mySite/shared/Documents/Consultation/Opinions/2007/07-09-05_Statistics_health_data_EN.pdf. 4 Jan 2011.

European Data Protection Supervisor. Opinion on the proposal for a council framework decision on the protection of personal data processed in the framework of police and judicial co-operation in criminal matters (COM (2005) 475 final). Available at http://www.edps.europa.eu/EDPSWEB/webdav/site/mySite/shared/Documents/Consultation/Opinions/2005/05-12-19_data_protection_EN.pdf. 23 Feb 2010.

European Data Protection Supervisor. Opinion on the communication from the commission on an action plan for the deployment of intelligent transport systems in Europe and the accompanying proposal for a directive of the European parliament and of the council laying down the framework for the deployment of intelligent transport systems in the field of road transport and for interfaces with other transport modes. Available at http://www.edps.europa.eu/EDPSWEB/webdav/shared/Documents/Consultation/Opinions/2009/09-07-22_Intelligent_Transport_Systems_EN.pdf. 23 Feb 2010.

European Data Protection Supervisor. The EDPS as an advisor to the community institutions on proposals for legislation and related documents. Policy Paper. Available at www.edps.europa.eu.

European Data Protection Supervisor. Glossary. Available at http://www.edps.europa.eu/EDPSWEB/edps/Home/EDPS/Dataprotection/Glossary/pid/84. 21 Jan 2010.

European Data Protection Supervisor. Opinion on a notification for prior checking received from the data protection officer of the European commission on "the implementation of flexitime—specific to DG INFSO". Available at http://www.edps.europa.eu/EDPSWEB/webdav/site/mySite/shared/Documents/Supervision/Priorchecks/Opinions/2007/07-10-19_Commission_flexitime_INFSO_EN.pdf. 25 Jan 2010.

European Data Protection Supervisor. Opinion on the communication from the commission to the European parliament, the council and the economic and social committee and the committee of the regions—"A comprehensive approach on personal data protection in the European Union. Available at http://www.edps.europa.eu/EDPSWEB/webdav/site/mySite/shared/Documents/Consultation/Opinions/2011/11-01-14_Personal_Data_Protection_EN.pdf. 29 Mar 2011.

European Data Protection Supervisor. Opinion on the evaluation report from the commission to the council and the European parliament on the data retention directive (Directive 2006/24/EC). Available at http://www.edps.europa.eu/EDPSWEB/webdav/site/mySite/shared/Documents/Consultation/Opinions/2011/11-05-30_Evaluation_Report_DRD_EN.pdf. 16 June 2011.

European Data Protection Supervisor. Opinion on the data protection reform package. Available at http://www.edps.europa.eu/EDPSWEB/webdav/site/mySite/shared/Documents/Consultation/Opinions/2012/12-03-07_EDPS_Reform_package_EN.pdf. Accessed 23 Sept 2012.

European Economic and Social Committee. 2012. Opinion on proposal for a regulation of the European parliament and of the council on the protection of individuals with regard to the processing of personal data on the free movement of such data (General Data Protection Regulation). SOC/45. 23 May.

European Parliament. Resolution on the ethical and legal problems of genetic engineering. (Official Journal C 96, 17/04/1989, p. 165–171). Available at https://www.codex.vr.se/texts/EP-genetic.html. 16 Feb 2009.

European Parliament. Swift: Meps to vote on backing or sacking eu/us data sharing deal. Available at http://www.europarl.europa.eu/news/public/story_page/019-68537-039-02-07-902-20100205sto68536-2010-08-02-2010/default_en.htm. 19 Feb 2010.

European Parliament. EU passenger name record talks on hold in council until Lisbon treaty is ratified. Available at http://www.europarl.europa.eu/news/expert/infopress_page/019-61958-279-10-41-902-20091006ipr61955-06-10-2009-2009-false/default_it.htm. 19 Feb 2010.

Expert Group on Credit Histories. May 2009. Report of the expert group on credit histories. Available at http://ec.europa.eu/internal_market/consultations/docs/2009/credit_histories/egch_report_en.pdf. 21 Jan 2010.

Fédération Bancaire Française (FBF). Charte relative aux conventions de compte de dépôt. Available at http://www.fbf.fr/web/internet/content_actualitebancaire.nsf/(WebPageList)/502AB0F373BE6762C1256DCD00490773/$File/AB_special.pdf. 22 Jan 2011.

Fédération Bancaire Française (FBF). Les min-guides. Repère n° 15. La protection de vos données personnelles. Available at http://www.fbf.fr/web/Internet2010/Content.nsf/DocumentsByIDWeb/87TFZB/$File/mini-guide_15_donnees_personnelles.pdf. 5 Oct 2010.

Garante per la Protezione dei dati Personali. General authorisation for the processing of genetic data. Decision of 27 Apr 2010. Available at http://www.garanteprivacy.it/garante/doc.jsp?ID=1395420. 22 Jan 2011.

Garante per la Protezione dei dati Personali. Relazione 2000 del garante per la protezione dei dati personali. Available at http://www.garanteprivacy.it/garante/doc.jsp?ID=1335443. 26 Mar 2009.

Garante per la Protezione dei dati Personali. Relazione 2004—L'attuazione del Codice nel quadro della Costituzione per l'Europa. Available at http://www.garanteprivacy.it/garante/document?ID=1093820. 15 Mar 2009.

Garante per la Protezione dei dati Personali. Provvedimento del 19 Dicembre 2008. Available at http://www.garanteprivacy.it/garante/doc.jsp?ID=1582849. 29 Mar 2009.

Garante per la Protezione dei dati Personali. Provvedimento del 26 Luglio 2006. Available at http://www.garanteprivacy.it/garante/doc.jsp?ID=1332498. 22 Jan 2010.

Garante per la Protezione dei dati Personali. Relazione 2000. Available at http://www.garanteprivacy.it/garante/doc.jsp?ID=1335443. 26 Mar 2009.

Garante per la Protezione dei dati Personali. Provvedimento del 25 Luglio 2007. Available at http://www.garanteprivacy.it/garante/doc.jsp?ID=1434791. 22 Jan 2009.

Garante per la Protezione dei dati Personali. Bollettino del n. 10 Ottobre 1997. Available at http://www.garanteprivacy.it/garante/doc.jsp?ID=47726. 28 Jan 2009.

Garante per la Protezione dei dati Personali. Bollettino del n. 20 Maggio 2001. Available at http://www.garanteprivacy.it/garante/doc.jsp?ID=39272. 28 Nov 2009).

Garante per la Protezione dei dati Personali. Provvedimento del 27 Ottobre 2005. Available at http://www.garanteprivacy.it/garante/doc.jsp?ID=1213613. 28 Jan 2008.

Garante per la Protezione dei dati Personali. Provvedimento del 12 Febbraio 2009. Available at http://www.garanteprivacy.it/garante/doc.jsp?ID=1598386. 28 Mar 2009.

Garante per la Protezione dei dati Personali. Provvedimento del 10 Novembre 2004. Available at http://www.garanteprivacy.it/garante/doc.jsp?ID=1103284. 21 Jan 2009.

Garante per la Protezione dei dati Personali. Newsletter n. 186 del 6–12 Ottobre 2003. Available at http://www.garanteprivacy.it/garante/doc.jsp?ID=346897. 28 Mar 2009.

Garante per la Protezione dei dati Personali. Quando identificare e fotocopiare i documenti di riconoscimento dei clienti. Available at http://www.garanteprivacy.it/garante/doc.jsp?ID=1189435. 27 Jan 2010.

Garante per la Protezione dei dati Personali. Opinion of 28 May 2009 (Dati bancari: Illecita comunicazione). Available at http://www.garanteprivacy.it/garante/doc.jsp?ID=1624734. 27 Jan 2010.

Garante per la Protezione dei dati Personali. Opinion of 23 July 2009 (Dati bancari: Accesso non autorizzato e misure di sicurezza). Available at http://www.garanteprivacy.it/garante/doc.jsp?ID=1640294. 27 Jan 2010.

Garante per la Protezione dei dati Personali. Relazione 2007—16 Luglio 2008—Parte II—L'atività del Garante. Available at http://www.garanteprivacy.it/garante/doc.jsp?ID=1549689. 22 Jan 2009.

Garante per la Protezione dei dati Personali. Guidelines for the processing of customers' data in the banking sector—25 Oct 2007—As published in Italy's official journal no. 273 dated 23 November 2007. Item 3.4. Available at http://www.garanteprivacy.it/garante/doc.jsp?ID=1478096. 29 Mar 2009.

Garante per la Protezione dei dati Personali. Resolution n° 9 on balancing of interests: Data collection by CRAs without consent. Adopted on 16 Nov 2004. Available at http://www.garanteprivacy.it/garante/doc.jsp?ID=1671380. 27 Jan 2010.

Garante per la Protezione dei dati Personali; Istituto per la vigilanza sulle assicurazioni private e di interesse collettivo. Join communication of 10 March 2003 (Communicato Congiunto del 10 marzo 2003). Available at http://www.garanteprivacy.it/garante/doc.jsp?ID=34907. Accessed 28 Jan 2009.

General Secretariat of the Council of the EU—Information Notice—Treaty of Lisbon (December 2009). Available at http://www.consilium.europa.eu/uedocs/cms_data/docs/pressdata/en/ec/111652.pdf. 21 Oct 2010.

Genetic Privacy. Available at http://epic.org/privacy/genetic/. 16 Feb 2008.

Genetics and Insurance Committee. Oct 2000. Huntington's disease (GAIC/01.1). Available at http://www.dh.gov.uk/dr_consum_dh/groups/dh_digitalassets/@dh/@ab/documents/digitalasset/dh_087703.pdf. 6 Feb 2010.

Human Genetics Commission. Nov 2009. Nothing to hide, nothing to fear? Balancing individual rights and the public interest in the governance and use of the National DNA Database. Available at http://www.hgc.gov.uk/UploadDocs/DocPub/Document/Nothing%20to%20hide,%20nothing%20to%20fear%20-%20online%20version.pdf. 10 Jan 2011.

Information Commissioner's Office. Guidance on electronic mail marketing. Available at http://www.ico.gov.uk/for_organisations/topic_specific_guides/marketing.aspx. 25 Jan 2010.

Information Commissioner's Office. Guidance on electronic mail marketing. Available at http://www.ico.gov.uk/for_organisations/topic_specific_guides/marketing.aspx. 25 Jan 2010.

Information Commissioner's Office. The guide to data protection. Available at http://www.ico.gov.uk/upload/documents/library/data_protection/practical_application/the_guide_to_data_protection.pdf. 23 Feb 2010.

Information Commissioner's Office. Data Protection Act 1998: Legal Guidance. Available at http://www.ico.gov.uk/upload/documents/library/data_protection/detailed_specialist_guides/data_protection_act_legal_guidance.pdf. 3 Mar 2010.

Information Commissioner's Office. Credit explained. Available at http://www.ico.gov.uk/upload/documents/library/data_protection/practical_application/credit_explained_leaflet_2005.pdf. 23 Feb 2010.

Information Commissioner's Office. Data protection technical guidance determining what is personal data. Available at http://www.ico.gov.uk/upload/documents/library/data_protection/detailed_specialist_guides/personal_data_flowchart_v1_with_preface001.pdf. 5 Feb 2010.

Information Commissioner's Office. May 2002. Use and disclosure of health data. Guidance on the application of the Data Protection Act 1998. Available at http://www.ico.gov.uk/upload/documents/library/data_protection/practical_application/health_data_-_use_and_disclosure001.pdf. 11 Feb 2010.

Information Commissioner's Office. Credit agreements — Data sharing. http://www.ico.gov.uk/upload/documents/library/data_protection/practical_application/credit_%20agreements%20-%20data_%20sharing.pdf. 12 Feb 2010.

Information Commissioner's Office. Use of personal information available on the electoral roll. Available at http://www.ico.gov.uk/upload/documents/library/data_protection/practical_application/use_of_personal_information_available_on_the_electoral_roll.pdf. 10 Feb 2010.

Information Commissioner's Office. Data protection technical guidance: Filling defaults with credit reference agencies.

Information Commissioner's Office. 2006. Credit agreements—Data sharing. 6 Nov. Available at http://www.ico.gov.uk/upload/documents/library/data_protection/practical_application/credit_%20agreements%20-%20data_%20sharing.pdf. 12 Feb 2010.

Information Commissioner's Office. What the ICO covers. Available at http://www.ico.gov.uk/what_we_cover.aspx. 6 Feb 2010.

Information Commissioner's Office. 2010. Consultation on the assessment notices code of practice. 10 Feb. Available at http://www.ico.gov.uk/upload/documents/library/corporate/research_and_reports/consultation_assessment_notices_code_of_practice_20120209.pdf. 12 Feb 2010.

Information Commissioner's Office. Data protection good practice note—When can I disclose information to a private investigator? Available at http://www.ico.gov.uk/upload/documents/library/data_protection/practical_application/disclosures_to_private_investigators_v1.0.pdf. 3 Mar 2010.

Information Commissioner's Office. 2009. Police cases: ICO's response to the Court of Appeal's judgement. 13 Nov 2009. Available at http://www.ico.gov.uk/upload/documents/pressreleases/2009/statement_police_cases_appeal_131109.pdf. 24 Feb 2010.

Information Commissioner's Office. Use and disclosure of vehicle information. Available at http://www.ico.gov.uk/upload/documents/library/data_protection/practical_application/its_your_information_dvla_vehicle_information_final.pdf. 14 Feb 2010.

Information Commissioner's Office. Compliance advice—Implications of the use and disclosure of vehicle keepers information. Available at http://www.ico.gov.uk/upload/documents/library/data_protection/practical_application/vehicle_keepers_information_-_implications_on_use_and_disclosures.pdf. 14 Feb 2010.

Information Commissioner's Office. Foreword by the information commissioner to the. UK home office, data sharing for the prevention of fraud—Code of practice for public authorities disclosing information to a specified anti-fraud organisation under sections 68 to 72 of the Serious Crime Act 2007.

Information Commissioner's Office; Financial Ombudsman Service Limited. Memorandum of understanding between the information commissioner's office and the financial ombudsman service limited. Available at http://www.ico.gov.uk/upload/documents/library/memo_of_understanding/documents/mou_fos_limited.pdf. 13 Mar 2010.

Information Society and Media Directorate General (INFSO). Reply to the interservice consultation launched by dg just on the draft proposal of a DP regulation and a draft proposal of a police and criminal justice DP directive. 22 Dec 2011.

Insurance Fraud Bureau. Background facts. http://www.insurancefraudbureau.org/files/misc_pdfs/ifb_background_information.pdf. 9 Feb 2010.

International Finance Corporation, World Bank Group. Credit bureau knowledge guide. Available at http://www.ifc.org/ifcext/gfm.nsf/AttachmentsByTitle/FI-CB-KnowledgeGuide-E/$FILE/FI-CB-KnowledgeGuide-E.pdf. 14 Apr 2009.

International Labour Office. Report of the Director-General. Equality at work: Taking the challenges (Global Report under the follow-up to the ILO Declaration on Fundamental Principles and Rights at work). International Labour Conference, 96th Session, 2007.

Joint Supervisory Authority. The Schengen Information System: A guide for exercising the right of access. Available at http://www.dutchdpa.nl/downloads_int/Guide_for_exercising_the_right_of_access.pdf. Accessed 7 Aug 2011.

National Cancer Institute. BRCA1 and BRCA2: Cancer risk and genetic testing. Available at http://www.cancer.gov/cancertopics/factsheet/Risk/BRCA. 8 Mar 2010.

Organisation for Economic Co-operation and Development. Guidelines on the protection of privacy and transborder flows of personal data. Available at www.oecd.org/document/18/0,2340,en_2649_34255_1815186_1_1_1_1,00.html. 20 Dec 2008.

Senato della Repubblica Italiana. 2011. Schede di Lettura: Disegno di legge A.S. n. 2809 "Istituzione di un sistema di prevenzione delle frodi nel settore dell'assicurazione della responsabilità civile derivante dalla circolazione dei veicoli a motore". Luglio. N° 303. Available at http://www.senato.it/documenti/repository/dossier/studi/2011/Dossier_303.pdf. Accessed 8 Aug 2011.

Steering Committee on Reciprocity (SCOR). Nov 2008. Information sharing: Principles of reciprocity. Available at http://www.experian.co.uk/www/pages/downloads/compliance/porVersion30.pdf. 12 Mar 2010.

The Oncologist. Oct 1996. More Ashkenazi Jews have gene defect that raises inherited breast cancer risk. *The Oncologist* 1(5): 335–335. AlphaMed Press. Available at http://theoncologist.alphamedpress.org/cgi/reprint/1/5/335. 14 Mar 2010.

UK Home Office. Data sharing for the prevention of fraud — Code of practice for public authorities disclosing information to a specified anti-fraud organisation under sections 68 to 72 of the Serious Crime Act 2007. http://www.crimereduction.homeoffice.gov.uk/organisedcrime/organisedcrime07c.pdf. 9 Feb 2010.

UK Home Office. Explanatory note to the data protection (Processing of sensitive personal data) order 2000. Available at http://www.opsi.gov.uk/si/si2000/20000417.htm. 2 Mar 2010.

UK Home Office. Explanatory note to the data protection (Processing of sensitive personal data) order 2009. Available at http://www.opsi.gov.uk/si/si2006/uksi_20062068_en.pdf. 2 Mar 2010.

UK House of Commons. Select committee on science and technology fifth report. Available at http://www.parliament.the-stationery-office.co.uk/pa/cm200001/cmselect/cmsctech/174/17404.htm#a1. 13 Jan 2011.

U.S.A. Records, computers and the rights of citizens. Report of the secretary's advisory committee on automated personal data systems, 1973. Available at www.aspe.hhs.gov/datacncl/1973privacy/c3.htm. 11 Apr 2011.

White House. 2012. Consumer data privacy in a networked world: A framework for protecting privacy and promoting innovation in the global digital economy. February, Washington. Available at http://www.whitehouse.gov/sites/default/files/privacy-final.pdf. 7 Apr 2012.

World Health Organization. 2008. WHO report on the global TOBACCO epidemic. Available at http://www.who.int/tobacco/mpower/mpower_report_full_2008.pdf. 16 May 2008.

World Medical Association. 2010. Declaration on the human genome project. Available at http://www.wma.net/en/30publications/10policies/20archives/g6/index.html. 26 Jan 2010.

MIX
Papier aus verantwortungsvollen Quellen
Paper from responsible sources
FSC® C105338

If you have any concerns about our products,
you can contact us on
ProductSafety@springernature.com

In case Publisher is established outside the EU,
the EU authorized representative is:
Springer Nature Customer Service Center GmbH
Europaplatz 3, 69115 Heidelberg, Germany

Printed by Libri Plureos GmbH
in Hamburg, Germany